CHURCH AND CHRONICLE
IN THE MIDDLE AGES

CHURCH AND CHRONICLE
IN THE MIDDLE AGES

ESSAYS PRESENTED TO
JOHN TAYLOR

EDITED BY

IAN WOOD AND G.A. LOUD

THE HAMBLEDON PRESS
LONDON AND RIO GRANDE

Published by The Hambledon Press, 1991

102 Gloucester Avenue, London NW1 8HX (U.K.)

P.O. Box 162, Rio Grande, Ohio 45672 (U.S.A.)

ISBN 1 85285 046 9

British Library Cataloguing in Publication Data
Church and chronicle in the Middle Ages.
  I. Wood, Ian, *1950–*
  II. Loud, Graham
  III. Taylor, John
  942.02

Library of Congress Cataloguing-in-Publication Data
Church and chronicle in the Middle Ages: essays
  presented to John Taylor/ edited by Ian Wood
  and G.A. Loud.
  Includes bibliographical references.
  1. Middle Ages — Historiography.
  2. Literature, Medieval — History and criticism.
  3. Church history — Middle Ages, 600–1500
    —Historiography.
  4. Taylor, John, 1925–
  I. Wood, I.N. (Ian N.)   II. Loud, G.A.
  III. Taylor, John 1925–
  D116.C53 1991   91–30968
  940.1 — dc20   CIP

Printed on acid-free paper and bound in Great Britain
by Cambridge University Press.

Contents

List of Illustrations

John Taylor

Preface

The occasion for this book was the retirement of John Taylor after forty years teaching medieval history at the University of Leeds. John's considerable distinction as a scholar and his many personal qualities are generously attested in a tribute written by his long-time friend and collaborator Professor Barrie Dobson. We, as editors, would like to feel that the volume as a whole is a fitting tribute to John as a scholar, teacher and friend, both by the contributors, all of whom have close connections with the University of Leeds or with John personally, and more particularly by ourselves as editors and as John's junior colleagues for a decade and more at Leeds. We hope that it shows not merely proper *fidelitas* to our former teaching director and head of department, but also something for our affection for John as friend and mentor.

There are also other debts of gratitude which we would like to acknowledge. We would first and foremost thank our fellow contributors for so generously making available the fruits of their research, and (almost all of them) for delivering their essays so promptly. We thank also the School of History at Leeds, and its Chairman, Christopher Challis, for a financial subvention towards the cost of production, and the Research Fund of the university for a grant covering the cost of the illustrations for the articles by Mrs. Kiff-Hooper and Professor Harvey. In addition we would like to thank the British Library, Lambeth Palace Library, the Biblioteca Laurenziana, the Biblioteca Nationale, Florence, and the Public Record Office for supplying the photographs. Production of this volume would have been impossible without the help of Mrs. Ann Dale and Mrs. Margaret Walkington on their wordprocessors. Our publisher, Martin Sheppard, has been both encouraging and patient.

It is a common criticism of *Festschriften* that they lack coherence. These essays however have two clear foci – those of John Taylor's own work – the study of history-writing in the middle ages and the late medieval church. We hope that John sees them as a fitting tribute from his friends and pupils and colleagues, and that other readers can enjoy them both in their own right and as a sign that medieval studies retain their vitality at

Leeds and at other 'provincial' centres, even when buffetted by the chill
winds of modern austerity. And we hope that at least a few of 'illae gentes
quae ad boream Humbri fluminis inhabitant' will rejoice at the presence
of so distinguished a scholar in their midst.

G. A. Loud
I. N. Wood

John Taylor: A Tribute

Barrie Dobson

As all his many friends and admirers – only a few of whom have contributed to this volume – will agree, John Taylor's modesty about his own considerable achievements is such as to make all other historians seem vain. Nothing, one supposes, would appeal to him less than the thought of breaking any sort of record; and it must come to him as something of a surprise that at the end of forty years' service in the School of History at the University of Leeds, he has studied the history of the later middle ages at a high professional level for a longer time than any other university teacher in northern England. During the last four highly volatile decades (volatile not for him but for the academic pursuit of history in this country) since John Taylor first came to Leeds in 1950 as a twenty-five-year-old Lecturer in Medieval History, he has remained a continuous source of benevolent stability. Not surprisingly, he has been most influential of all at the University of Leeds itself, a university which after all he has adorned for no less than a third of its entire history since 1877 when the long-forgotten Professor F.S. Pulling first announced a lecture course in that city on 'English History from the Norman Conquest'.[1] As for the two greater medieval historians whose outstanding achievements came to be most inseparably associated with his university, Alexander Hamilton Thompson and John Le Patourel, John Taylor himself has paid characteristically generous tribute to the way his two formidable predecessors 'laid the foundations for the professional study of medieval history at Leeds'.[2] The author of those words characteristically refrained from drawing attention to the many edifices he had himself personally built upon those foundations, all the more impressively so at times of acute financial attrition to his, as other, British university history departments. And if, as he remarked, *Anglia*

---

[1] J. Taylor, 'History at Leeds, 1877–1974: The Evolution of a Discipline', *Northern History*, x (1975), 141–46.

[2] *Idem*, 'John Le Patourel, F.B.A.', *Proceedings of the Leeds Philosophical and Literary Society*, xviii (1982), 7–8.

Sacra was the *patria* of Hamilton Thompson, and the Anglo-French connection that of Le Patourel, then the fourteenth-century English chronicle has provided John Taylor with a hunting-ground vast and important enough to keep both him and his readers happy for many years.[3] Long, in his quasi-retirement, may it continue to be so.

Born on 22 August 1925, John Taylor belongs to that large and familiar category of Lancastrians whose subsequent experience of the joys of residence in Yorkshire dissuaded them from ever reversing their tracks across the Pennines in later life. Nevertheless John's affection towards Bolton and especially towards Bolton School, which he attended from 1936 to 1943 when it was at the height of its academic prowess, has been undimmed by time; and his debt to that 'remarkable teacher' of booming voice and leonine appearance, Mr. F.R. Poskitt, Head of Bolton and previously History Master at Manchester Grammar School, was to be acknowledged fifty years later in *English Historical Literature in the Fifteenth Century*.[4] In the Sixth Form at Bolton School, John Taylor's interests lay as much with the study of English literature as of history, not least perhaps because of the literary interests of both his father and grandfather. Even to this day, John is almost as likely to become animated by a conversation about Cyril Connolly and Virginia Woolf (two of his favourite authors in the 1940s) as about the textual problems presented by the *Anonimalle Chronicle*. His reading in modern literature, above all in the field of literary biography, remains formidably extensive; but in the event, not only to his own good fortune, John Taylor was to read Modern History and not English Literature at Oxford in the late 1940s. However, there can be no doubt that his continued enthusiasm for the latter encouraged him to devote most of his career to research on medieval texts which are as 'literary' as they are historical. Indeed John's long-standing concern and respect for the authenticity of the written word has always been the leading characteristic of the way in which he has addressed the problems of late medieval English history during the last four decades. For him it seems unlikely that the pursuit of history has ever needed greater justification than a familiar rhetorical question posed by Virginia Woolf herself: 'Somewhere, everywhere, now hidden, now apparent in whatever is written down, is the form of a human being. If we seek to know him, are we idly occupied?'[5] Needless to say, John's own written work is an enduring testimony to the fact that we are not.

---

[3] *Ibid.*, 7.

[4] J. Taylor, *English Historical Literature of the Fourteenth Century* (Oxford, 1987), p.vii. I owe the description of Mr. Poskitt to another of his pupils, Professor Norman Hampson.

[5] Virginia Woolf, *The Captain's Deathbed*, 'Reading'.

Although John Taylor was awarded a scholarship at Balliol College, Oxford, in 1943, the following four years of his life were perforce preoccupied by a military career which eventually led him to India as a Lieutenant in the Royal Artillery. As an undergraduate at Balliol thereafter, between 1947 and 1950, his achievements – which included the Gladstone Memorial Prize as well as participating in memorable joint tutorials with Gerald Aylmer under the direction of Christopher Hill – were a portent of things to come. To be an undergraduate at Balliol in the late 1940s has no doubt always meant more to John than he usually admits; and he can surely not have been displeased at his recent discovery that of the fifty or so fellows of Oxford colleges in the fifteenth century who originated from the diocese of York, almost half were fellows of his own college.[6] However, even before he arrived at Balliol, John had already developed a close friendship with the highly talented family of the late Professor V.H. Galbraith; and during his undergraduate years that 'most lively English medievalist of his age' became, what he has always remained, the greatest intellectual and personal influence upon him. In 1947 Galbraith, who had just taken up the Regius Chair of History at Oxford, was at the height of his powers as a teacher, as a scholar and as a deflator of traditional academic pomposity. Not at all as conformist a figure as he sometimes allows even his friends to suppose, John Taylor warmed intensely to a medievalist who combined in unique fashion intense dedication to medieval historical research with a high-spirited irreverence towards the good and the great. Although John was always too intelligent, and too different by temperament, to adopt the inimitable Galbraith as what might now be called his 'role model', he continues to be enduringly influenced by his mentor's ability to lead the well-rounded life as well as to write the highly specialised book. 'Not even the latest article in the *English Historical Review* should stand in the way of a round of golf' was characteristic Galbraithian advice which John Taylor, himself an erstwhile golfer, might still be capable of passing on to his junior colleagues.

Much more obviously, the influence of V.H. Galbraith's written work lies heavily on almost all the research conducted by John since he left Oxford to become a Lecturer in History at the University of Leeds in 1950. Perhaps it was Galbraith's example above all which made him disinclined ever to venture far away from those fourteenth-century chronicles and other literary texts which he has made so very much his own. Certainly it seems almost too symbolically appropriate that in 1991 John, together with Dr. Wendy Childs of Leeds, should be editing

---

[6] J. Taylor, 'The Diocese of York and the University Connexion, 1300–1520', *Northern History*, xxv (1989), 47–48.

a section (relating the events of 1307–34) of the *Anonimalle Chronicle*, whose later and most celebrated folios provided the basis of a famous edition which first brought the young Galbraith himself to notice in 1927.[7] Few events in the history of the University of Leeds can have given John greater pleasure than that the Brotherton Library rather than the British Library acquired, somewhat surprisingly, the unique manuscript of the *Anonimalle* as recently as 1982. Not that Galbraith's shadow has ever lain uncomfortably upon John Taylor's own work on later medieval chronicles. Although both have high reputations as editors of texts, Galbraith was always most brilliantly perceptive when solving technical problems of provenance and authorship while Taylor is a greater practitioner of the art of 'analytical synthesis', at his most characteristic in his two most important books on historical writing in the middle ages, *The Universal Chronicle of Ranulf Higden* (1966) and *English Historical Literature in the Fifteenth Century* (1987). That said, it is now abundantly clear that, together with Dr. Antonia Gransden, John Taylor has done more than any scholar alive to continue and revivify the study of the late medieval English chronicle in the immediate post-Galbraith era. Despite his thoroughly deserved celebrity, V.H. Galbraith was perhaps too iconoclastic and varied in his interests to became a genuine *maître d'école*; but of his many individual disciples John Taylor has now become the most influential in his turn.

It is accordingly hardly surprising that when at Leeds John Taylor should have begun his scholarly career by applying a Galbraithian enthusiasm for medieval historical writing to the previously neglected field of Yorkshire chronicles. His first published work was in fact an edition, published by the Thoresby Society in 1952, of the so-called short and long chronicles of Kirkstall Abbey, originally written within what were to become the suburbs of Leeds itself. With its unexpected glimpses into the course of the Great Revolt of 1381 and of the deposition of Richard II eighteen years later, this edition might serve as the first of many demonstrations on John's part that Galbraith was absolutely correct to stress 'the necessity of scrutinising the nameless fragments of chronicles in our libraries'.[8] Such scrutiny has remained central to all his subsequent work; but it was increasingly combined as the 1950s progressed with a desire to set the late medieval chroniclers in a wider context and compare their aims and achievements with one another. This development is well exemplified in *The Use of Medieval Chronicles*, published by the Historical Association in 1965; while a paper on

---

[7] *The Anonimalle Chronicle, 1331 to 1381, from a MS. Written at St. Mary's Abbey, York*, ed. V.H. Galbraith (Manchester, 1927).

[8] V.H. Galbraith, *Studies in the Public Records* (London, 1948), p.18.

Medieval Historical Writing in Yorkshire, published in 1961 under the aegis of St. Anthony's Hall, York (now the Borthwick Institute of Historical Research) is still much the best introduction to its subject and touches on what was to become one of its author's most important themes: the beginnings of a lay as well as monastic audience for the histories written by Peter Langtoft of Bridlington Priory and other monastic chroniclers. By this time, however, John Taylor was coming to grips with one of medieval England's most voluminous as well as popular chroniclers of all, Ranulf Higden, apparently a monk of St. Werburgh's Abbey, Chester for no less than sixty-four years before his death in 1363/64. Once again it had been V.H. Galbraith who had suggested Higden's vast *Polychronicon* as a subject of research; and it would be hard to think of a more challenging topic in the entire field of medieval historical writing. After publishing several important preliminary articles on the problems raised by the *Polychronicon*, John's *The Universal Chronicle of Ranulf Higden* appeared in 1966, marking the first major achievement of his career as a scholar. Especially notable perhaps for its deft handling of the complicated textual problems raised by the manuscripts ('The Development of the Text'), here was the first lucid analysis of one of the most influential books of late medieval England. Within the compass of a comparatively small volume, the value of Higden's *Polychronicon* for his contemporaries and ourselves is sketched in a totally persuasive manner; and many of the book's incidental perceptions, not least on Higden's influence upon later writers, still await the further development they deserve.

Throughout most of the 1970s John Taylor's attention was temporarily distracted from fourteenth-century chronicles by two very different types of literary text, perhaps like each other only in being both notoriously controversial and heavily suffused with legend. In the case of both the medieval 'ballads' of Robin Hood and of the tract on the *Modus Tenendi Parliamentum*, several valuable articles on aspects of these topics preceded the publication of *Rymes of Robyn Hood: An Introduction to the English Outlaw* (1st edition, 1976) and *Parliamentary Texts of the Later Middle Ages* (1980). On both these projects too, John Taylor collaborated closely with another scholar, myself in the case of the Robin Hood poems and Nicholas Pronay in the case of the *Modus*. Given that authorial collaboration has a well-known tendency to lead to mutual recrimination and even to a breakdown in relations between the partners, it is a remarkable (if predictable) tribute to John Taylor that co-operation with him was, as it still is, a continuous demonstration of good sense, patience and forbearance. Where agreement in interpretation between the two collaborators was possible, John always found the quietest but most effective way of attaining that agreement; and on the few occasions where one had to agree to differ, that difference never left the slightest vestige of ill-feeling. In this, not the least demanding of professional relationships, to come to the end of a collaborative enterprise in John's company was to find oneself temporarily bereft, deprived of the pleasure of working with one of the wisest and most courteous counsellors among the English medieval historians of his generation.

Whether or not the collaborative *Rymes of Robyn Hood* fulfilled its modest purpose in making the texts fundamental to the study of the medieval greenwood legend more accessible to a wide audience, there can be no doubt of John Taylor's enthusiasm for the subject. Naturally enough, the difficult and unusually abstruse textual problems raised by this 'ballad' literature often tended to interest him most; and there is probably no scholar alive who knows the stanzas of the long and still enigmatic *A Lyttle Geste of Robyn Hood* with greater intimacy than himself. However, the whole extraordinary *mélange* of exciting and controversial issues raised by the Robin Hood legend fascinated, and still fascinates, John as much as it did twenty years ago. It might be a slight exaggeration to say that he never stops thinking about the problems raised by the greenwood outlaw at all; but there is indeed a tenacious curiosity with which he assesses and reassesses the evidence for Robin Hood's existence and milieu which might make even that most elusive hero in English literature tremble at the thought that he could at last be exposed for what he was. Scholarly tenacity, not perhaps that this is a trait he would readily recognise in himself, has indeed proved one of the fundamental qualities of John Taylor as a historian and textual critic.

Nowhere is this tenacity more apparent than in *Parliamentary Texts of the Later Middle Ages*, the triumphant outcome of an analysis of numerous manuscripts and transcripts of the English, Scottish and Irish *Modus Tenendi Parliamentum* (to which a brief guide is presented in Appendixes I and II of the book). Almost as interesting as the *Modus* itself, and certainly more unexpected, are the supplementary documents, including accounts from Rochester and Colchester of the parliaments of 1321 and 1485, included in *Parliamentary Texts*. No doubt, as very recent work has already made clear, a treatise as propagandist as the *Modus Tenendi Parliamentum* will always be a controversial work. Nor indeed would John Taylor wish it otherwise. However, both he and Nicholas Pronay deserve to enjoy the satisfaction of having produced not only the most critical edition yet to appear but also the most illuminating introduction to the *Modus* for our time. Here and there, notably in the General Introduction to *Parliamentary Texts*, the authors come as close as John ever has done in public to adopting the more general historical value judgements of V.H. Galbraith – and even of Bishop Stubbs. 'It was this kind of good sense and pragmatic maturity which, by this time [the fourteenth and fifteenth centuries], had set the parliament of England on a course vastly and fatefully different from those of all the other formerly sister institutions of the continent.'[9] However John might now like to qualify that remark at the end of a decade when he, like many others, is increasingly aware of the possible long-term disadvantages as well as advantages of the national political 'course' inaugurated in late medieval England, there can be no doubt that, if forced to choose, John Taylor would rather be a Whig than a Tory historian. As those who have observed his reactions to recent British and American politics are made cheerfully aware, he has a healthy suspicion of statesmen – and stateswomen – too convinced of their own rectitude. In assessing his own leading characteristics as a scholar too, 'good sense' and 'pragmatic maturity' are very much the *mots justes*.

Those two qualities, although always present (it would be impossible to imagine John Taylor as 'immature'), have become even more evident in the work he has produced during the 1980s. Increasingly assured and even magisterial, much of his recent writing is the most cogent and compelling he has ever produced. His familiarity with the chronicles of the reign of Richard II had long made John an authoritative guide to the political complexities of that reign, above all during the crisis year of 1399 itself. In the highly successful conference he organised at the School of History in Leeds on 8 March 1986, whose proceedings were later published under the editorship of Dr. Wendy Childs and himself, he turned his attention with equal skill to the sources for the Good Parliament of 1376. A more novel departure, and a tribute to his own 'northern connection', is a recent original exploration of the changing relationships between Yorkshire clerks and the Universities of Oxford and Cambridge during the later middle ages: a *locus classicus* of the potentialities in store for those who ponder the results of the computerisation of the late A.B. Emden's *Biographical Dictionaries* of Oxford and Cambridge Universities, this is a paper likely to inaugurate a highly profitable line of prosopographical research, and not in the north alone.

However, one supposes that it is for his *English Historical Literature in the Fourteenth Century* that John Taylor might most like to be remembered. There can be no doubt that he will be; and no doubt too that this is a book, both a survey and a work of original scholarship, which will forever be linked with C.L. Kingsford's *English Historical Literature in the Fifteenth Century* of nearly ninety years ago. John's conspectus of fourteenth-century English historical writing casts a refreshingly wide net; and even for readers of the relevant pages of Dr. Gransden's massive two-volume survey of medieval English historical writing it proves a

[9] N. Pronay and J. Taylor, *Parliamentary Texts of the Later Middle Ages* (Oxford, 1980), p.10.

mine of interesting, and often unexpected, information. That his book should be especially incisive upon 'Universal History' and the *Anonimalle Chronicle* was no doubt always likely; but no reader could have anticipated the skill with which John Taylor provides authoritative accounts of fourteenth-century letter collections and 'the missing literature'. Never a historian to make exalted claims for his own work, John Taylor's *English Historical Literature* has in effect done more than any book in recent times to make the fourteenth century seem a positively critical period not just for the writing of chronicles but for the triumph of a distinctively English mode of literacy. In the last resort, or so it now seems, John has never had any doubt that the reign of Richard II deserves to be remembered more for its literary and cultural rather than its political achievements.[10] In which case there are many worse candidates than *English Historical Literature* for a place in whatever an English National Curriculum in History should be. How could V.H. Galbraith not have been gratified to see the outcome of the labours set in progress so long ago?

Not that John Taylor's only, or greatest, debt is to the late Vivian Galbraith. Precisely how much he owes to his wife, Ella, it would be impertinent even to imagine. Only those with exceptionally long memories can now remember the life of 'bohemian bachelorhood' supposedly led by John in the more interesting *quartiers* of Leeds at the beginning of the early 1950s. It was a life he relinquished without regret; and there can be no doubt that since the future couple first met, after Ella had taken the time-hallowed step of moving south from her native Scotland to practise as a young doctor (appropriately enough in Lancashire), they have been inseparable in their generosity to their friends, colleagues and students, as well as in their dedication to their family. Within that family, both the Taylors' sons, Richard and Donald, have perpetuated their father's interests by following him to Oxford, the first to read English and the second History: as Yorkshire journalists of the 1990s they too may be occasionally gratified at the thought that they are the closest living heirs of the northern chroniclers of five and six centuries ago. As for John and Ella's place in the affections of their friends, to cite a phrase which could be echoed by countless others, 'their favours and kindnesses to us have been infinite'. To visit the Taylors at either Kirkby Overblow near Harrogate or at Ella's native home at Findhorn near Forres is *ipso facto* to enter what always seems a retreat from care; and their sensitivity to the *genius loci*, and to the literary association which might enliven that genius, makes them ideal travelling companions. It

---

[10] J. Taylor, 'Richard II's Views on Kingship', *Proceedings of the Leeds Philosophical and Literary Society*, xiv (1971), 201–2; *English Historical Literature in the Fourteenth Century* (Oxford, 1987), pp. 217–35, 257–73.

may indeed be an illuminating comment on John Taylor's temperament as well as his historical interests that if confronted by the decision whether to visit a medieval church or castle he would almost invariably prefer the former. But in the last resort, and despite such attractions as Sir Arthur Quiller Couch's Fowey and Scott Fitzgerald's Princeton (where they spent a highly enjoyable year in 1961–62), like all good Lancastrians it is to the charms of the Lake District that John and Ella are most continuously addicted. For the writer of these words, his very first and accidental meeting with a previously unknown young Lecturer in Medieval History at Leeds – against the background of Red Pike outside 'The Fish Inn' in Buttermere village during the summer vacation of 1952 – still seems to provide John with his most appropriate of all possible *mises en scène*. If, which seems unlikely, John Taylor might ever have liked to write a book other than *English Historical Writing in the Fourteenth Century*, one supposes it must have been *Swallows and Amazons*. Could it even be that John would have actually enjoyed being Arthur Ransome, that son of the second Professor of History at Leeds, born in 1884 but living long enough to receive an Honorary Degree from that University the year after John arrived there in 1950?

When receiving his honorary doctorate on that occasion, Arthur Ransome quoted Samuel Johnson to the effect that, 'Every man has a lurking wish to be thought considerable in his native place'.[11] To the extent that Leeds in Yorkshire and not Bolton in Lancashire can now be regarded as his own native place, the existence of this book may give some slight impression of how considerably John Taylor is now regarded. His commitment to Yorkshire and to Leeds has been complete and indefatigable. For nearly twenty years (1962–80) he served the Leeds Philosophical and Literary Society as a member of Council, as President and as Editor of its Proceedings. He was General Editor of the Yorkshire Archaeological Society's Record Series from 1984 to 1989; and he brought his many services to the most remarkable body of its sort in the country to a climax during his tenure of the presidency of the Yorkshire Archaeological Society between 1984 and 1989. Within the Yorkshire Archaeological Society, as within his own University School of History, John Taylor's integrity, his scrupulous fairness and his quiet distaste for unseemly emotionalism earned him the greatest of respect. Civilised behaviour among the staff of British universities has not been a quality much esteemed, or even mentioned, in recent debates about the future of higher education in this country; but it is of course as a thoroughly civilised scholar that John Taylor has been the greatest influence of all. A highly successful Chairman of his School of History

---

[11] H. Brogan, *The Life of Arthur Ransome* (London, 1984), p.419.

during the difficult years between 1979 and 1982, he is quite as much remembered for introducing a long succession of Leeds undergraduates to the pleasures of late medieval history with the minimum of display and the maximum of effect. His teaching commitments at Leeds, like his own historical interests, ranged very widely; and his many successful lecture courses over the years on the late medieval Church in Yorkshire, England and Christendom are only the most obvious demonstration of the manner in which he took up the baton dropped by Hamilton Thompson nearly fifty years ago. Those of us who were never taught by John Taylor or never worked with him as a close departmental colleague must be well aware of what good fortune we thereby missed; for central to John's life and work has been his total dedication to his students, his fellow members of staff and ultimately his University of Leeds. In serving the latter so loyally, he has placed many others in his personal and scholarly debt as well. The following pages are an inadequate tribute to a medieval historian it has been not only highly instructive to read but also invariably rewarding to know.[12]

[12] For their unfailingly enthusiastic comments upon their longtime colleague I am most indebted to the members of the University of Leeds School of History, above all to Mr. Gordon Forster. I am also grateful to Dr. Philip Jones for his reminiscences of John Taylor's early years at Leeds.

Bibliography
of John Taylor

1952

The Kirkstall Abbey Chronicles (Thoresby Society Publications, xlii).

1956

'Fourteenth-Century Chronicle Writing in the Diocese of York', *Proceedings of the Leeds Philosophical and Literary Society* (Literary and Historical Section), viii, part 1, 51–61.

'Notes on the Rise of Written English in the late Middle Ages', *Proceedings of the Leeds Philosophical and Literary Society* (Literary and Historical Section) viii, part 2, 128–36.

'Henry Wharton and the Lambeth Manuscript of the *Flores Historiarum*', *Notes and Queries*, cci, new series 3, 240–41.

1957

'The French Brut and the reign of Edward II', *English Historical Review*, lxxii, 423–37.

1958

'The Judgement on Hugh Despenser the Younger', *Medievalia et Humanistica*, xii, 70–77.

'The Missing Manuscript of the Plumpton Letters', *Notes and Queries*, cciii, new series 5, 140–41.

1961

Medieval Historical Writing in Yorkshire (St. Anthony's Hall Publications, xix, York).

'The Development of the *Polychronicon* Continuation', *English Historical Review*, lxxvi, 20–36.

1964

'A Wigmore Chronicle, 1355–77', *Proceedings of the Leeds Philosophical and Literary Society* (Literary and Historical Section), xi, part 5, 81–94.

Contributions to the *Encyclopaedia Britannica*, including Edward II; Isabella; Thomas of Lancaster.

1965

The Use of Medieval Chronicles (Historical Association, Helps for Students of History, lxx).

1966

The Universal Chronicle of Ranulf Higden (Oxford).

1967

'The Norman Conquest and the Church in Yorkshire', *University of Leeds Review*, x, part 3, 231–55.

Contributions to *Repertorium Fontium Historiae Medii Aevi, Fontes* (Rome, Instituto Storico Italiano).

1968

'The Manuscripts of the *Modus Tenendi Parliamentum*', *English Historical Review*, lxxxiii, 673–88.

1971

'Richard II's Views on Kingship', *Proceedings of the Leeds Philosophical and Literary Society* (Literary and Historical Section), xiv, part 5, 189–205.

1972

[with R.B. Dobson] 'The Medieval Origins of the Robin Hood Legend: A Reassessment', *Northern History*, vii, 1–30.

Film: *An Introduction to Palaeography*. (1) 'From Roman to Caroline'; (2) [with N. Pronay] 'From Gothic to Printing' (Interuniversities Film Consortium, T.V. Centre, Leeds University, 1972–74).

1973

'Higden and Erghome: Two Fourteenth-Century Scholars', *Économies et Sociétés au Moyen Age: Mélanges offerts à Edouard Perroy* (Paris), pp.644–49.

1974

[with N. Pronay] 'The Use of the *Modus Tenendi Parliamentum* in the Middle Ages', *Bulletin of the Institute of Historical Research*, xlvii, 11–23.

1975
'The Plumpton Letters, 1416–1552', *Northern History, x, Essays in Honour of John Le Patourel*, 72–87.

1976
[with R.B. Dobson] *Rymes of Robin Hood: An Introduction to the English Outlaw* (London and Pittsburgh); 2nd edition, 1989 (Gloucester).

1980
[with N. Pronay] *Parliamentary Texts of the Later Middle Ages* (Oxford).
'Letters and Letter Collections in England, 1300–1420', *Nottingham Medieval Studies*, xxiv, 57–70.
Audio-Learning [with R.B. Dobson], *England in the Fourteenth Century*.

1982
Contributions to J.R. Strayer, ed., *Dictionary of the Middle Ages*.

1984
'Representations of the Robin Hood Legend', *The Historian*, ii, 2–8.

1986
'The French Prose *Brut*: Popular History in Fourteenth-Century England', in W.M. Ormrod, *England in the Fourteenth Century* (Woodbridge), pp.247–54.

1987
English Historical Literature in the Fourteenth Century (Oxford).

1989
'The Diocese of York and the University Connexion, 1350–1520', *Northern History*, xxv, 39–59.

1990
'The Good Parliament and its Sources', in J. Taylor and W.R. Childs, ed., *Politics and Crisis in Fourteenth-Century England* (Gloucester), pp.81–96.

Forthcoming
[with W.R. Childs] *The Anonimalle Chronicle, 1307–1334* (Yorkshire Archaeological Society, Records Series, clxvii).
'Richard II in the Chronicles', in A. Goodman and J. Gillespie, ed., *Richard II: Power and Prerogative* (Oxford).

List of Contributors

Robert Black is Lecturer in History and Assistant Sub-Dean of Arts at the University of Leeds and author of *Benedetto Accolti and the Florentine Renaissance* (1985).

Brenda Bolton took her B.A. and M.A. at the University of Leeds. She is now Senior Lecturer in Medieval History at Queen Mary and Westfield College, University of London, and author of *The Medieval Reformation* (1983).

Wendy Childs is Senior Lecturer in Medieval History at the University of Leeds and author of *Anglo-Castilian Trade in the Later Middle Ages* (1978). Her edition, with John Taylor, of *The Anonimalle Chronicle, 1307–34* will be appearing shortly.

Barrie Dobson is Professor of Medieval History at the University of Cambridge and is the author among other works, of *Durham Priory, 1400–1450* (1973) and, together with John Taylor, *Rymes of Robin Hood* (1976).

Simon Forde is the editor of the *International Medieval Bibliography* and also teaches medieval history at the University of Leeds.

Gordon Forster is Senior Lecturer in History at the University of Leeds and is a former Chairman of the School of History. He is the founder editor of the journal *Northern History*, and has contributed extensively to the *Victoria County History of Yorkshire*.

Antonia Gransden has recently retired as Reader in Medieval History at the University of Nottingham. Her monumental study, *Historical Writing in England, c. 550–1307* (1974) was followed by a second volume *1307 to the Early Sixteenth Century* in 1982.

Paul Harvey has recently retired as Professor of Medieval History at the University of Durham. He is the author of *A Medieval Oxfordshire Village: Cuxham 1240–1400* (1965) and has also written extensively about manorial records and medieval cartography.

Lesley Johnson is Lecturer in English at the University of Leeds. She has published on Old French *fabliaux*, the medieval Troy story and fifteenth-century literature.

Jenny Kiff-Hooper offers tutorial assistance at the University of Leeds and is working on a Ph.D at Birkbeck College, University of London.

Joan Kirby has completed an M.Phil at the University of Leeds and is working on a new edition of the Plumpton Letters.

Graham Loud is Lecturer in Medieval History at the University of Leeds and is the author of *Church and Society in the Norman Principality of Capua, 1058–1197* (1985).

David Luscombe is Professor of Medieval History at the University of Sheffield and a Fellow of the British Academy. He is the author of *The School of Peter Abelard* (1969) and *Peter Abelard's Ethics* (1971).

Roger Mott is Second Master at King's College, Taunton, and completed his Ph.D under John Taylor's supervision.

Peter Sawyer was formerly Professor of Medieval History at the University of Leeds: among his publications are *The Age of the Vikings* (1961) and *Kings and Vikings* (1982). He will be giving the Ford Lectures at Oxford University in 1993.

Ian Wood is Senior Lecturer in Medieval History at the University of Leeds. He is co-editor of *People and Places in Northern Europe, 500–1600* (1991).

Anthony Wright is Lecturer in History at the University of Leeds and author of *The Counter Reformation: Catholic Europe and the Non-Christian World* (1982).

Chapter 1

Saint-Wandrille and its Hagiography

Ian Wood

The decline of the Merovingians and the rise of the Carolingians is a topic that is usually seen through Carolingian eyes.[1] In large measure this is the inevitable outcome of the distribution of source-material. Apart from the *Liber historiae Francorum* and the continuations to the chronicle of Fredegar, most of our evidence is not actually contemporary, and the continuations were commissioned by members of the Carolingian family.[2] This problem of the sources makes it particularly important for the Merovingianist to scrutinise his or her information with extreme care. Besides, in addition to casting light on Merovingian history, such scrutiny also illuminates the late eighth and ninth centuries.

One major group of documents covering the period of transition from the Merovingians to the Carolingians was produced by the monastery of Saint-Wandrille. The house was founded by Wandregisil in *c.* 649 at Fontanelle on the lower Seine, on an estate which had been held by the *maior palatii*, Erchinoald.[3] Prominent among early benefactors were the Merovingians Clovis II, Childeric II and Theuderic III.[4] Later the house fell into Carolingian hands, and it has, therefore, been seen as illustrating the transfer of power in eighth-century Francia.[5]

Between the death of the founder in *c.* 668 and the translation of his body first to Bloville and then in 858 to Quentovic,[6] the community

---

[1] This article was originally delivered as a lecture at the twenty-fourth International Congress on Medieval Studies, held in Kalamazoo in May 1989. I am indebted to Professor T.F.X. Noble for inviting me to deliver the paper, to Dr. Wendy Childs and, as always, to Dr. J.L. Nelson.

[2] On the *Liber Historiae Francorum* see R. Gerberding, *The Rise of the Carolingians and the Liber Historiae Francorum* (Oxford, 1987), esp. pp.146–72; on the continuations of Fredegar see J.M. Wallace-Hadrill, *The Fourth Book of the Chronicle of Fredegar* (London, 1960), pp.xxv–xxviii.

[3] F. Lot, 'Études critiques sur l'Abbaye de Saint-Wandrille', *Bibliothèque de l'École des Hautes Études*, cciv (1913), iii–xii.

[4] *Ibid.*, 3–6, nn.5–7, 8, 10.

[5] Gerberding, *op. cit.*, pp.97–98.

[6] Lot, *op. cit.*, xxx–xlvi.

produced a collection of hagiographic material which provides an unequalled opportunity for investigating the impact of the emergence of the Carolingians on an individual monastery, its cults and its lands. This dossier of texts is remarkable not least because of its size. It includes two Lives of Wandregisil, the first of which was written towards the end of the seventh century,[7] Lives of the second and third abbots of the community, Lantbert and Ansbert, as well as those of the hermit Conded, Bishop Erembert of Toulouse and Archbishop Wulfram of Sens.[8] Beyond these, there is also the first part of the *Miracula Wandregisili*,[9] and, above all, the *Gesta sanctorum patrum Fontanellensis coenobii*, more usually known as the *Gesta abbatum Fontanellensium*,[10] which has been described as the earliest monastic history from Western Europe.[11] Taken together this is a very substantial block of material, but it is one that has usually been treated piecemeal.[12]

The cults of Wandregisil, Ansbert and Wulfram were associated from the days of abbot Bainus, who translated all three saints from the church of St. Paul to that of St. Peter in 704.[13] Subsequently he transferred the body of Erembert to the place in St. Paul's where Wandregisil had been buried.[14] Conded was later moved to the same church.[15] The Carolingian hagiography of Saint-Wandrille, which is effectively a *corpus*, echoes this association of cult. Thus, the second Life of Wandregisil refers to a *libellus* containing the Lives of Lantbert and Ansbert, and associates these two saints with the religious careers of Wulfram, Erembert and Conded.[16] Further there are close stylistic relations between the Lives of Lantbert,

---

[7] *Vita Wandregisili*, ed. B. Krusch, *Monumenta Germaniae Historica: Scriptores Rerum Merovingicarum* [henceforth *MGH SRM*], v (Hannover, 1910), p.3; see also W. Wattenbach and W. Levison, *Deutschlands Geschichtsquellen im Mittelalter: Vorzeit und Karolinger* [henceforth Wattenbach-Levison] i (Weimar, 1952), p.138; *Vita II Wandregisili*, *Acta Sanctorum*, July v, pp.272–81.

[8] *Vita Lantberti*, ed. W. Levison, *MGH SRM*, v; *Vita Ansberti*, ed. Levison, *MGH SRM*, v; *Vita Condedi*, ed. Levison, *MGH SRM*, v; *Vita Eremberti*, ed. Levison, *MGH SRM*, v; *Vita Vulframni*, ed. Levison, *MGH SRM* v.

[9] *Miracula Wandregisili*, *Acta Sanctorum* July v, pp.281–90; for the starting date of composition, Wattenbach-Levison, v (ed. H. Löwe), (Weimar, 1973), pp.585–86.

[10] *Gesta sanctorum patrum Fontanellensis coenobii* [henceforth *GAF*], ed. F. Lohier and J. Laporte (Rouen and Paris, 1931). This edition superceded that of S. Loewenfeld, *MGH Scriptores Rerum Germanicarum in usum scholarum* (Hannover, 1886), although the Loewenfeld edition is useful as a reading of the Le Havre recension.

[11] W. Levison, 'Zu den *Gesta abbatum Fontanellensium*', in idem, *Aus rheinische und fränkischer Frühzeit* (Düsseldorf, 1948), p.532.

[12] But see A. Legris, 'Les vies interpolées des saints de Fontanelle', *Analecta Bollandiana*, xvii (1898), 265–306, and W. Levison, 'Zur Kritik der Fontaneller Geschichtsquellen', *Neues Archiv*, xxv (1899), 593–607.

[13] *GAF*, ii, 4.

[14] *Ibid.*, ii, 4.

[15] *Vita Condedi*, 12.

[16] *Vita II Wandregisili*, v, 25–6.

Ansbert, Conded, Erembert and the second Life of Wandregisil, which is intimately related to the *Gesta abbatum Fontanellensium*.[17] Not only are the texts related in style and content, they also refer to each other, thus providing a crucial indication of their order of composition. Among the most recent of them are the early parts of the *Miracula Wandregisili*,[18] and the *Gesta abbatum Fontanellensium*.[19] This last text cites the *Vita Lantberti*,[20] as do the *Vita Condedi*[21] and the *Vita Ansberti*, whose author claimed to have written the Life of Lantbert.[22] In other words, the *Vita Lantberti* seems to have been among the first of the Carolingian Lives to have been written; it was certainly earlier than those of Ansbert and Conded, and the *Gesta abbatum Fontanellensium*.

It is possible to go further than a mere relative chronology. Granted the comparatively early date of the surviving *Vita Ansberti*, it seems reasonable to assume that this is the same as the text transcribed, along with Lives of Wandregisil and Wulfram, by the priest Harduin.[23] Since the *Gesta abbatum Fontanellensium* gives him a death date of 811, it is likely that this provides a *terminus* for the surviving *Vitae* of Ansbert and Wulfram and, by extension, for the Life of Lantbert. It is unlikely, however, that these *Vitae* were composed long before 811. The Life of Conded seems to draw heavily on that of Ermenland of Indre,[24] who is the subject of a chapter of the *Vita Ansberti*.[25] The author of the *Vita Ermenlandi*, Donatus, may also have written the *Vita Trudonis* for Angilramn of Metz between 784 and 791.[26] Levison dated the Life of Ermenland to the late eighth century. Perhaps more important is the dependence of the Lives of Conded and Wulfram on Alcuin's *Vita Willibrordi*,[27] written for Beornrad of Sens, apparently between 785 and 797.[28] All this suggests that there was considerable hagiographic activity at Saint-Wandrille around the year 800, in other words during the lifetime of the priest Harduin. This was also the period of the abbacy of Gervold (789–807?), to whom the *Gesta* interestingly attribute the foundation of a school to improve literacy.[29]

[17] *MGH SRM*, v, pp.607, 615, 644–45, 652–53; *GAF*, ed. Laporte, pp.xxxix–xxx, xxxii.

[18] Wattenbach-Levison, v, pp.585–86.

[19] The *Vita II Wandregisili* is also dated late in the corpus; Wattenbach-Levison, i, p.139; Wattenbach-Levison, v, p.585; *GAF*, ed. Laporte, p.xxxiv.

[20] *GAF*, vi, 2.

[21] *Vita Condedi*, 8.

[22] *Vita Ansberti*, 11.

[23] *GAF*, xii, 3.

[24] *Vita Condedi*, 2–4, 6; *MGH SRM*, v, p.644.

[25] *Vita Ansberti*, 10.

[26] *Vita Ermenlandi*, ed. W. Levison, *MGH SRM*, v; see pp.675–76.

[27] *Vita Condedi*, 1–4, 7, 11; see *MGH SRM*, v, pp.644, 658.

[28] Alcuin, *Vita Willibrordi, praef.*, ed. W. Levison, *MGH SRM*, vii (Hannover, 1920); see now H.-J. Reischmann, *Willibrord: Apostel der Friesen* (Darmstadt, 1989).

[29] *GAF*, xii, 2.

For the *Gesta abbatum Fontanellensium*, Laporte, the work's finest editor, argued, on the grounds of the uneven nature of the coverage in the text, and of the absence of proper accounts of the abbacies of Lantbert, Ansbert and Hildebert, in the closing years of the seventh century, and those of Trasarus and Einhard, between 807 and 823, that the text was composed in four parts.[30] The first two, covering the period from Wandregisil to Gervold, he ascribed to *c*. 830, the third, concerned entirely with Ansigisus, he dated *c*. 845, and the final additions, covering the abbots Fulco, Joseph and Herimbert, he assigned to the period 850–67. Grierson accepted Laporte's division of the text but challenged his precise chronology, substituting instead a date of post-838 for the second part of the work, covering the eighth-century abbots, from Bainus to Gervold, and a date of pre-840 for the account of Ansigisus.[31] These modifications were suggested on the grounds that the second section depended on a list of the abbots of Saint-Vaast. Since Fulco was abbot of both Saint-Vaast and Saint-Wandrille between 838 and 842, this was the most likely moment for the composition of the second part. With regard to the third, Grierson denied Laporte's assertion that certain chronological references suggested that Louis the Pious was already dead. Neither of Grierson's arguments is watertight. Although Fulco was abbot of both Saint-Wandrille and Saint-Vaast, this was not the only period in which there was contact between the two monasteries. In his will Ansigisus remembered the community of Saint-Vaast.[32] Laporte may have been wrong to argue that there was evidence that Louis the Pious was dead by the time the abbacy of Ansigisus was written up, but Grierson's argument that Louis was still alive is equally unproven.

It may be that a straightforward assignation of dates of composition to various sections of the *Gesta abbatum Fontanellensium* is too simple an approach. The text could have been compiled and revised over a reasonably long period of time, without being the product of three or four bursts of activity. That a date of *c*. 830 is too late for some chapters of the second part is implied by the account of Wido's execution in *c*. 745; this the author learnt from 'a certain father who had been able to see him'.[33] It is just possible that a man who was very young in the 740s might have been an informant of someone who was reasonably old in the 830s, but it is not all that likely. Even less likely is the existence of many who could still testify in the 830s to Wando's piety in the years before his death, which can scarcely have been any later

[30] *GAF*, ed. Laporte, pp.xxviii–xxxiii.

[31] P. Grierson, 'Abbot Fulco and the Date of the *Gesta abbatum Fontanellensium*', *English Historical Review.*, lv (1940), 275–84.

[32] *GAF*, xiii, 7; it is less likely that continuing links were established under Wido, *ibid.*, vii.

[33] *Ibid.*, vii.

than 754.[34] Assuming that the author's claims about his informants were genuine, a date of composition for these sections rather closer to 800 would seem to be required.

But there are complications. In the chapter before that concerned with Wido there is an account of the spoliation of the abbey under Teutsind, who alienated estates as *precaria* and whose abbacy saw the diversion of the gifts of the faithful into worldly pursuits.[35] Such alienation is said to take ten times longer to repair than it took to build up the monastery's holdings in the first place. So appalling is the behaviour of such abbots, says the author, that they are worse than the pagans, 'since, if a pagan burns a place, he doesn't take the earth with him'.[36] It is very tempting to see such a comparison as belonging to the period of the Viking invasions, to understand the parallel with the pagans as having particular force, and to attribute this chapter of invective, which is actually a free-standing denunciation of *precaria*, to the 840s.[37] Otherwise the passage is a remarkable precursor of the rhetoric of the ninth-century episcopate.[38]

That the text of the *Gesta* was added to at various moments is clear enough; the account of Ansigisus's death and the entries on Fulco, Joseph and Herimbert only survive in one manuscript, Le Havre, MS A34, which is now reckoned to be the least satisfactory, not least because it omits much of importance, including the *Constitutio Ansigisi*.[39] Yet if the *Gesta* is seen as a work which was adapted and revised according to particular circumstances, then the opprobrium which has been heaped on the Le Havre manuscript may come to be seen as misplaced. For instance at the end of the Life of Wando this text alone has the word *explicit*,[40] which might suggest that at some point the *Gesta* only ran from Wandregisil to Wando. In such a text there would be a peculiar sense of balance, since Wandregisil happens also to have been known as Wando, and the opening words of the work compare Wandregisil/Wando with earlier monastic fathers.[41] That the second Wando continued to be regarded as a crucial figure in later recensions of the text is further implied

---

[34] *Ibid.*, ix, 3.

[35] *Ibid.*, vi, 1–2.

[36] *Ibid.*, vi, 3.

[37] For the context see *Chronicon Fontenallense*, ed. G.H. Pertz, MGH *Scriptores* ii (Hannover, 1829), pp.301–4.

[38] Councils of Rheims (813), c. 36–7, Tours (813), c. 51, ed. A. Werminghoff, *MGH Concilia* ii, i (Hannover, 1906); Meaux/Paris (845–6), cc. 21–2, Quierzy (858), c. 7, ed. W. Hartmann, *MGH Concilia* iii (Hannover, 1984).

[39] *GAF*, xiii, 8, xiv; or in Loewenfeld's edition, 18–19; for comments on Le Havre MS A34 see *GAF*, ed. Laporte, pp.xvii-xxi.

[40] *GAF*, ix, 4, ed. Laporte, p.71, note o; *GAF*, 13, ed. Loewenfeld.

[41] *GAF*, i, 1.

by his central position in the surviving versions of the Gesta, where the monastery's fortunes, having been established, are endangered by the behaviour of abbots, restored, endangered and restored again.

If a complex pattern of composition and reworking is envisaged, the absence of accounts of Lantbert, Ansbert and Hildebert ceases to be a criterion for understanding the chronology of the *Gesta*. These particular abbots may not have had any role in the original author's designs; in the cases of Lantbert and Ansbert, it may have been thought that their own *vitae* rendered lengthy accounts of them in the *Gesta* superfluous. Equally they may originally have been included, but then excised from the work at a later date.

The notion of a monastery creating and reworking an account of its history implies that the community must have regarded the memory of its abbots as a commodity to be exploited. This is also implied by the element of hagiographic forgery in the *vitae*. The Life of Ansbert, for instance, has a letter of dedication, which purports to be addressed by the author, Aigradus, to Hildebert, the fourth abbot of Saint-Wandrille, and Ansbert's successor.[42] Similarly the Life of Wulfram has a preface in which the author, supposedly called Jonas, addresses Hildebert's successor, Bainus.[43] The choice of the name, Jonas, was almost certainly intended to suggest that the author was also the biographer of Columbanus.[44] Further, the Life of Wulfram has a number of totally mendacious assertions about eyewitnesses.[45] It may be significant that two of the three *vitae* copied out by Harduin seem to have been forgeries.[46] The third Life which he transcribed was that of Wandregisil. Presumably this was the Merovingian text, but like the *vitae* of Ansbert and Wulfram, the second Life of Wandregisil, which is usually given a later date, has a forged prologue addressed to an abbot, Lantbert.[47] Perhaps Harduin himself was involved in forgery.

Such hagiographic activity must have had a purpose, or rather a number of purposes. Saint-Wandrille was concerned with the cults of its saints. This is apparent in the translations of Wandregisil, Ansbert and Wulfram effected by Bainus in 704, and of that of Erembert, perhaps in the same year.[48] Later the latter's vestments and crozier were translated to Saint-Wandrille.[49] The continuing significance of these cults for the

---

[42] *Vita Ansberti, praef.*; *MGH SRM*, v, p.615.

[43] *Vita Vulframni, praef.*

[44] *MGH SRM*, v, p.658

[45] *Vita Vulframni, praef.*, 6; see *MGH SRM*, v, pp.658–59.

[46] *GAF*, xii, 3; I.N. Wood, 'Forgery in Merovingian Hagiography', in *Fälschungen im Mittelalter, MGH Schriften*, xxxiii, v (Hannover, 1989), 372.

[47] *Vita II Wandregisili, prol.*

[48] *GAF*, ii, 4; *Vita Eremberti*, 6, 8.

[49] *Vita Eremberti*, 8.

monastery is also clear from its *vitae* and, for the period after 858, from the accounts of the translations of the relics of Wandregisil and Ansbert, following the Viking destruction of Saint-Wandrille.[50] Of the other saints, Wulfram continued to attract attention in this period,[51] but Conded and Erembert ceased to be of significance for the community. Lantbert had always been treated separately, which may suggest that he was buried at Lyons.

Corporeal relics were not the only aspects of the cult of the saints among the Saint-Wandrille community. The monks were careful to point out the places where Wandregisil, Audoin and Filibert had rested.[52] In addition, the sites of certain events were marked by buildings or crosses. Thus Wandregisil founded a church on the spot where a miracle had saved him from the spear of the royal forester, Batto.[53] A cross was erected at a place where Ansbert's body rested on its final journey from Hautmont to Saint-Wandrille, and a church was later built there.[54] There were other cults and relics, including those of Amantius of Rodez and Saturninus of Toulouse,[55] as of St. George, associated with a bizarre gospel reliquary washed up at Portbail.[56] For the most part, however, it was the house saints of the community who were most cherished.

Nevertheless, neither the *Gesta abbatum Fontanellensium* nor the Saint-Wandrille *vitae*, with the single and very important exception of the *Vita Ansberti*, are works in which the miraculous plays a major role. It seems that these texts were not concerned first and foremost to promote the shrines of the monastery as *foci* of pilgrimage. More important than the miraculous in much Saint-Wandrille hagiography is a concern with the activity of the saints as monks and abbots, and with their learning. Knowledge of the scriptures is discussed with regard to Ansbert,[57] and Hugo,[58] a zest for teaching and knowledge of music is noted for Gervold,[59] and gifts of books are recorded for Wando, Witlaic, Gervold, Harduin and Ansigisus.[60] Equally, the lack of education of

---

[50] *Miracula Wandregisili, passim*; see also A. Borias, 'Saint Wandrille et la crise mono-thélite', *Revue Bénédictine*, xcvii (1987), 42–43.

[51] *Miracula Wandregisili*, v, 52; see also Borias, 'Saint Wandrille et la crise monothélite', 43 on the *Sermo de adventu sanctorum Wandregisili Ansberti et Vulframni in Blandinum*.

[52] *GAF*, i, 6; *Vita II Wandregisili*, iv, 17.

[53] *Vita II Wandregisili*, iv, 18.

[54] *Vita Ansberti*, 34–35.

[55] *Vita II Wandregisili*, iii, 17; on the churches of these saints at St. Wandrille, *GAF*, i, 6, x, 5, xii, 3.

[56] *GAF*, x, 2–3.

[57] *Vita Ansberti*, 13.

[58] *GAF*, iv, 1.

[59] *Ibid.*, xii, 2.

[60] *Ibid.*, ix, 2; xi, 2, 3; xiii, 4, 6.

the archbishop of Rouen, Grimo, and of the abbots Wido, Reginfrid
and Witlaic is stressed.[61]

Alongside this interest in learning is a concern for the monastic life and
for the Rule. The importance of the monastic life in the Saint-Wandrille
community is already implicit in the Merovingian Life of Wandregisil,
where the saint's search for a model, at Bobbio and Romainmoutier
is emphasised.[62] The question of the monastic life is also important to
the *Gesta abbatum Fontanellensium*, which records the donation of several
monastic rules by Wando,[63] as well as providing an account of the
changing regular status of the abbey. This first becomes a significant
issue with Teutsind's undermining of Benedictine traditions, supposedly
instituted by Wandregisil.[64] Later Austrulf is praised for following the
Rule,[65] while Witlaic endangered it again.[66] Finally the Benedictine
reform of Ansigisus is described at length.[67] Wandregisil's prophecy
relating to the elections of Lantbert and Ansbert, recounted in their
vitae, may be explained by this concern with the Rule of St. Benedict.
Apparently the two abbots shared an abbacy. This may have been
regarded in the Carolingian period as uncanonical, and therefore needing
justification by divine intervention.[68] The emphasis which Ansbert's *vita*
places on his abbatial behaviour is also noteworthy;[69] this work is
particularly concerned with the question of monastic standards, and
one of its main literary models is, significantly, the Life of Honoratus,
the fifth-century founder of the great monastery of Lérins.[70] The Saint-
Wandrille hagiographers seem to have chosen their models with care.

Related to the concern about the Rule in the *Gesta abbatum Fontanellensium* is an emphasis on monastic immunity. Abbot Lando is first
reported as having been granted an immunity by Charles Martel in *c.*
732.[71] Later the monks of Saint-Wandrille managed to have Raginfrid
deposed for infringing it.[72] A further privilege was secured from Pippin
by Austrulf in 751–52.[73] The importance of immunities at the time of
the composition of the *Gesta* is clear from a charter of Louis the Pious

---

[61] *Ibid.*, viii, 1; xi, 2.

[62] *Vita Wandregisili*, 9–10; cf *Vita II Wandregisili*, ii, 9, 11.

[63] *GAF*, ix, 2. There is also mention of copies of the Rules of St. Basil and St. Benedict,
given by Ansigisus to St. Germer de Flay in xiii, 6.

[64] *GAF*, vi, 1.

[65] *Ibid.*, x, 1.

[66] *Ibid.*, xi, 2.

[67] *Ibid.*, xiii, 2.

[68] *Vita Lantberti*, 2; *Vita Ansberti*, 8.

[69] *Ibid.*, 5–6.

[70] *MGH SRM*, v, p.615.

[71] *GAF*, v, 2.

[72] *Ibid.*, viii, 1.

[73] *Ibid.*, x, 4.

from the year 815, which renewed a privilege of Charlemagne.[74] The Saint-Wandrille hagiographers were writing works with considerable contemporary reverberation.

This is particularly apparent if one turns to other diplomas of the reigns of Charlemagne and Charles the Bald. According to the *Gesta abbatum Fontanellensium*, Charlemagne restored to Abbot Gervold all those estates which had been taken unjustly from the abbey or which had been conferred on the king's followers.[75] That problems continued is clear from Charles the Bald's charter of 854 for his cousin, Abbot Louis, ensuring resources for the abbey, regardless of the negligence or niggardliness of abbots and the destructive effects of the Vikings.[76]

Land plays a major role in Saint-Wandrille texts, not least because the authors of the *Gesta* and the Carolingian *vitae* included a very considerable number of references to charters and archives in their works. The longest recensions of the *Gesta* include the *Constitutio Ansigisi*, which lists the dues owed by certain estates to the monastery.[77] The Saint-Wandrille texts are an important repository of charter material. Lot estimated that they contained references to sixty-three *acta*, fifty-one of which come from the *Gesta abbatum Fontanellensium*.[78] Five come either from the Life of Lantbert or that of Ansbert, three from that of Conded, two from that of Wulfram and two from that of Erembert. For most commentators this has made these texts valuable evidence, and has transformed the *Gesta* into something closer to history than hagiography. That this hagiographical sophistication might have had a purpose has somehow been ignored; yet the inclusion of charter material must indicate something of the purpose of the *Gesta* and the *vitae*.

The majority of these acts (fifty-six in all) belong to the period before the abbacy of Teutsind.[79] With him not only did the number of donations decline dramatically, but according to the *Gesta* one third of the abbey's estates were also granted out as *precaria*.[80] The author illustrates his case with a study of estates given to Lantbert by Childeric II and Bilichild. These were granted to Rathar in return for an annual levy of lights for the abbey, but Rathar ceased payment in the days of Witlaic.[81] This last abbot seems to have been as responsible as Teutsind for the parlous state

---

[74] Lot, *op. cit.*, recueil n.4, pp.28–30.

[75] *GAF*, xii, 2.

[76] Lot, *op. cit.*, recueil n.5, 31–6; also *Recueil des actes de Charles II le Chauve roi de France*, i, ed. F. Lot and G. Tessier (Paris, 1944), n.160, pp.419–26.

[77] *GAF*, xiii, 8.

[78] Lot, *op.cit.*, 3–20.

[79] *Ibid.*, 3–18.

[80] *GAF*, vi, 1.

[81] *Ibid.*, vi, 2.

into which the abbey had fallen.[82]

The diplomas of Charlemagne, Louis the Pious and Charles the Bald echo two of the salient features of the Saint-Wandrille texts written during their reigns; concern about monastic lands and immunity. The petitions which led to the restitution of lands by Charlemagne, the immunities of Charlemagne and Louis, and the arrangements made over resources with Charles the Bald, were backed by material which found its way into the Saint-Wandrille corpus. Perhaps the compilation of the *Gesta* was bound up with such petitions; Charles the Bald's visit to the monastery in 841, which included a discussion with the monks, might be related to one of the recensions of the text.[83]

The question of land must have encouraged the monks of Saint-Wandrille to emphasise the close association of the abbey with the Carolingians. On occasion this was certainly thought to have been a useful bargaining point. Although there is no mention of the fact in the first Life of Wandregisil, according to the second Life of the saint,[84] and to the *Gesta abbatum Fontanellensium*,[85] Pippin II and Wandregisil were related. This relationship is said to have prompted Pippin to release Ansbert from exile at Hautmont.[86] The link is probably fictitious.[87] Nevertheless the monastery of St. Wandrille did have close links with the Pippinids; Pippin II was certainly a benefactor of the abbey,[88] and Abbot Hugo was Charles Martel's nephew.[89]

Saint Wandrille, however, was not always a pro-Carolingian house. Wandregisil was provided with the site of his foundation by the Neustrian *maior* Erchinoald.[90] It is the Merovingians, notably the sons of Balthild, who feature prominently in the early history of the abbey.[91] Theuderic III, in particular, is singled out for the honour of a prophecy predicting

---

[82] *Ibid.*, xi, 2.

[83] *Chronicon Fontanellense*, *s.a.* 841, p.301.

[84] *Vita II Wandregisili*, i, 1.

[85] *GAF*, i, 2.

[86] *Vita Ansberti*, 12, 22.

[87] E.Vacandard, 'Saint Wandrille, était-il apparenté aux rois mérovingiens et carolingiens?', *Revue des Questions Historiques*, lxvii (1900), 214–28, rejected any familial link between Wandregisil and the Merovingians, but thought that a connection with Pippin II was possible but not proven; see, however, the review in *Analecta Bollandiana*, xix (1900), 235.

[88] *GAF*, ii, 1.

[89] *Ibid.*, iv, 1.

[90] *Vita II Wandregisili*, iii, 14; *GAF*, i, 4, 7; Lot, *op. cit.*, iii-xii.

[91] Lot, *op. cit.*, recueil nn.1, 2, 5, 6, 7, 8, 10, 21, 23, 24, 43, 50; the Merovingians may also have been involved in the original grant of Fontanelle, which is said by the first *Vita Wandregisili*, 14, to have been a royal gift of fiscal land, but, on the problem of the foundation, see Lot, *op. cit.*, iii-xii.

his accession.[92] Nor is there any real criticism of Dagobert III for his deposition of Abbot Benignus.[93]

By contrast it is worth looking at Carolingian involvement in the abbey. Benignus, who was restored to his post by Charles Martel, was well thought of as abbot,[94] as was Hugo, even though he did not owe his appointment to members of his father's family: the author of the *Gesta* is concerned to depict him less as the son of Drogo, than as the grandson of Ansfled, who brought him up in Rouen.[95] This powerful matron was one of the arbiters of power after the death of her husband, the Neustrian *maior* Waratto, in *c.* 684. She played a crucial role in the events surrounding the battle of Tertry.[96] In stressing Hugo's relationship with her the author of the *Gesta* was effectively emphasising the abbot's West Frankish origins and upbringing. Hugo himself seems to have been distinctly cool towards Charles Martel,[97] which is not surprising, granted the hostility between the latter and his step-mother, Plectrudis, who was Hugo's paternal grandmother.

Among later pro-Carolingian abbots, Teutsind, who can probably be seen as one of Charles's appointees on the grounds of his distribution of *precaria*, was a disaster,[98] nor was the secular Abbot Wido, a close relative of Charles, much better.[99] Raginfrid, Pippin's godfather, was so loathed by the monks of Saint-Wandrille that they persuaded Pippin to depose him. They also succeeded in having Dagobert III's appointee, Wando, brought out of exile and reinstated.[100] The last of the bad abbots, Witlaic, bought his office from Pippin III.[101] The Carolingian family was responsible for the policies which lost the abbey vast quantities of land, and it was personally involved in every bad abbatial appointment. Looked at in these terms the Saint-Wandrille corpus, with its emphases on good monastic standards and the preservation of church estates, is a flagrant denunciation of the results of the policies of Charles Martel and Pippin III.

The extent of this hostility can be seen in two instances. First, there is the death of Ansbert. According to the saint's *vita* Pippin exiled him to Hautmont, because of false suspicions.[102] He had intended to send the saint yet further away but Aldulf, the abbot of Hautmont, dissuaded

92 *Vita Ansberti*, 7.
93 *GAF*, iii, 1.
94 *Ibid.*, iii, 1.
95 *Ibid.*, iv, 1.
96 *Liber Historiae Francorum*, 48, ed. B. Krusch, *MGH SRM* ii (Hannover, 1888).
97 *GAF*, iv, 1.
98 *Ibid.*, iv, 3.
99 *Ibid.*, vii.
100 *Ibid.*, viii, 1.
101 *Ibid.*, xi, 1.
102 *Vita Ansberti*, 21.

him, reminding him of Wandregisil's connections with Pippin, and persuading him to let Ansbert return to Rouen.[103] The latter gave thanks, even though, as the hagiographer claimed, he would have been up to facing the Neronian or Decian persecution.[104] Before he could return, however, he died; what followed was a triumphal *translatio* across northern Francia, marked by miraculous cures.[105] The extent of feeling registered by the hagiographer can be gauged by the parallels drawn with Nero and Decius, by the lavish attention drawn to the *translatio*, and by the number of miracles recorded as having taken place at the time. It should be remembered that the *Vita Ansberti* has far and away the largest number of miracles of all the *vitae* of the Saint-Wandrille corpus. The erection of a cross and subsequently of a church to mark a place where the corpse of the saint rested must have been a permanent reminder of Carolingian persecution.[106] No wonder Pippin endowed Saint-Wandrille with the monastery of Fleury in an outburst of remorse;[107] a point omitted from the Le Havre manuscript of the *Gesta abbatum Fontanellensium*.[108]

The second episode is in certain respects a twin of the first, as it too concerns the return of an abbot from exile. After his victory at Vinchy Charles Martel deposed Ragamfred's appointee, Wando, for lending his patron a horse to escape from the battle. In his place he reappointed Benignus, who had previously been made abbot by Childebert III. Wando was sent into exile at Maastricht.[109] There he remained until the monks of Saint-Wandrille had secured the deposition of Abbot Raginfrid for his infringement of their privilege. The return of Wando, with crosses, banners and crowds of accompanying monks must have been another public rebuff to a Carolingian ruler, this time Pippin III.[110] The monks had gained the abbot they wanted, a Neustrian from the region of Béthune, with the same name as the monastery's founder.[111]

The hagiography of Saint-Wandrille, therefore, seems not to see the history of the monastery from a Carolingian viewpoint. Its attitudes are far more local, reflecting the concerns of the abbey, its inmates and benefactors. To judge from the origins of its abbots, and the main areas of its land-holding, these were from Neustria, particularly from the region between Boulogne and the lower Seine.[112]

103 *Ibid.*, 22.
104 *Ibid.*, 23.
105 *Ibid.*, 24–36.
106 *Ibid.*, 32, 34–35.
107 *GAF*, ii, 1.
108 *Ibid.*, ii, 1, ed. Laporte, p.14, n.1; compare with *GAF*, 2, ed. Loewenfeld, pp 17–18.
109 *GAF*, iii, 1.
110 *Ibid.*, viii, 1.
111 *Ibid.*, ix, 1; on Neustrian traditions see Gerberding, *op. cit.*, pp.146–72.
112 Lot, *op. cit.*, xiii-xxvi.

This specific viewpoint may help to explain the nature of the most peculiar of the Saint-Wandrille *vitae*, that of Wulfram of Sens. The Life is concerned with a saint who is known from other evidence, including the *Gesta abbatum Fontanellensium*, to have died before 696/7 and whose body was translated in 704.[113] Nevertheless, it makes him a leading figure in the conversion of Frisia, and depicts him as almost succeeding in converting the Frisian ruler, Radbod, before the devil tricked the latter into dying as a pagan.[114] Radbod, as the hagiographer tells us, died in 719.[115] Chronologically the Life of Wulfram is preposterous. But the dramatic story of Radbod withdrawing from the font at the last minute – he had already put one foot in the water – has been too good for historians to let pass.[116]

A number of factors seem to have been relevant to the writing of the Life. First, it was composed at the time of the Saxon wars and missions of Charlemagne.[117] These were not irrelevant to Saint-Wandrille: the *Miracula Wandregisili* records the capture and miraculous escape of one of the abbey's soldiers, Sigenand, during the wars.[118] More important is the relationship between the *Vita Vulframni* and another Life dealing with the Frisian mission, written at the same time; the *Vita Willibrordi* by Alcuin, a man intimately concerned with Charlemagne's missionary policy.[119] In the Life of Wulfram there are several parallels with that of Willibrord, and the latter saint is even given a walk-on role.[120] More suggestive is the question of dedication: Alcuin dedicated his work to Beornrad, archbishop of Sens, and formerly abbot of Echternach.[121] The author of the *Vita Vulframni* went one better, and wrote a Life of an archbishop of Sens, who did the work of Willibrord and was buried in Saint-Wandrille. The literary association of two archbishops of Sens with the Frisian mission can hardly be accidental.

That Saint-Wandrille might genuinely have had an interest in the Frisian mission is possible. Here the role of Wando is important. He features as a source of information about Wulfram, whom he is said to have accompanied.[122] Later Wulfram is said to have cured Wando's uncle.[123] It should, of course, be remembered that Wando was exiled to Maastricht or, as the *Gesta abbatum Fontanellensium* wrongly states, perhaps

[113] *MGH SRM*, v, p.657, *GAF*, II, 4, ed. Laporte, pp.20–21, n.48.
[114] *Vita Vulframni*, 3–11.
[115] *Ibid.*, 10; *MGH SRM* V, p.670, n.2.
[116] *Vita Vulframni*, 9.
[117] R. McKitterick, *The Frankish Kingdoms under the Carolingians* (London, 1983), pp.61–63.
[118] *Miracula Wandregisili*, i, 4–5.
[119] McKitterick, *op. cit.*, p.62.
[120] *Vita Vulframni*, 9.
[121] Alcuin, *Vita Willibrordi*, *praef.*
[122] *Vita Vulframni*, 5.
[123] *Ibid.*, 12.

deliberately, to Utrecht.[124] There he would have been a contemporary of Radbod and of Willibrord.

It is difficult not to see the *Vita Vulframni* as an attempt by the monks of Saint-Wandrille to claim a segment of late Merovingian history, which Alcuin had recently associated with Willibrord and the Carolingians. The claim as it stands is palpably fraudulent, although it may have some basis in Wando's period of exile. What is important is the author's decision to see the period in an explicitly non-Carolingian way. Here the depiction of Radbod is most telling. He may be damned because of his religion but, although he is a man hidebound by custom, he is prepared to listen to, if not follow, Wulfram. There is no question in the text of war or enmity with Charles Martel. This is surely the Radbod of the Neustrians, allied to Ragamfred, *maior* of Chilperic II and patron of Wando.[125]

The evidence from Saint-Wandrille is quite distinctly non-Caroling-ian,[126] even going to the extent of rewriting Frisian history to undermine the achievement of Willibrord and his patrons. It is anti-Austrasian,[127] and, more positively, Neustrian. In this respect it is close to the *Liber historiae Francorum*, even though its Neustrian concerns are those of the lower Seine, rather than those of Soissons.[128] It provides one more clue to the full complexity of late Merovingian and early Carolingian Francia. In the heartlands of the Franks this period needs to be approached with a sense of nuance and of regional differentiation, for which the standard Carolingian/Merovingian dichotomy does not allow.

[124] *GAF*, iii, 1; viii, 1; ix, 1; *GAF*, ed. Laporte, p.24, n.55, attributes the error to the author's dependence on Bede.

[125] Fredegar, continuations 8–9; *GAF*, iii, 1. Historians have consistently ignored the religious importance for Radbod of the alliance with the christians Ragamfred and Chilperic II. The latter earns a creditable assessment from the anonymous author of the *Historia abbatum*, 32, ed. C. Plummer, *Venerabilis Baedae opera historica* (Oxford, 1896), probably because he was the king who gave Ceolfrith permission to cross the Frankish kingdom in 716. He was also remembered as Helpric on fo. 12v, of the *Liber vitae* of Durham, ed. J. Stevenson, *Liber vitae ecclesiae Dunelmensis*, Surtees Society, xiii (1841), p.1.

[126] *Contra* Gerberding, *op. cit.*, p.98, n.33.

[127] *GAF*, ed. Laporte, p.xxxvii.

[128] See Gerberding, *op. cit.*, pp.150–59.

Chapter 2

Class books or Works of Art?: Some Observations on the Tenth-Century Manuscripts of Aldhelm's De Laude Virginitatis

J.A. Kiff-Hooper

The influence exerted by the tenth-century Benedictine reform movement upon the intellectual climate within England is unquestionable. By the preservation and copying of venerable and imported continental manuscripts the range of texts available within the monastic scriptoria increased. Authors of an earlier English 'Golden Age', such as Bede and Aldhelm, appear to have been particularly popular. Aldhelm's writings became established as an essential element in the school curriculum, and his major treatise on the merits of virginity, De laude virginitatis, was frequently copied by the scribes of the tenth century.[1] Many of these manuscripts were copied specifically for use in the classroom. The degree of glossing contained within them and the use of syntactical glossing provides ample evidence of their intended usage.[2] The De laude virginitatis, along with other works by Aldhelm, played an integral part in the educational process of the tenth-century monastic reform movement. The leading reformers were familiar with, and influenced by, the content and style of Aldhelm's writings.[3] The large number of copies of the De laude virginitatis made at Christ Church, Canterbury, have been linked to a general trend within that scriptorium which was intended to inculcate Christian moral teaching

---

[1] For a brief outline of the transmission of Aldhelm's manuscripts, see M. Lapidge and J. Rosier, *Aldhelm: The Poetic Works* (Ipswich, 1985), pp.1–4.

[2] Manuscripts containing syntactical glosses include London, B[ritish] L[ibrary], MS Royal 5.E.XI; Salisbury [Cathedral Library], MS38; Brussels, Bibliothèque Royale, MS lat. 1650. See R. Ehwald, *Aldhelmi Opera Omnia. Monumenta Germaniae Historica: Auctores Antiquissimi*, xv (Berlin, 1919), p.215; F.C. Robinson, 'Syntactical Glosses in Latin Manuscripts of Anglo-Saxon Provenance', *Speculum*, xlviii (1973), 443–75.

[3] On Aldhelm's influence on Bishop Æthelwold and Byrhtferth see M. Lapidge, 'The Hermeneutic Style in Tenth-Century Anglo-Latin Literature', *Anglo-Saxon England* (henceforth *ASE*), iv (1975), 67–111; M. Lapidge, 'Byrhtferth of Ramsey and the Early Sections of the *Historia Regum* Attributed to Symeon of Durham', *ASE*, x (1981), 113.

and the values of the monastery, as promoted by the reformers.[4] A policy of multiple copying has also been suggested, whether to facilitate the endeavours of its own students or to assist in the educational pursuits of other houses is unclear.[5] It is in this role, as a teaching aid, that the manuscripts of the *De laude virginitatis* are generally studied, either for the uses made of the extensive vocabulary and literary style or the range of the glosses.[6] The codicological aspects of these manuscripts, on the other hand, are frequently overlooked in these studies. It could easily be assumed that all of the extant manuscripts from the tenth century follow a 'standardised' format which is primarily concerned with presenting a functional rendition of the text. However, manuscripts produced for the classroom were not devoid of textual ornamentation and others would appear to have been produced for a luxury market. It is the purpose of this essay to make some observations relating to these deluxe manuscripts.

The most striking indication of a luxury manuscript is often considered to be the inclusion of illustrations, either forming an integral part of the whole composition or preceding the text. In the tenth-century manuscripts of the *De laude virginitatis* there are examples of this form of display. The earliest is contained within British Library, MS Royal 7.D.XXIV, although it is an illustration fraught with problems (Plate 1). The incomplete drawing, on fo.85v, appears to be a portrait of the author and faces the dedicatory passage of the prose version of the *De laude virginitatis* on fo.85r. It would appear to adhere to the standard iconography applied to Evangelistic portraits, and it is likely that the drawing was originally intended to be just that. Executed in a brown wash the artist shows a clean-shaven figure with flowing locks and stylus in hand, bent over a writing desk. Some of the features which are associated with Evangelistic portraits of this type are present, for example the draped desk and a curtain drawn to one side behind a column.[7] There also appears to be an indication that the figure was intended to be positioned within a frame. The lightly-sketched design seems to encorporate corner bosses as part of the overall design, although in the lower part of this outlined

---

[4] N. Brooks, *The Early History of the Church of Canterbury* (Leicester, 1984), pp.275–76, 277–78. The manuscripts referred to are London, BL, MS Royal 6.A.VI; BL, MS Royal 5.E.XI; C[ambridge], C[orpus] C[hristi] C[ollege], MS 326; Oxford, Bodleian Library, MS Bodley 577, and Salisbury, MS 38.

[5] *Ibid.*, p.273

[6] Lapidge and Rosier, *Aldhelm: The Poetic Works*, pp.27–33 provides a concise bibliography of the most important works related to these aspects of Aldhelm's writings.

[7] This composition also includes a 'horned' ink stand, a feature which forms part of a classical tradition; see A.M. Friend, 'The Portraits of the Evangelists in Greek and Latin Manuscripts', *Art Studies*, v (1927). It could be argued that the drawing in BL, Royal 7.D.XXIV was following a model influence by the Ada School; see R. Hinks *Carolingian Art* (Ann Arbor, 1974), p.168.

frame the composition has been altered to accommodate a rocky terrain. The inclusion of uneven ground beneath the feet of the Evangelists is commonplace.[8] In MS Royal 7.D.XXIV the landscaping varies from that found in some other tenth-century manuscripts, such as Cambridge, Corpus Christi College, MS 23, and the later cycle of drawings in Oxford, Bodleian Library, MS Junius 11, and is more reminiscent of the eleventh-century drawings to be found in British Library, MS Tiberius C.VI.[9] Whether the hand which later added to minor details of the original figure intended to adhere to the original composition is debatable, as both artists seem to have been unable to complete their labours.

The second artist, working in a darker ink, introduces solidity to the figure but makes no attempt to signify that this is intended to be a representation of Aldhelm. In this respect it is therefore doubtful whether one can categorise the drawing in MS Royal 7.D.XXIV as an Aldhelm 'portrait' as it makes little pretence to be one. In reality it is simply a reused sketch. A cursory look at the position of the drawing betrays this as it is not placed centrally on the folio but veers towards the right. The folio has obviously been trimmed to match the dimensions of the *De laude virginitatis*, as part of an additional sketch of a hand (which appears to be the work of the artist responsible for the additions to the original portrait) has been severed along with the prickings which aided in the ruling of the manuscript. A study of the quiring of the manuscript suggests that the illustration did not form an integral part of the main composition; for fos.82–85 form a separate quire, and the arrangement of the following quires is also problematic.[10] Although the portrait does not appear to be contemporary with the rest of the manuscript, the hand at work on the capitula section within this quire (fo.85) is identical to that of the main scribal hand. This may indicate that the inclusion of a capitula section was an afterthought. In addition, the manuscript also reveals evidence of exposure on folios 82 and 168 suggesting that once assembled in its present arrangement it spent some time without a cover.

Nevertheless, a detailed study of MS Royal 7.D.XXIV supports the

[8] Examples can be found in Oxford, Bodleian Library, MS Lat. lit. F.5, fo.13v, (St. Mark) and New York, Pierpoint Morgan Library, MS 708, fo.2v, (St. Matthew).

[9] It has been argued that the drawings in CCCC, MS 23 and Oxford, Bodleian Library, MS Junius 11 were executed by the same hand and are heavily reliant upon the stylistic influences exerted by the Utrecht Psalter; see E. Temple, *Anglo-Saxon Manuscripts, 900–1066* (Oxford, 1978), p.77.

[10] With the exception of quire 7 (fos.128–35), which fails to follow the main themes of the layout, London, BL. MS Royal 7.D.XXIV seems to be written by one scribe. It is unclear why one quire should have been written by another scribe who showed such scant regard for the design and layout applied to the manuscript as a whole. A more detailed discussion of this and other problems form part of my forthcoming London Ph.D. thesis on the layout and design of Anglo-Saxon manuscripts from the tenth and eleventh centuries.

theory that the manuscript was conceived of as a deluxe edition, even if the compiler did reuse an incomplete Evangelist portrait. It was produced during the reign of King Æthelstan (924–39) and contains many stylistic features which place it on a par with the best extant manuscripts from the period.[11] Although it is small (170 × 120 mm.), it contains a wealth of zoomorphic initials, painted in a range of colours, reminiscent of those found in the famous manuscript of Bede's Lives of Cuthbert, Cambridge, Corpus Christi College MS 183, which is perhaps unsurprising as the manuscripts appear to share the same scribe. The exact date and provenance of CCCC MS 183 has been discussed in detail elsewhere, and it is generally accepted that it was written between June 934 and October 939 in a scriptorium centred either at Glastonbury or Wells.[12] In every respect CCCC MS 183 is a deluxe manuscript and dispels the myth that English scriptoria suffered a 'dark age' in the early tenth century.[13] Both CCCC MS 183 and BL MS Royal 7.D.XXIV seem to have been products of a scriptorium that enjoyed royal patronage, and the two manuscripts have similarities in their approach towards layout and display. The initials used in both have many contemporary parallels and echo insular traditions.[14]

The skill of execution and the careful layout employed by a highly professional scribe suggests that MS Royal 7.D.XXIV may not have been intended for use within the classroom. Given the dimensions of the manuscript, it is possible that it was made for personal study, a pocket-sized *De laude virginitatis*, following in the tradition of the Irish pocket gospel books.[15] The amount of glossing in MS Royal 7.D.XXIV is extensive; the majority of the glosses were added during the course of the tenth century and are, therefore, not contemporary with the main scribal hand. However, some of the forty-three glosses written in Old English are executed in the same style of script as that used by the main scribe of the text, Anglo-Saxon square miniscule, although they appear to

[11] S. Keynes, 'King Athelstan's Books', *Learning and Literature in Anglo-Saxon England*, ed. M. Lapidge and H. Gneuss (Cambridge, 1985), pp.143–201.

[12] *Ibid.*, 184–85. Recent studies reject Winchester as the likely provenance for CCCC 183; see D.N. Dumville, 'English Square Minuscule Script: the Background and Earliest Phases', *ASE*, xvi (1987), 147–79.

[13] M.P. Brown, 'Paris, Bibliothèque Nationale, lat. 10861 and the Scriptorium of Christ Church, Canterbury', *ASE*, xv (1986), 119–137.

[14] F. Wormald, 'Decorated Initials in English Manuscripts from A.D 900 to 1100', *Studies in Medieval Art from the Sixth to the Twelfth Centuries* (Oxford, 1984), pp.47–75. Wormald regards the initial types found in these manuscripts as 'conservative', p.54.

[15] P. McGurk, 'The Irish Pocket Gospel Book', *Sacris Erudiri*, viii (1956), 249–70. I am grateful to Patrick McGurk for his comments on a draft of this essay and for all his assistance during my research.

be written by several different hands.[16] Given the lack of internal evidence it is impossible to determine whether MS Royal 7.D.XXIV was intended to be a presentation volume along the lines of CCCC MS 183, but intended for an individual rather than a community. The manuscript may well have been demoted in status as the tenth century progressed and fashions in manuscript production changed, but the quality of the execution does strongly suggest that in the early tenth-century Aldhelm's major treatise was considered to be a work worthy of such deluxe treatment.

The 'author portrait' which had been incorporated into the scheme of MS Royal 7.D.XXIV was an aspect of display which later artists were to adapt for their own purposes. The genre reappears in two late tenth-century manuscripts. The illustrations on fo.1 of Oxford, Bodleian Library, MS Bodley 577 occupy a single leaf, and it is unclear whether this is an added leaf, or a separate sheet. Unlike MS Royal 7.D.XXIV, this manuscript contains the metrical version of the *De laude virginitatis*, and provides us with two illustrations of the author. Although these drawings contain no specific rubric naming the figure as Aldhelm there is no ambiguity as in both instances he is shown tonsured, armed with his *magnum opus*, and the inclusion of the worthy nuns in the second drawing confirms his identity. As can be seen elsewhere, it is not unusual to find drawings which depict dedications of works at the opening of the relevant manuscript, although the recipient is more usually spiritual than temporal.[17] These drawings were intended to act as a frontispiece to the text and appear on the recto and verso. Both illustrations are surrounded by plain linear frames of similar size (130 × 82 mm. for the inner border and 150 × 98 mm. for the outer) which are devoid of any contemporary embellishment. This implies that the drawings were not intended to be heavily ornamented or possibly even coloured. The arrangement of the composition on fo.1v shows that in this instance the drawing was executed prior to the frame being added, as portions of Aldhelm's and the nun's garments have been partially drawn over. However, it would be a mistake to ascribe this to the artists lack of forethought regarding the composition. The practice of extending elements of the

[16] N.R. Ker, *Catalogue of Manuscripts Containing Anglo-Saxon* (Oxford, 1957), no.259; Dumville, 'English Square Minuscule Script: The Background and Earliest phases', 174.

[17] Examples include CCCC, MS 183, fo.1v, where King Athelstan is shown presenting the volume containing Bede's prose and metrical *Vitae* to St. Cuthbert and in BL, MS Vespasian. A.VIII, fo.2v, where King Edgar is depicted offering the New Minster Charter to Christ.

composition beyond the nominal confines of the frame was a feature of the Anglo-Saxon artist's considerable repertoire.[18]

In most examples an author portrait appears only once preceding the text, usually on the verso of the folio.[19] In this manuscript Aldhelm is depicted in two roles, as author and dedicator.[20] In the first drawing Aldhelm is shown seated, he is not writing but raising his right hand in blessing, while his left rests upon a book placed on a draped reading-desk. The iconography adheres to the Evangelistic model, including features noted in MS Royal 7.D.XXIV. Unlike the latter manuscript, this portrait follows a slightly different model. The artist employs a full frontal representation of the figure which contains aspects associated with an alternative iconographical tradition.[21] At a subsequent date blocks of colour have been added to the drawing, also a halo adorns the author portrait, which contains gold leaf and an etched design. This suggests that a later artist thought the drawing of sufficient merit to warrant some extra attention. The illustration of fo.1v has not received any additional embellishments, and is a great deal more lively than the static composition which precedes it. All of the figures are standing upon stony ground, and beneath the feet of Aldhelm there are two floral motifs. Aldhelm presents his tract on virginity to the nuns who at first glance appear to spring from a single body. Whether the full length figure is intended to depict the Abbess Hildelith it is impossible to determine. It is equally debatable whether the artist was attempting to make some, now obscure, reference to the role of an abbess in relation to the nuns, especially in the light of the political turmoils

[18] Examples can be found in Oxford, Bodleian Library, MS Junius 11, fo.61 (*c.* 1000); London, BL, MS Stowe 944, fo.7r (*c.* 1031); and London, BL, Cotton MS Claudius. B.IV, fo.36 (second quarter of the eleventh century); see H.R. Broderick, 'Some Attitudes towards the Frame in Anglo-Saxon Manuscripts of the Tenth and Eleventh Centuries', *Artibus et Historiae*, v (1982), 31–42.

[19] London, BL, MS Add 40618, fo.49v (St. John); London, BL, MS Royal I.E.VI, fo.30v (St. Mark). Some manuscripts contain a series of illustrations prior to the main text, for example, Paris, B[ibliothèque] N[ationale], MS lat. 943; London, BL, MS Stowe 944 and Cotton MS Tiberius C.VI.

[20] These drawings seem to be contemporary with the main text despite occupying a single folio, and have parallels with other manuscripts; see Temple, *Anglo-Saxon Manuscripts*, p.76, n.57. Other manuscripts with dedicatory portraits include Cambridge, Trinity College, MS B. 16.3., fo.1v, Rabanus Maurus offering his work to St. Gregory, and London, BL, MS Arundel 155, fo.133 which contains a drawing of a presentation of the Rule of St. Benedict by monks to the saint, a similar scene also appears in BL, MS Cotton, Tiberius A.III fo.117v.

[21] Evangelistic portraits of a similar style can be found in York Minster Chapter Library, MS Additional 1, fo.60v (St. Mark, late tenth century); New York, Pierpoint Morgan Library, MS 709, fo.2v (St. Matthew *c.* 1030–1050). The stool on which Aldhelm is seated can also be seen in London, BL, MS Cotton, Julius A.VI, fo.4v (early eleventh century); Cambridge, Pembroke College, MS 301, fo.10v (*c.* 1020) and CCCC, MS 23, fo.17v (late tenth century).

at Barking during the reign of King Edgar. If this were the case the subtlety of the artist was great, for in the realms of Anglo-Saxon iconography this economy of figures was widespread.[22]

In another tenth-century manuscript of Aldhelm's *De laude virginitatis*, Lambeth Palace Library, MS 200, on fo.68v a similar composition appears (Plate 2). The hunched form of the 'abbess' is repeated, attended by eight nuns, only one less in number than those referred to by name in Aldhelm's dedicatory preface.[23] Unlike MS Bodley 577 there are details in the decoration of the Lambeth drawing, for example on the sleeves and head-dresses of a few of the nuns, which need some consideration. It is possible that the artist was making a visual reference to part of the text of the *De Laude Virginitatis*, where Aldhelm castigates those who flout the rules relating to the correct monastic attire.[24] These concerns were not without parallel in the tenth century, which gives an added poignancy to these drawings.[25] The composition of the drawing represented in Lambeth Palace, MS 200 embraces both facets of those found in MS Bodley 577. Aldhelm is again shown tonsured and placed in a semi-Evangelistic pose, while the nuns humbly receive the work offered to them by the saint. However, there appear to be some inconsistencies within the composition. The drawing shows two bound volumes, presumably representing both the prose and the metrical versions of the *De laude virginitatis*. The largest is held by the nun at the extreme right of the composition while the other is held by Aldhelm, and is presented, presumably, to Abbess Hildelith. The text of the *De laude virginitatis*

[22] In most instances two or three figurse are shown in full length with additional heads springing from their shoulders to imply a larger gathering; examples can be found in London, BL, MS Cotton, Tiberius C.VI, fos.8v and 9r (*c.* 1050); BL, MS Cotton, Tiberius B.V, fo.85v (second quarter of the eleventh century); BL, MS Cotton, Claudius B.IV, fo.139v (second quarter of the eleventh century) and BL, MS Arundel 155, fo.133 (*c.* 1020–23).

[23] The close copying of one illustration from manuscript to manuscript is well-illustrated by London, BL, MS Cotton, Tiberius A.III, fo.2v (*Regularis concordia*) and Durham Cathedral Library, MS Lib. B.III.32, fo.56v (Aelfric's Grammar) where the figures of St. Aethelwold and St. Dunstan are almost identical. The Durham manuscript is slightly later in date and the artist was selective in those aspects of the exemplar which he chose to reproduce.

[24] Aldhelm attacks those who are 'adorned with forbidden ornaments and charming decorations . . . This sort of glamorisation for either sex consists in fine linen shirts, in scarlet or blue tunics, in necklines and sleeves embroidered with silk; their shoes are trimmed with red-dyed leather; the hair of their forelocks and the curls at their temples are crimped with a curling iron; dark-grey veils for the head give way to bright and coloured head-dresses, which are sewn with interlacings of ribbons and hang down as far as their ankles'. *De laude virginitatis* ch. lviii; trans. M. Lapidge and M. Herren, *Adlhelm: The Prose Works* (Ipswich, 1979), pp.127–28.

[25] The case of St. Edith of Wilton who was rebuked by Bishop Æthelwold of Winchester for her attire is the most renowned; see C. Fell, *Women in Anglo-Saxon England* (London, 1984), p.125.

makes it clear that the metrical work was completed after the prose.[26]
The logical conclusion would therefore be that since the nuns are shown
already in possession of one volume that Aldhelm is presenting the later
metrical work. Yet the text of Lambeth Palace, MS 200 is not that of
the metrical version but of the prose. Could it be that the drawing is
not contemporary with the text, but was copied at a slightly later date
from another manuscript which contained a metrical tract? There is not
doubt that Lambeth Palace MS 200 was intended to contain some form
of illustration as ample space has been allotted for it in the layout of
the dedicatory passage on fo.68v. Close inspection of the drawing shows
that parts of it have been added to, evident in the heavy ink blocking
of small details such as the shoes. However, the drawing appears to
be contemporary, as it is executed in the same ink as that used for the
main initial of the prologue, the latter being overlapped by parts of the
text, which is written in a slightly darker ink. It is therefore difficult to
argue that this apparent contradiction came about by the inappropriate
copying of an illustration from a metrical text. It is possible that the
artist was attempting to marry together two iconographical traditions,
or to convey the two-fold achievement of the author in writing both a
prose and metrical work. An exact interpretation has yet to be made.
Certainly the few later drawings of Aldhelm which are extant do not
seem to adhere to any of the iconographical patterns displayed in the
tenth-century manuscripts.[27]

The author portraits are not the only indicators of deluxe copies of the
De laude virginitatis; elaborate initial forms could be employed with equal
effect. The repertoire of major initial types utilised by Anglo-Saxon scribes
is well represented within the tenth-century manuscripts of Aldhelm's
work. For the major part of the text either ink or heavily painted initials
seem to have been favoured in the less elaborate classbooks, accompanied
by secondary capitals executed in a smaller but similar fashion.[28] The more

---

[26] The precise time lapse between the composition of the two versions is unclear, see
Lapidge and Rosier, *Aldhelm: The Poetic Works*, p.97 and Lapidge and Herren, *Aldhelm:
The Prose Works*, pp.130–31.

[27] London, BL, MS Royal 5.E.XI, fo.2r, contains a linear drawing of Aldhelm which
probably dates from the late twelfth or early thirteenth century. Aldhelm is depicted
in his episcopal regalia standing beside a lectern on which a book rests, apparently
emphasising his role as bishop/saint rather than that of author.

[28] London, BL, MS Royal 5.E.XI; fully-painted initials predominate at the opening of
each chapter with ink, Rustic capitals being used for the remaining parts of the word
or words. This basic pattern also appears in CCCC, MS 326. Fully painted initials are
employed by the scribe in BL. MS Royal 6.A.VI where there is some variation in the
colours used and the first line of each section is written in ink Rustic capitals. Oxford,
Bodleian Library, MS Digby 146 commences most of the chapters with ink initials,
followed by a line of rustic capitals.

1   London, British Library, MS Royal 7.D.XXIV, fo. 85v

2   London, Lambeth Palace Library, MS 200, fo. 68v

EVERENTISSIMIS

ΧΡΙ VIRGINIBVS OMNIQVE

deuotæ germanitatis affectu uenerandis. et non
solum corporalis pudicitiæ preconio celebrandis
plurimorum est. uerum etiam spiritalis castimo
niæ glorificandis. quod paucorum est. Hildelithe
disciplinæ et monasticæ conuersationis magistre.
Iustinæ ac cuthburgæ. necnon et osburgæ. mihi
necessitudinum nexibus conglutinatæ.
aldgydæ. ac scolasticæ. hydburgæ. et byrngydæ. eulaliæ ac teclæ.
rumore sericato concorditer æclesiam ornantibus: Aldhelmus
egenus epi ex et supplex æclesiæ uernaculus. optabilem per
petuæ prosperitatis salutem.

3   London, Lambeth Palace Library, MS 200, fo. 69r

4   London, Lambeth Palace Library, MS 200, fo. 80v

elaborate zoomorphic and interlaced initials tend to be limited to use at the opening of the dedicatory passage and the first chapter.[29] In some instances these sections incorporate a large and complicated initial form as well as varying sizes of secondary capitals, for example on fos.7v and 9r in British Library, MS Royal 5.E.XI. This treatment suggests that even classroom manuscripts of the *De laude virginitatis* in the later tenth century were considered worthy of some ornamentation, and possibly argues in favour of some of these manuscripts being produced for foundations other than Canterbury.[30]

The arrangement at the opening of chapter one in Lambeth Palace, MS 200, on fo.69r, illustrates a departure from the usual zoomorphic format, and contains the only example of a 'framed' initial in the tenth-century Aldhelm manuscripts (Plate 3). The elaborate interlacing contained within the heavily-inked panels of the frame follow two patterns, one of double-stranded interlace plaited into basketwork and, at the four corners, a design of foliate scrolls inhabited by birds and quadrupeds.[31] The initial 'I' has a shaft which is comprised of three panels, the central one contains a rosette pattern and the other two interlaced knotwork with foliate ornament terminating with birds heads.[32] The remaining secondary capitals are fully painted in red and green, the two colours being used alternately. Only two sizes of capitals are used, the first line being larger than the other eight. This contrasts with the varying sizes of capitals employed in such manuscripts as MS Royal 5.E.XI, where three to four lines of square capitals appear followed by a line of Rustics.

The design on fo.69r of Lambeth Palace, MS 200 is strongly reminiscent of the ornamental pages of Gospel books and Psalters, whence the artist may well have drawn his inspiration.[33] Its inclusion within the layout of the *De laude virginitatis* is unexpected, as are other features of the manuscript. In the conception of this manuscript there appears to have been no provision made for the inclusion of any capitula-listing which usually precedes the text. However, ample space has been left between chapters to accommodate both the numbers and

[29] For example in London, BL, MS Royal 5.E.XI. In BL, MS Royal 6.A.VI the ornamentation consists of two sizes of fully-painted red square capitals and one line of ink rustics arranged around a fully-painted green major initial.

[30] Brooks, *Early History of the Church of Canterbury*, p.273.

[31] Temple, *Anglo-Saxon Manuscripts*, p.63, no.39. Temple parallels the scrolls with stone carvings from the Tympanum at Knook, Wilts., *c.* 1000. Panelled frames have contemporary parallels, see London, BL, MS Cotton, Claudius B.IV, fo.2r.

[32] *Ibid.*, p.63; Temple suggests the intial was executed by the same artist as that in CCCC, MS 307 (part 1), where a similar 'I' opens the prologue to a *vita* of St. Guthlac.

[33] Temple, no.25, Paris, BN, MS lat. 987, fo.4; Temple, no.65., Cambridge, Trinity College, MS B.10.4, fo.60 and Temple, no.68., London, BL, MS Add. 34890, fo.115.

any rubrication that was required, neither of which has been added. Nor does any provision seem to have been made by the scribe for the inclusion of extensive glossing.[34] On fo.78v (chapter 19) the scribe has highlighted nine lines of the text which refer to the three states of virginity, *Ut sit virginitas*, by heavily inking the first letter of each line to create a visual sub-section within the chapter.[35] Other highlighted sub-sections within the chapters appear after chapter 20, as has been noted in other manuscripts of the *De laude virginitatis*.[36] In Lambeth 200 these are distinguished by fully-painted green square capitals placed within the double bounding lines beyond the main body of the text. This arrangement was also employed by the main scribe of MS Royal 7.D.XXIV, and is highly effective. This clear visual separation of versals and text has parallels with other tenth-century manuscripts.[37] In MS Royal 7.D.XXIV this separation becomes exaggerated to the extent that some of the versals are almost lost in the binding, for example in folio 104r. Specific ornamentation of the initial at chapter 20, which is a feature of the layout in many of the 'classbook' manuscripts, appears to be absent from both MS Royal 7.D.XXIV and Lambeth Palace, MS 200.

The initials used to open the individual chapters are generally well-executed and display a variety of zoomorphic and interlaced forms (Plate 4). On closer inspection some appear to be incomplete or sketchy, for example on fos.75r and 109v, where the ink has been partially smudged. In places paler ink has been retouched by ink, which is similar to that used for the text, and which cuts over parts of the surrounding letters, for example the fully-painted green secondary capital on fo.96v. The implication is that the initials were executed in two stages, a rough sketch prior to the writing of the text, followed by the final drawing in a darker ink once the text was complete. Some of the letter forms used for the chapter openings are a little unusual, for example on folios 85v, 109v and on fo.90r, where the artist has drawn a lion leaping from the tail to the bowl of the initial 'Q'. However, the initials are undoubtedly

---

[34] In some instances it is possible to detect ruling made in the margins to accommodate glosses which have not been added; for example in London, BL, MS Royal 6.A.VI.

[35] This highlighting would appear to be peculiar to Lambeth Palace MS 200, see Lapidge and Herren, *Aldhelm: the Prose Works*, p.75; Ehwald, *Aldhelmi Opera*, p.248, 11. 13–19.

[36] Chapter 20 in some manuscripts commences with an arrangement of major and secondary capitals which are employed to signify the start of the list of male virgins. This distinction seems less apparent at the opening of the list of female virgins at chapter 40. Manuscripts which illustrate this include CCCC, MS 326, Oxford; Bodleian Library, MS Digby 146; Salisbury, MS 38; London, BL, MSS Royal 6.A.VI and 5.E.XI. The number of highlighted sub-sections within these lists varies from manuscript to manuscript; some are denoted by inked or painted capitals and others by k. monograms.

[37] For example, Durham, Cathedral Library, MS A.IV. 19 and London, BL, MS Cotton, Tiberius A.II.

the work of an experienced and highly-skilled hand. Whether this scribe was also responsible for the writing of the main text is unclear. Links have been established between the textual hand and other manuscripts produced at St. Augustine's, Canterbury.[38] There are close similarities in the techniques and designs employed for the initial forms. Despite being such an elaborate copy of the *De laude virginitatis*, there is one aspect of display which is not present in Lambeth Palace, MS 200. The text ends simply; no attempt has been made to arrange the text in a decorative manner as appears elsewhere.[39]

The differences in the layout and display of the deluxe manuscripts of the *De laude virginitatis* and that adopted for the class-book manuscripts are apparently clear. Elaborate initial forms; drawings of the author and the absence of extensive contemporary glossing are all features contained within the range of the tenth-century deluxe manuscripts. In many ways these manuscripts mark the zenith of the *De laude virginitatis*'s popularity. The few manuscripts produced towards the end of the eleventh century and beyond fail to attain such an exalted status as that accorded to the production of Lambeth Palace, MS 200. Aldhelm's verbose and moralistic tone did not find the degree of favour in the Anglo-Norman scriptorium that it had apparently enjoyed at the height of the tenth-century monastic reform movement, becoming relegated to the role of curio or out-dated text-book. The manuscripts from this later period are lacking in any of the grandiose embellishments, and follow the traditions which appear to have formed part of the established repertoire for the tenth-century class-books. Yet it would be misleading to assume that the tenth-century classbooks should be regarded as inferior products to the deluxe manuscripts discussed here; they merely adhere to a different set of criteria. There is no justification for the view that the skills exhibited in the deluxe manuscripts were unknown to the scribes of the classbooks. Such a lengthy and complicated treatise as the *De laude virginitatis* must have been a challenge to any copyist. The sentiments of a late tenth-century

---

[38] In particular London, BL, MS Harley 5431. See Temple, *Anglo-Saxon Manuscripts*, p.62, no.38, where the scribe is linked to one at work in Oxford, Bodleian Library, MSS D.inf.2.9 and Auct. F.1.15. The latter manuscript contains additions from the scribe of London, BL, MS Royal 6.A.VI, who also appears in royal diplomas in the name of King Æthelred which are dated 995 and 1003, see Brooks, *History of the Church of Canterbury*, p.277.

[39] Salisbury, MS 38, fo.81v has a full page arrangement of the last section of the text contained within an enlarged rom of the opening initial. A similar arrangement on a smaller scale also completes the text in London, BL, MS Royal 7.D.XXIV.

scribe writing in one of the classbooks would have found sympathy amongst those engaged upon the more elaborate versions. At the end of the text the scribe adds two lines of dactylic hexameter verse as a testimony to his endeavours:

> Tres digiti scribunt totum corpusque laborat;
> scribere qui nescit nullum putat esse laborem.[40]

[40] London, BL, MS Royal 6.A.VI. It is tempting to regard these lines as being the impassioned cry of an exhausted scribe, although it is more likely to have been an exercise piece, as the Latin is arranged so rigidly to adhere to the verse format. The same lines reappear in a twelfth-century manuscript of the *De laude virginitatis*, London, BL, MS Harley 3013, with the addition of a third line,

> Dum digiti scribunt vix cetera membra quiescunt,

which seems to be an attempt to rephrase the preceding lines. The scribe of this latter manuscript also reveals his inept knowledge of Latin by incorrectly copying his exemplar, rendering *putat* as *potat* and *esse* as *elle*; see Ehwald, *Aldhelmi opera*, p.222.

Chapter 3

Swein Forkbeard and the Historians

Peter Sawyer

Swein Forkbeard has had a bad press. In the earliest accounts of Scandinavian history his remarkable achievements were either ignored or overshadowed by the humiliations he is supposed to have suffered in the first part of his reign. These early historians, like many of their successors, were greatly influenced by Adam of Bremen's description of Swein as an apostate who eventually repented after repeatedly suffering divinely ordained punishments. Stories of Swein's captivities, defeats, exile and rejection were repeated and elaborated with delight in nineteenth-century Denmark as well as in thirteenth-century Iceland. If poets ever sang his praises, their verses have not been preserved, and the one early text in which he is described favourably, the *Encomium Emmae Reginae*, was unknown in medieval Scandinavia and has been dismissed by most modern commentators as biased and less trustworthy than the combined testimony of Adam of Bremen and his predecessor Thietmar of Merseburg, despite their manifest hostility to the king, and their many errors.[1]

The bad press to which Swein was subjected is also present in the three main medieval accounts of early Danish history, written between about 1140 and 1220.[2] The Roskilde Chronicle, which was compiled in about

---

[1] Adam of Bremen, *Gesta Hammaburgensis ecclesiae pontificum* (henceforth, Adam), ed. B. Schmeidler, *Monumenta Germaniae Historica, Scriptores Rerum Germanicarum* (henceforth *MGH SRG*) (Hannover and Leipzig, 1917); English translation, F.J. Tschan, *History of the Archbishops of Hamburg-Bremen by Adam of Bremen* (New York, 1959); *Encomium Emmae reginae* (henceforth, *Encomium*), ed. A. Campbell, Royal Historical Society, Camden 3rd series, lxxii (London, 1949); *Thietmari Merseburgensis Episcopi Chronicon* (henceforth, Thietmar), ed. R. Holtzmann, *MGH SRG*, new series, ix (Berlin, 1935), pp.442–46.

[2] *Chronicon Roskildense*, ed. M.Cl. Gertz, *Scriptores minores historiæ Danicæ medii ævi*, fœrste hæfte (Copenhagen, 1917), pp.14–33; for Swein Forkbeard see ch. vi, pp.19–20; Sven Aggesen, *Brevis historia regum Dacie, ibid.*, pp.94–143; for Swein see ch. viii, pp.116–21. *Saxonis Gesta Danorum*, ed. J. Olrik and H. Ræder, 2 vols. (Copenhagen, 1931–57) is a heavily emended edition of the only authority for most of the text, *danorum regum heroumque historæ*, ed. Christian Pederson (Paris, 1514). A reduced facsimile of the 1514 edition of books x-xvi has been published, together with an English translation and voluminous notes full of acute observations and useful references, by Eric Christiansen, British Archaeological Reports, International Series 84, 118 i and ii (Oxford, 1980–81); the account of Swein Forkbeard's reign is in Book x, chs. 8–13; pp.276–85 in Olrik & Ræder vol.1, pp.12–27 in Christiansen.

1140, is a short summary beginning with the baptism of King Harald in 826. The other two, Sven Aggesen's *Brevis historia regum Dacie* and the *Gesta Danorum* of Saxo Grammaticus, which trace the history of the kingdom back to its supposed beginnings, were begun at the same time, in the 1180s, but they express very different attitudes: Sven wrote to praise kings; Saxo to criticise them.[3] Sven's book was completed before 1202, but Saxo's far more elaborate work was probably not finished until about 1216. For information about Swein Forkbeard all three relied on Adam of Bremen's *Gesta Hammaburgensis ecclesiae pontificum*,[4] written in the 1070s, but Sven and Saxo incorporated additional stories about the king; different versions also appear in Icelandic sagas, in particular those concerning Olav Tryggvason and the Jomsvikings.[5] The Roskilde Chronicle is the first evidence for the by-name *Tyuvskeg* (Forkbeard), and also amplifies Adam's account, presumably on the basis of local knowledge, by reporting that in Swein's reign a Bishop *Bernardus* came from Norway, and built a church in Skåne before crossing to Sjælland, where he died. Sven Aggesen has a version of the story of King Swein's capture and ransom, but says nothing about a battle with Olav Tryggvason or the conquest of England. All these episodes, and others, figure in Saxo.[6]

The anecdotes about Swein recorded in these Danish histories relate mostly to the first part of his reign and generally depict him a poor light. He is described as a rebel against his father Harald, who defeated him in battle. He is also said to have been captured in humiliating circumstances and ransomed for a large sum that impoverished his people. He was driven into exile and his kingdom conquered by the Swedish King Erik 'the Victorious'; Swein only recovered his throne after Erik's death. Further detailed accounts of the battle in which Olav Tryggvason was overthrown agree that Swein took part but his role is described as inglorious; Saxo

---

[3] B. Sawyer, 'Valdemar, Absalon and Saxo: Historiography and Politics in Medieval Denmark', *Revue Belge de Philologie et d'Histoire*, lxxxiii (1985), 685–705.

[4] A useful brief discussion of Adam's work is by S. Bolin in *Kulturhistorisk Leksikon for nordisk middelalder* (Copenhagen, 1956–57) (henceforth, *KHL*), v, cols. 283–89. A.K.G. Kristensen, *Studien zur Adam von Bremen Überlieferung* (Copenhagen, 1975) has some important comments on the way the text was compiled.

[5] The best-known of the sagas on Olav is *Oláfs saga Tryggvasonar* in Snorri Sturluson's *Heimskringla*, ed. B.A. Albjarnason, 1 (Islenzk Fornrit xxvi; Reykjavik, 1941); English translation by L.M. Hollander (Austin, 1977), pp.144–244. For the others see Olafur Halldórsson, *KHL*, xii, cols. 551–53. *The Saga of the Jomsvikings*, ed. N.F. Blake (London, 1962) has the Icelandic text with a parallel English translation. See also Jakob Benediktsson's article in *KHL* (Copenhagen, 1956–7), vii, cols. 607–8.

[6] The treatment of Swein in these works has most recently been discussed by I. Skovgaard-Petersen, 'Sven Tveskæg i den ældste danske historiografi: En Saxostudie', *Middelalder Studier Tilegnede Aksel E. Christensen på treårsdagen 11. September 1966*, ed. T.E. Christiansen *et al.* (Copenhagen, 1966), pp.1–38.

even claimed that Olav went into that battle knowing that 'Swein usually waged war without much success'. Such stories, although full of vivid details, are clearly unreliable evidence for Swein's reign, as we shall see. Even Adam's version of events contains many obvious mistakes and much more that is dubious.

Adam was manifestly hostile to Swein, regarding him as an apostate who was made to repent by suffering divine punishment. Some scholars have argued that in doing justice to God's wrath Adam invented some of the punishments, including exiles and Swedish conquests.[7] Others have pointed out that although Adam clearly interpreted events as exemplifying a moral lesson, and may be guilty of some exaggeration, that does not discredit all the details in his account.[8] One reason for treating Adam as an authority on the circumstances of Swein Forkbeard's reign is that he claims to have obtained much of his information from that king's grandson, Swein Estridsen.

Confidence in Adam's account has been reinforced by the even more hostile comments on Swein Forkbeard by his contemporary, Thietmar of Merseburg, who implied that Swein remained a pagan until his death and described him as 'a destroyer, not a ruler . . . an enemy of his own people'.[9] Thietmar's comments encouraged Erik Arup in 1925 to describe Swein as not so much a king as a viking, whose main domestic achievement was the destruction of the trading centre of Hedeby, 'the pearl in his crown'.[10] In coming to this conclusion Arup also seems to have been influenced, perhaps unconsciously, by the extravagances of the saga of the Jomsvikings in which Swein is described as persistently devastating Denmark. Thietmar also reports that soon after his father's death Swein was 'captured by revolting Northmen, and redeemed at an immense price by his subjects'. This apparently independent evidence has persuaded some scholars that the story of Swein's captivity and ransoming is plausible; it has even been suggested that Swein raided England in order to restore the wealth expended on the ransom.[11]

Although this interlocking chronicle evidence may seem strong, eleventh-century evidence from the British Isles and Flanders casts doubt on the reliability of Thietmar and Adam. The Anglo-Saxon

[7] Lauritz Weibull's conclusions, published in 1911 in *Kritiska undersökningar i Nordens historia omkring å 1000*, reprinted in his collected works *Nordisk Historia* 1 (Stockholm, 1948), pp.301–7, have been widely accepted, cf. *Encomium*, p.li, n.3.

[8] S. Ellehøj, 'Olav Tryggvesons fald og Venderne', *Historisk Tidsskrift* (Danish) xi, rk, 4 (1953–56), 1–51, at 36–38.

[9] Thietmar viii. 36–37, 39–40, translated in D. Whitelock *English Historical Documents, c. 500–1042*, 2nd edn. (London, 1979) (henceforth, *EHD*), no.27.

[10] *Danmarks Historie*, i (Copenhagen, 1925), p.127.

[11] Ellehøj, *op. cit.*, pp.39–40.

Chronicle, in describing raids by Swein in 994 and 1003–4, treats him as a feared enemy, but it nevertheless shows him to have been a remarkable military leader.[12] When, in the autumn of 1013, Swein conquered the English kingdom in a brilliant campaign, the chronicler reported that his troops began looting after they had crossed Watling Street, the boundary of the potentially friendly area that had previously been colonised by the Danes. This implies that Swein imposed a most unusual degree of discipline on his warriors. The Anglo-Saxon Chronicle does not apparently report all Swein's raids. An authentic charter of Æthelred implies that Swein was in England before 994; he may have taken part in the Maldon campaign in 991.[13] Swein's ability to recruit warriors to attack England twice in the first six years of his reign suggests that he was not such an ineffective ruler as Adam implied.

The *Encomium Emmae Reginae*, written at St. Omer between 1040 and 1042, presents a dramatically different picture of Swein from that found in the German sources.[14] The author was well-informed about the recent situation in Denmark and although in the judgement of his editor, Alistair Campbell, 'he was so severely selective a writer that nothing can ever be argued from his silence', his detected deceptions were generally achieved by implication, and his positive comments on Swein deserve to be taken seriously as reflecting the attitude of some contemporaries.[15] He described Swein as a fortunate king, loved by his people but envied by his father who wished to prevent his succession. The army 'deserted the father and adhered to the son'. In the ensuing battle the father was wounded and fled to the Slavs where he died shortly afterwards. Swein then ruled actively and wisely. Although in no fear of attack, he took care to strengthen his defences and was supported by troops whose loyalty was exceptional. When he embarked on the conquest of England he chose agents to secure his control of Denmark, leaving his son Harald 'at the head of the government' with a military force and 'a few of his chief men to instruct the boy wisely'.

Archaeological evidence reinforces doubts about the reliability of Thietmar and Adam. It gives no hint of any pagan revival. After Christianity was officially accepted by Swein's father in or shortly before 965, pagan burial customs continued for a while but were completely abandoned well before the end of the century; the youngest coin found in a pagan viking-age grave in Denmark was minted before

---

[12] Whitelock, *EHD*, no.1.
[13] *Ibid.*, no.121.
[14] *Encomium*, pp.6–15.
[15] *Ibid.*, p.lxix.

975.[16] Nor is there any sign of the devastation of Hedeby claimed by Arup; that place continued to function as a trading centre at least until the middle of the eleventh century.[17] The fact that the forts at Trelleborg and Fyrkat were not maintained during Swein's reign is significant. Whether they and the similar forts at Aggersborg, Odense, and perhaps also at Trelleborg in Skåne, all presumably built at much the same time, that is about 980, were intended to secure Harald's control of his scattered kingdom, or to provide bases in a system of defence against external attack, Swein apparently did not need them.[18] The Slav revolt of 983 had so weakened German influence in the region immediately south of the Danish frontier that Swein had no fear of an attack from that quarter, whatever the threats he may have had to face from elsewhere. We may assume that, like any other contemporary ruler, including the Emperor Otto III and the English king Æthelred, he had to cope with revolts, but he retained power despite absences abroad, and was succeeded by his sons. Excavations of both towns and villages suggest that his reign was a time of prosperity, in which several important towns, including Viborg, Roskilde and Lund were founded.[19] The development of Roskilde and Lund is especially significant, indicating a shift of the centre of the kingdom from Jutland to the shores of Øresund. Harald had created a complex monument at Jelling in Jutland with a large church in which the remains of his father Gorm were interred, but both he and Swein were buried at Roskilde in a mausoleum that, according to the Encomiast, was built by Swein.[20] The earliest known church in Lund was certainly built by the year 990, and that place soon became the main centre of Danish ecclesiastical and secular government, with a cathedral, several churches, and the most important mint of medieval Denmark.[21] The coins struck in Swein's name in the last decade of the tenth century and the far more numerous anonymous issues of his reign were most probably produced in Skåne, possibly in Lund.[22]

[16] E. Roesdahl, *Viking Age Denmark* (London, 1982), p.177.

[17] H. Ludtke, *Die mittelalterliche Keramik von Schleswig Ausgrabung Schild, 1971–1975* (Ausgrabungen in Schleswig: Berichte und Studien, iv; Neumunster, 1985), pp.134–38.

[18] Roesdahl, *op. cit*, pp.147–55. Indications of a fort at Trelleborg in Skåne have recently been reported, and the site is to be investigated more thoroughly this year (1990).

[19] *Ibid.*, pp.51–86.

[20] *Ibid.*, pp.171–76; *Encomium*, pp.18–19.

[21] A. Andren, *Den urbana scenen: Städer och samhälle i det medeltida Danmark* (Acta Archaeologica Lundensia, series in octavo, no. xiii; Bonn and Malmö, 1985) p.164; T. Nilsson, 'Drottenskyrkan och dess föregångare: Nya arkeologiska rön i Lund', *Kulturen* (1985), 173–82.

[22] *Viking-Age Coinage in the Northern Lands*, ed. M.A.S. Blackburn and D.M. Metcalf, part 2, British Archaeological Reports, International Series 122 (ii) (Oxford, 1981), pp.419–77.

The Anglo-Saxon Chronicle and the *Encomium* agree in describing Swein as a powerful ruler. Such a man would naturally inspire enmity as well as loyalty; it is therefore not surprising that Swein soon became the subject of stories, some of which tended to discredit him. The same spirit of *Schadenfreude* inspired both Thietmar and Adam of Bremen, for Swein ignored Otto III's claim to universal authority and refused to allow the archbishop of Hamburg-Bremen any jurisdiction over the Danish church. Both these writers tried to demonstrate that the Germans had been responsible for the conversion of the Danes. Thietmar summarised Widukind's account, but Adam claimed that Otto I successfully invaded Denmark and persuaded Harald to accept baptism in a ceremony in which Otto himself 'raised Harald's little son from the sacred font and named him *Sueinotto*'.[23] This story is pure invention, but it served its purpose, proving that the Danes were subject to the Germans and that Swein was a baptised Christian. For Adam the most important consequence of Swein's rebellion against his father was that the suffragan bishops of Hamburg-Bremen fled into exile. A charter of Otto III, dated 18 March 988, granting rights in Germany to Danish bishops, implies that they could no longer depend on support in Denmark.[24] Adaldag died later that year and, according to Adam, his successor Libentius endeavoured 'by suppliant legates and frequent gifts to soften the king's ferocious attitude to the Christians, but, as already noted, there is no archaeological evidence for a pagan reaction at that time.[25] Swein was opposed not to Christianity but to the suffragans and claims of the archbishop of Hamburg-Bremen. Adam, who equated conversion with acceptance of his archbishop's authority,[26] described the rebellion as a pagan revolt, thus making Swein an apostate. Adam had to provide for the king's repentance, for he knew that missionary activity continued in Denmark during Swein's reign, even though it was not directed from Hamburg-Bremen; he only mentions *one* bishop who worked in Denmark at that time, Gotebald, and he was from England.[27]

Adam claimed the support of the Danish king Swein Estridsen for his account of Swein Forkbeard's reign. Swein Estridsen was eager to collaborate with Hamburg-Bremen and apparently hoped to have Harald Gormsen recognised as a saint.[28] A royal saint was certainly an asset, and Swein Estridsen may well have been eager to counter

---

[23] Thietmar, ii, 14; Adam, ii, 3.
[24] *MGH Diplomata regum et imperatorum Germaniae II* (Hannover, 1884), no.41.
[25] Adam, ii, 29.
[26] *Ibid.*, iii, 72; iv, 36.
[27] *Ibid.*, ii, 41.
[28] *Ibid.*, ii, 28.

the spiritual authority of the Norwegian St. Olav, whose power he had himself experienced. In the conflict over the Danish kingship after 1042, Swein Estridsen was for five years successfully opposed by Magnus, who issued coins from a Danish mint depicting St. Olav, his father; the earliest evidence for that cult.[29] Harald was the ideal Danish candidate for sanctification; he was responsible for the official acceptance of Christianity by the Danes, and his miserable end in exile could be treated as martyrdom. The promotion of Harald's sanctity meant the denigration of his son who was responsible for that exile. Adam called him a parricide, and in support quoted Swein Estridsen as saying, with reference to Harald's death, 'Hoc est . . . quod ipse parricida suo piavit exilio'.[30] He was thus able to claim the king's authority for both the accusation of parricide and the penance of exile endured by Swein, but in taking such care to identify his source Adam may be suspected of disingenuousness; Swein Estridsen died while Adam was completing his *Gesta* and could be quoted without fear of contradiction.

Adam's treatment of the Danish conversion meant ignoring the tradition reported by Widukind. He could not, however, completely ignore the story of Poppo's ordeal. According to Widukind this took place in *c.* 965, and resulted in the conversion of Harald, but Adam placed it later, making Poppo, as the agent of the archbishop of Hamburg-Bremen, responsible for the conversion of the Swedish king Erik after he had conquered Denmark.[31] This served several purposes: it enhanced the claims of Adam's archbishop; it gave verisimilitude to the story of Swein's exile and the Swedish conquest, for which Adam is the sole witness; and it explained how Olof, Erik's son and successor as king of the *Sueones*, became a Christian, a conversion that Adam took for granted when describing Olof's missionary zeal and his later enthusiasm for Hamburg-Bremen.[32]

The 'punishment' of Swein that most historians have been prepared to accept is his capture by enemies. Thietmar's statement that after his father's death Swein was captured by 'revolting Northmen and redeemed at an immense price by his subjects' has been taken as independent confirmation of Adam's claim that Swein was twice captured by Slavs and ransomed. It may, however, be doubted that Adam wrote in complete ignorance of Thietmar's chronicle. It would, indeed, have been remarkable if Adam knew nothing of it. Thietmar's mother belonged to the comital family of Stade, about twenty miles from Hamburg, and

---

[29] C.J. Becker, 'Magnus den Godes Hedeby-mønter og slaget på Lyrskov hede', *Nordisk Numismatisk Unions Medlemsblad* (1983), 42–47.

[30] Adam, ii, 28.

[31] *Ibid.*, ii, 35.

[32] *Ibid.*, ii, 58.

from 1034 to 1049, his brother Bruno was bishop of Verden, which is about the same distance from Bremen.[33] Thietmar's chronicle was used by Adalbert, archbishop of Utrecht, very soon after his death, and was a source for many twelfth-century Saxon historical compilations.[34] The fact that Adam does not quote from it does not prove that he had never seen it; Thietmar said little to suit Adam's purposes. But even if Adam never saw Thietmar's book, he is likely to have heard about some of the stories it contained, especially those concerning Swein. Adam's treatment of the Poppo incident illustrates how such stories could be transmitted and distorted.

Thietmar may perhaps have invented the tale, or been very quick to accept its truth, for he had narrowly escaped being directly involved in something similar as a victim. In 994 Vikings who raided the Elbe valley killed one of his uncles, captured two others and demanded a huge ransom.[35] Thietmar himself was about to be handed over as a hostage when one of the prisoners escaped and the raiders took revenge by horribly mutilating the others before releasing them. It has been suggested that Swein was involved in that raid, but that seems unlikely.[36] Thietmar only identifies these raiders as pirates; it was Adam who described them as *Ascomanni* and as *Sueones et Dani*.[37] If Swein had been their leader, Thietmar would have said so, for it would have added substance to his otherwise very unspecific description of Swein's crimes. The episode, which must have been a traumatic experience for Thietmar, might have disposed him to believe that Swein suffered a similar fate.

Confidence in Thietmar is in any case reduced by the remarkable errors that he can be shown to have made in his account of the Danish attack on England.[38] This, combined with his manifest hostility to Swein Forkbeard, renders his unsupported testimony about that king untrustworthy. Adam's claim that Swein was captured twice by Slavs, hardly confirms Thietmar's story that he was captured once by Norsemen, and confidence in the story is not increased by its triplication in twelfth-century Denmark. Its dissemination in medieval Scandinavia does not prove that it was true, and Alistair Campbell's argument that 'some element of truth must lie under such a widely spread tradition' is not convincing.[39] It is, of course, possible that Swein was captured and ransomed at some time, but the available evidence does not prove that

33 Thietmar, pp.vii–xv.
34 *Ibid.*, p.xxxii.
35 *Ibid.*, iv, 23–25.
36 Christiansen, *Saxo Gramaticus: Books 10–16*, p.179.
37 Adam, ii, 31.
38 Whitelock, *EHD*, p.138.
39 *Encomium*, p.li, n.9.

he was, and the indirect evidence suggests that, if it did happen, it did not weaken his power.

According to Adam, who here again cites Swein Estridsen as his authority, Swein was further punished by suffering defeat in many naval battles against the *potentissimus rex Sueonum Hericus*, who conquered Denmark and drove Swein into exile.[40] Swein vainly sought refuge first with the Norwegian Tryggve, and then with the English king Æthelred. He was finally given shelter by an unnamed Scottish king, with whom he stayed for fourteen years until Erik died and he was able to reclaim his throne and marry Erik's widow. The story of exile has plausibly been explained as an extravagant elaboration of Swein's absence when raiding England. The story of Swein's defeat and a Swedish conquest has also been dismissed by many scholars as an invention, but some have accepted that Erik did invade Denmark, probably in 994 when Swein is known to have been in England.[41] A scholion added to Adam's *Gesta*, possibly by himself, adds the information that Erik married the daughter or sister of his ally Boleslav, the Polish king, and that the Swedes and Slavs jointly attacked the Danes.[42] Adam apparently only discovered that Erik's widow, who married Swein, was a Polish princess after he had completed his *Gesta*, but he was uncertain about her relationship with Boleslav. Thietmar, who was far better informed about the Poles than about the Danes, stated that Swein's sons were born to him by the daughter of the Polish ruler Mieszco and that she was long divorced from her husband. The Encomiast lends valuable support by reporting that, after Swein's death, his sons Knut and Harald went to '*Slavia*' to fetch their mother.[43]

The scholion in question, although revealing uncertainty about the woman's relationship to Boleslav, has been taken as confirmation that Erik did attack Denmark, apparently after 992, when Boleslaw succeeded his father Mieszco. There is no reason to doubt that a raid of this kind may have happened. Denmark may well have been raided by Swedes, and others, during Swein's reign, and was especially vulnerable when the king was absent. There is, however, no good reason to believe that the Swedes conquered the Danish kingdom, or that Swein only recovered his throne after Erik's death. The credibility of Adam's story is weakened by his assertion that Swein was exiled again when Erik's son Olof conquered Denmark.[44] A runic inscription erected by a King Swein, commemorating a man who died at Hedeby, and another in memory of

[40] Adam, ii, 30.
[41] Ellehøj, 'Olav Tryggvesons fald og Venderne', 40.
[42] Adam, scholion 24.
[43] *Encomium*, pp.18–19.
[44] Adam, ii, 39.

one of Swein's men who died during a siege of that place have been taken to refer to an incident in Swein's war with Erik, but that is only one of several possibilities.[45] These inscriptions have alternatively been associated with Swein's rebellion or with the expulsion of the Germans in 983, but the incident may, of course, have occurred during some other conflict.[46]

The combined evidence of Thietmar, the Encomiast and Adam shows that Swein married a Polish princess, the widow of a Swedish king called Erik who, on the evidence of the scholion discussed above, was alive in 992, but probably died a year or two after that. She was the mother of Erik's son and successor, Olof, and bore at least three of Swein's children: Harald, Knut and Estrid. There is no firm indication of the date of birth of any of her children; they could all have been born in the last decade of the century. Swein had at least two other daughters, one of whom, Gytha, must have been born well before 990. According to *Heimskringla* Gytha married Erik, the exiled son of the Norwegian jarl Håkon, in about 997, and their son Håkon was born a year later.[47] This tradition is confirmed by the fact that Håkon witnessed English charters as *dux* from 1019.[48] The identity of Gytha's mother is unknown. If she was Erik's widow, his death could be firmly dated before 990, but it is likely that she was Swein's daughter by an earlier but unmentioned liaison, and was born before Swein became king.

The date of Swein's accession is not known for certain. The Encomiast and Adam agree that he rebelled against his father who, after a battle, fled to the Slavs (Adam specifies *Iumne*, that is Wollin) where he soon died.[49] According to Adam, Harald died on 1 November, a date presumably taken from a calendar or list of obits at Bremen Cathedral. He does not state the year but says the rebellion was in the last days of Archbishop Adaldag (*nouissimis archiepiscopi temporibus*) who died on 29 April 988. The charter of Otto III dated 18 March 988

[45] *Danmarks Runeindskrifter*, ed. L. Jacobsen and E. Moltke (Copenhagen, 1942), nos. 1, 3; A.E. Christensen, *Vikingetidens Danmark* (Copenhagen, 1969), pp.256–57.

[46] P. Sawyer, *Da Danmark blev Danmark*, Danmarks historie, ed. O. Olsen, iii (Copenhagen, 1988), pp.232–33; O. Olsen, 'Tanker i tusindåret', *Skalk* (1980/3), 18–26, especially 23–25.

[47] *Heimskringla, Olafs saga Tryggvasonar* (see note 5), ch. 90.

[48] P.H. Sawyer, *Anglo-Saxon Charters: An Annotated List and Bibliography*, Royal Historical Society Guides and Handbooks, viii (London, 1968), nos 955, 960–62. No. 956, also dated 1019, is witnessed by *Hacun minister*. No. 963, an authentic original dated 1031, has *Hacun dux* as a witness, but that must be a mistake; he died in 1029 or 1030; see *Encomium*, p.72. The scribe made another mistake in calling *Æthelnoth Eboracensis basilice primas*!

[49] *Encomium*, pp.8–9; Adam, ii, 27–8

(mentioned above) suggests that the revolt occurred in 987, and that Swein's reign began then.

According to Adam, Swein was in exile for fourteen years and only recovered his kingdom on the death of his Swedish conqueror, Erik, whose widow he then married.[50] Adam made no attempt to explain this extraordinary turn of events but continued by reporting that once again Swein was expelled from his kingdom, this time by Erik's son Olof. He also reported that Swein at last repented, Olof 'restored him to his kingdom because he had married his mother', and the two kings entered into a pact to support Christianity.[51] Adam treated the Swedes as the dominant partner, but there are several indications that they were in fact subordinate to the Danes. Swein's marriage with Erik's widow seems rather to have been a sign of superiority, and may be compared with the marriage of Knut and Æthelred's widow after Knut conquered England. Olof's by-name *Skattkonungr*, now *Skötkonung*, implies that he was a tributary king (*skat* = tribute). That is, at least, the interpretation of the word offered by Snorri Sturluson in his explanation of poetic vocabulary.[52] The first evidence that Olof had this by-name is in two thirteenth-century king-lists which offer completely different explanations of its meaning, suggesting that it was by then an old name.[53] The fact that Olof supported Swein in the battle that established the Danish king's overlordship in Norway confirms that he acknowledged Swein as his superior. If Olof Skötkonung had been Swein's overlord, their battle against Olav Tryggvason and its consequences would have been presented in very different terms by Adam and by the twelfth-century Norwegian historians.[54]

Swein's death on 3 February 1014 gave Olof Skötkunung an opportunity to escape from this dependance. According to Adam, Knut made a pact with him before embarking on the conquest of England, but it did not last long.[55] Such a treaty is also mentioned by the twelfth-century English historian John of Worcester, who reports that soon after Knut

---

[50] Adam, ii, 34, 39.

[51] *Ibid.*, ii, 39.

[52] Snorri Sturluson, *Edda*, ed. F. Jónsson, 2nd edn (Copenhagen, 1926), p.123.

[53] H.S. Collin and C.J. Schlyter, *Samling af Sweriges Gamla Lagar, i, Westgötalagen* (Stockholm, 1827), p.298, '*Olawær skotkonongær ... skötte* (= gave, handed over, cf. 'shot') property to the bishopric'; *The Saga of King Heidrek the Wise*, ed. C. Tolkien (London, 1960), pp.60–61; 'He was then a child, and the Svear carried him about with them and therefore they called him *skautkonung* (lap-king)', an interpretation that has in turn been misunderstood to result in the description of Olaf as 'Lapp king', Tschan, *History of the Archbishops of Hamburg-Bremen*, p.91, n.181.

[54] Adam, ii, 40–41; G. Storm, *Monumenta Historica Norvegiæ* (Kristiania, 1880), pp.23–25 (Theodric), 117–19 (Historia Norwegiæ); *Ágrip: Ei liti norsk kongesoge* (Oslo, 1936), pp.46–49.

[55] Adam, ii, 52.

became king of the English, he sent two English princes to the king of the Swedes, presumably Olof Skötkonung, to be killed. 'He would by no means acquiesce in his requests, although there was a treaty between them, but sent them to the king of the Hungarians'.[56] An even clearer act of defiance was the marriage of Olof Skötkonung's daughter to Knut's Norwegian enemy, Olav Haraldsson.[57] Olof Skötkonung's request for a bishop from Unwan, who was consecrated archbishop of Hamburg-Bremen on 2 February 1013, appears to have been another demonstration of independence, for Olof died before Knut abandoned his father's policy by accepting that the archbishop of Hamburg-Bremen had authority over the Danish church.[58]

There are, therefore, indications that within a few years of his accession Swein was recognised as overlord by Olof Skötkonung, and that it was as a tributary king that Olof helped Swein to regain the overlordship of Norway. Swein thus consolidated and, by his influence in Sweden, extended the hegemony his father had established. Swein enlarged the Danish empire still further by conquering England in 1013 thus preparing the way for Knut's extensive claims.

The evidence, although slight, is sufficient to show that Swein was a remarkable, and remarkably successful, king. His achievements outside Denmark are better documented than those in it, but there is no good reason to suppose that his triumphs abroad were matched by failure at home. Swein's external successes, especially against the English, enabled him to retain the loyalty of the warriors on whom his power ultimately depended. Virtually nothing is known about the way he ruled his Danish kingdom. The neglect of the fortresses at Trelleborg and elsewhere suggests that his methods were not exactly the same as his father's. Both of them must, however, have depended on reliable agents. To retain power despite frequent, and perhaps prolonged, absences abroad, Swein needed men he could trust, like the warriors and advisers who, according to the Encomiast, supported his son Harald when he was given responsibility for the government of the kingdom in 1013. Such men were needed even when the king was not absent. At least some of the thegns and drengs commemorated in thirty-five Danish runic inscriptions probably helped to sustain Swein's royal authority.[59] The process of Christianisation continued in his reign. No weight can be put on Sven Aggesen's denial that Swein was an apostate, since his purpose

---

[56] Whitelock, *EHD*, no.9, *s.a.* 1017.

[57] Adam, ii, 61; Storm, *Monumenta Historica Norvegiae*, pp.29, 123–24.

[58] Adam, i, 55, 58. Icelandic annals record Olof's death in 1022, S. Axelson, *Sverige iutländsk annalistik, 900–1400* (Stockholm, 1955), pp.32, 47–48.

[59] P.H. Sawyer, *The Making of Sweden* (Alingsås, 1988), pp.34–35.

was to contradict the view of Swein given in the Roskilde Chronicle.[60] The Encomiast's description of him as a religious man, however, is more significant. The names of a few missionary bishops who worked in Denmark during Swein's reign are known: Bernard, Gotebald and Odinkar; there were probably others.[61] Churches were built; there was one in Lund by 990, and it seems likely that the church of the Holy Trinity in Roskilde, in which Harald was buried, was also completed early in the reign.

Most historians, medieval and modern, have given a much bleaker account of Swein's reign than that presented here. The main reason for the generally negative judgement of Swein is that the earliest comments on his reign were made by Germans who were fiercely hostile. Adam of Bremen has been especially influential; both the Roskilde Chronicler and Saxo Grammaticus were very willing to accept Adam's picture of a wicked king who was eventually forced to repent. For their patrons, Eskil and Absalon, both successively bishops of Roskilde and archbishops of Lund, this tale provided welcome support in their attempts to influence Danish kings.[62] For the earliest Norwegian historians Swein was a minor, incidental figure who they were happy to depict as less successful than their Norwegian heroes. Icelanders writing about Olav Tryggvason, Olav Haraldsson and the Jarls of Lade gave Swein a larger role, but with the same intention, and gleefully elaborated stories in which he was made to appear weak or ridiculous. Modern historians have recognised that Adam of Bremen's account has many errors and absurdities, but some scholars are nevertheless prepared to accept that there is substance in his stories of captivity, ransom and Swedish conquest, and that there was indeed a pagan revival in the early years of his reign. Thietmar's description of Swein as a destroyer rather than a ruler, pagan, vengeful and an enemy of his own people, has reinforced the impression that his reign was a disastrous time for the Danes, in marked contrast to the glorious reigns of his father Harald and his son Knut the Great. The more favourable comments in the *Encomium Emmae Reginae* have been dismissed as biased. In discussing that text Dorothy Whitelock posed the rhetorical question 'What are we to think of the reliability of a writer who can describe Swein Forkbeard as a generous and religious king, whose end was happy "from both the spiritual and worldly point of view"?'[63]

[60] Skovgaard-Petersen, 'Sven Tveskæg i den ældste danske historiografi', pp.11–12; but see C. Breengaard, *Muren om Israels Hus: Regnum og Sacerdotium i Danmark, 1050–1170* (Copenhagen, 1982), pp.51–81.

[61] Bernard: *Chronicon Roskildense*, ch. vi; see above, p.27; Gotebald: Adam, ii, 41; Odinkar: Adam, ii, 36; Thietmar, vi, 18.

[62] Breengaard, *Muren om Israels Hus*, pp.51–72, casts doubt on Eskil's role in the compilation of the Roskilde Chronicle.

[63] Whitelock, *EHD*, p.138.

The evidence discussed here suggests that the answer is that we should take him seriously; his judgement was sounder than Thietmar's, and he was better informed than Adam.[64]

[64] I should like to thank my wife, Bibi, and Niels Lund for their help in writing this essay.

Chapter 4

Anna Komnena and her Sources for the Normans of Southern Italy

G.A. Loud

Byzantine historians of the eleventh century took little interest in the Normans of southern Italy. Their viewpoint was derived from Constantinople, and only when Italian affairs impinged upon the wider destiny of the Empire as a whole, as with the revolt of Giorgios Maniakes which came close to toppling Constantine IX from the imperial throne in 1043, did they take any notice of events in the west.[1]

This was not however to be the case with the biography of her father, the Emperor Alexios I, by Anna Komnena. Indeed, the Normans of southern Italy loom very large in the *Alexiad*. At times it seems hardly very fanciful to think this literally the case given Anna's descriptions of the gigantic stature of Robert Guiscard and Bohemond. We have, except for Orderic Vitalis's account of the latter's birth (which itself seems to owe more to legend than sober fact), no comparable western descriptions against which we can check those in the *Alexiad*, and one suspects that these pen-portraits were literary idealisations of the archetypal barbarian.[2] But leaving aside their physical attributes, the threat from the Normans played a major part in Alexios's reign and in

---

[1] The only exception was a short section in the anonymous continuation of Skylitzes, printed in Giorgios Kedrenos, *Historiarum Compendium*, ed. I. Bekker, 2 vols. (Bonn, 1838–39), ii, 720–4. Skylitzes's account of the revolt of Maniakes does give some details of the Apulian campaign of 1041–2, *ibid.*, ii, 545–9, or (better) John Skylitzes, *Synopsis Historiarum*, ed. H. Thurn (Berlin, 1973), pp.425–28. Cf. on the revolt Michael Psellus, *Chronographia*, ed. E. Renaud 2 vols. (Paris, 1926–8), ii, 1–6 and Michael Attaliates, *Historia*, ed. I. Bekker (Bonn, 1853), pp.11, 18–19. This article benefited from the comments of James Howard-Johnston, Bernard Hamilton and John Cowdrey, and from the linguistic assistance of Colin Johnson. It grew out of a paper given at a conference on Alexios Komnenos organised by the Department of Greek and Latin, Queen's University of Belfast, in April 1989.

[2] *Alexiad*, i, 10; xiii, 10. All references are by book and chapter to the edition by B. Leib 3 vols. (Paris, 1937–45, reprint 1967). Quotations are from the English translation by E.R.A. Sewter (Harmondsworth, 1969). One may note that the verse biography of Robert

continued

in Alexios's reign and in Anna's biography. Georgina Buckler went so far as to write of Robert Guiscard that 'like Milton's Satan he is in truth the hero of Book IV'.[3]

Yet, given that Anna was writing long after the events in question, a generation after her father's death and sixty years after Guiscard's Balkan campaign, it seems worthwhile to assess the value of the *Alexiad* as a source for southern Italy in the age of the Normans. A crucial aspect of this problem is the question of Anna's own sources. How much did she really know about southern Italy and her father's enemies there?

The Byzantine government was far from ignorant of events, circumstances and personalities in the south of Italy in the later eleventh century. Until very recently parts of the peninsula had been under Byzantine rule. There was still a substantial Greek population in Calabria, north-east Sicily and the Terra d'Otranto, and emigrés from those areas could be found in Constantinople itself, notably the philosopher John Italos whom Anna so disliked.[4] Furthermore the diplomatic expertise which was so important a part of the Byzantine tradition, and indeed common prudence, dictated a continued interest. Because of Guiscard's and Bohemond's invasions of the Balkans southern Italy was of more than usual concern to Alexios Komnenos, and in both conventional diplomacy and subversion (assuming that any clear distinction can be made between the two) it had a high priority. Throughout the eleventh and early twelfth century the Empire was in contact with the great south Italian monastery of Montecassino, not least during the First Crusade when Alexios used it as an intermediary in his communications with Pope Urban II.[5] But not all his attentions towards southern Italy were so innocuous. Potentially disaffected members of the south Italian aristocracy were an obvious target for Byzantine

continued
Guiscard by William of Apulia expressly contrasted the relatively modest stature of the Normans with the excessive tallness of their German adversaries at the battle of Civitate in 1053, Guillaume de Pouille, *La Geste de Robert Guiscard*, ed. M. Mathieu (Palermo 1961) [henceforth WAp] book ii, 11. 93–97, 235–41, pp.136,144. For Anna the tallness of the Normans seems to have been a *topos*, as evinced by her story of the gigantic cousin of Bohemond captured by a tiny Pecheneg, *Alexiad*, xiii, 6. Cf. however *The Ecclesiastical History of Orderic Vitalis*, ed. M. Chibnall, 6 vols. (Oxford, 1969–81), vi, 70.

[3] G. Buckler, *Anna Comnena: A Study* (Oxford, 1929), p.453.

[4] *Alexiad*, v, 8–9. Another important exile at the end of the eleventh century was Archbishop Basil of Reggio, for whom D. Stiernon, 'Basile de Reggio, le dernier metropolite grec de Calabre', *Rivista di storia della chiesa in Italia*, xviii (1964), 189–222.

[5] H. Bloch, *Montecassino in the Middle Ages*, 3 vols. (Rome, 1986), i, pp.110–112. H. Hagenmayer, *Die Kreuzzugsbriefe aus den Jahren* 1088–1100, (Innsbruck, 1902), pp.140–41, 152–53.

blandishments, most notably Guiscard's nephews Abelard and Herman, the counts of Canne, sons of his deceased elder brother Humphrey. Their resentment at being displaced in the overall rule of south Italy by their uncle was expressed in no uncertain terms by a whole series of rebellions, in the mid 1060s, 1071–72, 1075–76, 1078 and 1082.[6] And to all those seeking independence from Guiscard's far from mild rule the Byzantine Emperor was, at the very least, the obvious figurehead for rebellion, as the frequent use of his regnal years in Apulian charters long after the fall of Bari, Byzantium's last direct bastion in Italy, attests.[7] In the last resort too the Emperor was their refuge if they were forced to flee from Guiscard's wrath, as was Goscelin of Molfetta in the 1060s and Abelard himself in the early 1080s.[8]

The attack on the Byzantine Empire only intensified this process of subversion as Alexios tried to undermine the morale and cohesion of Guiscard and Bohemond's victorious army, especially after Robert had returned to Italy in 1082 to combat the rebellion there. Not surprisingly spies kept the Byzantine authorities well-informed about the movements of the Norman forces; for example the 'Kelt', about whom Anna informs us, who confirmed that Bohemond's fleet was about to sail in 1107.[9] Anna even claimed that in 1085 Guiscard's own son Guy was offered

---

[6] The best general discussion is still F. Chalandon, *La Domination Normande en Italie et en Sicile*, 2 vols. (Paris, 1907), I, pp.182–84, 223–24, 240–42, 251, 273–74, who sorts out the problems of chronology. The best source is Amatus of Montecassino; see *Storia de' Normanni di Amato di Montecassino*, ed. V. de Bartholomeis (Rome, 1935), books v, 4; vii 17–22; viii, 34; pp.224–27, 308–14, 373, though his account is by no means complete. *Amatus*, vii, 20, p.312 records that Duchess Sichelgaita was particularly incensed by Abelard because he was the one Apulian lord who refused to acknowledge the succession of her son Roger when Guiscard was believed to be dying. According to WAp, iv, ll. 530–32, p.232, Abelard and Herman were in fact half-brothers. Cf. also Geoffrey Malaterra, *De rebus gestis Rogerii Calabriae et Siciliae comitis*, ed. E. Pontieri (Bologna, 1927–28), iii, 4, p.59.

[7] The regnal years of Alexius were for example still used in charters at Monopoli in 1086 and 1099, Conversano in 1099, Molfetta in 1100, Canne in 1116 and 1117, Corato in 1098, 1100 and 1110, Trani in 1095 and 1112, and Barletta in 1097 and 1102; *Regii Neapolitani Archivii Monumenta*, 6 vols. (Naples, 1854–61), v, 108–9 no.440, 255–56 no.498; *Codice Diplomatico Pugliese*, xx, *Le Pergamene di Conversano* (109–1265), ed. G. Coniglio (Bari, 1975), 141–44 no.60; *Codice Diplomatico Barese*, vii, *Le Carte di Molfetta* (1076–1309), ed. F. Carabellese (Bari, 1912), 8–9 no.4; viii *Le Pergamene di Barletta. Archivio Capitolare* (897–1285), ed. F. Nitti di Vito (Bari, 1914), 53–54 no.31, 56 no.33; ix, *Documenti storici di Corato*, ed G. Beltrani (Bari, 1923), 21–24 nos. 13–14, 27–29 nos. 17–18; x, *Pergamene di Barletta del R. Archivio di Napoli* (1075–1309), ed. R. Filangieri di Candida (Bari, 1927), 6–9 nos. 3–5. Many of these charters were issued by the lords of the particular cities.

[8] WAp, iii, ll. 116–19, 649–653, pp.170, 200. *Malaterra*, ii, 43, p.51.

[9] *Alexiad, xii*, 8.

bribes and a Byzantine bride as inducements to desert his father's army. There is, perhaps not surprisingly, no corroborative evidence for this, and it may be that Anna was reading backwards from Guy's later employment as a mercenary commander in the Byzantine army at the time of the First Crusade and Alexios's attempts to stir up dissension between him and his elder brother in 1107. It may also be the case that these later incidents provide circumstantial evidence for the truth of Anna's claim about 1085.[10] The particular instance is not necessarily that important; the more general issue is. The south Italian chronicler William of Apulia wrote of Normans entering Greek service after Guiscard's death;[11] such enlistments proved an obvious source of intelligence for the Byzantine authorities. The incident in the 1107–8 campaign when the Emperor devised false letters to convince Bohemond of the treachery of his chief supporters, even among his close relatives, would have been impossible without the most detailed knowledge of the relationships and circumstances within the south Italian army. Other obvious sources for such information were members of the indigenous aristocracy of southern Italy displaced or threatened by the Normans. One of the Emperor's intermediaries in his attempt to destabilise Bohemond's army in 1108 was a member of the ruling family of Naples, a city still acknowledging the nominal rule of Byzantium, and which was to maintain a precarious independence from the rule of the Norman dukes of Apulia until the 1130s. The commander of the Byzantine fleet at the same period was, to judge by his name (Landulf), a south Italian Lombard.[12]

The level of contact between southern Italy and Byzantium was therefore high. The recent suggestion that Bohemond himself spoke Greek, and presumably this ability was not wholly exceptional among south Italian Normans, is surely important in this context. Indeed in 1108 Alexios was worried about contact between his army and that of the Normans because he feared that the latter might suborn his own men. For this to be possible there must have been mutual

[10] *Ibid.*, vi, 5; xiii, 4. *Gesta Francorum*, ed. R. Hill (London, 1956), pp.63–65. W.B. McQueen, 'The Relations between the Normans and Byzantium, 1071–1112', *Byzantion*, lvi (1986), 445–47 argues that Guy did enter Byzantine service in the 1080s, not least because he cannot be traced in southern Italy between 1085 and the First Crusade. This is however in error, cf. R. Pirro, *Sicilia Sacra* (alermo 1733), p. 75 (1089), Reg. Neap. Arch. Mon., vi, 137–9 no. 444 (1092). *Orderic*, vi, 102 believed that Guy and Robert de Montfort did accept Alexios's bribes in 1107 and actively sabotaged Bohemond's plans, but the *Alexiad* does not support this. That however it was believed in the West suggests that the emperor's scheme was effective.

[11] WAp, v, ll. 387–90, p.256.

[12] *Alexiad*, xii, 8–9.

communication, and not just with the western mercenaries in the Byzantine army.[13]

That the government of Alexios Komnenos knew a great deal about the Normans does not of course necessarily imply that Anna herself did, writing as she was in her embittered old age. She lamented her lack of visitors (diplomatic isolation?) and alleged that she drew on 'insignificant writings' and conversations with former soldiers, now monks; as well as her youthful memories of listening to conversations between her father and GiorgiosPaleologos, and to her various uncles.[14] It would not therefore be surprising·if she was relatively ill-informed about peoples beyond the Empire's bounds. She lacked access to official archives, and (by her own account) contact with witnesses at the centre of events. Yet although her chronology is often vague, and gaps and distortions inevitably appear given the passage of the years between the events in question and the composition of the *Alexiad*, Anna in fact tells us a great deal about the Empire's neighbours and competitors. For all the difficulties she endured, or alleged she endured, in the reign of her despised brother John, Anna hardly lacked resources or the position to procure information. Moreover the Emperor John seems to have treated her disloyalty towards him with singular mildness.[15]

Occasionally in the *Alexiad* Anna mentions her own role as an eyewitness, as when she helped to save the conspirator Michael Anemas from blinding.[16] She was almost certainly present in Constantinople when the leaders of the First Crusade visited the city. For events of which she had no direct knowledge then first and foremost among her potential sources was her husband Nikephoros Bryennios. The Caesar Nikephoros may well have gathered material for his own uncompleted history which Anna later used; more importantly he was both a participant and an eyewitness. It was, Anna tells us, he who was instrumental in persuading Bohemond to agree to the Treaty of Devol in 1108, and he had played a prominent role too in the reception of the First Crusade at Constantinople. It is hardly coincidental that one of only three official documents which Anna quoted verbatim in

[13] *Alexiad*, xii, 8; xiii, 4. 'The object of this new strategy was to prevent easy access from our side to the Franks, and also to stop letters reaching our army from the enemy or the sending of friendly greetings'. For Bohemond, J. Shepherd, 'When Greek meets Greek: Alexius Comnenus and Bohemond in 1097–8', *Byzantine and Modern Greek Studies*, xii (1988), 251–56, largely based on *Alexiad*, v, 6. Anna was naturally very dismissive of such foreigners who had learnt Greek, as can be seen by her comments on Bohemond's accent in this passage, and on John Italos. She also mentions Latins learning Greek at the orphanage founded (or refounded) by her father. *Alexiad*, v, 8, xv, 7.

[14] *Ibid.*, xiv, 7. Buckler, *Anna Comnena*, pp.42–43.

[15] Niketas Koniates, *Historia*, ed. I. Bekker (Bonn, 1835), pp.16–17.

[16] *Alexiad*, xii, 6.

her history was the text of the Treaty of Devol.[17] Secondly there is the importance of those conversations overheard between the Emperor Alexios and Giorgios Paleologos. Since the latter had been governor of Durazzo in 1081 when Guiscard had first attacked (and his father had been one of those who had died in the emperor's attempt to relieve the besieged city), he would seem to have been a prime source for relevant information about the south Italian Normans.[18] Since there was quite a colony of Amalfitans at Durazzo in the 1080s, Giorgios may in turn have been particularly well-informed about southern Italy.[19] Anna also mentions personal information from another eyewitness of the 1081 invasion, a Latin messenger from the [arch]bishop of Bari to Robert during that campaign. Since Archbishop Ursus of Bari was a ducal *familiaris* whose promotion to that see was almost certainly at Robert's behest, his envoy would also have been a most valuable witness.[20]

It is certainly true that Anna's discussion of the south Italian Normans does contain mistakes, misinformation and an element of legend or gossip. Anna admitted, for example, that she was ignorant of Tancred's exact relationship to Bohemond (but note that her speculation that Tancred was his nephew on the maternal side was in fact correct).[21] She made other minor errors about Guiscard's family – Bohemond was his elder son not his younger, and his other alleged son *Boritilas* (Count Robert of Loritello) was actually his nephew.[22] But such mistakes are easily explicable – particularly given Roger Borsa's succession to the duchy of Apulia in preference to his elder half-brother Bohemond – and are hardly that serious. Indeed in the context of the family relationship of the

---

[17] *Ibid.*, x, 9; xiii, 11–12. The others were the chrysobull delegating administrative authority to the Emperor's mother Anna Dalassena, and a letter of Alexios to Henry IV of Germany, *Alexiad*, iii, 6 and 10.

[18] *Ibid.*, iii, 9; iv, 1 and 6. Nikephoros Bryennios calls Paleologos 'a brave soldier, of great military prowess' and 'a most experienced commander, valiant of arm and heart', *Nicephori Bryennii historiarum libri quattuor*, ed. P. Gautier (Brussels, 1975), iii, 15; iv, 36; pp.239, 307. His wife, Anna Ducaena was the sister of the Empress Irene.

[19] A. Ducellier, *La Façade maritime de l'Albanie au moyen âge* (Thessaloniki, 1981), especially pp.71, 105. I owe this reference to John Cowdrey.

[20] *Alexiad*, iii, 12. On Ursus see particularly F. Babudri, 'Le Note autobiografiche di Giovanni arcidiacono barese e la cronologia dell'arcivescovato di Ursone a Bari (1078–89)', *Archivio storico pugliese*, ii (1949), 134–46. Ursus was a frequent recipient or witness of ducal charters. *Recueil des actes des ducs Normands d'Italie* (1046–1127), i, *Les premiers Ducs* (1046–1087), ed. L.R. Ménager (Bari, 1981), nos. 31 (1080), 41 (1082), 44 (1084), 45 (1085), 46–49 (all 1086) and 61–62 (both 1087). An earlier group of charters from Venosa in which he was purported to be a witness are all forged or heavily interpolated. For these H. Houben, 'Urkundenfälschungen in Süditalien: Das Beispiel Venosa, *Fälschungen im Mittelalter, MGH Schriften*, xxxiii, iv (Hannover, 1988), 35–65, esp. 50–52.

[21] *Alexiad*, xii, 8.

[22] *Ibid.*, i, 14.

Hautevilles what Anna gets wrong is far less interesting than what she gets right, as with her guess as to Tancred's relationship to Bohemond. She knew, for example, about the marriages of Guiscard's daughters,[23] that Bohemond had married a daughter of the king of France and Tancred her sister,[24] that Guiscard had been buried at Venosa and that his brothers had been buried there before him. She was more or less correct when she said that he died in his twenty-fifth year as duke (actually twenty-sixth), although she probably considerably overestimated his age at death as seventy (only perhaps an estimate for one who had lived to a good age; he was probably about sixty).[25] Probably her most serious error in this context was to allege that Bohemond had no lands at all in southern Italy. Here she seems to have drawn the wrong conclusion from Roger Borsa's succession as duke.[26]

Anna's chronology is also difficult to follow and some events are misplaced or out of sequence. For example, she placed the episode when Robert dammed the River Glykys to refloat his ships in the spring of 1082 – and even there it was probably out of sequence since she put it before the battle outside Durazzo, which the western chroniclers would seem to date to 1081. William of Apulia, writing little over a decade after the campaign, rather than half a century later as Anna did, placed the refloating of the ships in the spring of 1085. Indeed, as Buckler pointed out sixty years ago, her whole chronology of the Durazzo siege poses numerous difficulties.[27] She also contradicts herself. In Book One she writes that Robert decided to sail to Albania from Brindisi rather than Otranto because the journey was shorter, in Book Six she has him sail on his second expedition from Otranto rather than Brindisi for precisely the same reason.[28]

But it is easy to overestimate how significant all this is, or to be influenced by Anna's predictable (one might almost say pardonable) exaggeration of the personal exploits of her father. Comparison of Anna's account of the Balkan campaign of 1081–85 with the account of William of Apulia (by far the most detailed Latin source for these events) is instructive. In almost all significant aspects the two accounts are very

[23] To Raymond Berengar II of Barcelona and Count Ebulus of Roucy, *Alexiad*, i, 12; cf. WAp, iv, ll. 8–15, p.204.

[24] *Alexiad*, xii, 1.

[25] *Ibid.*, vi, 6; cf. WAp, v, ll. 400–5, p.258 for Robert's burial, and ii ll. 379–80, p.152 for the burial of his elder brother Humphrey. But if Guiscard was really seventy in 1085 then he must have been over thirty when he first came to Italy *c.* 1046 which seems unlikely, particularly given the testimony of Geoffrey Malaterra that the younger sons of Tancred de Hauteville came to Italy 'as soon as age permitted', *Malaterra*, i, 11, p.14.

[26] *Alexiad*, x, 11. Shepherd, 'When Greek meets Greek', 242.

[27] *Ibid.*, iv, 3. WAp, v, ll. 235–54, pp.248–50. Buckler, *Anna Comnena*, pp.406–414.

[28] *Alexiad*, i, 16, vi, 5.

close to each other. Both are for example agreed that the expedition was preceded by a meeting between Robert and Pope Gregory VII at Benevento during which a peace was concluded between them, then go on to describe the German rebellion against Henry IV and the death of Rudolf of Rheinfelden.[29] Both mention the impostor who claimed to be the Emperor Michael VII, although while William dismisses him in a few lines, the *Alexiad* gives a much more elaborate and at times fanciful account.[30] Both sources say that before leaving Italy Robert designated his son Roger as his successor and at least nominal regent. They then go on to describe the capture of Butrinto and Avlona by the advance guard, and the storm at sea which imperilled Robert's fleet.[31] Both accounts describe the inhabitants of Durazzo jeering the pseudo-Michael when he was exhibited to them.[32] Both emphasise Duchess Sichelgaita's role at the battle outside Durazzo, though where Anna ascribes to her a virago's heroic part William was more conventional and less flattering, describing her as 'terrified by her wound'.[33]

The accounts then diverge insofar as Anna, in a fairly brief passage, ascribes the primary role in the surrender of Durazzo to the pusillanimity of various of its inhabitants originally hailing from Amalfi, while both William of Apulia and Geoffrey Malaterra assigned the chief responsibility to a Venetian called Domenico.[34] But, if Anna's account is less circumstantial – and it is again worth stressing that she was writing long after the two south Italian chroniclers – there is nothing directly contradictory in the two versions; Anna may well have simply been less well informed about the exact circumstances. Both Anna and William of Apulia specifically mention the chapel of St. Nicholas near Durazzo. Anna has first Alexios's, then Robert's, headquarters there, William says that the traitor arranged a rendezvous there with Duke Robert.[35]

Both accounts now deal with Guiscard's return to Italy, though William ascribes this specifically to the revolt of the Apulian towns, Anna to the German threat. Again neither explanation contradicts the other, both agree that Bohemond was left behind as leader at Durazzo. The *Alexiad* certainly telescopes events in southern Italy in 1082–85,

[29] *Ibid.*, i, 13. WAp, iv, ll. 16–34, pp.204–6. The most detailed examination of the parallels between the two accounts is by Ja. I. Ljubarskij, 'Ob istochnikakh "Aleksiady" Anny Kominoy' [On the sources of Anna Komnena's *Alexiad*], *Vizantijskij Vremennik*, xxv (1964), 110–17, esp. 110–11.

[30] *Alexiad*, i, 12, 15. WAp, iv, ll. 160–70, p.212.

[31] *Alexiad*, iii, 12. WAp, iv, ll. 185–234, pp.214–16.

[32] *Alexiad*, iv, 1. WAp, iv, ll. 264–71, p.218.

[33] *Alexiad*, iv, 6. WAp, iv, ll. 425–431, p.236.

[34] *Alexiad*, v, 1. WAp, iv, ll. 450–505, pp.228–30. *Malaterra*, iii, 28, pp.74–75.

[35] *Alexiad*, iv, 7. WAp, iv, ll. 461–6, p.228.

but rightly has Guiscard going to Rome and then returning to Salerno (1084).[36]

We can once again see the two accounts running closely parallel in describing events in the Balkans in Guiscard's absence. Both Anna and William of Apulia associate a certain Briennus/*Bryennios* with Bohemond in command of the expeditionary force; he is probably to be identified with Briennus the Constable, lord of S. Mango sul Calore.[37] Both describe Bohemond twice defeating Alexios in open battle, establishing his base at Jannina, Alexios using wagons to try to break up the impact of the Norman charge, the capture of Tzimiskos at the siege of Larissa, the prominent roles of Nikephoros Melissinos on the Byzantine side and Briennus on the other at the battle of Larissa, and Alexios capturing Bohemond's camp. After the battle both agree that Briennus was left to guard Kastoria.[38]

Agreement again largely prevails when both sources turn to Robert Guiscard's second expedition of 1084–85. Admittedly Wiliam has the duke sailing from Brindisi rather than Otranto because the former was more sheltered, while Anna says that he changed his mind and decided to sail from Otranto not Brindisi. This is however hardly a very serious divergence.[39] William agrees with Anna that this time Roger Borsa accompanied his father to Albania, that Corfu was in revolt against the Normans, that a naval battle was fought with the Venetians en route, and that the fleet stopped at Vonitsa. Though both add different rhetorical and highly unlikely details, their accounts of Robert Guiscard's death have significant features in common: that he fell ill at Kephalonia, that his wife arrived when he was already desperately ill, and that immediately after his father's death Roger Borsa announced to his troops that he must

---

[36] WAp, iv, ll. 524–35, p.232. *Alexiad*, v, 3. *Malaterra*, iii, 32, p.77, wrote that Robert returned to aid the Roman church in response to anxious letters from Gregory VII.

[37] *Alexiad*, v, 5 and 7. WAp, iv, ll. 526–27, v, ll. 4–5, pp.232, 236 and commentary p.325. Briennus witnessed charters of Roger Borsa to the cathedral of Melfi in November 1093 and December 1097, F. Ughelli, *Italia Sacra*, 2nd. ed. N. Colleti, 10 vols. (Venice, 1717–21), i, 923–4. He died apparently before September 1112.

[38] *Alexiad*, v, 4–7. WAp, v, ll. 1–79, pp.236–40. However, while William (who knew that Melissinos was the emperor's brother-in-law) also mentioned the prominent role of Alexios's younger brother Adrian, Anna does not refer to him. John Zonaras, *Epitomae Historiarum*, ed. M. Pinder, 3 vols. (Bonn, 1897), iii, pp.735–36, also singles him out as commanding one division of the Byzantine army, though generally his account is too compressed to be very useful. Melissinos had been a rival for the imperial throne in 1081, but had been bought off with the title of Caesar. He was married to Alexios's sister Eudocia, *Alexiad*, ii, 8, 10–111, 111.4. Bryennios, *Historiarum*, iv, 31, p.301.

[39] *Alexiad*, vi, 5. WAp, v, ll. 130–39, p.242. *Malaterra*, iii, 40. p.81 wrote that the fleet was collected at Otranto, WAp, v, ll. 128 that the army was mustered at Taranto. Clearly all three ports were involved in mounting the expedition.

return home.[40]

That the chief features of Anna Komnena's account of the Norman invasion of the Byzantine Empire are essentially the same as those of a more contemporary western source suggests two possibilities. Either there was some close relationship between the two sources or they coincide because both, independently, were well-informed and accurate about the events in question. It must be said at once that the latter is far the more probable, for it seems in the highest degree unlikely that Anna can have had access to the *Gesta Roberti Wiscardi*, a work with a very limited manuscript distribution even in the west,[41] and only a shade less unlikely that both texts depended upon a lost common original. Anna did not read Latin and how such a transmission could have occurred seems difficult to envisage, particularly given the early date of William's poem, written almost certainly in the second half of the 1090s.[42]

There are still difficulties which must be faced. The learned and highly competent modern editor of the *Gesta Roberti* discussed three passages where there seemed to be close textual links between it and the *Alexiad*: the discussion about the origin and name of Durazzo (*Dyrrachium*), the abuse directed against the imposter claiming to be Michael VII by its inhabitants, and the episode of the refloating of Guiscard's ships. She concluded that in all three cases oral sources, and not a written one, explain the similarities.[43] But there are other, and really rather disturbing, parallels, primarily at the start of book four of William's poem. Admittedly the first of these, about the marriage of Guiscard's daughters, may well be explicable simply in terms of common and accurate information.[44] William then goes on to describe a meeting at Benevento between Robert Guiscard and Gregory VII, at which Robert swore fealty on the Gospels to the Holy See. William adds that 'the pope was said to have promised to him the crown of the Roman Empire'.[45] After this the poem refers to the excommunication of Henry IV, the Saxon revolt led by Guelf IV and Rudolf of Rheinfelden (whose rebellion William wrongly ascribes to the pope's initiative) and

---

[40] *Alexiad*, vi, 5–6. WAp, v, ll. 144–363, pp.244–56.

[41] WAp introduction pp.70–75, The only two known MSS. (one of which is now lost) were from the monasteries of Bec and Mont-Michel in Normandy, although the chronicler of the monastery of St. Bartholomew, Carpineto, in the Abruzzi must also have had access to it, parts of which he incorporated into his own work. The *Chronicon Sancti Bartholomei* is printed by Ughelli, *Italia Sacra*, x, pp.350–82.

[42] WAp, introduction pp.11–13.

[43] WAp, introduction pp.39–46. The three passages are WAp, iv, lines 234–43, 264–71, v lines 235–74, cf. *Alexiad*, iii, 12, iv, 1 and 3. By contrast Ljubarskij, 'Ob istochnikakh', 113–15 argued for a lost common original.

[44] See above note 23.

[45] WAp, iv, ll. 16–30, p.204.

Rudolf's subsequent death at the battle of Elster.[46] The story then turns to the background of Guiscard's expedition against Byzantium, and describes an embassy from Henry IV to Robert asking for an alliance against the pope. William said that although the duke's response was (outwardly) favourable the envoys achieved nothing. Robert promptly notified the pope of these communications and assured him of his loyalty, while refusing to call off his expedition against the eastern empire.[47]

All these features of William's poem are present in the *Alexiad*. The *Alexiad* has them in a different order, and the texts even of particular incidents are not identical, but they are close. Anna tells us, for example, that while Robert thought that Henry IV, as well as Gregory VII, was a fool to ask for his aid, 'he made some sort of verbal reply to the king, but wrote a letter to the pope'. This letter Anna claims to quote – surely a rhetorical exercise on her part – but the version she gives us has as its purport to reassure the pope of his loyalty but also to emphasise that he himself is going ahead with his war against Byzantium. Perhaps most serious is the *Alexiad's* agreement with the *Gesta Roberti Wiscardi* that Robert met with Gregory and then swore fealty to him at Benevento, and that the pope offered to make him a king (which the *Alexiad* accepts as fact, not just rumour).[48] That Benevento was described as the place of the meeting seems to derive from confusion between the actual encounter of the duke and pope in June 1080, which took place at Ceprano on the borders of the papal states, and the abortive and disastrous meeting between the two at Benevento in August 1073, which ushered in a long period of difficult relations only brought to a close by the Ceprano agreement. That the 1080 meeting was at Ceprano there can be no doubt, for the text of Robert's oath survives, dated at Ceprano on 29th June 1080. Only the *Gesta Roberti* and the *Alexiad* make the mistake of placing this meeting at Benevento, in contradiction to all the other sources both south Italian and papal, which either put it correctly at Ceprano or at Aquino, only a few miles away.[49]

[46] WAp, iv, ll. 31–64, pp.204–6.

[47] WAp, iv, ll. 171–84, pp.212–14.

[48] *Alexiad*, i, 13.

[49] *Gregorii VII Registrum*, VIII. la, ed. E. Caspar, 2 vols., MGH Epistolae Selectae (Berlin, 1920–3), ii, 514–15. Cf Romuald of Salerno, *Chronicon*, ed. C.A. Garufi (Città di Castello, 1935), p.191. *Liber Pontificalis*, ed. L. Duchesne, 2 vols. (Paris, 1886–92), ii, 366. Bonizo of Sutri, *Liber ad Amicum, MGH Libelli de Lite*, 3 vols. (Hannover, 1891–97), i, 612. Although Gregory's itinerary between late July and mid September 1080 is uncertain there is no evidence that he was at Benevento at any point during that year. Unfortunately the Beneventan annals for this period are thin and unhelpful; see O. Bertolini, 'Gli Annales Beneventani', *Bolletino dell'Istituto Storico Italiano per il Medio Evo*, xlii (1923), 145.

Such coincidences would seem to suggest that one cannot lightly dismiss ideas about a common source, although how such a transmission occurred is by no means easy to envisage. It still seems more probable that the reason for the agreement between the *Alexiad* and the *Gesta Roberti Wiscardi* was that both reported what actually happened. But the occasional parallels in the texts, not just in terms of events, suggest, at the very least, that the *Alexiad* author had access to information from the Norman side. In that case, though the archbishop of Bari's envoy was one source to whom Anna herself had access, it may be that we should be looking, as argued by Dr. Howard-Johnston,[50] to Nikephoros Bryennios as the intermediary (since his direct contact with the Normans was surely much greater than Anna's), and perhaps 1108 and the treaty of Devol as the time. Whatever the nature of the links, that the *Alexiad* does reproduce details found in the *Gesta Roberti Wiscardi* of William of Apulia suggests that Anna was both well-informed and accurate about the Norman invasion of the Byzantine Empire.

Confidence in the credibility of her sections about the south Italian Normans is surely enhanced by the reliability of the names she mentions, whatever the problems she encountered with the phonetic transcription of barbarian nomenclature. She correctly identified the leaders of the Apulian rebels as Herman (*Ermanos*) and Abelard (*Bagelardos*), the archbishop of Capua whom she claimed had received a letter from Alexios as Hervé (*Erbios*) – attested as archbishop from 1078 to 1082;[51] and though no western sources cite him in this context the *Amiketas* whom she mentioned at the battle of Durazzo may well be identified with Count Amicus of Giovenazzo, one of the most prominent leaders of the Apulian Normans of this period.[52] Similarly one's confidence in the text of the treaty of Devol which she quotes is strengthened by the witness list, where both the [arch]bishops mentioned are well-attested in other sources.[53]

There are however three instances which, at least at first sight, suggest that Anna's grasp of matters western is less sure, and in each of these what looks like legendary material, folk tales, gossip (call it what you will) has been used. The first of these episodes concerns the Normans

[50] In an unpublished lecture delivered at the same conference as the first draft of this essay.

[51] *Alexiad*, iii, 9. For Archbishop Hervé, *Chronica Monasterii Casinensis*, ed. H. Hoffman, *MGH Scriptores*, (Hannover, 1980), iii, 42, p.420; *Gregorii VII Registrum*, viii, 48, vol.ii, 609.

[52] For him WAp, iii, ll. 392–95, 522, 542–66, 645–9, pp.184, 192–94, 200, who describes his involvement in the revolts against Guiscard in the 1070s. It would certainly have been prudent to make him accompany the expedition against Byzantium.

[53] Maurus was archbishop of Amalfi 1103–28, and was sent as envoy by Paschal II to Alexios in November 1112. Rainald is attested as archbishop of Taranto between 1108 and 1113. *Italia Pontificia*, ed. P.F. Kehr, 10 vols. (Berlin, 1905–74), viii, 390–91; ix, 438.

of southern Italy only indirectly, but is nonetheless indicative of Anna's command of western issues. Anna recounts, in her first book, the breach between Henry IV and Gregory VII and the barbarous revenge taken by the pope on Henry's envoys. Needless to say the latter detail is not attested elsewhere. Anna's remarkable coyness in describing what actually happened: 'I would have given a name to the outrage, but as a woman and a princess modesty forbade me', is hilariously at variance with the equally remarkable anatomical frankness with which, according to Niketas Koniates, she reproached her husband for his pusillanimity (or prudence?) in refusing to lead a coup against her brother John in 1118. But it is worth noting that just before she becomes carried away by her anti-papal bias Anna gives a succinct and notably accurate account of the origins of the Investiture Contest, one which it would be difficult to better in a single paragraph. If she had no direct knowledge of Henry IV's 1076 letter calling on 'Hildebrand, false monk' to descend from the papal throne (and it seems improbable, if not one supposes quite impossible, that she, or the Byzantine government, did have such knowledge), then she certainly gives a good general description of its 'most insulting and reckless language'. A little later she more or less correctly identifies the leaders of the German opposition to King Henry, Rudolf of Rheinfelden (*Landolfos*) and Welf IV (*Velikos*), and then provides a brief, highly-coloured, but in essence not inaccurate, account of the battle of the Elster in 1080 at which Rudolf was killed at the moment of victory. This last part is, as was noted above, not dissimilar to William of Apulia's poem, but for the letter and for the general political context Anna was surely drawing on information obtained at the time by Byzantine diplomats.[54]

Secondly, there is her description of Bohemond's pretended death and journey from Antioch to Corfu in a coffin. This, as is well-known, is yet another variant on an old chestnut occurring in almost a dozen western sources in a variety of contexts. But most of these were in some way connected with the Normans, southern Italy or both. The earliest variant comes in Dudo of St. Quentin's *Historia Normannorum Ducum*. Among the other authors who reproduced the legend was William of Apulia, with Robert Guiscard himself as the protagonist, using the strategem to capture an (unnamed) monastery. In turn Matthew Paris, the latest writer to reproduce the story, names this monastery as Montecassino.[55] What Anna tells us here is therefore myth, but it

---

[54] *Alexiad*, i, 13. *Monumenta Bambergensia* ed. P. Jaffé (Berlin, 1868), pp.101–2, no.47. Niketas, *Historia*, p.15.

[55] *Alexiad*, xi, 12. Dudo, *De Moribus et Actis Primorum Normanniae Ducum*, ed. J. Lair (Caen, 1865), pp.49–51. WAp, ii, ll. 332–54, p.150. Matthew Paris, *Chronica Majora*, ed. H.R. Luard, Rolls Series, 7 vols. (London, 1872–84), iii, 538. For other references WAp, introduction, pp.46–52.

is myth within a specifically Norman, or Normanno-Italian context, and related to other, primarily oral, tales, fragments of which only are preserved in the written sources. Anna therefore reflects at second-hand something of the myth-making of the 'Norman Achievement', a concept which despite the scepticism of R.H.C. Davis and others should not be too hastily relegated to the historical scrapheap, even if its implications need careful examination.[56]

The third such story which requires attention is the most interesting of the three. This is Anna's account of the strategem employed by Robert Guiscard during the earlier part of his career to capture his father-in-law, William Mascabeles, supposedly the 'ruler of most of the territory adjacent to Langobardia'. The *Alexiad* tells how Robert arranged a meeting with William, persuaded him to dismount, and then overpowered him with the help of his men concealed nearby, acting so suddenly that Mascabeles' bodyguard, lulled into a false sense of security, were unable to react in time to prevent it. Their abortive rescue attempt was then foiled by the rapid appearance of more of Robert's troops and by a notable feat of arms by Guiscard himself, killing one of the bodyguards who charged to the rescue of his master. The unfortunate William was then led off to Robert's castle and forced to disgorge his money through the painful process of having each of his teeth extracted in turn to force another payment.[57]

The particular interest of this story is that it was a variant upon one which had already been reproduced in no less than three Latin and one Greek texts, all written well before the *Alexiad*. In the likely order of composition these are the *Strategikon* of Kekaumenos (late 1070s), the History of Amatus of Montecassino (*c.* 1080), the 'Deeds of Count Roger of Sicily' by Geoffrey Malaterra (*c.* 1100) and (a very brief version this and probably dependent on that of Amatus) in the Montecassino chronicle of Leo of Ostia (probably before 1103).[58] The details in these versions vary, but all repeat the basic story of the great wealth of the victim, the meeting, and of Robert's personal seizure of his unfortunate opponent. All four sources however claim that the latter came from the town of Bisignano in Calabria. Kekaumenos, who calls him 'Teras the Calabrian', and Leo of Ostia make him respectively the governor (*phylax*) and the lord of the town; Amatus and Malaterra merely a very rich inhabitant. All three western chroniclers call him Peter de Tyra or

[56] See G.A. Loud, 'The *Gens Normannorum:* Myth or Reality?', *Proceedings of the Fourth Battle Conference on Anglo-Norman Studies*, 1981, ed. R.A. Brown (Woodbridge, 1982), pp.104–16.

[57] *Alexiad*, i, 11.

[58] *Strategikon*, ed. B. Wassiliewsky and V. Jernstedt (St. Petersburg, 1896), p.35. *Amatus*, iii, 10, pp.122–3. *Malaterra*, i, 17. pp.17–18. *Chronica Monasterii Casinensis*, iii, 15, p.377.

Peter son of Tyre (Amatus). The account of Amatus is notable in his claim that Robert made an agreement with Peter that he 'took him for father, and Peter took him for [his] son'. No mention is however made of any marriage, and indeed in the very next chapter the author goes on to tell the story of Guiscard's marriage to Alberada of Buonalbergo. The two most detailed Latin sources suggest that the fateful meeting took place in a plain outside Bisignano, Kekaumenos in the dry moat or ditch (*kantax*) outside the main gate of the town, not in a marshy valley between two hills as Anna would have it.[59]

The basis of Anna's story would thus seem to be genuine, but she or her direct source embellished it with details which were not included in any of the other versions of the same incident. The significant alterations are four-fold: (1) that the victim was Robert's father-in-law; (2) that his name was William Mascabeles; (3) that Robert killed in single combat one of his guards; and (4) that he was forced to disgorge a ransom by having all his teeth extracted; All of these details were actually based on some sort of fact or legend concerning Robert Guiscard, but none of them was connected with this particular incident. That the *Alexiad* used them suggests once again that Anna or her source had access to the legends which had developed about the spread among the Normans of south Italy. To prove this these four features need to be examined more fully.

That Robert Guiscard fell out with his father-in-law can only be based on some distant knowledge of his repudiation of his first wife Alberada of Buonalbergo *c*. 1058–59 in order to marry Sichelgaita, the sister of Gisulf II, the Lombard prince of Salerno.[60] Why however was Anna's usually good knowledge of Norman names so deficient in this instance as to call the father-in-law William Mascabeles rather than Gerard of Buonalbergo, as was really the case? The answer may in fact be connected with the First Crusade. Among the leaders of the

---

[59] The relevant passage in the *Strategikon* is as follows: 'Let me tell you another thing (if you have the grace of God you will be an accomplished general) which happened to Teras the Calabrian who was guardian of the town of the Bisiniani. For he was very wealthy and well-born and the leading man in the district. Now Robert the Frank, having by the will of God become tyrant, desired to overpower him. But every device he made was beaten off. What should he do? He comes outside the town as a friend and sends a message to him to come outside the gate on the pretext of some important and secret discussion. So Teras went out of the gate of the fort, but inside the moat. Then the Frank pretended to be afraid of those who accompanied Teras. Then Teras ordered them to withdraw and was left alone; the two stood talking. Now the Frank had three picked men ready sitting valuable horses, who with a kick of their heels leapt the moat and overpowering him [Teras] instantly turned back with him and subdued that estimable man as a slave. What torments they applied to him I am not able to tell. So guard against the plots of your enemies and do not trust them'. I am indebted for the translation to Janet Hamilton.

[60] *Amatus*, iv, 18, pp.194–5, *Malaterra*, i, 30, p.22. *Chron. Cas.*, iii, 5, pp.377–78, all of which refer to consanguinity as the (ostensible) motive for Alberada's repudiation.

south Italian contingent on that Crusade was a cousin of Bohemond's called Geoffrey of Montescaglioso, who was subsequently killed at the battle of Doryleum. Geoffrey's brother Ralph, count of Montescaglioso, and the latter's son Roger both had the nickname *Maccabeus*.[61] It would need the alteration in a written source of only two characters and the insertion of a third for that *Maccabeus* to become *Mascabeles*. It is therefore my suggestion, albeit tentative, that the knowledge that Robert had a kinsman called Maccabeus was, through scribal error, transformed into Mascabeles; and from being a kinsman he was somehow conflated with the father-in-law with whom Guiscard had indeed fallen out.

The other two notable features of Anna's account would also seem to be garbled recollections, of two of the most famous incidents in the career of the Hauteville family. Robert's killing of the charging bodyguard recalls the notable feat of arms during Maniakes' campaign in Sicily in 1038 from which Robert's eldest brother, William 'the Iron Arm', acquired his famous nickname.[62] And the nasty tale of the extraction of the victim's teeth must surely refer to Guiscard's acquisition of the tooth of St. Matthew when he captured Salerno from his brother-in-law Gisulf in 1077. According to Amatus, not one of Gisulf's admirers, the prince was offered his freedom in return for this relic but attempted to play false by substituting the tooth of a recently-deceased Jew for that of the Evangelist. The fraud was however exposed, and Robert threatened the prince that unless he produced the genuine tooth of St. Matthew all of his own teeth would be forfeit. The resemblances between this and Anna's story are too obvious to be laboured further.[63]

Even therefore when she appears to be at her most fanciful Anna Komnena was not inventing material about the Normans of southern Italy. She had access to sources which repeated, albeit not always very accurately, stories circulating in southern Italy which were part of the legend of the Norman conquest of the peninsula. That conquest, which modern commentators tend to see, and rightly so, as an epic undertaking, like all good epics grew in the telling. The obvious comparison is the growth of legendary material which occurred soon after the conquest of the Holy Land by the First Crusade, but whereas the works of men

[61] *Gesta Francorum*, pp.8 (which wrongly calls the crusader Humphrey), 21. E. Gattula, *Accessiones ad historiam abbatiae Casinensis* (Venice, 1734), p.213 (1096); J. Mabillon, *Annales Ordini S. Benedicti* (Lucca, 1740), pp.631–32 (September 1099); *Reg. Neap. Arch. Mon.*, vi, 168–170 nos. 12–13 (May and November 1099), 184–96 nos. 20–24 (1110, 1115, July and August 1119). E.M. Jamison, 'Some Notes on the *Anonymi gesta Francorum*, with Special Reference to the Norman Contingent from South Italy and Sicily in the First Crusade', *Studies in French Language and Literature Presented to Professor Mildred K. Pope* (Manchester, 1939), pp.200–1.

[62] *Malaterra*, i, 7, p.11.

[63] *Amatus*, viii, 23, 370–71.

like Graindor of Douai preserved much of the crusade cycle the legends of Norman Italy survived only in fragmentary form in the overtly more sober chronicle literature, although one would suggest that this was part of a larger body of oral legend. Anna Komnena, who in other respects was well-informed about southern Italy in the age of Alexios and Robert Guiscard, drew at second-hand on these legends. Yet this does not diminish the importance of the *Alexiad* as a source for the history of Norman Italy, rather it reinforces it.

Chapter 5

The Question of the Consecration of St Edmund's Church

Antonia Gransden

The origins of the abbey of Bury St Edmunds are veiled in obscurity,[1] and so is the question of the consecration of the conventual church. It vexed Bury monks from the late twelfth until at least the mid fourteenth century, and can still puzzle an historian today. The main problem was and is whether the magnificent Romanesque church of St. Edmund was ever consecrated at all. Inevitably such an important matter gave rise to historical research in the middle ages, and it is still worth investigating. The monks themselves had a particular cause for anxiety. If St. Edmund's church had never been consecrated, what effect would that have on their chances of salvation? This worry led to legal inquiry.

Abbo of Fleury in his *Passio sancti Eadmundi* recorded the earliest tradition about St. Edmund's church.[2] He says that when the martyr's body was first moved to Beodricesworth, the faithful of the vill built a large wooden church to house it. *Hermann's De miraculis sancti Eadmundi* contains the next piece of research into the church's early history. He relates that in the time of King Cnut and his wife Emma the monks replaced this church with a larger stone one, and that Eadnoth, archbishop of Canterbury 'dedicated' it.[3] Dedication does not of course necessarily include consecration; it can mean that the church was only solemnly blessed, not that its high altar and walls were also anointed with holy oil, but in the texts cited below it seems to be used synonymously with 'consecration'. Hermann is imprecise in that he gives no date for the dedication. By about 1131, however, the

---

[1] See. A. Gransden, 'The Legends and Traditions concerning the Origins of the Abbey of Bury St. Edmunds', *English Historical Review*, c (1985), 1–24. I am indebted to Dr. Mary Cheney and the Right Reverend Eric Kemp for kindly reading this article in typescript and making many useful comments. I am also especially indebted to Dr. Cheney for invaluable help in identifying the citations from canon law and its glosses in the document printed in the appendix below. I am grateful to Professor Peter Stein for help in particular with the identification of citations from civil law in the same document.

[2] *Three Lives of English Saints*, ed. Michael Winterbottom (Toronto, 1972), 82.

[3] *Memorials of St. Edmund's Abbey*, ed. Thomas Arnold, Rolls Series, lxxxxvi, 3 vols. (1890–96), i, 84–5.

Bury monks claimed to be better informed. Shortly after 1131 they made a copy of the chronicle of 'Florence' and John of Worcester, into which they interpolated details about their abbey's (in some cases supposed) history.[4] One interpolation states that on 15 Kal. November (18 October) 1032 Archbishop Eadnoth consecrated the church in honour of St. Mary and St. Edmund.[5] However, the question of the consecration of St. Edmund's second church was of subsidiary importance after the Norman Conquest. Although that church remained standing it was soon replaced as St. Edmund's mausoleum and shrine by the splendid new church built by Abbot Baldwin (1065–97). It is with the consecration of this church that we are primarily concerned.

Baldwin began building shortly after he became abbot. Hermann, a Bury monk in Baldwin's time and author of the *De miraculis sancti Eadmundi*, which includes much abbatial history, records that the presbytery of the new church was completed in 1094, ready, in Baldwin's eyes, for consecration. Hermann relates the sequel.[6] Baldwin asked the king, William Rufus, for licence, as the king required, to have the church consecrated and for St. Edmund's translation into it.[7] William promised a licence but did not fulfill his promise. Instead he gave permission for the martyr's translation and specifically not for consecration. He then went abroad. (Baldwin's request must have been early in 1094, for Rufus was in Normandy from 19 March until 29 December in that year.) Meanwhile Baldwin made sumptuous preparations, still hoping for licence to consecrate the church as well as to translate the martyr. Time passed, the king returned, but in 1095 a rumour began to circulate at court that St. Edmund's uncorrupt body did not lie at Beodricesworth. And the wicked courtiers advised that his shrine be stripped of its riches to pay the king's soldiers. Baldwin now apparently despaired of obtaining Rufus's licence to consecrate. It happened that on Wednesday 25 April 1095, Walkelin, bishop of Winchester, and Ranulf, the king's chaplain (Ranulf Flambard, later, 1099–1128, bishop of Durham), came to Bury

[4] Oxford, Bodleian Library, MS Bodley 297. Described and eighteen passages printed, *Memorials*, i, pp.lxi–lxiii, 340–56. See also *The Chronicle of John of Worcester, 1118–1140*, ed. J.R.H. Weaver, Anecdota Oxoniensia (Oxford, 1908), p.9.

[5] *Memorials*, i, p.342. The *Annales Sancti Edmundi* date the consecration to the feast of St. Luke the Evangelist, i.e. 18, not 28, October. See the *Annales* printed in *Ungedruckte Anglo-Normannische Geschichtsquellen*, ed. F. Liebermann (Strassburg, 1879), and, from 1032, in *Memorials*, ii, p.3.

[6] *Memorials*, i, p.85–88.

[7] A royal licence was necessary presumably because the king was the abbey's patron. The incident is an example of the power of the Anglo-Norman kings over the church. See Frank Barlow, *William Rufus* (London, 1983), p.177, and Eadmer, *Historia novorum in Anglia*, ed. Martin Rule, Rolls Series, lxxxi (1884), pp.10, 60, 83–84. For this example see Barlow, *op.cit.*, pp.207–8.

to discuss the king's business. Baldwin took advantage of their presence to ask them to conduct St. Edmund's translation. This they gladly agreed to do; indeed it seems that the king had instructed them to do so. The ceremony was therefore performed, with all due solemnity and splendour, before a vast multitude on Sunday 29 April.

Hermann is careful to note that Walkelin and Ranulf acted at Baldwin's free request and in defiance of the bitter opposition of the diocesan, Herbert Losinga, bishop of Norwich. Throughout his abbatiate Baldwin was in conflict with the East Anglian bishops, first with Arfast (or 'Herfast'), bishop of Elmham (1070–72) and of Thetford (1072–84), and then with Losinga, bishop of Thetford (1091–94 × 1096) and of Norwich (1094 × 1096–1119).[8] Arfast and Losinga in turn tried to move the see to Bury, a plan which the monks adamantly opposed. At the centre of the dispute was the abbey's claim to exemption from diocesan control, indeed from any ecclesiastical authority except the pope and his legate. The privilege, the monks asserted, had been granted by King Cnut[9] and Pope Alexander II,[10] Baldwin having obtained the latter's bull on 27 October 1071. One result of the privilege of exemption was that the abbot could choose whichever bishop he liked to perform pontifical offices. The monks of Bury valued this right highly. Hermann gives a particularly full account of Baldwin's struggle with Arfast.[11] He records that at Easter 1081 the king sent Archbishop Lanfranc to try to settle the dispute. On this occasion Baldwin won the case by appealing to the past; he argued that the three abbots of Bury since the monastery's foundation, Uvius, Leofstan and himself, had all been blessed or consecrated by the bishop of their choice – by the bishop of London, the bishop of Winchester and the archbishop of Canterbury respectively.[12] Hermann is less detailed about Losinga's quarrel with Baldwin than about that with Arfast, but he does record that Losinga was gravely offended when Baldwin chose Walkelin and Ranulf to officiate at St. Edmund's translation. As the diocesan,

[8] For this dispute see: David Knowles, 'Essays in Monastic History, iv. the Growth of Exemption', *Downside Review*, i (1932), 208–13; V.H. Galbraith, 'The East Anglian See and the Abbey of Bury St. Edmund's', *English Historical Review*, xl (1925), 222–28; A. Gransden, 'Baldwin, Abbot of Bury St. Edmunds, 1065–1097', *Proceeedings of the Battle Abbey Conference on Anglo-Norman Studies*, iv (1981), 70.

[9] Cnut's charter of privilege is printed e.g. J.M. Kemble, *Codex diplomaticus aevi Saxonici*, 6 vols. (London, 1839–48), iv, p.16 (no.735), and calendared P.H. Sawyer, *Anglo-Saxon Charters* (London, 1968), pp.293–94 (no.980). It is of doubtful authenticity at least in its present form; see F.E. Harmer, *Anglo-Saxon Writs* (Manchester 1952, 2nd edn. Stamford 1989), pp.433–34.

[10] For Alexander II's bull see *Regesta pontificum Romanorum*, ed. Philippe Jaffé, 2 vols. (Leipzig, 1885, 1888), i, p.587. The text is printed in *The Pinchbeck Register*, ed. Francis Hervey, 2 vols. (Brighton, 1925), i, pp.3–4.

[11] *Memorials*, i, pp.60–7.

[12] *Ibid.*, i, p.66.

Losinga wanted to participate and, failing that, to forbid the ceremony. The abbey, however, as Hermann points out, was fortified by royal and papal privileges. The king supported its claim to exemption, and plans for the translation proceeded as arranged.[13] The abbey's claim to exemption was linked to the question of its church's consecration: whenever that event should take place, the abbot would insist on choosing the celebrant. Moreover, if the church remained unconsecrated for an unreasonably long time, the bishop of Norwich, the diocesan, might use that as an excuse for intervening, to bring about its consecration.

St. Edmunds was again in conflict with the diocesan early in Henry II's reign. Almost nothing is known about the dispute except what can be inferred from an incidental reference in the *Gesta abbatum sancti Albani* and the existence of a tract on the dedication of altars, chapels and churches at Bury. The *Gesta abbatum* records in detail the dispute between the bishop of Lincoln and the abbot of St. Albans in the late 1150s and the early 1160s over the latter's claim to exemption (an agreement was made between the parties in March 1163). Henry II was in France when the quarrel broke out and appointed commissioners to try the case. The parties appeared before them at Winchester, the abbot of St. Albans being supported by, among others, both the abbot (Hugh) and the prior (Theobald) of Bury.[14] In the course of the trial the bishop of Lincoln suddenly produced a letter of Pope Alexander III, dated 16 March [1161], to the abbot of St Albans enjoining him to prove his case before the bishop of Chichester and the bishop of Norwich. Henry II was angry at this interference with his jurisdiction and accused the abbot of St. Albans of having solicited the papal letter. However, the abbot's party assuaged his anger by pointing out that both bishops were the bishop of Lincoln's friends, not his, 'and were engaged in similar cases, one against St. Edmund's monastery and the other against St Martin's, Battle'.[15]

David Knowles could find nothing to support the statement that the then bishop of Norwich, William Turbe (1146–74), challenged St. Edmunds' claim to exemption.[16] He therefore concluded that the reference must merely mean that the bishop 'was the inheritor of an opposition to St. Edmund's'. However, the *Gesta abbatum* provides further evidence which throws light on the matter. The final stages of

---

[13] *Ibid.*, i, p.87.

[14] *Gesta abbatum monasterii sancti Albani*, ed. H.T. Riley, Rolls Series, xxviii, 3 vols. (1867–9), i, p.139. For the course of the dispute see *ibid.*, i, pp.137–58 and M.D. Knowles, 'Essays in Monastic History, iv, The Growth of Exemption', 215–17.

[15] This must be the meaning of the passage although the text seems to be corrupt. It reads: '. . . judices impetrati erant suspecti Abbati, ut dictum est, tanquam Episcopo familiares, et consimilem habentes causam adversus Monasterium Sancti Edmundi; alter, adversus Monasterium Sancti Martini de Battle'. *Gesta abbatum*, ed. Riley, i, p.145.

[16] Knowles, *op.cit.*, 212–13.

the trial of the dispute between the bishop of Lincoln and the abbot of St. Albans took place at Westminster before the king himself early in 1163. The abbot submitted St. Albans' papal and royal privileges for Henry's inspection. He also produced witnesses prepared to swear that the bishop of Lincoln had never exercised authority over the abbey, and that ordinations, the dedication of St. Albans' altars and churches, and other episcopal acts had always been performed by various bishops of the abbot's own choosing. Lest there should be any doubt in the future, the author of the *Gesta Abbatum* included a brief record of the witnesses' testimony about the ordinations and dedications.[17]

The section on the St. Albans' dedications in the *Gesta abbatum* resembles the tract on the dedication of altars, chapels and churches at Bury St. Edmunds. The Bury tract specifies which pontiff consecrated individual altars and chapels in the conventual church, the chapels in the monastery's precincts, and churches within St. Edmund's *banleuca* (the town and its suburbs, the area of the abbey's spiritual jurisdiction). Unlike the St. Albans record, it does not mention witnesses, but in other respects it is much fuller. It includes a fair amount of incidental material about the history of the abbey's sacred buildings and objects. The earliest known text of the tract is late thirteenth century,[18] but the contents suggest a date of composition considerably earlier, although, as will be seen, two paragraphs were added later on two separate occasions. The last abbot whom it mentions is Ording (1148–56) and the last king Stephen (1135–54), and all the buildings mentioned had been erected by the time of Ording's death or well before. This suggests that the tract was composed fairly soon after 1156,[19] a rough date which fits in witth another clue. The tract speaks of a boy, Walter, a pupil at the monks' school, whom Ralph d'Escures, bishop of Rochester (1108–14) had confirmed; it remarks that 'he is still alive' (*qui adhuc est*).[20] Confirmation of baptism usually took place before a boy reached his teens. Therefore in the late 1150s and early 1160s William would have been in his sixties or thereabouts.

The tract was, so far as is known, the first attempt at writing a history

[17] *Gesta abbatum*, i, p.147. The passage reads: 'Ne ergo de hiis posterorum notitiae aliquid dubietatis relinquatur, de ordinationibus monachorum seu clericorum, de consecrationibus altarium seu basilicarum, aliisque sacramentis, ipsorum testium veridica relatione confirmatis, pauca ex multis brevibus concludentes, ad futurae successionis memoriam transmittimus.' The record, first of dedications and then of ordinations, follows; *ibid.*, i, pp.146–49.

[18] Printed *The Customary of the Benedictine Abbey of Bury St. Edmunds in Suffolk*, ed. A. Gransden, Henry Bradshaw Society, xcix (1973), pp.114–21. The tract is in the same hand as the Customary, for the date of which see *ibid.*, p.xxxvi.

[19] *Ibid.*, p.xl.

[20] *Ibid.*, pp.114–15.

of the sacred buildings and objects at Bury. It records, for example, that John, bishop of Rochester, at the request of Abbot Anselm (1121–48) dedicated various altars and chapels including the altar of St. Saba. It comments that Anselm had previously been abbot of St. Saba in Rome and that he had had the altar erected and the reredos painted in St. Saba's honour, and in honour of God. Again, it records that Anselm, with the sacrist Hervey, had had the chapel of St. Andrew built and painted. It replaced a tiny, formerly much venerated, stone chapel next to the sacrist's guest house. They pulled down this chapel in order to widen the stream and because it was not conveniently situated. The new one was in the monks' cemetery, a place suitable for the daily commemoration of the dead.[21] The author's account is in general, as far as it can be checked, remarkably accurate (although one, possibly significant, error will be noticed below). If he does not know, he readily admits it.[22]

Nevertheless, despite the tract's strongly antiquarian touch, its main purpose was not to satisfy the objective curiosity of monks or of pilgrims coming to the shrines at Bury. It was a record. It demonstrated that a variety of pontiffs, freely chosen by the abbot, had consecrated altars, chapels and churches within St. Edmund's *banleuca*. This is explicitly stated at the end of the first of the two additional paragraphs. It says: 'praemissa ideo maxime scripsimus, ut quisque sciret a diversis provinciarum episcopis dedicaciones hic celebratas, ut in privilegiis apostolicorum confirmatum et statutum per omnia legitur.'[23] The contents of the tract confirm that such was its main intention. Possibly this was why William Turbe is wrongly called archbishop of Canterbury, not bishop of Norwich.[24] The tract says that at Abbot Anselm's request he dedicated the church of St. James at Bury and the chapel of St. Michael the archangel in the infirmary. Of course the error may have been caused simply by confusion with William of Corbeil, archbishop of Canterbury (1123–36), but it seems more likely that the author was deliberately hiding the fact that a bishop of Norwich had actually consecrated at Bury. Thus both the probable date of the original tract and its content suggest that it should be seen as the counterpart, so to speak, of the St. Albans record. While the abbot of St. Albans was struggling against the bishop of Lincoln, the abbot of Bury was similarly employed against the bishop of Norwich.

The first addition to the Bury tract on dedications, the penultimate paragraph, was probably made during the abbatiate of Samson

21 *Ibid.*, pp.116, 117.
22 See e.g. *ibid.*, p.115, 11. 21–22.
23 *Ibid.*, p.120, 11. 19, 21.
24 *Ibid.*, p.119, 1. 12.

(1182–1211). This dating is indicated by a reference to the new infirmary which was built by William, the last sacrist to hold office under Abbot Hugh.[25] Latterly William was served as subsacrist by Samson, the future abbot.[26] He carried on in office under Abbot Samson, but was soon dismissed for insolvency.[27] It is possible that Samson himself was interested in the tract. Although there is no evidence that when abbot he had any conflict with the bishop of Norwich, he might have valued the tract for another reason. It provided a permanent record that the altars, chapels and churches which it mentions had been consecrated. Early in his abbatiate Samson studied canon law, to help him deal with ecclesiastical litigation.[28] (The abbey had at least three copies of Gratian's *Decretum*, besides owning copies of Justinian's *Institutes* and *Code*.)[29] Canon law would have impressed on Samson the need for having churches consecrated and also for keeping records of consecrations. The third part of the *Decretum, de consecratione*, opens with the statement that 'mass should only be celebrated in places consecrated to the Lord, except in cases of great necessity, according to the precepts of the New and Old Testaments'.[30] It also stated that a church should be consecrated if there was any doubt whether it had been consecrated in the past, even though this risked it being consecrated twice. Doubt arose when 'there was no reliable written record or personal witness'.[31] The Bury tract provided just such a 'reliable written record'.

Moreover, the tract on dedications highlights the fact that, although numerous altars, chapels and churches had been consecrated within St. Edmund's *banleuca*, the monastery's centrepiece, the great abbey church itself, had not. This is made apparent by a passage which foresees its future consecration. It records that Archbishop Eadnoth dedicated the church built by King Cnut, Queen Emma, Ælfwine,

---

[25] *Ibid.*, p.120, 11. 7–8.

[26] *Gesta Sacristarum* printed *Memorials*, ii, p.291. Cf. M.R. James, *On the Abbey of S. Edmund at Bury*, Cambridge Antiquarian Society (1895), p.147.

[27] *The Chronicle of Jocelin of Brakelond*, ed. H.E. Butler (Oxford, 1949), pp.30–31 (cf. *ibid.*, pp.2, 9, 10).

[28] *Jocelin*, pp.33–34.

[29] R.M. Thomson, 'The Library of Bury St. Edmunds Abbey in the Eleventh and Twelfth Centuries', *Speculum*, xlvii (1972), 641.

[30] *Decretum*, canon 1, D. 1, *de cons.*: 'De ecclesiarium consecratione, et missarum celebrationibus non alibi quam in sacratis Domino locis absque magna necessitate fieri debere, liquet omnibus, quibus sunt nota noui et ueteris testamenti precepta'.

[31] *Ibid.*, canon 16, D.1, *de cons.*: 'Solempnitates dedicationum ecclesiarum, et sacerdotum, per singulos annos sunt celebrandae. De ecclesiarum consecrationibus Quociens dubitatur, ut nec certa scriptura, nec testes existunt, a quibus consecratio sciatur, absque ulla dubitatione scitote eas esse sacrandas; nec talis trepidatio facit iterationem, quoniam non monstratur esse iteratum quod nescitur factum.' For a gloss on this see below pp. 74 n. 79, 86 n. 45.

bishop of East Anglia, and the monks to St. Mary and St. Edmund. It continues: 'ac nouum ut credo monasterium, quod nunc videmus, in memoria amborum similiter cum fiet dedicacio consecrabitur'.[32] The monks at the time when the tract was written would have known that the abbey church had not been dedicated because, in the first place, of the testimony of Hermann's *De miraculis sancti Eadmundi*: a beautiful copy of this, bound with Abbo of Fleury's *Passio sancti Eadmundi*, was one of the abbey's prized possessions; it had St. Edmund's name in gold throughout and was kept in the martyr's shrine itself.[33] Secondly, presumably no monk had seen or heard of the consecration taking place after Baldwin's time. Samson must have been aware of both these pieces of evidence.

Hermann's testimony might have made a particularly deep impression on Samson. Associated with him is an updated version of Hermann's *De miraculis*.[34] This new edition was composed at Bury in the late twelfth century. It comprises the substance rather than the actual words of Hermann's text, with many additions (a number of miracles were borrowed from a now lost work on St. Edmund by Osbert de Clare). It follows Hermann's account of Baldwin's unsuccessful attempt to get William Rufus to agree to the church's consecration as well as to St. Edmund's translation.[35] The author's historical research enabled him to add one detail. To Hermann Ranulf Flambard, who helped solemnise the translation, was simply *Ranulfus capellanus regis*; to the new author he was also 'tunc regalium provisor et exactor vectigalium, postea quoque Dunelmensis antistes' (a correct description). Its modern editor, Thomas Arnold, attributed the new version of the *De Miraculis* to Samson.[36] The reason for the attribution is that extracts from it are in the late fourteenth-century version of the *Historia Aurea* (Oxford, Ms Bodley 240) compiled at Bury, with the source variously given as *Sampson abbas Sancti Edmundi*, *Ex libro de miraculis [Sancti Edmundi]*, *Sampson*, and *Ex libro primo miraculorum Sampsonis abbatis*. However, the attribution presents a problem. The author states in the prologue that he wrote at the command of superiors and with the encouragement of fellow monks.[37] Samson would not have written thus after he became abbot (in 1182). But the work was probably written after the death of Henry II (in 1189) since it speaks of his reign as if in the past: one

---

[32] *Bury Customary*, p.116.

[33] BL, Cotton MS Tiberius BII. See Gransden, 'Baldwin', 75 and n. 146, and Thomson, 'The Library of Bury St. Edmunds Abbey', 626 and n. 49.

[34] Described and printed *Memorials of St. Edmund's Abbey*, i, pp.xxxix–xli, 107–208.

[35] *Ibid.*, i, p.155–56.

[36] *Ibid.*, p.xxxix–xl. Thomson, *op. cit.*, 389–408, comes to the same conclusion, but his arguments, which are mainly stylistic, are not wholly convincing.

[37] *Ibid.*, i, p.108.

chapter begins *Regnante rege Henrico secundo*.[38] Unless those words are, as
Arnold contended, an interpolation (the best surviving text is thirteenth-
century), Samson could not have composed the work. Nevertheless, the
evidence of Bodley 240 is at least sufficient to prove that Samson owned
a copy of the late twelfth-century *De Miraculis*.

Samson was a great builder, first as subsacrist and then as abbot. By
the time of his succession to the abbacy the abbey church was more or
less complete. Samson's ambition was to improve it and above all to finish
what remained to be done. He built the choir screen and had it painted
with biblical stories, each with explanatory verses;[39] he roofed the
chapels at the western end of the church, St. Catherine's and St. Faith's,
besides the chapel of St. Andrew in the monks' cemetery, with lead;[40] and
he started building two turrets at the two extremities of the west front,
completing the first story of the southern one and the stonework of the
one to the north.[41] But his greatest achievement was the construction and
eventual completion of the great west tower.[42]

The *Decretum* would have impressed on Samson the necessity of the
church being consecrated; according to Jocelin of Brakelond, the need
became an obsession with him. Jocelin devotes some pages of his chronicle
to a summary of Samson's merits and achievements. This ends:

> Abbot Samson performed these and similar deeds, worthy of eternal record and renown,
> but he himself said that he would have achieved nothing in his lifetime unless he could
> bring about the dedication of our church. That done, he asserted, he would die content.
> He said he was ready to spend 2000 marks of silver on the ceremony, provided the king
> was present and all was done with due solemnity.[43]

Samson's desire to have the church consecrated may well have reached
a peak after the fire which devastated St. Edmund's shrine on 22 June
1198.[44] According to Jocelin of Brakelond, the martyr's body excaped
unscathed. But the virtual destruction of the shrine could have done
incalculable injury to the abbey's prestige and prosperity. Immediate
steps had to be taken to assure not only the public at large, but even the
monks and people of Bury, that St. Edmund's body still lay uncorrupt in
his church, and to restore the shrine to its previous splendour. The work
of repair and refurbishment began at once, and on 25 November Samson,

---

[38] *Ibid.*, i, p.148.

[39] *Jocelin*, p.9; and *Memorials*, ii, p.291.

[40] *Jocelin*, p.96, and n. 5; and *Memorials*, ii, p.291.

[41] *Memorials*, ii, p.291.

[42] *Ibid.*, ii, p.291. Cf. the prophetic dream which a Bury monk claimed to have had about
Samson during the period when his candidature for the abbacy was being canvassed. Part
of it foresaw Samson's success as a builder: 'Uelauit autem pedes sancti martiris, quando
turres ecclesie a centum annis inceptas perfecte consummauit.' *Jocelin*, p.20.

[43] *Ibid.*, pp.47–48

[44] See *Jocelin*, pp.107–9, 111–16.

with a few chosen monks as witnesses, viewed St. Edmund's body. It was then put back in its coffin which was placed in the renovated shrine. It does seem not unlikely that the new *De Miraculis* was composed at this time, perhaps commissioned by Samson, in order to boost St. Edmund's reputation. The substantial additions to Hermann's text are of miracles; most of these are cures, most of which took place at St. Edmund's shrine. Thus the new version stressed the martyr's power as a healer, encouraged visits to his shrine and generally enhanced his glory. It must have been in this same autumn or early winter that Samson applied to Innocent III for a licence to have St. Edmund's church consecrated. The pope issued the necessary bull on 1 December.[45] It gave Samson and the convent leave to dedicate their church. An endorsement adds: 'Quod episcopus potest vocari ad dedicandam et. . . .'[46] The date of the issue of the bull, just a week after St. Edmund's body was viewed, surely suggests a connection between the two events. Indeed, what would shed greater lustre on the martyr than the splendid ceremony of the consecration of his church? Its publicity value would be inestimable if the king and the chief ecclesiastics of the land were there. Significantly enough, Innocent's bull ordered those bishops invited to the ceremony to come at the summons of the abbot and convent.

But the consecration did not follow. Maybe Samson delayed until he could secure the king's attendance, but Richard I died on 6 April 1199, and John was in France during most of the first three years of his reign. The church was still not properly finished. As has been seen, Samson was an energetic builder but, although he completed the west tower, the two turrets at the extremities of the west end were still unfinished when he died.[47] Then in 1210 the great central tower fell and the slow process of rebuilding had to begin.[48] In Baldwin's day, of course,

---

[45] The licence, dated Lateran, 1 December 1198, is to Samson and the convent of St. Edmund to dedicate their church without removing the very large crosses and images. Those bishops invited to attend the dedication ceremony are ordered by apostolic authority to come at the summons of the abbot and convent. Calendared *The Letters of Innocent III (1198–1216) concerning England and Wales*, ed. C.R. and M.G. Cheney (Oxford, 1967), p.13 (no.63). Printed *Die Register Innocenz III: Pontifikatsjahr 1198–1199* (Graz and Cologne, 1964), p.682 (no.457). The bull is now in Lambeth Palace Library. It is listed in two medieval inventories of Bury charters, BL, MS Harley 638, fo.120, and Harley 1005, fo.228.

[46] Dr. Jane Sayers called my attention to this endorsement.

[47] *Memorials*, ii, p.291. Cf. above p.67.

[48] 'Turris apud Sanctum Aedmundum fortissima absque omni impulsu turbinis aut tempestatis magis prodigiosaliter quam causaliter cecidit 9 kl. Octobris;' *Annales Sancti Edmundi, s.a.* 1210 in *Ungedruckte Anglo-Normannische Geschichtsquellen*, ed. Liebermann, p.149. *Decretum*, Canon 1, D.1, *de cons.* (see above p. 65 and n. 30) seems to assume that a 'sacred place' should be consecrated after completion. It was specified by the legatine and episcopal reformers later in the thirteenth century; see below p. 69 and n. 50, pp. 70–1 and n. 61, appendix, pp. 82–3 and nn. 1–5.

the church was much less finished than it was in Samson's, and its incompleteness may have been one reason why William Rufus refused to licence consecration. Even under Samson its imperfections may have been an obstacle. Whatever the case, the papal interdict on England from 1208 to 1214 would have barred consecration during that period.

The general question of the consecration of churches did not escape the attention of ecclesiastical reformers in the thirteenth century. The papal legates to England, Otto and Ottobuono, both gave it high priority. In deference to the *Decretum*, canon I, D.I, *de cons.*,[49] Otto put the consecration of churches first among the constitutions he issued at the legatine council he held in London in 1237. He begins with an allusion to the *Decretum*'s ruling that mass should only be celebrated in consecrated places except in cases of necessity. The constitution continues:

Porro quia vidimus per nosipsos et a plerisque audivimus tam salubre ministerium contempni vel saltem negligi a nonnullis, dum multas invenimus ecclesias et aliquas etiam cathedrales que licet sint ab antiquo constructe nondum tamen sunt oleo sanctificationis consecrate, volentes huic tam periculose negligentie obviare statuimus et statuendo precipimus ut omnes ecclesie cathedrales, conventuales, et parochiales que perfectis parietibus sunt constructe, infra biennium per diocesanos episcopos ad quos pertinet, vel eorum auctoritate per alios, consecrentur. Sicque infra simile tempus fiat in decetero construendis. Et ne tam salubre statutum transeat in contemptum, si loca huiusmodi non fuerint infra biennium a perfectionis tempore dedicata, a missarum solempniis usque ad consecrationem manere statuimus interdicta, nisi aliqua rationabili causa excusentur. Ad hec ne presumant abbates aut ecclesiarum rectores antiquas ecclesias consecratas sub pretextu pulcrioris vel amplioris fabrice faciende diruere absque licentia diocesani episcopi et consensu, presenti statuto districtius inhibemus. Diocesanus vero diligenter consideret utrum expediat dari licentiam vel negari et, si dederit, attendat et intendat ut opus quam celerius poterit consummetur; quod extendi statuimus et volumus ad iam cepta. De capellis vero minoribus nil novi duximus statuendum, consecrationes earum quando et qualiter fieri debeant diffinitionibus canonicis relinquentes.[50]

Clearly Otto was deeply concerned about the number of unconsecrated churches in England. Reforming bishops responded promptly to his challenge. Within a year or so Robert Grosseteste, bishop of Lincoln, wrote to one of his archdeacons instructing him to see that all rectors of unconsecrated churches in the diocese should have them ready for consecration, in obedience to the constitution of the council of London which ordered consecrations within two years.[51] (A chronicler notes

[49] Above 65 and n. 30.
[50] *Councils and Synods with other Documents Relating to the English Church*, ii. A. D. 1205–1313, ed. F.M. Powicke and C.R. Cheney, 2 vols. (Oxford, 1964), i, pp.245–46.
[51] *Ibid.*, i, p.263.

under 1238 that 'Robert bishop of Lincoln dedicated many churches and monasteries'.)[52] Another reforming bishop, Walter Cantilupe, bishop of Worcester, put a statute to the same effect third amongst the 102 he issued for his diocese in 1240.[53] William Raleigh, bishop of Norwich, and Nicholas Farnham, bishop of Durham, also included similar statutes amongst those they issued for their dioceses in 1240 × 1243 and 1241 × 1249 respectively.[54] Later the bishops of Salisbury, Wells and Winchester did likewise in their statutes issued variously in 1257 × 1268, ?1258 and 1262 × 1265.[55] As the century advanced concern grew that the anniversaries of consecrations should be properly observed. This particularly preoccupied the bishops of Salisbury (the cathedral was consecrated in 1258), as appears in the statutes of 1238 × 1244 and 1257 ×?1268.[56] It also appears in the statutes of Wells and Winchester.[57]

In addition the reforming bishops recognised the importance of keeping careful records of when and by whom an altar, chapel or church was consecrated. Already before Otto's constitutions, William of Blois, bishop of Worcester, an active reformer, had legislated about this. One of his statutes of 1229 rules that the date, the name of the consecrator and of the patron saint should be clearly written in a suitable place by the high altar of every church.[58] This ruling was copied into the statutes of Worcester of 1240, the 1238 × 1244 Salisbury statutes and those of Wells.[59] One of the Durham statutes of 1241 × 1249 orders archdeacons, having diligently enquired which churches had been consecrated and which had not, to see that every consecrated altar should be marked with the sign of the cross.[60]

Despite the persistence of the reforming bishops, many churches remained unconsecrated. Ottobuono, in the third constitution he issued at the legatine council he held in London in 1268, reiterated Otto's constitution on the consecration of churches and then added a new paragraph. He said that he knew that Otto's excellent statute had been neglected and scorned and that many churches remained unconsecrated. To achieve the statute's implementation he ordered all rectors and other 'rulers' (*gubernatores*) of churches, and their vicars, on pain of suspension, to ask the bishop, or an archdeacon, within a year of the construction of any church, to consecrate it or to authorise another to do so. If the

[52] The annals of Dunstable, cited *ibid.*, i, p.264.
[53] *Ibid.*, i, p.296–97.
[54] *Ibid.*, i, pp.353–54 (c.52), 426–27 (c.17) respectively.
[55] *Ibid.*, i, pp.564 (c.35), 600 (c.17), 708 (c.32) respectively.
[56] *Ibid.*, i, pp.367 (c.3), 563–64 (cc.33, 34) respectively.
[57] *Ibid.*, i, pp.600 (c.18), 708 (c.33) respectively.
[58] *Ibid.*, i, p.172 (c.7).
[59] *Ibid.*, i, pp.296–97 (c.3), 367 (c.3), 600 (c.18) respectively.
[60] *Ibid.*, i, pp.426–27 (c.17).

bishop did not act, he was to be suspended from the use of dalmatic, tunic and sandals, unless he had a good excuse, such as a great number of other churches to consecrate.[61] The response to Ottobuono's constitution would appear to have been tepid. The only synodal statutes printed by Powicke and Cheney which deal with the matter are those of Exeter, issued in 1287, nearly twenty years later.[62]

There is no certain evidence as to how the monks of Bury reacted to these legatine constitutions, or indeed whether they reacted at all. The only possible clue seems to be the fact that the tract on dedications was preserved and copied at least once, that is in the late thirteenth century. The only known text is a copy of that date in the same hand as the abbey's customary,[63] which was composed c.1234.[64] The method used by the author of the customary in places strongly resembles that of the author of the tract on dedications. He too on occasion leaves the reader to make up his own mind on a debatable point. Twice he gives alternative views on an uncertain matter;[65] the author of the tract does the same thing once.[66] The internal evidence for the dating of each work makes it impossible that they are both by the same man.[67] There is of course the possibility that the extant text of the tract on dedications is a revised version by the author of the customary of some earlier, now lost, tract composed in the 1180s. This, however, seems unlikely since the tract is stylistically homogeneous. On the other hand its author's method could have influenced the way the author of the customary treated his subject. Whatever the truth on this matter, there is no sound evidence that the monks of Bury took much, if any, notice of Otto's canon. Nor is the evidence better with regard to Ottobuono's constitution of 1268. A paragraph was added to the tract on dedications shortly after 1275. It records that in that year Abbot Simon de Luton destroyed the ancient chapel of St. Edmund and built the Lady Chapel in its place. As St. Edmund's chapel had belonged to the prior, he was given the chapel

---

[61] *Councils and Synods*, ii, pp.750–51 (c.3).

[62] *Ibid.*, ii, p.1004 (c. 10). To judge from the absence of entries about the consecration of churches in England in Wilkins' *Concilia* it would appear that bishops' interest in the subject had lapsed.

[63] For the manuscript of the Bury customary see *Bury Customary*, ed. Gransden, p.xxxvi. For that of the tract see *ibid.*, p. xli (the identity of the handwriting with the handwriting of the customary is not noted there).

[64] *Ibid.*, pp.xxxiii–iv.

[65] *Ibid.*, pp.5, ll. 19–34, 28, ll. 35–41.

[66] *Ibid.*, p.115, ll. 13–19.

[67] I here reverse the opinion I previously expressed, that they were by the same man; *Historical Writing in England*, i, *c.550-c.1307* (London, 1974), p.391. For the date of the tract see above p. 63.

of St. Stephen instead and the remains of the old chapel were carefully buried there. William, archbishop of Edessa in Media (a bishop *in partibus infidelium*), dedicated this chapel to St. Edmund and St. Stephen.[68] The Bury Chronicle dates the dedication 28 December, 1275. This paragraph must therefore have been added to the tract more than seven years after the issue of Ottobuono's constitutions. The reason why the monks made no move to have the abbey church consecrated could have been that building work was still in progress.[69]

Although the monks of Bury seem at the time to have taken little, if any, notice of Otto's and Ottobuono's constitution on the consecration of churches, this was not always the case in the fourteenth century. As before, the evidence is scanty and hard to understand. Sometime, apparently around the middle of the century, an (unidentified) canon lawyer was asked about the canonical position of St. Edmund's church if in fact it had never been consecrated. The question was whether a celebrant in a church not consecrated two years after the constitution of Otto and Ottobuono was irregular and the church itself interdicted. The question and the canonist's answers are preserved in a copy of c.1325 – c.1375 in the abbey's 'Kempe' register (BL, MS Harley 645, fos.142v–43),[70] and are printed for the first time below. The answers are of interest primarily because they illustrate the application of canon law to an individual case. They are also interesting for other reasons. They throw light on the relations between St. Edmund's abbey and the diocesan, the bishop of Norwich. They also show how, in the absence of written justification, tradition could be used as grounds for continuing as before. And they hint in passing at the condition of parts of the church's fabric.

Briefly, the canonist argued that St. Edmund's church was not interdicted and celebrants in it were not irregular, despite Otto's and Ottobuono's constitution, for various reasons. The constitution said that the church must be consecrated once it was finished; St. Edmund's church was still unfinished because it had round chapels not yet properly faced

68 *The Chronicle of Bury St. Edmunds, 1212–1301*, ed. A. Gransden (London, 1964), pp.58–60 *passim*; James, *On the Abbey of S. Edmund*, pp.188–89.

69 See below p. 78.

70 I owe this dating to Dr. Michelle Brown of the British Library who wrote to me on 20 January 1990 saying: 'The hand of fos.142v–43 employs a *cursiva anglicana* of the 'reformed' type introduced in *c.* 1300, and although practised longer, continued in the present style with secretary features, absent here, often intruding from *c.* 1375. Stylistically I would have said second or third quarter of the fourteenth century.' Dr. Brown also pointed out that the same hand occurs on fo.139 and refers to 11 Edward III (1337–38).

with stone.[71] The constitution itself was of limited application. It related only to churches under a bishop's jurisdiction, and Bury was exempt. It said that churches not consecrated within two years of completion were interdicted only from the celebration of mass; other offices were, therefore, not affected. The constitution also said that this ruling did not apply if there were good reason why it should not. Ignorance was a good excuse. The present monks of Bury St. Edmunds were merely following the example of their predecessors, who in their turn were following their predecessors who had lived many years ago, at the time of Ottobuono's constitutions in 1268. The present monks had accepted that what their predecessors had done was right; either their predecessors had some knowledge that the church had been consecrated, or were otherwise satisfied about their salvation. Nevertheless, the canonist advised the monks to complete the church as soon as possible and to have it consecrated, since there was doubt whether it ever had been consecrated, even though by so doing they ran the risk that it might be consecrated twice. Otherwise, the canonist warned them, the bishop of Norwich might intervene.

The canonist supported his arguments with numerous references to canon law (the *Decretum*, the *Decretals*, and the *Sext* of Boniface VIII) and to its glosses and commentaries. He made considerable use of the commentary on the *Decretals* by Innocent IV (1243–54),[72] and refers to the *Summa aurea* of Henry of Susa ('Hostiensis', d. 1271)[73] and to the *Rationale Divinorum officiorum* by Guilelmus Durandus (d. 1296).[74] Possibly he also used the glosses by Bartholomew of Brescia (d. 1250 or 1258)[75] and Bernard de Bottone (d. 1266).[76] He ends his answers with a reference to a *Summa confessorum*. He refers the reader to a section in it entitled *De ecclesie consecracione* for further discussion

---

[71] The translation of one of the two relevant passages is obscure. See below p. 80 and nn. 35–7. Nowadays canon law forbids the consecration of a church built of wood (or of iron or other metal). *Code*, canon 1165. The medieval ceremony for the consecration of a church has a number of references to stone in its imagery and seems to assume that it will be of stone. See e.g. the pontifical of the last half of the twelfth century from the province of Canterbury, printed *The Pontifical of Magdalen College*, ed. H.A. Wilson, Henry Bradshaw Society, xxxix (1910), pp.113 (antiphon: 'Erexit iacob lapidem in titulum fundens oleum desuper', and prayer: '. . . ut qui per totum mundum fidem aspersit et ecclesiam congregauit quam lapis excisus sine manibus angulari compage solidauit . . .'), 115 (antiphon: 'Lapides pretiosi omnes muri tui et turres ierusalem gemmis edificabuntur', and prayer beg.: 'Deus qui de uiuis et electis lapidibus eternum maiestati tue condis habitaculum . . .'), 116 (prayer: '. . . Sit tibi altare hoc sicut illud quod moyses susceptis mandatis tuis in prefiguratione apostolica duodecim lapidum constructione firmauit . . .').

[72] Below pp. 79 and nn. 13, 15, 17, p. 80 and nn. 29, 31.

[73] Below p. 80 and n. 40.

[74] Below p. 80 and n. 44.

[75] Below p. 80 and n. 43.

[76] Below p. 80 and n. 27.

of what action should be taken if there is doubt whether or not a church has been consecrated.[77] In fact the *Summa confessorum* by the Dominican John Rumsik (d. 1314) has no titulus *De ecclesie consecratione*. It has one headed *De reconciliatione ecclesie* which mainly discusses the reconciliation of a church polluted, for example, by blood.[78] However, the very popular version of the *Summa confessorum* by another Dominican, Bartholomew San Concordio (d. 1347), the *Summa de casibus concientiae* (also called *Summa Pisana, Pisanella, Bartholomaea* and *Magistruccia*), does have such a section. Bartholomew arranged John Rumsik's material alphabetically and supplemented it from canon law. One section is headed *Consecratio*. The second entry under that general heading is *Consecratio . . . ecclesie vel etiam reconciliatio eius*. It deals with the subject at length, including three reasons for reconsecration. The last is relevant to the Bury case. It reads: 'Tertius casus est quando dubitatur an fuerit consecrata nec apparet aliqua probatio de his que dicta sunt supra scilicet proximo'.[79]

If indeed the canonist did use Bartholomew of San Concordio's work, it would be his latest source. This gives a clue to the date of the question and answers, sometime around the middle of the fourteenth century, during the abbacy of William de Bernham (1335–61). Such a date would fit in with other evidence. The only known manuscript of the question and answers, *c.* 1325 – *c.* 1375, does not make a mid fourteenth-century date impossible.[80] The text itself makes clear that 1268, the year of Ottobuono's constitutions, was a long time ago, beyond living memory.[81] But it is unlikely to be later than the 1360s since, as will be seen,[82] it was known to Henry of Kirkstead, successively notice master, *armarius* and subprior of Bury, who died *c.*

---

[77] Below p. 80 and n. 46.

[78] For John Rumsik *alias* John of Freiburg see the *New Catholic Encyclopedia*, vii (New York etc., 1966), 1051c. For his *Summa Confessorum* see: *The Catholic Encyclopedia*, ii (New York, 1907), 317a; *ibid.*, xii (New York, 1911), 364b; *ibid.*, xiv (New York, 1912), 606a. For the titulus 'De reconciliatione ecclesie', see *Summa Confessorum* (Hispali [Seville], 1526), fos.clii-cliiv. [See G* 14. 33 (F) in Cambridge University Library].

[79] For Bartholomew of San Concordio see *The Catholic Encyclopedia*, ii. 316d–17a. For his very successful version of Rumsik's work see *Summa de Casibus Conscientiae* (unknown place in Italy, 1473), fo.28c. [See Inc.3. B. 74. Bii (2269) in Cambridge University Library.] The reference, 'de his que dicta sunt scilicet proximo', is to a paragraph beginning 'Presumitur ecclesia consecrata quando apparet de hoc aliqua scriptura uel instrumento dotationis uel in libro ecclesie uel in columna uel in tabula marmorea et huiusmodi uel etiam si unus testis appareat de uisu uel auditu. De consecratione, distinctio j. solemnitates dedicationum.' This reference is to the *Decretum* (Canon 16.D.1, *de cons.*) cited above p. 65 n. 30. Cf. the gloss of Innocent IV, cited below p. 86 n. 45.

[80] Above p. 72 and n. 70.

[81] Above p. 73.

[82] Below p. 77.

1379. If a mid fourteenth-century date is accepted, St. Albans would provide a parallel. It was about then that Thomas de la Mare, abbot of St. Albans 1349–96, obtained the opinion of a canonist, Master Richard de Wymundeswolde (d. 1356), on various questions relating to St. Albans' privilege of exemption, particularly with regard to its dependent priories and cells.[83] Wymundeswolde studied at Cambridge and by 1338 was a D.C.L. By 1343 he was an advocate at the papal curia and was one of the five English proctors appointed to negotiate for peace with France under the auspices of Innocent VI in 1354. He died in Avignon early in 1356.[84] Exactly when Abbot Thomas consulted him is unknown, but it must have been sometime in the mid fourteenth century. Nor is it known why Abbot Thomas did so. However, it is not unlikely that the diocesan, the bishop of Lincoln, was putting some kind of pressure on St. Albans, making further definition of its privilege of exemption desirable.[85]

The St. Albans parallel, and the references in the Bury question and answers to the abbey's exemption from the authority of the bishop of Norwich, suggests the possibility that Abbot William de Bernham, like Thomas de la Mare, consulted a canonist in order to strengthen the abbey's defences against the diocesan. William had good reason to fear William Bateman, bishop of Norwich 1343–55. In some respects Bateman's education and career were remarkably like Wymundeswolde's. He too studied law at Cambridge. He was a D.C.L. by 1328, a papal chaplain by 1330 and auditor of the sacred palace by 1332. He was also, by 1343, a king's clerk. He was employed by Clement VI and Edward III on Anglo-French relations from 1340 to 1343 and on similar diplomatic missions from 1344 to 1353. He died in Avignon in 1355, little more than a year before Wymundeswolde's death there.[86]

Bateman's knowledge of canon law makes it not unlikely that he may have raised the question of the uncanonical position of St. Edmund's church. He was certainly on very bad terms with the Bury monks.[87] One of his first acts as bishop was to raise an aid from his clergy, both secular and regular. He proceeded without due regard for Bury's exemption, but worse still, when he held a general visitation of his diocese in 1345, he tried to visit the abbey. A bitter dispute ensued which was eventually referred to Rome.[88] Abbot William appealed to his charters and in 1346 the king's

[83] See J.E. Sayers, 'Papal Privileges for St. Albans Abbey and its Dependencies,' in *The Study of Medieval Records: Essays in Honour of Kathleen Major*, ed. D. A. Bullough and R. L. Storey (Oxford, 1971), pp.75–78.

[84] For Richard de Wymundeswolde's career see A. B. Emden, *A Biographical Register of the University of Cambridge to 1500* (Cambridge, 1963), pp.659–60.

[85] See Sayers, *op.cit.*, p.73.

[86] For William Bateman's career see Emden, *op.cit.*, p.44.

[87] For his dispute with the abbey see *Memorials*, iii, pp.xi–xv, 56–73, 320 and n.1, 321–27.

[88] *Ibid.*, iii, pp.68–72, 323.

court decided in his favour. It is recorded that in the course of the quarrel the abbot consulted 'those skilled in the law' (*juris periti*) and appealed to civil and canon law.[89] Nor did the 1346 judgement allay his fears. The monks suspected that Bateman was plotting against them at the papal curia up to the time of his death.[90] There is no reference, at least in the printed records of the dispute, to the question of the consecration of St. Edmund's church. Maybe the matter was not at issue between abbot and bishop, but Abbot William might nevertheless have feared that Bateman would use the probability that the church had never been consecrated as ammunition, and so tried to forearm himself.

It is likely that two short memoranda in the 'Kempe' register, on fo.133v, in a hand very similar to that of the question and answers text, were made in connection with the problem of the church's consecration. They were the result of historical research undertaken to discover whether the church had been consecrated or not. Whoever made them had taken some trouble. The first is an extract from Matthew Paris's *Flores historiarum*. It copies the annal for 1032 recording that Archbishop Eadnoth dedicated St. Edmund's monastery, which had been nobly built at 'Beatrichesworth', in honour of the Mother of God and St. Edmund himself. The memorandum is headed *In libro de gestis Anglorum qui intitulatur flores historiarum in ecclesia sancti Pauli London*. A version of the *Flores* from St. Paul's, copied sometime in the fourteenth century after 1341, still survives. Although an abbreviated version, it has the relevant entry; perhaps it was the Bury researcher's examplar.[91] Not only did the researcher go to St. Paul's for evidence, he also consulted his abbey's charters of privilege. To corroborate the statement in the *Flores* he concludes the memorandum with a reference to the charter of 'William I, king of England.' The privilege of William the Conqueror to Abbot Baldwin (which is almost certainly spurious, at least in its present form) was one of the monks' most treasured possessions.[92] In fact it does not confirm in detail the *Flores* statement. It merely records that Eadnoth, archbishop of Canterbury, dedicated the monastery; the dedication to the

[89] *Ibid.*, iii, pp.68.

[90] *Ibid.*, iii, pp.325–26.

[91] Lambeth Palace Library, MS 1106, fo.40. I am grateful to Miss Melanie Barber, Deputy Librarian and Archivist of Lambeth Palace Library, for checking the reading for me. The manuscript is described: *Chronicles of the Reigns of Edward I and Edward II*, ed. William Stubbs, Rolls Series, lxxvi, 2 vols. (1882–83), i, pp.xlii *et seq.*; M. R. James, *The Manuscripts in the Library of Lambeth Palace: The Mediaeval MSS* (Cambridge, 1932), pp.818–21.

[92] The 'original' charter is now BL, MS Cotton Augustus II, no.25. A more or less contemporary copy is at the end of the illuminated Gospel book which was kept in the feretory, now BL, MS Harley 76, fo.140. Printed *Regesta regum Anglo-Normannorum*, i, *1066–1100*, ed. H.W.C. Davis (Oxford, 1913), p.36 no.137, and *Feudal Documents from the Abbey of Bury St. Edmunds*, ed. D. C. Douglas (London, 1932), pp.50–55 (no.7). Douglas, *op.cit.*, pp.xxv, n.7, xxxii-v, discusses the charter, taking a more favourable view as to its authenticity than I do; see Gransden, 'Baldwin', pp.71, 191 n.89.

'Mother of God' and St. Edmund and its date are first given in the Bury version of the Worcester chronicle.[93] The second memorandum is headed *Alia cronica* and is copied from the passage in the tract on dedications or derives from a common source. It records the foundation, first, of St. Mary's church and, secondly, of Cnut's monastery and the latter's dedication by Archbishop Eadnoth.[94]

Despite the advice given by the canonist to William de Bernham, St. Edmund's church was not consecrated during his abbacy. This is proved by two notes, one to each of the two memoranda, by Henry of Kirkstead (d. *c*. 1379), a tireless antiquary and bibliographer.[95] He spotted that the first memorandum was irrelevant to the question of the consecration of the post-Conquest abbey church. 'Sed cave', he writes, 'quia Baldewinus abbas anno lx sequente, basilicam ab Agelnotho dedicatam destruxit et aliam quam adhuc stat construxit.' He then adds 'que non (*dum* deleted) adhuc est consecrata'. Kirkstead's note to the second memorandum is longer but its substance is much the same. However, Kirkstead concluded with what is clearly a reference to the text of the question put to the canonist and the canonist's answers. The whole of Kirkstead's note to the second memorandum reads.

> Anno domini m.xxxij. Agelnothus archiepiscopus Cant' dedicauit basilicam a Cnutone rege et alwino episcopo estanglorum constructam in honorem Christi sancte marie et sancti edmundi.
>
> Anno domini m.lxv. Baldewinus factus est abbas sancti edmundi, qui destructa basilica ab alwino episcopo et cnutone rege constructa et ab agelnotho archiepiscopo consecrata, construxit aliam eminenciorem et eam perfecit anno domini m.xciiij. que non dum est consecrata. Vide infra de hac materia folio x. notabilia.

These notes by Kirkstead occur in the Kempe register exactly ten folios (fo.133v) before the first page of the question and answers' text (fo.143v).

No evidence of later date than Kirkstead's notes have come to light on the matter of the consecration of St. Edmund's church. If the consecration had taken place subsequently it is perhaps strange that such an important event apparently left no mark in the abbey's records. It is tempting to speculate that the church was never consecrated at all. It is clear that the monks were fairly certain, at least until towards the end of the fourteenth century, of their church's unconsecrated state. Why, therefore, did they not take steps to remedy the omission, especially after the canonist strongly advised Abbot William de Bernham to do so? The reason why the canonist's advice was not taken could have been that the Black Death intervened, to overshadow other preoccupations. Then there was the Peasants' Revolt

[93] See above p. 60 and n. 4.

[94] Above pp. 59–60.

[95] See R. Rouse, 'Bostonus Buriensis and the Author of the *Catalogus Scriptorum Ecclesiae*,' *Speculum*, xli (1966), 471–94.

and the troubles which accompanied it at Bury. But the reason in the long run was perhaps that almost until the Dissolution the church did not meet Otto's stipulation that it should be complete before consecration. Building work on it was more or less continuous.[96] In the late fourteenth century a new campanile was constructed above the choir. In 1403–4 the west tower fell and had to be rebuilt. In 1465 the church suffered a terrible fire which seems to have almost gutted it; its restoration was only completed shortly before the monastery was dissolved, on 4 November 1539.

Appendix: British Library, MS Harley 645

(The text is heavily abbreviated and apparently corrupt in places. I have extended abbreviations wherever possible, indicating cases of doubt by square brackets or in a footnote.)

[fo.142v] In questione proposita an celebrans in ecclesia non consecrata post biennium a constitutione Ottonis et Ottob[oni] sit irregularis et an talis ecclesia sit interdicta,[1] videtur quod dicte constitutionis auctoritate ecclesia sancti Edmundi non sit interdicta nec ibi celebrans irregularis, primo quia constitucio dicit a tempore perfectionis ecclesiarum imfra biennium debent consecrari, sed nichil videtur perfectum dum aliquid resistat ad agendum. C[odex] Ad Sillan[ianum], Cum Sill[anianum].[2] *Extra[vagantes]*, De bap[tismo], Maiori [*sic.*].[3] Et constat quod ecclesia vestra non est perfecte dum supersunt capelle rotunde in pluribus locis [?non] operi lapideo ecclesie vestre contigue,[4] sine quibus non posset ecclesia vestra consecrari nec in partes diuidi, cum integra sit consecranda prout dicunt verba earundem constitutionum.[5]

Item, cum constitutio illa sit odiosa et per consequens restringenda;[6] et in ea dicatur quod ecclesie per diocesanos locorum ad quos pertine[n]t vel eorum auctoritate per alium debent consecrari,[7] videtur constitutio arcare tantummodo episcopis [loca] subdita et tunc loca exempta in quibus diocesani nullam habeant excercere potestatem; ar[gumentum] *Extra[vagantes]*, De Regulis Iuris, liber *Sext*,[(a)] c[apitulum] *Odia*,[8] cum priuilegiorum vestrorum tenore.[9] Item, in constitutione Otonis cum hec sola pona sit statuta,[(b)] ut ecclesia non

---

[96] For the abbey's architectural history in the later middle ages see A. B. Whittingham, 'Bury St. Edmunds Abbey: The Plan, Design and Development of the Church and Monastic Buildings,' *The Archaeological Journal*, cviii (1952), 175–76.

[a] liber Sext] t vj. in MS.   [b] ecclesie *sic.* MS (and Otto).

consecrata[c] a missarum solempniis sit usque ad consecracionem eius interdicta,[10] ad alia ecclesiastica officia in eadem non debet extendi; ar[gumentum] dicti c[apituli] *Odia*.[11] Et sic de aliis ecclesiasticis officiis non est dubitandum. Item, cum in eadem constitutione Octonis dicatur quod ex tunc ecclesia sit interdicta nisi aliqua[d] causa rationabili excusetur,[e][12] causa rationabilis impedit ipsum iure[f] interdictum; allegans ergo interdictum, habet probare causam rationabilem cessare; alium non probat intentum; sicut legitur de illo instrumento quo continetur nisi constiterit talem tali die pecuniam soluisse, sit excommunicatus; non habetur excommunicatus post diem nisi probetur eum dicto die non soluisse; no[ta] Innocentius *Extra[vagantes]* De Ac[cusationibus], c[apitulum] *Super hiis*, super verbo excludatur.[13] Item, cum dicat constitutio quod eadem ecclesia a dicto biennio remaneat usque ad consecracionem interdicta,[14] interim in ea celebrans eciam sciens, non est irregularis, sicut nec suspensus quousque peniteat interim celebrans non sit irregularis, ut n[otat] Innocentius ii[i]j, c[apitula] *Si celebret*,[g][15] *Quum medicinalis*[h][16] et De Cohabitatione Clerici *Sicut*.[17]

Cum igitur in iure non caueatur expressim quod celebrans in ecclesia non consecrata sit aliquali pena irregularitatis vel alia afficiend[us] vel ipsa ecclesia interdicta sit affecta, preter quam ex rigore constitucionum Octonis et Octoboni predictorum, ipso iure cessante processu superior[um] a compulsione procurandi huiusmodi consecracionem, videtur interemptum cuiuslibet interdicti vel irregularitatis celebrancium in ecclesiis huiusmodi iusti timoris[i] fundamentum; nec videtur ex causis premissis quod ipsa ecclesia sancti Edmundi aliquo tempore fuerit aut sit interdicta nec diuine laudis organa suspendenda in eiisdem rationibus suprascriptis.

Plane pro informacione pleniori ad iura vestram consideracionem mouencia videtur r[atio][j] ad c[apitulum] *Is, qui in ecclesia*[18] s[upposita] i[nterdicta];[k] dicit ibi, Is qui scienter celebrat in loco interdicto etc'; no[ta] verbum scienter. Ergo ignoranter cel[ebrans] [?non sit] excommunicatus, maxime si ignorancia huiusmodi non sit crassa vel supina,[19] que non potest in vestro casu legitime reputari, qui more maiorum hucusque in dicta ecclesia continue celebrancium, eorum estis vestigia secuti a tempore dictarum constitutionum, videlicet Octoboni, que fuer[un]t pupplicate anno domini m.mccl xviij, a quo tempore subscriptibilia et ultra iam fluxerunt, et imfra que tempora credendum est religiosos viros antecessores ibidem vel tunc memoriam dedicacionis habuisse vel aliter [fo.143] scie[nter] saluti providisse; per contumacionem[l] antecessorum tanto tempore debet presencium ignorancia priorum vestigia sequentes probabil[iter] non inmerito reputari; ar[gumentum], quia ignorancia facti alicui excusat, *Extra[uagantes]*, De Regulis Iuris, videlicet vj.[m] c[apitulum] *Ignorancia*.[20] Et cum quis in alterius locum succedit, iustam habet ignorancie causam; eodem

---

c consecrate *sic*. MS (and Otto).

d alia *sic*. MS.

e excusentur *sic*. MS (and Otto).

f iur' in MS.

g celebret *sic*. MS.

h Circa *sic*. MS (for 'Cum'?).

i timorid' *sic*. MS.

j R in MS

k s.i. in MS.

titulo, l[ex] *Cum quis in ius*.[21] Et maxime quia presumitur ignorancia nisi sciencia probetur; eodem titulo, c[apitulum] *Presumitur*.[22] Et ex eo quod olim factum fuerat, presumitur modo licitum esse, *C[odex]*, De Prescriptione xxx, *Sicut*,[23] ff.[i.e. *Digesta*], De Statu Hominum, lex penultima,[24] *C[odex]*, De Rei Vendicatione, lex *Partum*,[25] et quod iustam habens ignorancie causam interdicti vel excommunicationis, si celebret excusetur a qualibet irregularitate, penultima probatur optime, *Extra[vagantes]*, De Clerico Excommunicato, iiii[i] t[itulus] *Apostolice*[26] in textu et glossa B[ernardi de Bottone].[(n)27]

Per eandem rationem respondeo ad illa iura De Clerico Excommunicato, vii.[(o)] *Postulastis*[28] vltimo cum glossa Innoc[entii][29] et c[apitulum] *Tanta*,[30] ubi sit mencio in textu et glossa[31] de celebrante in ecclesia interdicta, et ad illa c[apitula] cum eterni,[(p)32] c[apitulum] *Si celebret*[33] et c[apitulum] *Quum*[(q)] *medicinalis*[34] ubi loquitur de suspenso[(r)] celebrante; quod contrahat irregularitatem verum est, si scienter sine causa rationabili siue ignorancia probabili in loco sciuit effecialiter et simpliciter interdictum; que omnia cessant in casu proposite uestre questionis, ut patet per iura et rationes superius allegata.

Ad hoc securum videretur et honestum pro exaltacione catholice deuocionis ad ecclesiam vestram et detractionum refrenacionem, quod capelle ecclesie vestre contigue inperfecte et lutamine[35] fedate[(s)] perficientur opere mediocr[e] ballato[(t)36] in summitate operis lapidei, et plana summitate lapideum opus non transcendente cooperirentur.[37] Et extunc tota ecclesia simul procuraretur consecrari, primo quia tante deformitatis reparacio ad arbitrium episcopi potest inducere causam consecrandi ecclesiam.[38] De consecratione, di[stinctio] j. *Si motum*,[39] et no[ta] Hostiensis in *Summa*, De consecratione etc, c[apitulum] *Et an sit iteranda*,[40] ubi de hac materia tractat habunde. Item, quociens probabiliter dubitatur de consecratione, est propter dubium ecclesia consecranda. De consecratione de[stinctio] 1 c[anon] *De ecclesiarum*[41] et c[anon] *Ecclesie vel altaria*[42] vbi de hoc in glo[ssa] hanc materiam de ecclesiarum consecratione et reconciliatione tractat habunde.[43] T[estis?][(u)] Durandi in *Summa* sua *Rationale Diuinorum* in tit[ulo] De ecclesie consecracione cuius distinctiones in multis conueniunt suprascriptis.[44] De hoc eciam nota Innoc[entius] eodem titulo super Rubricam.[45] Item de hoc plene eodem titulo in *Summa Confessorum*.[46]

---

1 The reading seems to be 'contumacionem' but it just could be 'continuacionem.' But apparently sometimes a scribe copied 'contumacio' in error for 'continuacio.' See Latham, *Revised Medieval Latin, Word–List*, p. 113 under 'contumatio.'

m vt in MS.

n b in MS.

o iiij. *sic*. MS.

p *sic*. MS (? for eadem)

q causa *sic*. MS (? for cum). Cf above, p.79, and note h.

r Suspens' in MS.

s or sedate.

t *sic*. MS (for belliato?).

u T in MS.

Translation

[fo.142v] With regard to the question whether a celebrant in a church which is still unconsecrated two years after the constitution of Otto and Ottobuono is irregular and whether such a church is interdicted;[1] it appears that St. Edmund's church is not interdicted nor a celebrant in it irregular for various reasons. First, the constitution says that a church must be consecrated within two years of completion. But nothing is complete while anything remains to be done. See *Codex*, Ad Sillanianum, *Cum Sillanianum*,[2] and *Decretals*, De Baptismo, *Maiori* (sic).[3] Clearly your church is not perfect as long as round chapels remain (without proper stone work) in many places adjacent to your stone built church;[4] your church cannot be consecrated without them, nor if divided into parts, since the actual words of the constitutions say that the entire church must be consecrated.[5]

Item, since the constitution is open to exceptions it must be restricted.[6] It says that churches should be consecrated by their diocesans, or by those authorised by a diocesan.[7] Therefore the constitution must be limited to places subject to bishops; places where diocesans have no power are exempt. See *Decretals*, De Regulis Iuris, *Sext* chapter *Odia*,[8] together with your own privileges.[9] Item, since the only penalty imposed in Otto's constitution is that an unconsecrated church should be interdicted from the celebration of mass until it is consecrated,[10] the constitution ought not to be applied to other ecclesiastical offices. See the same chapter *Odia*.[11] Item, since Otto's constitution says that an unconsecrated church is interdicted unless excused for some reasonable cause,[12] a reasonable cause rightly prevents interdict. Therefore whoever alleges an interdict has to prove any 'reasonable cause' invalid, but he does not prove another intention. A similar case can be seen in the document which stipulates that a man should be excommunicated unless he pays such-and-such a sum of money on such-and-such a day; he is not excommunicated after that day unless it is proved that he did not pay on that day. Note Innocent on the word 'excludatur' in the *Decretals*, De Accusationibus, chapter *Super hiis*.[13] Item, since the constitution says that a church still not consecrated after two years is interdicted until its consecration,[14] a celebrant in it, even if he knows this, is not irregular, just as a celebrant who has been suspended *is* irregular until he repents. This is noted by Innocent, in his gloss on the chapter *Si celebrat*,[15] and in *Quum medicinalis*[16] and in De Cohabitatione Clerici, chapter *Sicut*.[17]

Since therefore the law does not expressly warn that a celebrant in an unconsecrated church suffers the penalty of irregularity or any other penalty, or that the church itself is interdicted, except by the rigour of Otto's and Ottobuono's constitutions, and [their] law itself stops short of compulsion to procure such a consecration by act of superiors, the basis of any just fear of any interdict on, or the irregularity of celebrants in, [such] churches is destroyed. Nor does it seem from the foregoing reasons that St. Edmund's church ever was, or should have been, either interdicted or suspended from divine service.

For more detail on these points of law here offered for your consideration, you should obviously look at [*Sext.*], chapter *Is, qui in ecclesia*.[18] It says 'He who knowingly celebrates in an interdicted place' and so on. Note the word 'knowingly'. Therefore, anyone celebrating in ignorance should not be excommunicated, especially if his ignorance is neither crass nor supine.[19] This cannot rightly be supposed in your case, since you, like those before you who celebrated in your church, have followed in the footsteps of predecessors, from the time of the said constitutions, that is of Ottobuono, which were published in 1268. From that date both recordable and more recent times have passed. We must assume that during that period the monks who preceded you remembered a dedication or [fo.143] consciously provided for their salvation in some other way. It is probably fair to attribute the ignorance of the present generation to the long observed practice of its predecessors, in whose steps it has followed. The argument runs: 'ignorance of a fact excuses a person'; *Sext*, De Regulis Juris, chapter *Ignorancia*.[20] And he who succeeds to the place of another has just cause for ignorance; see under the same title the law *Cum quis in ius*.[21] This is especially true because ignorance is to be assumed unless knowledge is proved; see under the same title chapter *Presumitur*.[22] From that it follows that what was done in the past must be assumed to be lawful in the present. See: *Codex*, De prescriptione xxx, *Sicut*;[23] *Digest*, De Statu Hominum, the penultimate law;[24] *Codex*, De Rei Vendicatione, the law *Partum*.[25] It also follows that anyone, having just cause for ignorance of suspension and interdict, who celebrates, is excused from any irregularity. This is best proved by the penultimate chapter of the *Decretals*, De Clerico Excommunicato, titulus v, *Appostolice*,[26] both in the text and in Bernard de Bottone's gloss.[27]

For the same reason I reply to the law De Clerico Excommunicato, vii, *Postulastis*,[28] at the end, with the gloss of Innocent[29] and the chapter *Tanta*,[30] both text and gloss[31] mention the question of a celebrant in an interdicted church. I reply again with [?Innocent's gloss][32] and also with the chapters *Si celebret*[33] and *Quum medicinalis*,[34] where the question of a suspended celebrant is discussed. It is true that he incurs irregularity if he celebrates with full knowledge without reasonable cause, or is probably not ignorant, in a place which he knows to be effectively and simply interdicted. But none of this applies in the case you have asked me about, as the laws and reasons set forth above show.

On this matter it would seem safest and most honourable, for the exaltation of catholic worship in your church and to silence detractors, that the chapels adjoining your church, which are unfinished and disfigured by plaster work,[35] should be completed with sufficiently handsome stonework,[36] that is at least the surfaces should be faced with stone.[37] Then the consecration of the whole church, complete, should be arranged. This should be done in the first place because the bishop might undertake to correct such deformity at his own discretion, for the sake of having the church consecrated.[38] See the *Decretum*, De Consecratione, distinction 1, *Si motum*,[39] and note Hostiensis in his *Summa*, De Consecratione etc., chapter *Et an sit iteranda*,[40] where this matter is fully discussed. Item, whenever there is justifiable doubt about a consecration, the church should be consecrated because of that doubt. See *Decretum*, De Consecratione, distinction 1, *De ecclesiarum*[41] and canon *Ecclesie vel altaria*,[42] in the gloss where the question of the consecration and reconciliation of churches is dealt with at length.[43] See the evidence of Durandus in his *Summa rationale divinorum* under the title *De ecclesie consecratione*;[44] the distinctions there agree with much of what has been said above. On this also note Innocent on the rubric under the same title.[45] In addition, see the full treatment of this matter in the *Summa confessorum*.[46]

Subject Notes to Appendix

All references to the *Corpus iuris canonici* in the footnotes are to the edition by Emil Friedberg (Leipzig, 1879–81, 2 vols., repr. 1922–28).

1   'si loca huiusmodi non fuerint infra biennium a perfectionis tempore dedicata, a missarum solempniis usque ad consecrationem manere statuimus interdicta . . .' Otto's constitution, cited above p. 69.

2   *Codex Justinianus*, VI. 35. 11; the last line reads 'nihil etenim actum esse credimus, dum aliquid addendum superest.'

3   X [i.e. Decretals of Gregory IX].3. 42. 3 begins *Maiores*. However its contents seem irrelevant to the canonist's argument. Possibly *Maiori* is a corruption of *Morosiensi*; X. 3. 42. 5 is addressed *Morosiensi*. . . and decrees that there can be no true baptism without the Word and the Water i.e. if things are incomplete.

4   The reference is presumably to apsidal chapels in the abbey church, which were numerous. See Whittingham, 'Bury St. Edmunds Abbey: The Plan, Design and Development of the Church and Monastic Buildings,' the plan facing p. 192. Two such chapels, St. Catherine's and St. Faith's, were improved by Abbot Samson (above p. 67). A later passage in the canonist's answers repeats that some of the chapels were incomplete and indicates that they were faced with plaster not stone. See above p. 80 and below n.35. For the importance of stone in the medieval consecration ceremony see above p. 73 n. 71.

5   Otto stipulated that consecration should be within two years 'a perfectionis tempora'; above p. 69.

6   Vi [i.e. *Sext*], end, De Regulis Iuris, xv, 'Odia restringi, et favores convenit ampliari'.

7   quod ecclesie . . . consecrari: ut omnes ecclesie . . . per diocesanos episcopos ad quos pertinet, vel eorum auctoritate per alios, consecrentur'; Otto's constitutions cited above p. 69.

8   See above n.6.

9   See above p. 61 and nn.9, 10.

10   ut ecclesia . . . interdicta: cf. Otto's constitutions, cited above p. 69 and n.1.

11   Above, and n.6.

12   nisi . . . excusentur: nisi aliqua rationabili causa excusentur; Otto's constitutions,

cited above p. 69.

13　X. 5.1.16 (copied from a letter of Innocent III). The passage with 'excludatur' in it reads: 'Sed quum opponitur, ut quis a promotione officii vel beneficii excludatur, si ante confirmacionem obiicitur, non cogitur quisquam inscribere, quia crimen, hoc modo probatum, impedit promovendum, sed non deiicit iam promotum.' Innocent IV (1243–54) wrote a long gloss on *Super hiis* including an excursus 'excludatur' in his Commentary on the Decretals. (See *Apparatus decretalium* [Venice, 1491], fos.181v–82 of the modern foliation in Inc. I. B. 3. 97 in Cambridge University Library). It includes this passage (fo.182): 'Sed quod dices obijcies electo periurium probans eum iurasse certo die se soluturum non sufficit nisi et probes per confessionem eius vel alio modo eum in termino non soluisse, probasti enim quod peccatum non est, scilicet eum iurasse non quod te probaturum obtulisti, scilicet quod esset periurus: quis enim probare debet quod asseuerat. Ff. [*Digest*] de proba, ei que, et excipiens exceptionem suam, ff. [*Digest*] de proba, in excep. et idem dicendum videtur etiam si sententia excommunicationis lata sit sub conditione: puta excommunico te nisi ad talem diem solueris.' The relevant passages in the *Digest* are: XXII. 3. 2, 'Ei incumbit probatio qui dicit, non qui negat;' XXII. 3. 19. 'In exceptionibus dicendum est reum partibus actoris fungi oportere ipsumque exceptionem velut intentionem implere: ut puta si pacti conventi exceptione utatur, docere debet pactum conventum factum esse.'

14　See above, and n.1.

15　X. 5.27.10. Begins: 'Si celebrat minori excommunicatione legatus, licet graviter peccet, nullius tamen notam irregularitatis incurrit'. Innocent IV wrote a long gloss on this decretal in his Commentary. See *Apparatus decretalium*, fos.194–94v.

16　VI. 5.11.1. ends: 'Caveant autem ecclesiarum praelati et iudices universi, ne praedictam poenam suspensionis incurrant; quoniam, si contingeret eos sic suspensos divina officia exsequi sicut prius, irregularitatem non effugient iuxta canonicas sanctiones, super qua non nisi per summum Pontificem poterit dispensari.' This chapter of the Sext is c. 19 of the First Council of Lyons which Innocent IV summoned; printed Mansi, xxiii, pp.646–47 (from the text in Matthew Paris's *Chronica maiora*).

17　X. 3.2.4. Clerks should be admonished to put away their concubines. If they do not they should be suspended; if they still fail to comply they should lose their benefices. Innocent IV wrote a long gloss on this decretal; *Apparatus decretalium*, fo.131.

18　VI. 5.11.18. The relevant passage reads: 'Is vero qui scienter in loco celebrat supposito interdicto (nisi super hoc privilegiatus exsistat, aut a iure sit concessum eidem), irregularitatem incurrit.'

19　'crassa et supina': a citation from X. 5.27.9. See below, n. 26. See textual note.

20　VI. De Regulis Iuris, xiii: 'Ignorantia facti, non iuris, excusat.'

21　VI. De Regulis Iuris, xiv: 'Quum quis in ius succedit alterius: iustam ignorantiae causam censetur habere.'

22　VI. De Regulis Iuris, xlvii: 'Praesumitur ignorantia, ubi scientia non probatur.'

23　*Codex*, vii. 39.3. begins: 'Sicut in rem speciales, ita de universitate ac personales actiones ultra triginta annorum spatium minime protendantur': ends: 'Post hanc vero temporis definitionem nulli movendi ulterius facultatem patere censemus, etiamsi se legis ignorantia excusare temptaverit.'

24　*Digest*, I. 5.26, the penultimate law of De hominum statu hominum: reads: 'Qui in utero sunt, in toto paene iure civili intelleguntur in rerum natura esse. Nam et legitimae hereditates his restituuntur: et si praegnas mulier ab hostibus capta sit, id quod natum erit postliminium habet, item patris vel matris condicionem sequitur: praeterea si ancilla praegnas subrepta fuerit, quamvis apud bonae fidei emptorem pepererit, id quod natum erit tamquam furtivum usu non capitur: his consequens est, ut libertus quoque, quamdiu patroni filius nasci possit, eo iure sit, quo sunt qui patronos habent.'

25 *Codex*, III. 32. 7. reads: 'Partum ancillae matris sequi condicionem nec statum in hac specie patris considerari explorati iuris est.'

26 X. 5.27.9. (the penultimate chapter) reads: 'Apostolicae sedis (*Et infra*) Verum, quia tempore suspensionis ignari celebrastis divina, vos reddit ignorantia probabilis excusatos. Ceterum, si forte ignorantia crassa et supina [cf. above, and n. 19] aut erronea fuerit, propter quod dispensationis gratia egeatis, eam vobis de benignitate apostolica indulgemus.'

27 'B' is the sign for 'Bernard de Bottone,' of Parma (d. 1266), author of the *Summa Decretalium*. See G. Mollat, *Introduction a l'étude du droit canonique et du droit civil* (Paris, 1930), p.18. For Bernard's gloss on X. 5.27 see *Bernardi papiensis . . . summa decretalium*, ed. E.A.T. Laspeyres (Regensburg, 1860, repr. Graz 1956), p.253. It does not seem relevant to the canonist's argument.

28 X. 5.27.7. The last part reads: 'Quaesivitis praeterea, qualiter puniri debeant clerici ac monachi vel moniales ecclesiarum conventualium, qui post latam interdicti sententiam in locis suppositis interdicto praesumpserunt hactenus, et adhuc etiam non verentur divina officia celebrare, quamvis propter hoc sint excommunicationis vinculo innodati. Ad hoc breviter respondemus, quod clerici, qui talia prae-sumpserunt, sunt ecclesiasticis beneficiis spoliandi; monachi vero vel moniales in arctioribus monasteriis ad peragendam poenitentiam detrudendi.'

29 Innocent IV's gloss on *Postulastis* reads: 'dispensatum, cum papa non retineat dispensationem sibi episcopus dispensare potest in dicta sententia excommuni-cationis nuper (propter hoc) quia celebrant in locis interdictis (innodati) sententiam in eos spiritualiter latam non ipso iure (talia), scilicet celebrare in ecclesiis interdictis ex quo propter hoc sunt excommunicati, nos dicimus idem siue propter hoc sint excommunicati siue non: nam ex quo celebrant in loco interdicto hanc penam subeunt per testes. . . .' *Apparatus decretalium*, fo.194.

30 X. 5.31.18.

31 Innocent IV gives a long gloss on *Tanta*. *Apparatus decretalium*, fo.196v.

32 The text appears to be corrupt here. Perhaps the reference is to 'the same [gloss],' i.e. Innocent IV's (see textual note).

33 X. 5.27.10. Cf. above, and n.15.

34 *Quum medicinalis*; vi. 5.11.1. Cf. above, and n.16.

35 I cannot find a word 'lutamen.' However, a possible meaning could be that the interiors of the chapels were faced with plaster, not stone, and the word related to '*lutum*' (mud), '*luto*' (to daub with mud or clay), *lutamentum* (that which is made of mud, a coating of mud, a mud or clay wall). In medieval Latin 'lutarius' meant a dauber, plasterer, and '*luteo*' to daub, plaster; R.E. Latham, *Revised Medieval Latin Word-List* (Oxford, 1965), p.283, under '*lutum philosophorum*.' Cf. above p. 79 and n.4.

36 The suggested emendation to 'belliato' (see textual note t) makes some sense of an otherwise problematical passage. '*Belliatus*' means pretty, beautiful, from '*bellus*', pretty, handsome, admirable, excellent, etc.; *Oxford Latin Dictionary*, i, p.228 under '*belliatus*', and *ibid.*, i, p.229 under '*bellus*.'

37   'lutamine fedate . . . cooperirentur': the meaning of this passage is obscure and my translation a very tentative, free rendering. The text may be corrupt.

38   This warning that the diocesan bishop might intervene to ensure consecration responds to the passage towards the end of Otto's constitution (repeated by Ottobuono), which stipulates that abbots and other rectors of churches should not pull down old, consecrated churches, under pretext of building more beautiful or larger ones, without the licence and consent of the diocesan. The diocesan had to decide whether to give a licence, and if he did so, to ensure that the building was completed as soon as possible. Otto's constitutions, cited above p. 69.

39   *Decretum*, Canon 19, D. I, *de cons*. The canon reads: 'Si motum fuerit altare, denuo consecretur ecclesia; si parietes mutantur, et non altare, salibus tantum exorcizetur. Si homicidio uel adulterio ecclesia uiolata fuerit, diligentissime expurgetur et denuo consecretur.'

40   *Henrici cardinalis Hostiensis summa aurea* [Henry of Susa, d. 1271], Bk. III, dist. De consecratione ecclesie vel altaris, cap.5, *Et an sit iteranda consecratio*. For a printed text see e.g. Cambridge University Library, Acton a.2. 115 (Venice, 1670), fos.306, 306v.

41   *Decretum*, canon 1, D.1, *de cons*.

42   *Ibid*., canon 18, D.1, *de cons*. reads: 'Ecclesiae uel altaria, que ambigua sunt de consecratione, consecrentur, et superflua altaria destruantur.'

43   There is a long gloss on the above by Bartholomew of Brescia (d. 1250 or 1258). He gives seven reasons for the reconsecration of a church or altar. The first is 'quando dubitatur de consecratione'.

44   *Rationale divinorum officiorum* by Guilelmus Durandus (d. 1296), Bk. I, cap.6, *De ecclesiae dedicatione*, and cap.7, *De altaris consecratione*. See the modern edition (Naples, 1859), pp.39–57.

45   Innocent IV's gloss on the decretal *De consecratione* (x. 3.40) starts with three reasons for reconsecration. The first reads: 'Si dubitetur an sit consecrata: quia non apparet aliqua scriptura: vel in libro ecclesie vel columna vel tabula marmorea vel etiam unus testis de visu: et quedam de auditu.' *Apparatus decretalium*, fo.168v.

46   A *Summa confessorum* was written by the Dominican John Rumsik, lector of Freiburg (d. 1314), but it has no titulus headed 'De ecclesie consecratione'. It seems likely that the work referred to here is the version of Rumsik's *Summa* by Bartholomew San Corcordio (d. 1347). If so, the reference provides a valuable clue to the date of the canonist's answers. See above p. 74 and n.79.

Chapter 6

Too Important to Neglect: The Gesta Innocentii PP III

Brenda Bolton

It is the purpose of any *gesta*, that most particularly medieval genre of historical prose, to provide a contemporary background to the outstanding deeds of its principal character, usually portrayed as the hero of the piece.[1] The form of the *gesta* originally followed the simple chronological framework used in the widely diffused *Liber pontificalis*.[2] Basic details such as family origins and length of career were followed by an account of striking achievements, concluding with a brief description of the subject's death. By the twelfth century it had become standard practice for material to be organised explicitly according to its bearing on separate topics such as personal attributes, the defence of lands and castles and gifts to local monasteries and churches. As kings began to realise the considerable potential of *gesta* their form was adapted to a more courtly context, while the authors became concerned to describe and justify the growth of royal authority.[3] By the second half of the twelfth and by the early thirteenth century, the *gesta* was at the height of its development and fashion. The Emperor Frederick Barbarossa (1152–90)[4] and Henry II of England (1154–89)[5] had their *gesta* as did Philip II Augustus (1179–1223).[6] One pope seems to have merited a *gesta*, namely Innocent III (1198–1216).[7] From this we should not be

---

[1] R.D. Ray, 'Medieval Historiography through the Twelfth Century: Problems and Progress of Research', *Viator*, v (1974), 32–59; C.B. Bouchard, *Spirituality and Administration: The Role of the Bishop in Twelfth-Century Auxerre*, Speculum Anniversary Monographs, v (Cambridge, Mass., 1979), pp.5–13; B.F. Reilly, 'The *Historia Compostelana*: The Genesis and Composition of a Twelfth-Century Spanish *Gesta*', *Speculum*, xliv (1949), 78–85.

[2] *Le Liber Pontificalis*, ed. L. Duchesne-C. Vogel, 3 vols., 2nd ed. (Paris, 1955–57); T.F.X. Noble, 'A new look at the *Liber pontificalis*', *Archivum Historiae Pontificae*, xxiii (1985), 347–58.

[3] R.R. Bezzola, *Les origines et la formation de la litterature courtoise en occident, 500–1200* (Paris, 1958–1963).

[4] *Ottonis et Rahewini, Gesta Friderici I imperatoris*, ed. G. Waitz and B. von Simson, *Monumenta Germaniae Historica, in usum scholarum* (Hannover, 1912); *The Deeds of Frederick Barbarossa: Otto of Freising and his Continuator Rahewin*, trans. C.C. Mierow (Columbia, 1953).

[5] *Gesta regis Henrici secundi Benedicti abbatis*, ed. W. Stubbs (London, 1867).

[6] *Oeuvres de Rigord et de Guillaume le Breton*, ed. H.-F. Delaborde, i, (Paris, 1882).

[7] *Gesta Innocentii PP. III*, in *Patrologia Latina*, ed. J.P. Migne, (Paris, 1855) ccxiv, i–cl, cols. xvii–ccxxviii.

misled into an overemphasis of Innocent's political activities. His *Gesta*, however, provides us with an important source, just as valuable as those of his secular contemporaries.

By Innocent's day the *gesta* had evolved into something far more dramatic and interesting than a mere factual chronicle. The worthy deeds of the individual could now be supplemented by the inclusion of *instrumenta* or documentary evidence from the growing collections of archives, charters, registers and judicial rolls. If the patron was sufficiently powerful, a Philip Augustus for example, the prose *gesta* might subsequently be transformed into verse.[8] If a suitable villain could be found to act as counterpoint to the hero the dramatic effect of prose or verse was all the more intense. The approach was strongly biographical and a *gesta* written from first-hand experience would enjoy an improved standing over one based merely on 'common report'. Many *gesta*, of course, incorporated a variety of approaches and methods. Often the work of several authors, although sometimes of one alone, they were frequently reworked to suit changing circumstances. Where an eyewitness was involved events and suitable anecdotes could sometimes be interwoven with privileged information obtained from private archival or documentary sources. In some ways then a *gesta* might have had something in common with a modern festschrift the purpose of which is well understood.[9]

To honour John Taylor's retirement and to convey my thanks, I want to attempt to rehabilitate Innocent III's *Gesta*,[10] that neglected and

---

[8] J.W. Baldwin, *The Government of Philip Augustus: Foundations of French Royal Power in the Middle Ages* (Berkeley, 1986), pp.362–93, 420–23.

[9] I stand eyewitness to John Taylor's excellence as a tutor. Thirty years on I can still relate a particular event which typifies the concern for and availability to students which was always linked to the fine teaching and scholarship of the Leeds History School. One typically Yorkshire autumn day five of us, two of the three History Johns (John Cox and John Taylor; the third was John Le Patourel, Professor of History, 1945–1974, died July 1981) and three students, drove deep into the Dales. Our conveyance was a splendid and aged Rolls-Royce hearse; our mission was to rub the great brass of Simon of Wensley as a joint effort for the department. Mission accomplished saw us playing darts in the local inn where three inexperienced students were encouraged to defeat two kindly and considerate staff. I cherish my memories of John Taylor's encouragement in other fields as well, although neither of us would have suspected at the time that I might come to work on the Medieval Church, that area which he has made so much his own.

[10] H. Elkan, *Die Gesta Innocentii III im Verhältnis zu den Registen desselben Papstes* (Heidelberg, 1876); Y. Lefevre, 'Innocent III et son temps vus de Rome: étude sur la biographie anonyme de ce pape', *Mélanges d'archéologie et d'histoire de l'École Française de Rome*, lxi (1949), 242–45; V. Pfaff, 'Die Gesta Innocenz' III und das Testament Henrichs VI', *Zeitschrift der Savigny-Stiftung für Rechtesgeschichte: kanonische Abteilung*, 1 (1964), 78–126, especially 79–90; W. Imkamp, *Das Kirchenbild Innocenz' III (1198–1216)*, Päpste und Papsttum, xxii (Stuttgart, 1983), pp.10–46.

undervalued source which seems to have lain so long dormant, as did my interest in church history after my time at Leeds. The *Gesta Innocentii PP III* is a unique source for the life and work of its hero during the first ten years of his pontificate. The *Gesta* was apparently not well known in the middle ages[11] and seventeenth-century copies seem to have survived in greater number than manuscripts of the time. The transmission of the text of the *Gesta* has been painstakingly reconstructed by Imkamp who identifies two sources, one in France, the other in Rome.[12] In France, two fourteenth-century manuscripts,[13] one possibly from Toulouse, the other from Autun, both end at chapter CXLV and make no mention of Innocent's *Commentary on the Penitential Psalms*. These appear to have been used in the editions of Bosquet (1635)[14] and Baluze (1682).[15] In Rome, Vat. Lat. 12111, written in a late thirteenth- or early fourteenth-century hand, can be identified from the Papal Library Catalogue as being in Avignon in 1411.[16] It seems to have arrived back in Rome before the end of 1604.[17] The death of Giacomo Grimaldi, Archivist of St. Peter's, on 7 December of that year is recorded on the first folio.[18] This manuscript may well have been Vallicelliana J49, used by La Porte du Theil and Brequigny in 1791 and published again by Migne in 1855.[19] More comprehensive than its counterparts it includes a further six chapters, CXLVI to CL, with detailed and significant lists of gifts and promotions made by Innocent to the Roman church. The manuscript also includes the pope's *Commentary on the Psalms*.

Today the text of the *Gesta* is still most readily accessible at the beginning of Migne's four-volume edition of Innocent's *Opera omnia* where it occupies 211 columns.[20] As Innocent is the first medieval pope to have anything approaching a complete set of surviving registers, the attention of historians has been concentrated on the official chancery documents which make up the main body of Migne's four volumes. The *Gesta* has usually been discounted in a few dismissive words. How

---

[11] K.W. Pennington, *Pope and Bishops: The Papal Monarchy in the Twelfth and Thirteenth Centuries* (Philadelphia, 1984), p.54.

[12] Imkamp, *Das Kirchenbild*, pp.10–20.

[13] Paris Bibliothèque Nationale, MS Lat. 5150; 5151.

[14] F. Bosquet, *Epistola Innocentii pontificis maximi notae* (Toulouse, 1635), pp.1–150.

[15] E. Baluze, *Epistolarum Innocentii III Romanorum pontificis libri undecim; accedunt Gesta eiusdem Innocentii et prima collectio decretalium composita a Rainerio diacono et monacho Pompostino; Stephanus Baluzius Tutelensis editionem Tolosanum innumeris propemodum in unum colligit, magnam partem nunc primum editit, reliqua emendavit*, 2 vols., (Paris, 1682).

[16] Imkamp, *Das Kirchenbild*, p.14.

[17] *Ibid.*, p.15.

[18] MS Vat. Lat. 12111, fo. 1r.

[19] Imkamp, *Das Kirchenbild*, pp.17–19.

[20] *Gesta*, I-CL, cols. xvii-ccxxviii.

could a biography by an anonymous contemporary, which does not even cover the whole pontificate match more official sources of greater validity? It was all too easy to denigrate with the words 'enigmatic',[21] 'partisan', 'panegyric' and 'pro-papal'.[22] It is now high time to redress the balance. This will reveal the *Gesta* to be unique as a source for the better appreciation of Innocent III's activities, particularly as they apply to Rome and the Papal States.

The official biography of Innocent III, entered in the *Liber pontificalis* by Martin of Troppau (d. 1279),[23] merely outlines Innocent's career to 1216 as it would have been known and remembered in the third quarter of the thirteenth century. A poor thing it is too, both brief and uninspiringly terse. It follows a simple chronological framework: a few sentences on his family origins in Campania; the length of his pontificate; an account of his main achievements; and finally a brief description of his death. Martin's work cannot be compared either in quality or in quantity with the *Gesta*'s rich detail and vivid narration of events.

The *Gesta* of Innocent III is attractive and exciting. Its author must have seen the pope frequently, worked closely with him and understood and sympathised with his feelings. It helps us to come closer to the person of the pope. Other eyewitness accounts that we have of the pontificate serve to increase the credibility which the *Gesta* has for the period it covers. Two of these are chance survivals. One is a private letter from an official of the Curia at its summer retreat at Subiaco in 1202 and possibly addressed to Rinaldo, archbishop-elect of Capua.[24] This reveals how by sheer force of his personal example, Innocent inspired his officials to work through the full heat of every day no matter how they yearned for their siesta.[25] The so-called Giessen Manuscript contains a letter by a German cleric,[26] who attended the Fourth Lateran Council (11–30 November 1215) and who records not only Innocent's impressive chairmanship of the greatest assembly of the church since Chalcedon (451) but also registers the pope's spontaneous and proprietorial delight in showing Rome to his distinguished visitors. The third eyewitness, a continuator of the Chapter Archives of S. Costanzo in Orvieto, is perhaps more conscious of the need

---

[21] Lefevre, 'Innocent III', p.243.

[22] T.C. Van Cleve, *Markward of Anweiler and the Sicilian Regency* (Princeton, 1937), pp.119–21.

[23] *Liber pontificalis*, pp.451–53.

[24] K. Hampe, 'Eine Schilderung des Sommeraufenthaltes der römischen Kurie unter Innocenz III in Subiaco, 1202', *Historische Vierteljahrschrift*, viii (Leipzig, 1905), 509–35.

[25] *Ibid.*, p.531.

[26] S. Kuttner and A. Garcia y Garcia, 'A New Eyewitness Account of the Fourth Lateran Council', *Traditio*, xx (1964), 115–78.

to record his account of what he saw.[27] He describes the papal visit to that city on Sunday 1 May 1216, where Innocent's charismatic preaching encouraged more than 2,000 men and women of every sort to take the Cross. The Orvietan canon even tells us of Innocent's physical appearance within two months of his death. At fifty-seven the pope, of middling height, shone with interior as well as exterior beauty.[28] This description, reminiscent of St. Francis, matches contemporary Mendicant perceptions and accords well with the *Gesta*, whose author speaks similarly of Innocent's medium height and attractive and inspiring appearance.[29]

The *Gesta*'s value as an historical source goes far beyond these chance survivals about the personality of the pope which serve only to enhance its contents, not to diminish them. It is not merely a diary recounting day-to-day events during the first ten years of the pontificate. Instead it is a single author's presentation of carefully organised themes, rigorously selected. The biographer must have lived and worked at the Papal Curia. He certainly had privileged access to the Papal Registers and they were, in fact, his only documentary source.[30] At all times he followed his subject as a skilled and sensitive diplomatist. He begins with a short section on the pope's early career, his education and cardinalate, his election and consecration. He moves rapidly and in an ordered fashion to deal with his chosen themes. He examines in sequence Innocent's policy for the recovery of the Papal States and the reform of the church in Rome. He considers the influence of the church throughout Christendom and includes in this theme relations with Greeks in the East and the Fourth Crusade of 1204. The account concludes with the continuing struggle against the commune for control of the city of Rome. The last six chapters enumerate Innocent's charitable activities and benefactions, not only to churches and religious institutions within the city of Rome but throughout the Patrimony and beyond. These and the list of promotions amongst his household and familiars provide information which is to be found only in this source.

The biographer's first theme is the desperate situation which arose from the German occupation of the Papal States. A harsh and tyrannical repression of the pope's subjects approached the gates of Rome itself.[31] Innocent's purpose was to return the Patrimony to the sphere of influence of the church. It was to be a programme of *recuperatio* or recovery but could not be undertaken without many qualms on the pope's part.[32] Here the author of the *Gesta* comes closest to understanding his subject's innermost

[27] Pierpont Morgan Library M. 465, fo. 90v; M. Maccarrone, *Studi su Innocenzo III*, Italia Sacra, xvii (Padua, 1972), pp.3–9.

[28] *Ibid.*, p.9, 'Statura modicum, formosum interiori et exteriori pulcritudine vegetavit'.

[29] *Gesta*, I, col. xvii, 'statura mediocris et decorus aspectu'.

[30] Lefevre, 'Innocent III', 243.

[31] *Gesta*, VIII, cols. xxi-xxv; IX, cols. xii-xxv.

[32] *Ibid.*, XVII, cols. xxix-xxx.

feelings, expressed through the text from Ecclesiasticus 13:1, 'Whosoever touches pitch shall be defiled'.[33] Innocent's anguish reveals his disquiet, *sollicitudo*, at the impropriety implicit in this armed recovery of his temporal power. The sense of danger and of the limitations on papal power are clearly articulated by the biographer. So well is this point made that the pope may have actually spoken of his anxieties to the author. In the event, papal rule brought positive benefits. Innocent made the roads safer and did not exact those harsh tolls taken by his German predecessors in the area.[34] He was, however, well aware of the heavy burdens he would have to place upon his subjects in the Patrimony and aimed to make these more acceptable by claiming that 'his yoke is easy and his burden light'.[35]

Accepted literary form is given dramatic expression in Innocent's conflict with Markward of Anweiler, the villain and anti-hero of the *Gesta*.[36] The hatred Innocent here displays is unique. Markward, German adventurer, *dapifer regis* and seneschal to the late Emperor Henry VI (1190–97), was duke of Ravenna, margrave of Ancona and count of Molise. Markward not only claimed his right to the regency and the Regno on behalf of the young Frederick II but also initially wrecked Innocent's plan to rebuild the Patrimony. After his siege of the great Benedictine abbey of Cassino in January-February 1199 and his subsequent excommunication,[37] Markward's activities are closely documented by the author of the *Gesta*. On the whole the biographer seems to have selected his information carefully. In July 1199 Markward is shown attempting to make a secret and underhand agreement with Archbishop Conrad of Mainz. If he agreed to represent Markward at the Curia he would receive 20,000 ounces of gold from the customary *census* usually given to the pope in the Patrimony.[38]

Markward made a dramatic attempt in August of the same year at Veroli to prevent the issuing of Innocent's sentence of excommunication. The *Gesta* shows that this very nearly succeeded when Markward threatened force against the cardinals concerned. Only Hugolino's courage managed to save the situation when he is reported as saying 'Behold the mandate of the Lord Pope. We cannot do otherwise'.[39] Innocent's propaganda campaign is continually highlighted. Not only is Markward *perfidius* but

---

[33] Maccarrone, *Studi*, pp.9–12.

[34] *Gesta*, xv, col. xxix.

[35] O. Hageneder and A. Haidacher eds., *Die Register Innocenz III*, i, *Pontifikatsjahr 1198–99* (Graz-Koln, 1964), pp.127–28; *PL*, cciv, 76; Maccarrone, *Studi*, pp.14–15.

[36] Van Cleve, *Markward*, pp.108–23; E. Kennan, 'Innocent III and the First Political Crusade: a Comment on the Limitations of Papal Power', *Traditio*, xxvii (1971), 231–49.

[37] *Gesta*, xxiii, cols. xxxviii-xlii.

[38] *Ibid.*, col. xlii.

[39] *Ibid.*, col. xliv; 'Ecce mandatum domini Papae. Nos aliud facere non valemus'.

also *ingeniosus et subdolus*.[40] Memories of previous cruelties by the Germans in the peninsula doubtless helped to rally the people against him. The fortuitous discovery by papal forces of Markward's baggage lost in his flight from defeat was used to the full in the *Gesta*.[41] In a cloak, the suppressed will of Henry VI complete with a golden bull was discovered. This will gave all to the church and, forgery or not, it suited Innocent's case. Markward's only claim to legality was the Declaration of Speyer where he was named as the Staufen regent in Sicily.[42] Markward's invasion of Sicily in October 1199 and his alliance with the local colony of Saracens had further fuelled the Pope's fury. This was a threat coming from the 'other Saladin'.[43] When Markward died in September 1202, the *Gesta*'s anti-hero description concludes with the agony he suffered in his final illness, reflecting vividly the view that the sinner was being suitably punished.[44]

Resistance continued in spite of Markward's death. When the pope fell gravely ill at Anagni in 1203, news spread that he had died.[45] An uprising took place in the Regno where Matera, Brindisi and Otranto were lost to him. German influence in the south lasted until 1205 when Innocent's former confessor, the Cistercian and papal diplomat Brother Rainier, received the homage of a number of leading nobles including Diepold of Acerra and another Markward, this time of Laviano.[46] The theme ends with the creation of Innocent's brother Richard as count of Sora, an important lordship at the frontier between the Patrimony and the Regno.[47] Finally Innocent, as the overlord, was able to take oaths of homage and fidelity from all the counts and barons. It was an important and highly symbolic ceremony that was held at S. Germano in June-July 1208 marking the full recovery of the southern part of the Patrimony.[48]

The second theme of the biographer is the power, influence and probity of the Roman church throughout all Christendom. He explains the reforms

---

[40] *Gesta*, ix, col. xxiii.

[41] *Ibid.*, xxvii, col. lii; Pfaff, '*Die Gesta* Innocenz' III', 79–90.

[42] *Regestum Innocentii III papae super negotio Romani imperii*, ed. F. Kempf, *Miscellanea Historiae Pontificiae*, xii (1947), pp.33–38.

[43] *Die Register Innocenz III*, ii, *Pontifikatsjahr 1199–1200*, eds. O. Hageneder, W. Maleczek and A. Strnad (Rome-Vienna, 1979), pp.411–14; *PL*, ccxiv, col. 780; Potthast, 877. Markward is also 'Dei et Ecclesiae inimicus', *Register*, i, pp.811–13; *PL*, ccxiv col. 516; Potthast, 601. Compare Innocent's letter of June 1212 to James, the papal marshal in *PL* ccvi, cols. 624–25 where the same title is used, even ten years after Markward's death.

[44] *Gesta*, xxv, col. lxvi.

[45] *Ibid.*, xxvii, col. lxvi; cxxvii, col. clxxxviii.

[46] *Ibid.*, xxxviii, col. lxviii.

[47] *Ibid.*, xxix, cols. lxxi-lxxiii.

[48] *Ibid.*, xl, cols. lxxiv-lxxx, with the text of his ordinance and a letter to the faithful of the Regno. 'Cum propter necessitatem urgentem in regnum personaliter descendimus . . . ut in ipso videlicet pacem et justitiam reformemus'.

which Innocent had instituted for the spiritual wellbeing of the church. Whilst curial officials were forbidden from taking fees, a sliding scale was established for scribes and *bullators*.[49] Porters were to allow free access to the notarial chambers without taking *douceurs* for themselves, and within the Lateran Palace Innocent, *solertissimus pontifex*, threw out the moneychangers' tables. The Consistory was to meet three times a week where the pope himself would hear the most significant cases, *cum multa maturitate*.[50] The biographer then lists those major cases: Compostella versus Braga; the Canterbury monks in their dispute over Lambeth Palace; the archbishop of Milan against the abbot of Scozula. This last case clearly intrigued the biographer.[51] He gives details, to add to evidence from elsewhere, of Innocent's ever-present concern to establish the validity of documents. He describes the pope's flamboyant act of seal-breaking as part of his campaign to root out forgery wherever it should appear.[52] Another case was the abasement of the excommunicated Conrad of Hildesheim who spread himself on the floor in front of the pope in the shape of a cross.[53] Anticlimax followed with a description of the bishop's open attempt to influence Innocent by presenting silver vases. The quick-witted Innocent immediately responded with a greater gift, of a more precious gold cup, and in so doing showed that he could not be corrupted. Both episodes, seals and vases, are used by the biographer to increase the liveliness of his reporting. After listing other significant cases of papal arbitration the biographer concludes with the case of Ingeborg of Denmark, the divorced wife of the king of France who had appealed to Rome.[54] Her case with its notoriety and pathos and her cries of *mala Francia, mala Francia* and *Roma, Roma*, shows the extent of the problems which Innocent had inherited and is used by the author to expand further on the marital theme, including incestuous marriages in Iberia and in the east.[55]

The second theme concludes with Innocent's desire in the tenth year of his pontificate to visit personally the now peaceful northern part of his Patrimony.[56] In Viterbo in September 1207 he held his great three-day parliament, receiving homage, hearing disputes and on the third

---

[49] *Ibid.*, XLI, cols. lxxx-lxxxi.

[50] *Ibid.*, XLII, cols. lxxxi-lxxxxii.

[51] *Ibid.*, col. lxxxiv.

[52] R.L. Poole, *Lectures on the Papal Chancery down to the Time of Innocent III* (London, 1915), pp.147–62. See also the case of 19 May 1198 in *Register* i, pp.333–35; *PL.* cciv, cols. 202–3.

[53] *Gesta*, XLIV, cols. lxxxvii-lxxxxviii; Pennington, *Pope and Bishops*, pp.32–33.

[54] *Gesta*, XLIX, cols. xciv-xcv.

[55] *Ibid.*, LVIII, cols. ciii-cviii.

[56] *Ibid.*, CXIII, cols. clxi-clxii.

day enacting several statutes against heresy.[57] The derelict monastery of S. Martino al Cimino nearby was given 'magnificent privileges' and its incorporation into the Cistercian order encouraged in order to help in holding the line against heresy.[58] Innocent's peacemaking and pastoral roles were evident in ending the local conflict amongst the citizens of Todi and providing suitable pontificals for the poverty-stricken archbishop of Ravenna.[59] After visiting his newly fortified palace at Montefiascone, where he spent twelve days,[60] he moved on to Tuscania to the new palace he had built at S. Niccola. There he demanded and received the oaths of his subjects. From Vetralla he went to Sutri, where he remained three days solemnly dedicating the cathedral before returning to Rome.

Further cases of Innocent's wider role as peace-maker are detailed in a small sub-section:[61] Henry, king of Hungary, brought to peace with his brother Andrew; the Milanese with the citizens of Pavia; the Lombard communes and the kings of France and England aided by the special effort of the Cistercian, Gerald, abbot of Casamari.[62] This peace-making often entailed ecclesiastical reform. Long list of provinces visited by papal agents and of bishops removed from their sees are provided.[63] Control by Rome is always evident. Even in its 'profound servitude', the church in England is shown to be ultimately responsible to Innocent. His consecration of Stephen Langton, cardinal-deacon of S. Crisogono is given as evidence of this.[64]

The third and major theme of the *Gesta* is the pope's relationship with Rome, its prefect, its commune and its citizens. From the biographer we have a clear eyewitness account of Innocent taking possession of his city after his consecration when 'all the city was crowned' and rejoicing.[65] Although the prefect, Peter de Vico, a former imperial supporter, is shown performing his act of homage and receiving a red mantle from the pope, the Romans were much less easily won over. They demanded their traditional money gifts given at the election of a new pope and bitterly protested against the

[57] For the texts of the three statutes promulgated, see *PL*, ccv, cols. 1226–28; Maccarrone, *Studi*, pp.51–61.

[58] *Gesta*, cxxvi, cols. clxii-clxiv; *PL*, ccv, cols. 1309–12; Potthast, 2997. For the gift of a red and gold altar frontal and 100 pounds in money of Siena, *Gesta*, cxlv, cols. ccviii, ccxxvii.

[59] *Ibid.*, cxxvii, cols clxv-clxvi.

[60] *Ibid.*, xiv, cols. xxviii-xxix; *PL*, cciv, col. 112; Maccarrone, *Studi*, pp.21–22.

[61] *Gesta*, cxxviii, cols. clxviii-ix.

[62] *Ibid.*, cxxx, col. clxix. Gerald, abbot of Casamari (1183–1209) was a nephew of Gerald, sixth abbot of Clairvaux.

[63] *Ibid.*, cxxx, clxxii-clxxv.

[64] *Ibid.*, cxxxi, cols. clxxv-clxxvii.

[65] *Ibid.*, vii, cols. xx-xxi; 'Coronata est tota civitas'.

parish by parish oath enforced on them to prevent fraud.[66]

Nor were the nobles any less docile. Using the imagery of the Psalms (63:90), as the virtue of gold is proved in the fiery furnace,[67] a text incidentally used later by Innocent in his call to crusade,[68] the *Gesta* shows the pope, wounded more by his enemies' tongues than by their arrows, successfully resisting the harmful taunts of hiis chief enemies, John Pierleone and John Capocci. They accused him of misusing and despoiling the properties of the city as a sparrowhawk might strip the feathers from a smaller bird.[69] They in their turn tried to extort money from the pope who steadfastly refused to submit to what he regarded as a *pessima consuetudo*.[70] The *Gesta* is at pains to show Innocent as the strong defender of Rome.

In the Romans' two difficult wars against Viterbo his brother Richard gave 1,000 pounds to provision the small, embattled fortress-town of Vitorchiano.[71] The pope himself showed where he stood by insisting upon the return of the bronze doors and fountain grills which the Viterbans had broken and removed from St. Peter's in 1167.[72] The impression given here is that the biographer is struggling hard to show Innocent and the Romans working together. The other side of the picture which he also reports, is a grim catalogue of physical molestation and downright humiliation – of masses disrupted at St. Peter's: of physical attacks on the person of the pope; and of open rebellion during his absence at Velletri in 1202. There is no underestimation of the violence of the Tower Wars between the clans of the Orsini-Boboni-Capocci-Pierleone on the one hand and the papally-supported Conti-Annibaldi-Romani de Scorta (Scotti) on the other.[73] The widespread distaste felt by the Romans for Richard Conti is clearly described including his territorial ambitions which extended from Poli near Tivoli to Sora.[74] In July-August 1208 he was invested as count of Sora at the hands of his brother. From those dark days, the pope, the Bishop of Rome, is shown as emerging triumphant. John Pierleone is publicly excommunicatted and Innocent shows that he is not 'like a dumb dog who does not know how to bark',[75] words identical to those he

[66] *Ibid.*, vIII, cols. xxi-xxii.

[67] *Ibid.*, cxxxIII, col. clxxvii.

[68] In *Quia maior*. J. and L. Riley-Smith, *The Crusades: Idea and Reality, 1095–1274* (London, 1981), p.119.

[69] *Gesta*, cxxxIII, col. clxxxiii; 'sicut anceps deplumat avem omnibus pannis'.

[70] *Ibid.*, col. clxxix.

[71] *Ibid.*, cxxxIv, col. clxxxii.

[72] *Ibid.*, cxxx, col. clxxxiii; 'Praecipiens Viterbiensibus ut portas aereos quos de cantharo ante basilicam dicebantur extulisse, vel confregisse, tempore Frederici imperatoris, facerent restauri'.

[73] *Ibid.*, cols. clxxxiv-cxcvi.

[74] *Ibid.*, xxxIx, cols. lxx-lxxiii.

[75] *Ibid.*, cxlII, col. cxcvi.

so frequently used to his own bishops. The steps of the basilica of St. Peter on the feast of its dedication was a most fitting setting for such a declaration where pope and commune finally came to terms.

The language of the *Gesta* is neither highly coloured nor overelaborate. It is surely written, as Lefevre suggested, by a single well-placed curial official whose exposition flows easily along maintaining his readers' interest.[76] The papal registers are the only written source which the biographer appears to have used and he moves stylistically from personal account to the straightforward citation of papal correspondence. Clearly, the *Gesta* is an official work produced by a cleric with privileged access to the chancery and its flow of documents. Up to this point most historians have agreed. On questions of motive and dating there has been far less unanimity. Elkan believed that the text was written between June and August 1208 by a close relative of Innocent himself with the aim of justifying papal policy towards Sicily.[77] Lefevre (1949) dismissed Elkan's examination of the *Gesta* as both incomplete and partial.[78] He agreed that the author was well-placed in the curia but was no relation and had composed his work in two separate stages. A primitive text of *c.* 1203 in biographical form with supporting documents, *pièces justicatives*, was completed in draft. The reason for the speed of this compilation must have been the severe illness and rumoured death of the pope at precisely that time in Anagni. By 1208 a second version had been created without any alteration to the primitive text save the insertion of paragraphs here and there to update his information. In 1207 the biographer had access to the papal registers and incorporated large extracts directly into his work correcting and amplifying the primitive version but without modifying the early form of the text.

Lefevre has argued that this evolution of the *Gesta* indicates the historian working rigorously to select events he wished to highlight and waiting to write about them until he had access to the documents. He would thus diminish the risks of misinterpretation.[79] Lefevre has also suggested that this is the reason the author never deals with the imperial question or the situation in Germany as the outcome is always too uncertain. He considers that the approach to the Fourth Crusade also confirms the policy of waiting to use relevant documents until the registers were written up. The Crusades are written about not in 1203 but in 1208, when the use of the pope's correspondence confirm the author's reliability and trustworthiness in

---

[76] Lefevre, 'Innocent III', p.245.

[77] *Ibid.*, p.244

[78] *Ibid.*, pp.244–45.

[79] *Ibid.*, p.244.

regard to the capture of Zara.[80] Lefevre has concluded that the author of the *Gesta* wished to present a clear but classified exposition of events. Through his use of papal documents he echoes curial thought and opinion. In a very real sense, therefore, his is a 'view from Rome'.[81]

More recent discussion of the *Gesta* by Pfaff and Imkamp has concentrated on specific issues such as the reported will of Henry VI, whether suppressed or forged, and the accuracy of the details of Innocent's early education and his training in theology. All this is valuable but adds little to our attempt to understand why the *Gesta* stops in 1208 or 1209 and why the biographer selected the themes he did.

One almost contemporary work which may help in this attempt is Boso's *Life of Alexander III* (1176).[82] This history of the Papal Schism of 1159–76 has a classic hero in the pope and an equally classic anti-hero in Frederick Barbarossa. The subject matter is rigorously selected with an eye to dramatic effect, for this is indeed a drama. There is a hero, a villain, a beginning and an end. Far more literary in form than the *Gesta*, it was intended to describe Alexander's formal repossession of Rome. It finished in 1176 before the pope's death not, as was once thought, because Boso himself had died but because the work's purpose had been accomplished.[83] The *Gesta* may have been the same: a work deliberately designed to carry a message about the celebrated achievements of a pope. There is no evident break or sharp change at any point in the narrative which might have been expected had the anonymous biographer died suddenly. The work proceeds to its conclusion calmly and purposefully, ending with a long balance sheet of the benefactions which had been achieved during the period.[84] This is a piece of justicative writing, a prose *geste* directed to a local audience in the Patrimony to show Innocent, a true Roman with roots in the Campania, surmounting tribulation, overcoming the machinations of villains, particularly that 'other Saladin' and at length taking possession of the lands, rights and subjects of the Patrimony of St. Peter. By 1208 it must have seemed both to Innocent and to his biographer that he was at last more or less secure in his homeland. Ten years of struggle had been carefully and honestly described and documented; reverses included as well as triumphs. In the

[80] *Gesta*, LXXXIII, cols. cxxxi–cxxxii; A.J. Andrea and I. Motsiff, 'Pope Innocent III and the Diversion of the Fourth Crusade Army to Zara', *Byzantinoslavica*, xxx (1972), 6–25, especially 8–15.

[81] Lefevre, 'Innocent III', p.245.

[82] *Boso's Life of Alexander III*, intro. P. Munz, trans. G.M. Ellis (Oxford, 1973), especially pp.1–39.

[83] *Ibid.*, pp.1–5.

[84] *Gesta*, CXLIX, cols. ccxxv–ccxxviii.

carefully structured thematic approach of our author persons and events of Roman and Campanian interest take first place against a background of events of wider significance in contemporary Christendom. The reshaping of the Patrimony demonstrated what its people owed to their bishop, the pope *Innocentius PP III*.

Chapter 7

An Unknown Thirteenth-Century Manuscript of Ianua

Robert Black

It has long been recognized that in later medieval Italy the fundamental text of elementary education was not Donatus's *Ars minor* but a manual spuriously attributed to Donatus which Sabbadini christened *Ianua* after the first word of its verse prologue.[1] Seventeen Italian manuscripts of the *Ianua* have been identified by Bursill-Hall, whose catalogue lists twenty-seven manuscripts in all;[2] Schmitt, the author of the fundamental study of *Ianua*, lists eight manuscripts, of which four are Italian.[3] However, there is a further Italian manuscript of *Ianua*. Biblioteca Laurenziana, MS Strozzi 80 is a school anthology, containing Cato's *Disticha*, Prosper of Aquitaine's *Epigrammata*, a set of *Regule grammaticales* by Thebaldus, and Aesop's fables in the translation by Walter the Englishman;[4] the first text in the collection is a treatise which has variously been described as 'Anon, *De octo partibus orationis* + prologue',[5] as 'Pseudo-Donatus, *De octo partibus*'[6] or *Donati prima grammaticae rudimenta, seu de octo partibus orationis*,[7] but nowhere is this text described as a version of *Ianua*.

Nevertheless, there can be no doubt that Laurenziano Strozzi 80 contains a full text of this work. It offers the following version of the characteristic eight-line verse prologue:

> Ianua sum rudibus primam cupientibus artem
> Nec sine me quisquam rite peritus erit.

---

[1] R. Sabbadini, *La scuola e gli studi di Guarino Guarini Veronese* (Catania, 1896), pp.35, 42–44; W. O. Schmitt, 'Die Ianua (Donatus) – ein Beitrag zur lateinischen Schulgrammatik des Mittelalters und der Renaissance', *Beiträge zur Inkunabelkunde*, ser. 3, iv (1969), 45, 73–74; E. Garin, *Il pensiero pedagogico dello umanesimo* (Florence, 1958), p.98; P. Grendler, *Schooling in Renaissance Italy: Literacy and Learning, 1300–1600* (Baltimore and London, 1989), pp.174–82.

[2] G. Bursill-Hall, *A Census of Medieval Latin Grammatical Manuscripts* (Stuttgart, 1981).

[3] Schmitt, 'Die Ianua', 50–51.

[4] The manuscript has been given a paleographic and codicological description by Paul Gehl, 'Latin Readers in Fourteenth-Century Florence: Schoolkids and their Books', *Scrittura e civiltà*, xiii (1989), 419–20.

[5] Bursill-Hall, *Census*, p.79.

[6] Gehl, 'Latin Readers', 420.

[7] A.M. Bandini, *Catalogus codicum manuscriptorum Bibliothecae Mediceae Laurentianae* (Florence, 1774–78), supplement, ii, col. 412.

Non [*sic* for nam] genus et casum speciem numerumque figuram
Hiis que flectuntur partibus insinuo
Pono modum reliquis quid competat optime pandens
Et quam non doceam dictio nulla manet
Ergo legas studiumque tibi rudis adiscete [*sic* for adisce] lector
Nam celeri studio discere multa poteris.[8]

As a schoolbook, the actual treatise itself appears with wide variations among manuscripts and early printed versions, schoolmasters freely adapting the text according to their own needs and preferences.[9] However, there is no question that all the works prefaced by the *Ianua* poem, including Laurenziano Strozzi 80, are versions of a common text.

Like other *Ianua* versions, Laurenziano Strozzi 80 is divided into eight sections, each of which treats a part of speech in catechistic form. The core of each section is made up of an analysis of a particular example of one of the parts of speech, beginning with the question, 'Poeta que pars est?' for the noun, and using *amo, legens, ego, ad, nunc, heu* and *et* as basic examples for the questions about the other parts of speech.[10] After identifying the various parts of speech, each section then proceeds to a definition, as for example, 'Quare est nomen? Quia significat substantiam [et] qualitatem propriam et comunem',[11] or, 'Quare est verbum? Quia cum modis et temporibus est significativum agendi vel patiendi.'[12] Next come questions and answers about accidence: 'Nomini quot accidunt? Quinque. Que? Species, genus, numerus, figura, casus. Cuius speciei? Primitive. Quare? Quia a nullo derivatur' etc.,[13] or, 'Participio quot accidunt? Sex. Que? Genus, casus, tempus, significatio, numerus et figura. Cuius generis? Omnis set in hoc loco masculin' etc.[14] Accidence – discussed through question, answer and example – is the only topic treated in the sections devoted to the four indeclinable parts of speech (preposition, adverb, interjection and conjunction),[15] but for the four declinable parts (noun, verb, participle and pronoun), the text also gives extensive paradigms, declensions and conjugations.[16]

Laurenziano Strozzi 80, therefore, provides a full text of *Ianua*, even concluding with the usual 'Explicit liber Donati',[17] and so it must be

---

[8] Biblioteca Laurenziana, Florence (henceforth BLF), Strozzi, 80, fo.1r.
[9] Schmitt, 'Die Ianua', 55–69.
[10] BLF, Strozzi, 80, fos.1r, 9v, 22v, 24r, 27v, 28v.
[11] *Ibid.*, fo.1r.
[12] *Ibid.*, fo.9v.
[13] *Ibid.*, fo.1r-v.
[14] *Ibid.*, fo.22v.
[15] *Ibid.*, fos.27v-29v.
[16] *Ibid.*, fo.1r-27r.
[17] *Ibid.*, fo.29r. Cf. Biblioteca Nazionale, Florence (henceforth BNF), Magliabecchiano, I, 45, fo.15v: Explicit liber Donati.

wondered why this text has not previously been identified. The answer is that Laurenziano Strozzi 80 has another five-verse prologue preceding the usual *Ianua sum rudibus*:

> Incipiunt partes per quas properamus ad artes,
> Has quisquis nescit, piger in levitate quiescit.
> Harum Donatus fuit auctor, in arte probatus,
> Quas tradens turbe, Romana scripsit in urbe,
> Monstrans dificile, pueri cito carpere callent.[18]

In his catalogue of the Biblioteca Laurenziana, Bandini gave only the first four of these verses, and he omitted entirely the *Ianua sum rudibus* prologue.[19] Moreover, the actual text of this version begins not immediately with 'Poeta que pars est?' but with the following general questions and definitions preceding the usual 'Poeta que pars est?':

Quot sunt partes orationis secundum gramaticos? VIII. Que? Nomen, verbum, participium, pronomen, prepositio, adverbium, interiectio et coniunctio. Et quia nomen est principalis pars orationis, ideo ab ipso incipiamus. Quid est nomen? Nomen est pars orationis declinabilis que unicuique subiectorum corporum seu rerum propriam vel communem qualitatem distribuit, communem quidem corporum ut homo, propriam ut Virgilius. Unde dicitur nomen? Nomen dicitur a noma greco vel a notamini, eo quod per ipsum notemus qualitatem uniuscuiusque substantie. Quid est proprium nominis? Proprium nominis est significare substantiam, qualitatem cum casu.[20]

The initial five-line verse prologue is unique to this text of *Ianua*, but this type of general discussion of the parts of speech is sometimes found in other *Ianua* versions. Each of the eight sections of Laurenziano Strozzi 80's *Ianua* opens with similar general questions and answers,[21] but in other versions of *Ianua*, if such general discussions and definitions are included, they are usually relegated to an appendix.[22] These definitions mainly derive from Priscian, whose definition of the noun and its 'property' was directly followed in Laurenziano Strozzi 80:

Nomen est pars orationis, quae unicuique subiectorum corporum seu rerum communem vel propriam qualitatem distribuit. Dicitur autem nomen vel a Graeco, quod est '$\nu\acute{o}\mu\alpha$' vel, ut alii, notamen quasi nomen, quod hoc notamus uniuscuiusque substantiae qualitatem. et communem quidem corporum qualitatem demonstrat, ut 'homo', propriam vero, ut 'Virgilius'. . . . Proprium est nominis substantiam et qualitatem significare.[23]

---

[18] BLF, Strozzi, 80, fo.1r.
[19] Bandini, *Catalogus*, Supplement, ii, col. 412.
[20] BLF, Strozzi, 80, fo.1r.
[21] *Ibid.*, fos.1r, 11r, 22v, 24r, 27r-v, 28v.
[22] Schmitt, 'Die Ianua', 67–69.
[23] Priscianus, *Institutiones grammaticarum*, ii, 22, 18.

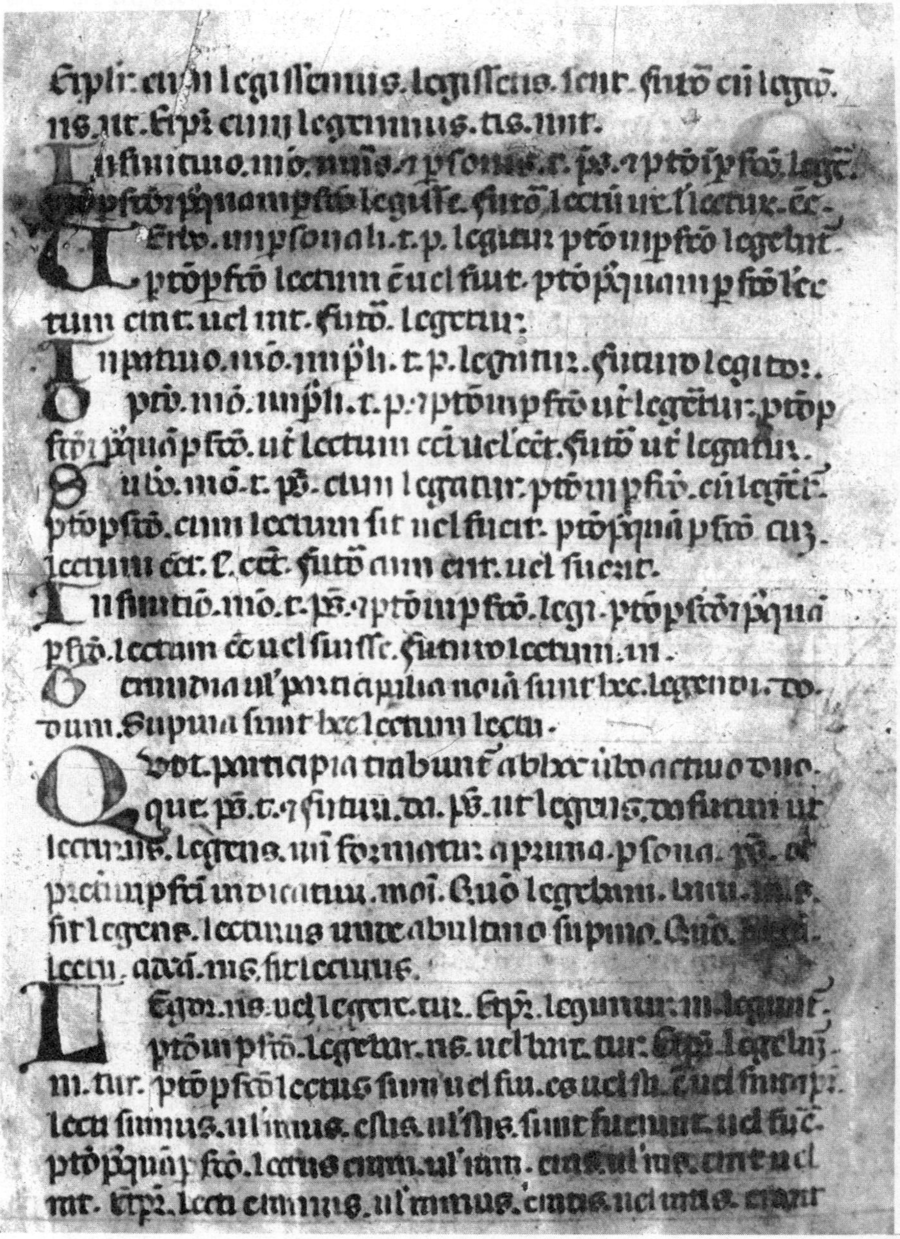

5 Florence, Biblioteca Laurenziana, Fondo Strozzi, MS 80, fos. 14v-15r

uel fuerint. futuro legar: leges. ul legerit. tur: Ex p̃i. le
gumur. legimini. tur:

Inperativo. mo. t. p̃s. ad sam. ꝛ tꝛiam p̃sonam legeꝛe
degatur. Ex p̃i legamur: mini. tur: futuro. legito. ꝼi. le
gitoꝛ ille. Ex p̃i. legamur. nor. tor.

Opto. mo. t. p̃s ꝓ p̃tum ipfec̃o. ut legar. reris. ul l̃ge
tur. Ex p̃i. ut legeremur. mini. tur: ꝓ p̃fec̃o ꝑquã ꝓ f̃co
ut lectus eẽm ul eẽ. eẽs. ul eẽs. eẽr. ul eẽr. ꝑi. ut le
ti. eẽmus. ul inus. eẽtis. ul eẽtis. eẽnt. ul eẽnt. futuꝛo.
ut legar: legaris. ul legar. tur: Ex p̃i. ut. legamur. ni. tur:

Sublo. mo. t. p̃s. cum legar. ris. ul legar. tur: Ex p̃i. c̃
legamur. ni. tur: ꝓ p̃m ipfec̃o. cum legerer. ris. ul legar
tur: Ex p̃i. cum legeremur. ni. tur: ꝓ p̃ pfec̃o cum lecʼ. sis.
ul inn. sis. ul fuerus. sit. ul eẽt. Ex p̃i. cum lectisimus. l̃
fuimus. sitis. ul fueritis. sint ul siunt. ꝓ ꝑquã pfec̃o ci
lectus eẽm. uel eẽm. eẽs. uel eẽs. eẽr. uel eẽr. Ex p̃i. cũ lecti
eẽmus. uel inus. eẽtis. uel eẽtis. eẽnt. ul eẽnt. fu. cũ ʼeʼ
cir. uel ro. ens uel eris. cir. uel rit. Ex p̃i cum loti eẽmus.
uel mus. eẽtis. uel tis. cint. uel nnt.

Infinitio. mo. numeris ꝛ p̃sonis. t. p̃s. ꝓ p̃tʼ ul p̃fec̃o. le
gi. ꝓ p̃fec̃o ꝓ ꝑus pfec̃o. lectu eẽ. uel eẽ. futuꝛo lectum. iri.

Qvot ꝑmo ap ꝓ ab hac ꝛ ab hoc ũlo passiuo. duo.
que. p̃til. t. ꝛ futuꝛu. ꝑ p̃titi. ut lectus. de futuꝛu
ut legedus. lectus in formatur a butritio supi̇o. qd.
lectum. ni. a doʼ. ꝛ sit lectus legedus. isn. aguʼ. fu. p̃s.
ꝑ ma p̃ꝛ. qd. leges. ris. ris. indus. sit legitꝛ bus.

Avdio. audis audit. audiam. audimus fit. audiʼtur
audi. audiat. audiat. audiuiste. audieris eꝛit
audiritur audiui. audiens ꝛ audiuitus.

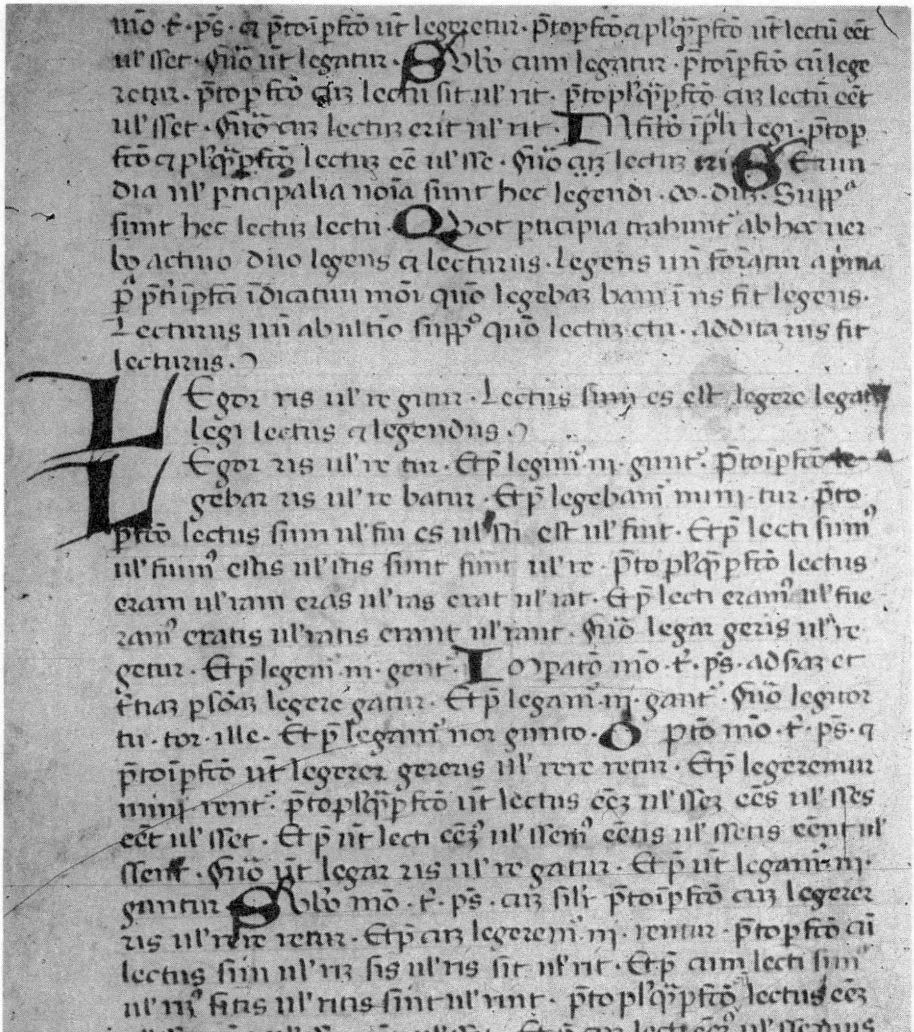

6 Florence, Biblioteca Nazionale, Fondo Magliabecchi, MS I, 45, fos. 6v-7r

eens ul' ssens ceut ul' ssent· ssio aut lectus eo ul' to eus ul'
ns eut ul' nt· Etp eum lecti euni' ul' rmi' eeus ul' rtus·
eeut ul' nut· In stio mo miis a psonis· t· ps· q pto
ipsto legi· proptsto q plussepsto lecti ee ul' sse· ssio lec
tus tu· Quot pnapia trahunt abhec uerbo passiuo duo
que lectus a legendus· Lectus uni soiat abultio suppt
quo lectus etu addita ·s· sit lectus· Legendus uni agto
sui puts· t· pnapij· quo legens legentis tis iudus sit
legendus·)

Audio is dit· Audiui sti iut· audi audiat· audne i
audiuisse· Audiendi· eo· diz· Auditur audiui· au
diens q auditurus·)

Audio is dit· Et p audiui' tis duit· ptoipsto audie
baz bas bat· Etp audiebam' tis bant· proptsto au
diui sti iut· Etp audiui' sus unt ul're· proptssep psto
audiueraz tus rif· Etp audiueram' tis runt· Quo au
diaz audies et· Etp audiem tis ent· Compato mo· t· ps·
ad saz q trtaz psonaz audi at· Etp audiam' dite ant· Quo
audito tu· to ille· Etp audiam' tote uinto· Q pto mo· t·
ps· q ptoipsto ut audnez res ter· Etp ut audnez reus
rent· proptsto q plssep psto ut audiuissez sses sset· Etp ut i
audiuissez tis ssent· Quo ut audiaz as diat· Etp ut audia
mus tis ant· Solo mo· t· ps· an silt· proptsto az
audnez res rif· Etp eum audnem rens rent· proptsto·
az audiuerit tis nt· Etp an audiueriz tis rmt· pto
plssep psto az audiuissez sses sset· Etp az audiuissem'
tis ssent· Quo az audiuero tis nt· Etp an audiueriz
tus rmt· In stio mo miis a psonis· t· ps· q pto
ipsto audne· proptsto q plssep psto audiuisse· Quo audiui
ue ul' auditur ee·)

Getto ipsonali· t· ps· audit· ptoipsto audiebatur·

Schmitt has shown that *Ianua* is mainly a reworking of material from Priscian into an elementary catechism, in the manner of Donatus's *Ars minor*;[24] Laurenziano Strozzi 80 contains additional material not apparently found in other *Ianua* versions and it is not surprising that some of this extra content consists of further extracts of Priscian:

Priscian, Institutiones	*Laurenziano Strozzi 80*
Secunda declinatio terminationes	Secunda declinatio . . . quot terminationes
habet nominativi sex: in 'er', in 'ir', in'ur', in 'us', in 'eus', in 'um'.[26]	habet? Sex. R. ir. ur. eus. us. um.[25]
Quarta declinatio terminationes habet in nominative duas, in 'us' cooreptam et. in 'u'.[27]	Quarta declinatio quot literas terminales habet? Habet duas, 's' et 'u', et duas terminationes, 'us' et 'u'.[28]
Quinta declinatio terminationem habet nominativi unam in 'es' productam, et sunt omnia feminini generis . . . in plurali vero semper masculini invenitur, 'hi dies', sicut etiam ab eo compositum semper masculini generis est, 'hic meridies'[29]	Quinta declinatio quot literas terminales habet? Unam scilicet s. Et quot terminationes habet? Unam, s . . . Omnia nomina quinte declinationus sunt femini generis . . . in singulari numero, in plurali vero est masculini generis tantum, et meridies eius compositum guod est masculini generis tantum.[30]

Indeed, Priscian is the only author explicitly cited in Laurenziano Strozzi 80 (and this seems to be the only attributed quotation in any version of *Ianua*):

Priscian	*Laurenziano Strozzi 80*
Tertia declinatio habet nominativi septuaginta octo vel paulo plus.[31]	. . . tertia declinatio . . . quot terminationes habet? Septuaginta octo vel paulo plus quas Priscianus bene numeravit.[32]

---

24 Schmitt, 'Die Ianua', 58–70.
25 Priscian, vii, 12
26 Fo.2v.
27 Priscian, vii, 87.
28 Fo.7v.
29 Priscian, vii, 92.
30 Fo.8v.
31 Priscian, vii, 29.
32 Fo.4r-v.

Other direct derivations from Priscian found only in this manuscript seem to be the statement that the noun is the principal part of speech,[33] the defining features of the declensions of nouns,[34] and figures in participles,[35] while some other passages not paralleled in other *Ianuae* seem to be more roughly derived from Priscian, such as the discussions of the gender of trees and fruits,[36] vocatives in pronouns[37] or the treatment of comparison.[38]

Excurses, such as the last three examples, are a typical feature of Laurenziano Strozzi 80, and at least one other version of Ianua has a similar excursus. This is the reconstructed Latin text which was used to make the Greek translation of *Ianua* in the early fifteenth century:

Reconstructed Latin Text	*Laurenziano Strozzi 80*
Omnis vocativus est similis suo nominativo apud Latinos ut pater, o pater, praeter quam in nominibus secundae declinationis desinentbus in us quae faciunt vocativum per mutationem us in e . . . praeter unum appellativum, quod facit . . .[39] vocativum in e quam in i ut filie vel fili.[40]	Omnia nominia cuiuscumque declinationis sint aut cuiusque generis hunc vocativum [faciunt] similem nominativo, hoc templum vocativum o templum, exceptis nominibus secunde declinationis que faciunt vocativum in e ut dominus vocativo domine . . . preter unum appellativum ut filius quod facit

This section on the vocative of *filius* closely recalls Priscian: 'excipitur unum, quod tam in e quam in i facit vocativum, quamvis sit appellativum, "o filie" et "o fili"',[41] but, more directly, seems to be a verbatim repetition of the wording of Petrus de Isolella of Cremona's mid thirteenth-century grammar:

Petrus	*Laurenziano Strozzi 80*
praeter unum appellativum, quod est filius, quod facit tam in e quam in i, ut filie vel fili.[42]	preter unum appellativum ut filius quod facit vocativum in e quam in i ut filie vel fili.[43]

Otherwise, the various excurses of Laurenziano Strozzi 80 (dealing with such topics as the declension of patronymics,[44] irregular dative and ab-

---

[33] BLF, Strozzi, 80, fo.1r (Priscian, xiv, 1).

[34] *Ibid.*, fos.2v, 3r, 4r (Priscian, vii, 10, 13, 45).

[35] *Ibid.*, fo.23v (Priscian, xi, 31).

[36] *Ibid.*, fo.3v (Priscian, v, 3).

[37] *Ibid.*, fo.27r (Priscian, xiii, *passim*).

[38] *Ibid.*, fo.7v (Priscian, iii, 6–11).

[39] Schmitt, 'Die Ianua', 59, note 142.

[40] Fo.3r.

[41] Priscian, vii, 22.

[42] Schmitt, 'Die Ianua', 59, note 142.

[43] Fo.3r.

[44] Fo.2v.

lative plurals of the first declension,[45] gender changes in singular and plural nouns,[46] nouns lacking singular or plural forms,[47] nouns lacking various cases,[48] nouns requiring special word order in construction with verbs,[49] peculiar features of some fourth and fifth declension nouns,[50] defective verbs,[51] species in participles[52]) do not seem to have derived directly from Priscian and appear to be without parallel in other *Ianua* manuscripts.

Laurenziano Strozzi 80 seems to have some features in common with particular *Ianua* manuscripts. One of these is MS Magliabecchiano I, 45.[53] In the questions about the *genera* of verbs, only these two versions have this additional sentence regarding active verbs: 'in prima vel in secunda persona vel saltem in secunda per assumptionem R',[54] and this answer about passives: 'Quia in "or" [desinens et format ab activo] per aditionem R.'[55] Only these manuscripts add the phrase 'circa actionem vel passionem'[56] to the end of the answer regarding the present tense of the verb, and the definitions of optative, subjunctive and infinitive modes,[57] of the derivative species,[58] of the composite figure,[59] and of the four verbal conjugations[60] show a unique resemblance. These two manuscripts alone preserve the catechistic form in the discussion of the first, second and fourth pronominal modes,[61] and all the four modes are defined with peculiar similarity in Laurenziano Strozzi 80 and Maglibecchiano I, 45,[62] which alone give paradigms of *unus* and *totus* for the second mode.[63] Particularly striking is the appearance in only these manuscripts of a summary of the conjugation of the exemplary verbs before the full paradigms: e.g. 'Amo amas amat. Amavi amavisti amavit. Ama et amare amavisse. Amandi [amando] amandum amatum. Amatum amatu. Amans et amaturus. Amor amaris [vel amare amatur]

---

45 Fo.2v.
46 Fo.3v-4r.
47 Fo.5r-v.
48 Fo.8v.
49 Fo.7v.
50 Fo.8r-v.
51 Fo.22r-v.
52 Fo.23v.
53 On this manuscript, see Schmitt, 'Die Ianua', 50–73, *passim*; Grendler, *Schooling*, p.179; Gehl, 'Latin readers', 420–21; Bursill-Hall, *Census*, p.82; Garin, *Pensiero pedagogico*, p.98.
54 BLF, Strozzi, 80, fo.9v; BNF, Magliabecchiano, I, 45, fo.3r.
55 BLF, Strozzi, 80, fo.9v; BNF, Magliabecchiano, I, 45, fo.3r.
56 BLF, Strozzi, 80, fo.10r; BNF, Magliabecchiano, I, 45, fo.3r.
57 BLF, Strozzi, 80, fo.10r; BNF, Magliabecchiano, I, 45, fo.3v.
58 BLF, Strozzi, 80, fo.10r; BNF, Magliabecchiano, I, 45, fo.3v.
59 BLF, Strozzi, 80, fo.10r; BNF, Magliabecchiano, I, 45, fo.3v.
60 BLF, Strozzi, 80, fo.10v; BNF, Magliabecchiano, I, 45, fo.3v.
61 BLF, Strozzi, fo.25r, 25v, 26v; BNF, Magliabecchiano, I, 45, fo. 12v, 13v.
62 BLF, Strozzi, 80, fo.25r-26v; BNF, Magliabecchiano, I, 45, fo. 12v-13v.
63 BLF, Strozzi, 80, fo.25v; BNF, Magliabecchiano, I, 45, fo. 12v-13r.

amatus sum es est. Amare. Ametur. Amari. Amatus et amandus'.[64] This pattern is repeated for most of the irregular verbs as well only in these two manuscripts. Another unique similarity is the addition of these rules for the formation of participles at the end of the active and passive conjugations of each of the paradigm verbs; e.g. 'Amans. Unde formatur? A prima persona [presentis et] preteriti [im]perfecti indicativi modi. Quomodo? Amabam. bam in ns fit amans. Amaturus. Unde? Ab ultimo suppino. Quomodo? Amatum, amatu addita rus fit amaturus'.[65]

But the manuscript with which Laurenziano Strozzi 80 has the most in common is Bibliothèque Nationale, Paris, MS 15972.[66] Like Laurenziano Strozzi 80, this manuscript apparently has definitions of the parts of speech and their 'property' interspersed throughout the text; e.g:

> Quid est nomen? Nomen est pars orationis declinabilis, que unicuique subjectorum corporum seu rerum communem vel propriam qualitatem distribuit: communem quidem corporum, ut *homo*; propriam, ut *Virgilius*; comunem quidem rerum, ut *scientia*; propriam, ut *Grammatica Aristarci*. – Unde dicitur nomen? – A *noto, notas*, quia per ipsum notatur substantia et qualitas; vel nomen dicitur a greco *noma*, et addita *o* fit *onoma*, dicto a tribuendo, grece enim *nemein* tribuere dicitur. Vel dicitur nomen quasi *notamen*. – Quid est proprium nominis? – Significare substantiam et qualitatem.[67]

Both manuscripts have many more exemplary paradigms that other texts, for example, in the third declension of nouns;[68] moreover, a catechism regarding how many *species, genera, numeri, figure* and *casus* of nouns appears only in these two texts.[69] Most striking, however, is the inclusion of mnemonic verses in each of these two versions. Thus, for example, in Paris 15972:

> Hec sunt pronomina que precedunt sua regimina que in istis versibus continentur:

> > *Quis, qualis* et *quantus*, talis, *quotus* quoque, *tantus*
> > Nu[nc] aliud nemo precedere verba videbo;
> > *Cujus, uter* cum *quot* sociatur, atque *quotennis*.[70]

---

[64] BLF, Strozzi, 80, fo.11r; BNF, Magliabecchiano, I, 45, fo.4r, 4v.
[65] BLF, Strozzi, 80, fo.12r; BNF, Magliabecchiano, I, 45, fo.4v.
[66] I have not yet been able to see this manuscript, but it has been extensively described by Ch. Fierville, *Une grammaire latine inédite du xiiie siecle* (Paris, 1886), pp.200–1, and by Schmitt, 'Die Ianua', 51–67, *passim*. See also Bursill-Hall, *Census*; p.202; L. Delisle, 'Inventaire des manuscrits latins de la Sorbonne', *Bibliothèque de l'école des chartes*, xxxi (1870), 32; Ch. Thurot, *Notices et extraits de divers manuscrits latins pour servir à l'histoire des doctrines grammaticales au moyen âge* (Paris, 1868), p.47; É. Pellegrin, *La bibliothèque des Visconti et des Sforza ducs de Milan au xve siècle* (Paris, 1955), p.382, note 2.
[67] Fierville, *Une grammaire*, pp.200–1.
[68] Schmitt, 'Die Ianua', 59; BLF, Strozzi, 80, fos.4r-7v.
[69] Schmitt, 'Die Ianua', 67, note 185; BLF, Strozzi, 80, fos.1v-2r.
[70] Fierville, *Une grammaire*, p.201.

Or:

Nota quod pronomina quedam sunt demonstrativa, quedam relativa, sicut in his versibus continentur:

> *Is, suus, ipse, sui* referunt, sed cetera monstrant;
> *Ille* sed officium servat utrumque sibi.[71]

In Laurenziano Strozzi 80, after the declension of *cepe*, the author writes, 'cuius versus:

> Guasape presepe non mutant cum cepe.[72]

Similarly for *nemo*:

Hoc nomen nemo componitur ex non et homo et caret vocativo, quia est negativum et non declinatur in plurali, quia est negativum substantivum. Unde versus:

> Fixa negativa nunquam pluralia summit.[73]

Or for *plus*:

Hoc nomen plus in nominativo et acusativo et vocativo singulari est generis neutri; in ceteris vero casibus est generis omnis. Unde versus:

> Cum per tres casus neutrum genus optineat plus,
> Casibus in reliquis optinet onne genus.[74]

To clarify the meaning of *ubera*, the author cites the verses:

> Uber abundat, habet lac, copie dicitur uber.
> Ubera sunt bovium, mamille sunt mulierum.[75]

To recall the neuter passive verbs, there are the verses:

> Quinque, puer, numero neutra passiva tibi do:
> Gaudeo cum fio soleo, simul audeo fido.[76]

[71] *Ibid.*

[72] BLF, Strozzi, 80, fo.3v.

[73] *Ibid.*, fo.5v.

[74] *Ibid.*, fo.6v.

[75] *Ibid.*, fo, 7r.

[76] *Ibid.*, fo.9v. This particular set of verses appears also in the *Catholicon* of Giovanni da Genoa (completed in 1286: see note 99 below): 'Et sunt quinque (verba neutropassiva) que continentur in his versibus:

> Quinque puer numero neutropassiva tibi do
> Gaudeo cum fio soleo simul audeo fido.'

However, it is impossible to know whether the *Catholicon* was quoting this version of *Ianua* or vice versa, or whether indeed both were drawing on a common source (possibly a version of Alexander of Villedieu's *Doctrinale*, which presents this variant of the lines:

> Audeo cum soleo, fio quoque, gaudeo, fido
> Quinque, puer, numero neutropassiva tibi do.)

See W. K. Percival, 'The Historical Sources of Guarino's *Regulae Grammaticales*: A Reconsideration of Sabbadini's Evidence', in *Civiltà dell'umanesimo*, ed. G. Tarugi (Florence, 1972), p.268.

or the verbs belonging to no conjugation:

> Quattuor hiis verbis est coniugatio nulla,
> Sum volo fero et edo, compositisque suis.[77]

It is perhaps not entirely surprising that Laurenziano Strozzi 80, Paris 15972 and Magliabecchiano I, 45 have such pronounced affinities, because they are probably the three oldest manuscripts of *Ianua*. All three have been variously dated to the thirteenth or thirteenth/fourteenth centuries,[78] but I myself would agree with Bursill-Hall and place Laurenziano Strozzi 80 in the thirteenth century, but Magliabecchiano I, 45 at the turn of the fourteenth:[79] the hand of Laurenziano Strozzi 80 is much more angular, with many fusions and compressions, whereas Magliabecchiano I, 45 seems to be more of a fourteenth-century gothic rotunda.[80] A precise *terminus post quem* for Laurenziano Strozzi 80 is 1199, the date of the completion of Alexander of Villedieu's *Doctrinale*,[81] five verses of which are cited in the text:

> Campester volucer alacerque saluber equester
> silvester celeber acerque celerque pedester
> Hiis nominibus quinque tenet hic et hec, is et hoc.[82]

> Bis duo sunt odi novi cepi et meminique
> Que retinet sensum presentis et preteritique.[83]

The early to mid thirteenth century is suggested by the parallels which this manuscript shows with the work of Pietro de Isolella of Cremona, active at this time,[84] and similarly the versification of the opening five-line prologue, with its rhymes within lines,[85] suggests the poetic style of this thirteenth-century preface to Everard of Bethune's *Graecismus*:

---

[77] BLF, Strozzi, 80, fo.10v. For other mnemonic verses in this manuscript, see *ibid.*, fos.2v, 3v-4r, 5r, 5v, 6r, 7r, 8r, 8v, 9v, 14r, 22r, 22v, 25v, 26r.

[78] Schmitt, 'Die Ianua', 50–51; Gehl, 'Latin Readers', 420. Schmitt cites the various datings of BNF, I, 45 and Paris 15972, but it should be noted that E.M. Sanford's eccentric dating of I, 45 to the eleventh century ('The Use of Classical Latin Authors in the *libri manuales*', *Transactions and Proceedings of the American Philological Association*, lv [1924], 218) is to be discarded because she did not actually inspect the manuscript.

[79] Bursill-Hall, *Census*, pp.79, 82.

[80] See plates 5 and 6.

[81] D. Reichling, *Das Doctrinale des Alexander de Villa-Dei* (Berlin, 1893), pp.xxxvi-vii.

[82] Vv. 583-85 (ed. Reichling, 41). Cf. BLF, Strozzi, 80, fo.7r.

[83] Vv. 983–84 (ed. Reichling, 65). Cf. BLF, Strozzi, 80, fo.22r.

[84] Schmitt, 'Die Ianua', 59, note 142. See W.K. Percival, 'The Place of the *Rudimenta grammatices* in the History of Latin Grammar', *Respublica litterarum*, iv (1981), 235; R.W. Hunt, 'Hugutio and Petrus Helias', *Medieval and Renaissance Studies*, ii (1950), 177, note 3; F. Novati, *La giovinezza di Coluccio Salutati* (Turin, 1888), p.72, note 3.

[85] See above, p. 103.

Hoc excusetur, quod materiale tenetur,
Si quid longatur contra metra vel breviatur.
Intima scruteris, vocum sensus imiteris.
Utilis est brevitas mentes factura peritas.[86]

Moreover, Laurenziano Strozzi 80 has two long excurses devoted to gerunds and supines;[87] these had never been treated as distinctive grammatical units before Petrus Helias's work in the mid twelfth century,[88] and they became a preoccupation of important thirteenth-century grammarians, including Bene da Firenze[89] and the anonymous author of the gloss *Admirantes* on the *Doctrinale*.[90]

What is noteworthy about the chronology of *Ianua* manuscripts is that the two earliest versions of the text – Laurenziano Strozzi 80 and Paris 15972 – are much fuller grammatical treatises on the parts of speech than the jejune summaries typical of the fourteenth- and fifteenth-century versions. The process of condensing and abbreviating is clear even in comparisons with Magliabecchiano I, 45, which contains many longer explanatory passages found in Laurenziano Strozzi 80 but omitted in later versions.[91] A particularly striking example of the kind of compression which this text underwent is the catechism on the *genera* of participles:

Laurenziano Strozzi 80	*Magliabecchiano I, 45*
Cuius generis? Omnis set in hoc loco masculini. Quare? Quia sic est illud cui adheret. Quod est illud? Virgilius. Cuius generis? Omnis set in hoc loco feminini. Quare? Quia sic est illud cui adheret. Quod est illud? Berta. Cuius generis? Omnis set in hoc loco neutri. Quare? Quia sic est illud cui adheret. Quod est illud? Scamnum.[93]	Cuius generis? Omnis sed in hoc loco masculini feminini vel neutri. Quare? Quia sic est illud cui adheret. Quod est illud? homo mulier vel mancipium.[92]

Indeed, the later abbreviators of *Ianua* occasionally lost the sense of the text in their desire to condense; for example, the opening of the section on pronouns in fourteenth- and fifteenth-century manuscripts reads:

Ego que pars est? Pronomen est. Quare est pronomen? Quia ponitur in loco proprii nominis et certam significat personam. Pronomini quot accidunt? Sex. Que? Species

---

86 Thurot, *Notices et extraits*, p.27.
87 BLF, Strozzi, 80, fos.8v-9v.
88 Thurot, *Notices et extraits*, pp.376 ff; Schmitt, 'Die Ianua', 72.
89 C. Marchesi, 'Due grammatici latini del medio evo', *Bullettino della società filologica romana*, xii (1910), 25.
90 Thurot, *Notices et extraits*, pp.376 ff.
91 See above pp. 106–7.
92 Fo.23r.
93 Fo.11v.

genus numerus figura persona et casus. Cuius speciei? Primitive. Quare? Quia a nullo derivatur. Cuius speciei? Derivative. Unde derivatur? A [genitivo sui primitivi] mei.[94]

This text does not make sense, because *ego* does not derive from its own genitive. What has actually happened is that the abbreviator has omitted the form *meus* to which the question about derivative *species* refers and which then begins an entire catechism on derivative pronouns; this is omitted in later *Ianue* but given in full in Laurenziano Strozzi 80:

Meus cuius speciei? Derivative. Unde derivatur? A genitivo sui primitivi mei.
Noster cuius speciei? Derivative. Unde derivatur? A genitivo nostrum vel nostri.
Tuus cuius speciei? Derivative. Unde derivatur? A genitivo sui primitivi tui.
Suus cuius speciei? Derivative. Unde derivatur? A genitivo sui primitivi sui.
Vester cuius speciei? Derivative. Unde derivatur? A genitivo vestrum vel vestri.[95]

This shortening of the text of *Ianua* after the thirteenth century may suggest a changing function of the work in the classroom. It is usually acknowledged that grammar had languished in Italy during the earlier middle ages and especially in the twelfth century,[96] but the thirteenth century saw the first great flowering of Italian grammatical studies, initiated by the *Magnae derivationes* of Hugutio of Pisa.[97] Noteworthy participants in this renaissance of Italian grammar were Bene da Firenze and Pietro da Isolella, mentioned above,[98] and the century's work culminated in 1286 with the completion of Giovanni da Genoa's *Catholicon*,[99] which became a standard grammatical reference work over the next two centuries.[100] This was also a period in which many copies were made in Italy of Alexander's *Doctrinale* and Everard's *Graecismus*.[101] In this educational climate, a fulsome text of *Ianua*, such as is provided by Laurenziano Strozzi 80, could have served the aims of ambitious grammar masters anxious to furnish a broad foundation in their subject.

However, by the fourteenth century the text had been abbreviated, and only condensed versions appear among later manuscript copies and

[94] E.g. BLF, Palatino, 63, fo.17v; cf. Schmitt, 'Die Ianua', 78.

[95] BLF, Strozzi, 80, fo.24r-v.

[96] See G. Manacorda, *Storia della scuola in Italia: il medioevo*, (Milan, Palermo and Naples, 1914), ii, pp.218ff., 231ff.; Hunt, 'Hugutio and Petrus Helias', 176–78; Percival, 'The Place', 234–35. On the grammatical sections of *Papias*, an encyclopedic dictionary of the mid eleventh century, *see ibid.*, pp.248ff.; Percival, 'The Place', 234 and note 4; Garin, *Pensiero pedagogico*, p.98; Grendler, *Schooling*, p.113.

[97] Manacorda, *Storia*, ii, 251ff.; Percival, 'The Place', 234 and note 5; A. Marigo, *I codici manoscritti delle 'Derivationes' di Uggucione Pisano: saggio d'inventario bibliografico con appendice sui codice del 'Catholicon' di Giovanni da Genova* (Rome, 1936); Garin, *Pensiero pedagogico*, pp.98–99.

[98] See above, p. 110.

[99] Manacorda, *Storia*, ii, pp.236 ff.; Percival, 'The Place', 234–35; Garin, *Pensiero pedagogico*, p.99; Marigo, *I codici*.

[100] Manacorda, *Storia*, ii, pp.236 ff.; Marigo, *I codici*.

[101] Reichling, *Das Doctrinale*, pp.cxxi ff.; Manacorda, *Storia*, ii, pp.228 ff., 231 ff.

early printed editions.[102] This new appearance for the text coincides with new educational aims and a new class of teachers. These were specialist elementary masters, or *doctores puerorum*, who have been noted as early as 1277 in Florence and were numerous there by the turn of the fourteenth century.[103] Their aims were not to teach grammar but rather elementary reading and writing, as is clear from the contract which Lippo Casini of the Florentine parish of San Lorenzo signed in 1304 with 'd. Clementia doctrix puerorum' of the parish of Santa Maria Maggiore, who, for the fee of 40 *soldi*, 'promisit . . . eidem . . . tenere, docere et instruere Andream, fratrem ipsius . . ., legere et scribere, ita quod convenienter sciat legere Psalterium, Donatum et instrumenta, et scribere, sine aliquo alio pretio'.[104] Such practical educational aims did not require the grammatical excurses, mnenomic verses, prolonged definitions and numerous paradigms of Laurenziano Strozzi 80, but rather the streamlined format of a text such as Magliabecchiano I, 45. It is hardly surprising that the abbreviated *Ianua* became the standard version of 'Donatus' used in elementary education in Florence and throughout Italy in the fourteenth and fifteenth centuries.

With the appearance of the *doctores puerorum* at the turn of the fourteenth century, a marked distinction had arisen between Italian elementary and secondary education; this new specialisation is evident in the many outlines of school curricula which first began to appear in the fourteenth century. Such syllabuses were laid out by the communes usually because teachers were allowed to charge higher fees to more advanced pupils. In an Aretine example from 1440 the fees were: 'a scolaribus nondum legentibus Donatum usque ad soldos quadraginta . . . pro anno quolibet; a scolaribus vero legentibus Donatum nondum lactinantibus usque ad libras tres pro anno; a lactinantibus vero et auctores audientibus usque ad florenum unum pro anno quolibet'. Thus there were three levels of teaching: the most elementary class was for pupils not yet reading Donatus; the second was for pupils actually reading Donatus; the third and most advanced was for the study of Latin language ('lactinare') and literature ('auctores').[105] This kind of division was typical throughout fourteenth- and fifteenth-century Italy,[106] and it holds true for private

[102] Schmitt, 'Die Ianua', 44–80, *passim*.

[103] S. Debenedetti, 'Sui più antichi "doctores puerorum" a Firenze', *Studi medievali*, ii (1906–7), 327–351.

[104] *Ibid.*, 333.

[105] Archivio di Stato, Arezzo, Deliberazioni del magistrato dei Priori e del Consiglio Generale, (henceforth ASA, Provv.) 7, fos.33v-34r (8 March 1439 ab inc.).

[106] Manacorda, *Storia*, i, pp.180–83; F. Gabotto, *Lo stato sabaudo*, iii (Turin, 1895), pp.274–76; V. Rossi, *Dal rinascimento al risorgimento* (Florence, 1930), pp.14–15; M. Battistini, *Il pubblico insegnamento in Volterra* (Volterra, 1919), pp.49–50; A. Zanelli, *Del pubblico insegnamento in Pistoia* (Rome, 1900), pp.35–38; P. Barsanti, *Il pubblico insegnamento in Lucca* (Lucca, 1905), pp.115, 120 are a few examples.

tutors as well as public elementary and grammar schools.[107] There was usually a clear division between elementary and grammar or Latin education, towns often employing one type of teacher for reading and writing and a real grammarian for Latin.[108] The *doctores puerorum* of the fourteenth century became the *maestri di leggere e scrivere* or *maestri di fanciulli* of the fifteenth:[109] men (or very occasionally women) of little education, drawn from the artisan class,[110] who seem to have known little or no Latin. As distinct from grammar teachers, who almost always corresponded in Latin, these elementary teachers usually wrote their letters and submitted their petitions in the vernacular.[111] Their tax returns were written in mercantile script,[112] in contrast to grammar teachers, who tended to write in notarial or later in the fifteenth century sometimes in humanist italic script.[113] These elementary teachers usually took boys from their ABCs through their primers and finished with Donatus.[114]

[107] Bernardo Machiavelli, *Libro di Rocordi*, ed. C. Olschki (Florence, 1954), pp.31, 45, 103, 183.

[108] ASA Provv. 12, fo.119r (22 May 1471) and 13, fo.122r (10 April 1482); Archivio di stato, Prato, Comune, Diurnali (henceforth ASPCD), 82, fo.27r (7 January 1408 ab inc.); ASSColle, 101, fo.xli verso (25 March 1359) and 105, fo.xlii verso (18 September 1365); Archivio Comunale, Sangimignano, NN (henceforth ACSGNN), 71, fo.lxxvi recto (17 June 1359); Zanelli, *Pistoia*, p.38, note 2; Rossi, *Dal rinascimento*, p.13.

[109] ASF, Catasto, 15, fo.901r; 17, fo.341r; 20, fo.1103r; 28, fo.148v; 45, fo.691r; 51, fo.64r.

[110] ASF, Catasto, 17, fo.341r; 45, fo.691r.

[111] ASAProvv. 12, fo.119r (22 May 1471); ASPCD, 82, fo.27r (7 January 1408 ab inc.); 83, fos.38v-39r (12 February 1410 ab inc.); 84, fos.52v-53r (27 January 1412 ab inc.).

[112] ASF, Catasto, 15, fo.901r; 17, fo.341r; 20, fo.103r; 37, fo.1189v; 45, fo.691r. An exception is Maestro Piero di Lorenzo Malamma, who 'insegnia a fanciulli legiere' and who wrote in a formal gothic hand: ASF, Catasto, 51, fo.64r.

[113] ASF, Catasto, 224, fos.60r-62r (Portata of Maestro Giovanni d'Ubertino da Asti, grammar teacher in Pistoia); 225, fo.617r (Portata of Ser Federigo di Giovanni, schoolmaster in Castelfiorentino); 213, fo.547r-v (Portata of Ser Guido d'Antonio da Isola Maggiore, near Perugia, grammar teacher in Cortona); 203, fo.323r-v (Portata of Maestro Francesco di ser Feo di Nigi da Arezzo, grammar teacher there). For a selection of autograph letters by fifteenth-century grammar masters, see ASF, Mediceo avanti del principato, V, 270 (Girolamo di Marco, grammar teacher in San Miniato, before 1434); V, 10, 551, 554, VI, 305, 337, VII, 57, VIII, 160, 380, IX, 117 (Giovanni di Niccolò Peregrini da Volterra, grammar teacher in Poggibonsi, Livorno, Colle di Valdelsa, Grosseto and Massa, 1444–1459); XCIII, 148 (Jacopo da Pistoia, grammar teacher in Prato, 1471); XXII, 484 (Cantalicio, grammar teacher in San Gimignano, 1472).

[114] ASPCD, 82, fo.27r (a *maestro di fanciulli* in Prato who taught boys to 'legere la tavola, il saltero e il donadello'; for the *tavola* and *saltero*, see Grendler, *Schooling*, pp.142–56). Except for Florence, in Tuscan curriculum outlines reference is usually made to Donato or Donatus, but there are a few occasions where *donatello* or *donadello* is substituted, suggesting that these terms meant Donatus. See the above Pratese text and the statutes of Bucine of 1411: 'insegnatore di fanciulli in gramaticha o in el saltero o donadello': C. Mazzi, 'Cartiere, tipografie e maestri in Valdelsa', *Miscellanea storica della Valdelsa*, iv (1896), 186.

The 'Donatus' of Laurenziano Strozzi 80, with its extensive paradigms, examples, mnemonics, rules and excurses, was obviously a text to form the basis of an active knowledge of Latin, but the condensed *Ianua* of the fourteenth and fifteenth centuries was used, not primarily as a manual for learning the rudiments of Latin grammar but rather as a reading text. This is suggested, in the first place, by the format of early printed versions which, as Grendler observes, 'often ran lines on for more than a page without paragraphing, and . . . made no attempt to set off declension and conjugation paradigms' whereas in the early runs of Guarino's *Regulae*, 'the layout included more paragraphing and the partial paradigms of the four principal parts of the verb'.[115] The inference (not actually drawn by Grendler) is that these differing formats may have represented different use of these books in the classroom. Further evidence that *Ianua* had become more a reading text than a grammar manual, is provided by appointment documents, for it is clear that the specialist teachers of this text were elementary reading masters.[116] Donatus was no longer part of the grammar syllabus: distinctions were drawn between schooling in 'grammaticalibus' on the one hand and 'lettura seu doctrina donati' on the other,[117] and Donatus was distinguished even from 'primum latinum'.[118] Donatus was read, Latin was done: 'Facientes latinum, legentes Donatum',[119] 'lactinare', 'legere Donatum',[120] 'legentes Donatellum', 'lactinantes in latino.'[121] This vocabulary is making a point: *Ianua* was being used not as a manual to learn Latin but as a reading text.

How *Ianua* was actually taught to boys who did not yet know Latin is suggested by the distinction frequently made between two stages of reading this text: 'Donato per lo testo et per lo senno'.[122] 'Per lo testo' is sometimes

---

[115] P. Grendler, 'The Teaching of Latin in Sixteenth-Century Venetian Schools', in *Acta conventus neo-latini bononensis. Proceedings of the Fourth International Congress of Neo-Latin Studies*, ed. R.J. Schoeck (Binghamton, 1985), p.262.

[116] ACSGNN, 71, fos.lxxviiii verso – lxxx recto (18 June 1359); Barsanti, *Lucca*, p.120; Zanelli, *Pistoia*, pp.138–39.

[117] 'tam in gramaticalibus quam in lettura seu doctrina donati, libricioli, carte et alii pertinentis ad dictum ministerium seu artem': Archivio di Stato, Siena, Colle di Valdesa (henceforth ASSColle), 110, fo.2v (March, 1368).

[118] Gabotto, *Stato sabaudo*, pp.335–36.

[119] ASSColle, 94, fo.lviii verso – lviiii recto (5 August 1352); fo.lxvi recto (23 August 1352); 100, fo.ci recto (6 November 1357); 107, fos.lxxxxii verso – lxxxxiii recto (31 March 1367). ACSGNN, 78, fo.cxiii verso (5 April 1372).

[120] ASSColle, 121, fo.lxiiii recto (29 January 1380 ab inc.). Archivio di Stato, Pistoia, Consigli, Provvisioni, 22, fos.55v-56r (4 June 1389); ACSGNN, 107, fos.44r-45v (23 February 1406 ab inc.), 150v-51v (21 October 1407); see L. Pecori, *Storia della terra di San Gimignano*, [Florence, 1853], p.618; 109, fos.27v-28v (8 March 1408 ab inc.); 111, fos.161r-162r (1 December 1412); 115, fos.14r-15r (14 October 1417).

[121] Battistini, *Volterra*, pp.34–35.

[122] Zanelli, *Pistoia*, p.139.

rendered 'a veduta',[123] 'testualiter',[124] 'cum textu' or 'syllabicando',[125] whereas 'per lo senno' is often translated 'cum sensu'[126] or 'sensualiter'.[127] 'Per lo testo' means 'syllibicare' or 'compitare',[128] that is, sounding out, whereas 'cum sensu' 'sensualiter' or 'per lo senno' signifies with meaning. At first the *doctores puerorum* or *maestri di fanciulli* had their pupils simply read the works of *Ianua* without meaning; if their pupils went on to the next stage, 'per lo senno', these humble, ill-educated *maestri* might arm themselves with a vernacular translation of *Ianua* (significantly called *Donato al senno* or 'Donatus with meaning') and when this version was printed it appeared as an interlinear or interverbal translation.[129] This means that pupils at this elementary level read Latin without comprehension, then with the teacher's translation. Pupils were not yet learning the language for themselves; hence the distinction made just after this level between *non lactinantes* and *lactinantes*: this now represented the fundamental division between elementary and grammar education. In this new world of 'Donato per lo testo et per lo senno' the generous text of Laurenziano Strozzi 80 was an anachronism, and the changing format of *Ianua* illustrates some of the great changes which were taking place in Italian education around the turn of the fourteenth century.

---

[123] Ch. Klapisch-Zuber, 'Le chiavi fiorentine di barbablù: l'apprendimento della lettura a Firenze nel XV secolo', *Quaderni storici*, lvii (1984), 767.

[124] ASSColle, 121, fo.lxiiii recto (29 January 1380 ab inc.).

[125] Piero Lucchi, 'La santacroce, il salterio e il babuino: libri per imparare a leggere nel primo secolo della stampa', *Quaderni storici*, xxxviii (1978), 601.

[126] *Ibid.*; L. Colini-Baldeschi, 'L'insegnamento pubblico a Macerata nel trecento e quattrocento', *Rivista delle biblioteche e degli archivi*, xi (1900), 23.

[127] ASSColle, 121, fo.lxiiii recto (29 January 1380 ab inc.).

[128] For 'sillabicare' in St. Bonaventura's scheme of learning to read, see Manacorda, *Storia*, ii, p.172; see also Lucchi, 'La santacroce', 601. For 'compito' and 'compitare', *ibid.*, 600; Klapisch, 'Le chiavi', 767.

[129] Grendler, *Schooling*, pp.184 ff. He mistranslates *Donato al senno* as 'Donatus to wisdom': *ibid.*, p.184

Chapter 8

Personal Seals in Thirteenth-Century England

P.D.A. Harvey

English medieval seals are a virtually untapped source of historical information. For centuries seals have been collected, they are often used to illustrate books on medieval history, and particular seals have been discussed in a limited, antiquarian context: successive seals of a magnate, a monastery or a borough. But systematic study of their design, their manufacture, their use, their significance, has largely been confined to the royal Great Seal and its surrogates in various courts and departments. For most other sorts of seal we have not even the most elementary typology, the simplest chronological outline of their development.[1] Given that seals have been the subject of continuous antiquarian interest for at least 350 years it is amazing that we have had to wait until the 1980s for answers to the basic questions on the form and use of the earliest English seals recently discussed by Dr. T.A. Heslop.[2]

But if English medieval seals in general are a little-explored and under-exploited area, personal seals of the non-armigerous classes – or, indeed, any personal seals without coats of arms – are all but virgin territory. Guides to it are lacking. W. de G. Birch's catalogue of seal impressions in the British Museum (now British Library) is by far the largest catalogue of seals to have been published in Britain and is the primary work of reference on the subject.[3] It lists nearly 15,000 English and Welsh seals under headings which include only three sorts of personal seals of laymen other than rulers: 'Equestrian seals', 'Figures

---

[1] Two valuable works do, however, look at these questions and draw attention to their interest and significance: H. Jenkinson, *Guide to Seals in the Public Record Office* (London, 1954), especially pp.4–9, 56–62, and M.T. Clanchy, *From Memory to Written Record: England 1066–1307* (London, 1979), especially pp.35–36, 244–48.

[2] T.A. Heslop, 'English Seals from the Mid Ninth Century to 1100', *Journal of the British Archaeological Association*, cxxxiii (1980), 1-16, pls. I-III; *idem*, 'Seals as Evidence for Metalworking in England in the Later Twelfth Century', in *Art and Patronage in the English Romanesque*, ed. S. Macready and F.H. Thomson (Society of Antiquaries of London, 1986), pp.50–60.

[3] W. de G. Birch, *Catalogue of Seals in the Department of Manuscripts in the British Museum* (London, 1887–1900).

of noble and other ladies' and 'Heraldic seals'. As he continues with a further 8,500 entries of Scottish, Irish and foreign seals, Birch can hardly be blamed for excluding the vastly larger number of English and Welsh personal seals that fell outside these categories. However, this limitation is reflected in the only two general books on seals written in English: each has just one chapter, one of the shortest in the book, on the seals of non-armigerous laymen. In J.H. Bloom's work, in 1906, it is called 'Seals of Private Gentlemen and of Merchants' and in Birch's own book, published the following year, 'Miscellaneous Designs and Devices of English Seals'.[4] As Mr. R.H. Ellis pointed out in 1978, in introducing his catalogue of seals in the Public Record Office, 'sigillography . . . cannot be fully or systematically studied until our record repositories have compiled, and made accessible, catalogues of all the seals . . . which they hold'.[5] Knowing what seals there are is an essential first step; and Mr. Ellis's own work has contributed significantly to it. The first two volumes of his catalogue cover the personal seals on the Ancient Deeds 'S series', those documents selected and set aside from the main classes of Ancient Deeds for the fineness of their seals. In contrast to Birch's catalogue, every kind of personal seal is represented, though as the criteria of selection for the 'S series' included fineness of design and of engraving as well as of condition there is still a disproportionate number of the seals of the armigerous classes.

Among the seals catalogued are those on the 331 'S series' Ancient Deeds in the records of the Duchy of Lancaster (Public Record Office class D27). The observations that follow on thirteenth-century personal seals derive primarily from work, in continuation of Mr. Ellis's, cataloguing the seals in the other series of Duchy of Lancaster Ancient Deeds (classes D25, D26); these comprise 3,757 documents on which there survive impressions of nearly 2,500 different personal seals. The majority date from the thirteenth and fourteenth centuries and they are probably a reasonably typical sample of the many thousands of English medieval seals that survive.[6] Their geographical spread is good: the documents concern transactions in most parts of England and the Welsh Marches, but Essex, north Lancashire and north-east Lincolnshire are particularly well represented. Sixteen per cent of the seals are heraldic, and a further two per cent are equestrian or bear figures of ladies; the remaining

    [4] J.H. Bloom, *English Seals* (London, 1906), pp.177–85; W. de G. Birch, *Seals* (London, 1907), pp.189–93.
    [5] R.H. Ellis, *Catalogue of Seals in the Public Record Office: Personal Seals* (London, 1978–81), i, vii.
    [6] The primary listing of the seals on P.R.O., DL25/1–640 was by Mr. R.H. Ellis and I am grateful for his permission to draw on this work; I accept full responsibility, however, for all descriptive references made here to these documents and their seals.

a   b

c   d

7a   Privy seal of Robert de Breteuil, Earl of Leicester, 1191-1204.

       A large (30mm diameter) armorial privy seal, with owner's name in the legend, used here as a counterseal (*P.R.O., E42/266*)

7b   Privy seal of William Percy, *c.* 1200

       A gem with legend, 'Sigill' secreti', not naming the owner, used here as a counterseal (*P.R.O., DL27/83*)

7c   Privy seal of William de Ashford, early thirteenth century

       A gem with legend, 'Cela segreti Will'i', used here as a counterseal (*P.R.O., E212/68*)

7d   Seal used by William de Micheldever, 1252

       An early example of an anonymous seal, inscribed like a privy seal 'Sigillvm secreti' but used by itself to authenticate a formal document (*P.R.O., DL25/2066*)

8a   Seal used by Alan le Charman, 1296-1301

       An anonymous seal showing a dog and a hare gaming, with the motto 'Hasard in hod is min' (*P.R.O., DL25/1684*)

8b-d   Three seals of William son of Osbert le French, mid thirteenth century

       Each seal has a different design: a fleur-de-lis, a five-petalled flower and a five-rayed star (*P.R.O., DL25/2670, 2807, 2864*)

9 Seals of four heirs of Robert le Frere, 1280

All four seals were probably made by a single engraver for this transaction;
note, for instance, reversed S and the E with straight upright and converging
bars (*P.R.O., DL25/2050*)

10 Seals of four tenants at Westfen, Lincolnshire, between 1217 and 1232

A further example of seals probably engraved as a set for a particular transaction; here note the angular S (almost a reversed Z) and the distinctive form of G (*P.R.O., DL25/2423*)

eighty-two per cent are types of seal that were excluded from Birch's catalogue, the seals confined to one small chapter in his and in Bloom's monographs. The potential interest of these seals is considerable. They probably have much to tell us about the craftsmen who made the dies as well as about the men and women who owned and used them. In 1953 Professor R.H. Hilton discussed the significance of a group of peasant seals from thirteenth-century Gloucestershire, but then – and still now – there was no way of seeing them in their sigillographic context.[7] What is offered here is no more than a first scratching of the surface: certain points that leap to the eye in working through all the seals in this group. If it is as good a sample as it seems, these points will be generally valid, but they will need testing against other substantial collections of original thirteenth-century deeds. At best they can be no more than a starting-point for the detailed investigation that is needed of every aspect of the manufacture and use of personal seals in medieval England.

'It was not the custom in the past', said the king's chief justiciar, 'for every little knight to have a seal.' He was speaking perhaps in the 1160s.[8] By the end of the twelfth century the use of seals had spread far beyond the humblest knights, beyond the ranks even of those whom J.H. Bloom called 'Private Gentlemen'. The land market might involve anyone who held land that could be sold and, though the detailed chronology has still to be elucidated, it was commonplace for transfers at least to religious houses and other important landholders to be confirmed with written charters. Being a party to a charter meant owning a seal. It was practically unknown in the early thirteenth century for a grantor, having no seal of his own, to use someone else's or, like one late twelfth-century grantor in Nottinghamshire, to impress the wax with his wife's key instead.[9] Almost certainly the number of people owning seals increased in the first half of the thirteenth century as it became more and more usual for all transfers of free land, as well as many other transactions, to be confirmed by written charters. It is less certain that seal ownership descended any further down the social scale, for it may effectively have had no further to go: those who had seals in 1200 may already have included villeins as well as townsmen and the smallest freeholders. In fact we seldom learn the legal or economic status of those who sealed documents. It is most unusual for a charter to identify as a villein – or as a free man – the man who sealed it, as one Gloucestershire lease

---

[7] R.H. Hilton, *The English Peasantry in the Later Middle Ages* (Oxford, 1975), pp.153–55 (reprinting 'Gloucester Abbey Leases of the Late Thirteenth Century', *University of Birmingham Historical Journal*, iv [1953], 1–17).

[8] *The Chronicle of Battle Abbey*, ed. E. Searle (Oxford, 1980), pp.214–15.

[9] *Documents Illustrative of the Social and Economic History of the Danelaw*, ed. F.M. Stenton (British Academy, 1920), p.275.

did in 1274.[10] And in our present state of knowledge we cannot begin to correlate particular sorts of seal with the standing of their owners beyond what is self-evident: that only the armigerous had heraldic seals and only the well-to-do had elaborate, finely-engraved ones.

One change that occurred in the thirteenth century is very clear: in 1200 a personal seal almost always named its owner, in 1300 it did not necessarily do so. At some date between 1217 and 1232 the grant to Ranulf, earl of Chester and Lincoln, of 500 acres of marshland at Freiston and Butterwick, Lincolnshire, was confirmed in a document bearing seals of fifty of the local tenants; most survive intact and every one of these bears the same name as is written on the tag to which it is attached.[11] In 1274, on the other hand, an indenture leasing two mills at Langham, Essex, was sealed not only by the two lessees but also by their twelve sureties; of the eight seals that survive only two bear the owner's name.[12] There may have been some regional variation in this: of the fifty-seven seals of men from Roos and Reqaynok cantreds in Denbighshire that were once attached to an agreement of 1295 only seventeen survive and are in poor condition, but most, perhaps all, of these bear the name of the signatory.[13] However, the broad trend appears clearly in comparing the thirteenth-century personal seals in classes DL25 and DL26 with those of the fourteenth century:[14]

	1201–1300	1301–1400
	Per cent	Per cent
Equestrian	2	0
Figures of ladies	1	0
Heraldic	9	32
Others with names	80	25
Anonymous	8	42

In the early thirteenth century we very occasionally find armorial seals that instead of the owner's full name have the surname alone or the family motto.[15] They may be seen as precursors of the anonymous

[10] Hilton, *English Peasantry*, p.154.

[11] P.R.O., DL27/270, illustrated in Jenkinson, *Guide to Seals*, pl. II.

[12] P.R.O., DL25/1512.

[13] P.R.O., DL25/2064.

[14] Seals on undated documents with estimated date encroaching on two centuries (e.g.'late thirteenth or early fourteenth') have been counted in both. 'O' means less than 0.5 per cent. Seals bearing no name but two initials have been counted with those with names, those with a single initial have been counted as anonymous, but it was not until the fifteenth century that seals with a single letter as the device became common.

[15] E.g., P.R.O., DL25/2388 (surname alone: Richard Bacon, early or mid thirteenth century), DL25/522 (Motto alone: Thomas Hawtrey, temp. King John).

seals of the late thirteenth century, but these have a clearer direct line of descent from the seals that important people had as privy seals. This privy seal might be used as a counterseal, impressed on the back of the wax that bore the formal seal on the front, or by itself to authenticate less important documents. Usually it was inscribed 'Secretum' or 'Sigillum secreti' (or similar wording) with the owner's name. Sometimes the privy seal bore a coat of arms and might be not much smaller than a formal seal. An example is that of Robert de Breteuil, earl of Leicester 1191–1204 ('Zecretum Roberti Bretuil'), 30 mm. across and used as a counterseal to his 70 mm. equestrian seal.[16] More often the privy seal was an engraved gem set with the inscription around it and probably often worn in a signet ring. The privy seal of John de Lacy, constable of Chester in the early thirteenth century ('Secretum Iohannis de Lacy'), was a gem engraved with a man's head.[17] Occasionally these privy seals made of gems omitted the owner's name: those of William Percy about 1200 and William de Lancaster between 1220 and 1246 read simply 'Sigill' secreti', 'Sigillum secreti'.[18] More unusual is the counterseal of Henry de Beaufou about 1200 (neither a gem nor armorial: a fleur-de-lis) which has no inscription at all.[19] At the same period William son of William de Ashford used as a counterseal a gem with the inscription 'Cela segreta Will'i', while the seal of Osbert, chaplain of William Brewer, again a gem, was inscribed 'Lecta cela nec revela';[20] unlike the others, privy seals of the well-to-do, this last may well have been its owner's sole seal, though, as we shall see, it was not only the great who owned more than one seal at this time. These two last inscriptions are of particular interest. First they remind us that the primary purpose of a privy seal at this period was probably not only to authenticate but also to close securely a private communication.[21] Second they are forerunners of the mottoes inscribed on anonymous seals from the 1270s onwards.

This is the sigillographic background to the appearance of anonymous seals that are neither counterseals nor gems. The earliest that can be dated in the Duchy of Lancaster Ancient Deeds is that of William de Micheldever in 1252,[22] and another two also date from the 1250s;[23] all are inscribed 'Sigillum secreti' (or a variant). There are none from the

[16] Ellis, *Catalogue of Seals*, i, nos.P295, P296. Here and subsequently inscriptions from seals are given with lower-case letters where appropriate and with the use of i and j, u and v normalised.

[17] *Ibid.*, ii, no.P1639.

[18] *Ibid.*, ii, no.P1867; P.R.O., DL25/578.

[19] Ellis, *Catalogue of Seals*, i, no.P61.

[20] *Ibid.*, ii, no.P956; i, no.P910.

[21] Cf. Heslop, 'English Seals', pp.14–16.

[22] P.R.O., DL25/2066. It is undated but must have been drawn up not much more than seven weeks after DL25/2065.

[23] P.R.O., DL25/173, 2102.

1260s, but from 1272 onwards there are many more: over twenty from 1272 to 1280, mostly with a general motto,[24] but at least one with no legend at all.[25] There are of course others on undated documents, and as it was only in the 1270s that it began to be a common practice to give the date on private charters it may well be that the anonymous seal arrived much more rapidly on the scene in the 1250s or 1260s. But at latest by the reign of Edward I the anonymous seal must have been fully accepted as authenticating a document, and in the anonymous seals of the late thirteenth century we find already designs and mottoes (in English and French as well as Latin) that recur over and over again in the next century: the sleeping lion with 'Wake me no man', the stag's head with 'Timete deum', the squirrel, the lamb and flag, the hawk and its prey, the mottoes 'Frange lege tege', 'Mater die memento mei', 'Sohou' (a hunting-cry) and more besides.[26] From the same period we have a few armorial seals, without the owner's name or family motto; the earliest that can be dated in the Duchy of Lancaster deeds is of 1269.[27] Some are inscribed 'Sigillum secreti', some have the same sorts of motto as the non-armorial seals, and some have no inscription at all. If a seal did not bear its owner's name there was no reason why it need be used by only one person. But to judge from the Duchy of Lancaster deeds an anonymous seal by 1300 was normally still as personal to an individual as a seal that bore his name. Where a duplicate impression has been found the signatory has always been the same, even where the charters are years apart; thus Adam le Charman of Rickling, Essex, used in 1296 and again in 1301 an unusual anonymous seal showing a dog and a hare, probably playing dice, and inscribed 'Hasard þin hod is min'.[28]

However, it was not necessarily by the seals of the parties to the transaction that a charter was authenticated in the thirteenth century. The seal of a local official might be attached as well, like the seal of the reeveship of Southampton, added to local charters (no doubt against a fee) 'for greater security'.[29] The charter for one small grant of land to Beaulieu Abbey before 1230 apparently bore the seal not of the grantor at all, but of his overlord, again 'for greater security'.[30] When the clergy of the deanery of Holderness wrote to the archbishop of York in 1281 their letter bore the deanery seal instead of (perhaps as well as) their

---

[24] E.g., P.R.O., DL25/3423, dated 1272, 'Crede ferenti'.
[25] P.R.O., DL25/1512.
[26] E.g., P.R.O., DL25/1694, 1375, 384, 3190, 1512, 2315, 185, 24.
[27] P.R.O., DL25/2231.
[28] P.R.O., DL25/1684, 1685.
[29] E.g., Southampton City Record Office, SC 4/2/1. 4/2/9.
[30] *The Beaulieu Cartulary*, ed. S.F. Hockey (Southampton Records Series, 1974), pp.94–95.

own, 'since our own seals are not known to you';[31] and it was this or some similar phrase that was normally used in the fourteenth and fifteenth centuries if a document was given added weight by bearing the seal of some great person or official besides or in place of the seal of the actual party.[32]

It was not only for corroboration that other people's seals were used in the thirteenth century, for sealing was not always carried out with the careful formality that these examples might suggest. Where husband and wife were a party to a charter it would normally bear both their seals; but one charter of Robert de Veilly and his wife Joan about 1300 has a single seal and says in the sealing clause that it was sealed only by Robert, while another of Robert Acca and his wife Alice in the mid or late thirteenth century, again said to have been sealed by the husband alone, was in fact sealed only by Alice.[33] Rose, widow of John Smith of Pleshey, Essex, again in the mid or late thirteenth century, attached what the sealing clause calls 'my seal' to her charter; but the seal is actually that of John Smith himself.[34] At Poyntington, Dorset, in the late thirteenth century we find a man using his father's seal, apparently during his father's lifetime, and on the face of it the seal used by Gilbert, son of Gilbert, son of Richard of Mablethorpe, Lincolnshire, was also his father's, for it bears the name of Gilb' fil' Ric'.[35] It may be, though, that a clerical error gives his name incorrectly in the charter, and a similar mistake may possibly explain why Margaret, daughter of William son of Christian of Skidbrooke, Lincolnshire, used a seal with the name Margaret daughter of John.[36]

Possibly but not certainly, for already in the thirteenth century we occasionally find someone using a seal with another person's name on it, a name that does not appear to belong to a close relative. In the 1230s Roger son of William de Moorcroft used the seal of Hugh de Frodsham.[37] A charter of Alice de la Hill and her son Walter de la Hill bore two seals when it was drawn up in 1274; only one survives and this bears the partly illegible name of Richard -y, clerk.[38] That this last was a clerk's seal suggests that these may be early examples of what demonstrably

---

[31] *The Register of William Wickwane, Lord Archbishop of York* 1279–1285, ed. W. Brown, Surtees Society (1907), p.249.

[32] E.g., *Calendar of Close Rolls 1364–8*, p.463 (in 1368); *The Boarstall Cartulary*, ed. H.E. Salter, Oxford Historical Society (1930), p.199 (in 1452).

[33] P.R.O., DL25/3628, 3111.

[34] P.R.O., DL25/1443.

[35] B.L. Egerton Ch. 1577; P.R.O., DL25/2768.

[36] P.R.O., DL25/2950.

[37] P.R.O., DL25/594.

[38] P.R.O., DL25/1380.

occurred in later centuries: the clerk who wrote the document owned the seal and used it on the acts of any of his clients.[39] Alternatively Roger and either Walter or Alice may simply have borrowed the seals they used or (perhaps more likely) acquired them secondhand: there are various possibilities. These however were only precursors of what was to come. Before long any remaining inhibitions over using another person's seal were cast aside, whether or not it bore a name. Thus five seals on a charter of 1315 include two impressions of the seal of one William whose surname is obscure on both but who was certainly not one of the five named signatories.[40] Twelve seals on a charter of 1340 include two impressions of each of three seals, all anonymous; of the other six, four are anonymous, one heraldic seal bears a name that does not appear in the charter and only one seal bears the name (and also the arms) of a signatory.[41] From very early in the fourteenth century it seems to have been no longer the norm for a signatory to a document to have a seal of his own. Important or well-to-do persons who often put seals to documents would of course have their own seals, but many lesser people would sign with a seal that the clerk, or perhaps a friend, supplied. The seal-owning proportion of the population indeed increased in the early part of the thirteenth century, but by, say, 1320 it was probably much smaller than a hundred years earlier. This is one reason why the proportion of heraldic seals rose so sharply from the thirteenth to the fourteenth century, in DL25 and DL26 from a tenth to a third of the total, as the table above shows: fewer of the non-armigerous now owned seals.[42]

But in the early and mid thirteenth century the humbler person who sealed a document need not own just one seal: he might own two or more, each with his name on it. These were not like the formal and privy seals of the great, each serving a distinct function; they were seals of similar form and identical use, sometimes of similar design, sometimes not. Two seals of John, son of Peter Gall of Saltfleetby, though from different dies, have the same design of a flower with eight

[39] Thus a seal bearing the (partly illegible) name of Geoffrey Le--ur occurs on two charters written in the same hand, one on 10 January 1308, where it is the seal of Mabel, wife of William ate Notek, and the other on 14 May 1308, where it is the seal of Hugh de Neville (P.R.O. DL25/1722, 1698). An anonymous seal (but with the letter W as its device) appears on charters written in a single hand on consecutive days in 1465, on 27 November as the seal of William Bernard (two copies) and on 28 November as the seal of Felicia Wood (P.R.O. DL25/1104–1106).

[40] P.R.O., DL25/1311. The seal may possibly read 'Sigillum Willelmi Syrugoni', i.e. William Surgeon.

[41] P.R.O., DL25/1016.

[42] Others include the growing fashion for displaying coats of arms and an increase in the number of people bearing them.

petals;[43] of three with the name of William, son of Osbert le French of Saltfleeby, one has a five-petalled flower, one a fleur-de-lis and one a five-rayed star.[44] These examples, and most others in the Duchy of Lancaster archives, are from the many Lincolnshire charters, especially those from the Saltfleetby area, a large group of conveyances of which most seem to be by very small landholders.[45] But duplicate seals seem to be found among the greater local landholders as well as the lesser and in all parts of the country: examples elsewhere include those of Adam de Marton in north Lancashire and Thomas de Hurtmore in Surrey.[46] It is always possible of course that two seals with the same name belonged not to the same man but to namesakes – the more likely in that in the thirteenth century two brothers might have the same Christian name. Sometimes this was certainly the case. One grant at Saltfleetby was by two brothers; both were named Thomas son of Hugh on their seals, and if the seals had appeared on separate documents one might have thought they were different seals of the same man.[47] But the contents of the documents occasionally show that two seals must belong to the same person – two of the three seals bearing the name of Henry Beck of Lusby are a case in point[48] – and the phenomenon is anyway too common to be explained simply by the existence of namesakes: in the Duchy of Lancaster charters from the Saltfleetby area more than twenty names occur on seals from two, three or even four different dies.[49] And if some seeming duplicate seals were really the seals of namesakes, others owned by a single person may pass unrecognised because an individual might be known by more than one bye-name. William, son of Geva, whose seal is on a charter of William, son of Walter of Saltfleetby, is presumably the same as William, son of Walter, whose seal is on a charter of William, son of Geva, again of Saltfleetby; but if each seal had been attached to the other charter, so that in each case the same man was on charter and seal alike, this would have escaped us.[50] Seal-dies do not wear out as coin-dies do; nor can they have been lost or thrown away with careless abandon. Why then do we find people owning more than one seal?

A method has yet to be established, the criteria worked out, for identifying the work of a single engraver of these small personal seals.

---

[43] P.R.O., DL25/2155, 2441.

[44] P.R.O., DL25/2670, 2807, 2864.

[45] The group would repay detailed investigation, along with the Saltfleetby charters in the archives of Magdalen College, Oxford; I am grateful to Dr. C.M. Woolgar for details of these.

[46] P.R.O., DL25/443 (Marton); E210/3559, E326/4013, 4018 (Hurtmore).

[47] P.R.O., DL25/2886.

[48] P.R.O., DL25/2929, 2930.

[49] One on four is William de Redbourne: P.R.O., DL25/2996, 3020, 3031, 3046.

[50] P.R.O., DL25/2786, 2787.

When this can be done we shall be in a position to learn a great deal more about a little-known medieval craft. Sometimes, however, two or more seals are so alike in design, style and execution that we cannot doubt that the same engraver made the dies together. Usually there is a clear family connection between the owners of these seals. Among the charters from the Saltfleetby area, for instance, we find several pairs of seals, clearly engraved together, belonging to husband and wife,[51] one belonging to two sisters, one belonging to two brothers.[52] Occasionally, however, a charter bears a group of seals so alike that they must have been engraved together yet with no obvious connection between their owners beyond what was involved in the particular transaction. An example is a document drawn up at Monmouth in 1280 by which the five heirs of Robert le Frere quitclaimed a piece of meadow to Edmund, earl of Leicester and Lancaster. The seals of four survive: Juliana and Margery, the daughters of John Baldekat, Felicia le Frere and Margery widow of Walter (named Margery Frere on her seal). It seems to have been only their kinship to Robert that connected all four, yet their seals have every appearance of having been engraved together as a set: all are pointed ovals, uniform in style, with a different but similar device on each.[53] Another example is a group of affidavits by which five prisoners held for King John by H. (presumably Hugh) de Neville undertook on the security of their lands not to escape; each is written in the same hand, each has a seal in the same uncoloured wax on the same yellow and red silk cord, and each seal is round, about 35 mm. across and in a uniform style but with a different device.[54] Other groups are on two agreements made between 1217 and 1232 with Ranulf, earl of Chester and Lincoln, over rights of marsh and pasture in Westfen in Lincolnshire. Each has uniform seals. One has four, all pointed ovals with variously elaborated forms of a fleur-de-lis or stylised spray as the device.[55] On the other, eight seals survive and seven of them are uniform, being round and about 31 mm. across; four of these again have variations of a fleur-de-lis or a spray, while the other three have a cartwheel, one with six spokes, one with seven and one with eight. These last three seals may admittedly have belonged to one family: their owners were William, son of Reginald, and Reginald and William, nephews of Toli.[56] But in all there can be little doubt that it was a known practice for seal-dies to be cut and supplied expressly for a particular transaction, a particular act of sealing.

51 E.g., P.R.O., DL25/1257, 3163.
52 P.R.O., DL25/2733, 2554.
53 P.R.O., DL25/2050.
54 P.R.O., DL25/724, 725, 1343, 1344, 3452.
55 P.R.O., DL25/2423.
56 P.R.O., DL25/2422.

This may explain how people came to possess duplicate seals. In using written charters to record the oral conveyance of small pieces of land it seems to have been the monasteries and perhaps lay magnates that led the way: at the beginning of the thirteenth century the villager selling his land to one of his fellows would do so simply by public ceremony, but if the purchaser was a religious house it would seek to have this confirmed by a charter. It was the monastery that drew up the charter (it was, after all, the monastery that wished to have it) and if the smallholding vendor had no seal of his own one would be supplied, which he would then keep as a perquisite or souvenir. Sometimes a seal may have been supplied inadvertently to a grantor who already had one of his own; indeed, the practice may for a while have hardened into custom, so that the grantor expected a new seal whether or not he already had one. This would explain how a person's two or three seals might all have the same design: the recipient would select his own device and might stick to the same one each time, making it a kind of personal mark which may have been used in other contexts as well – to mark livestock or other property for instance. This is merely guessing; but it is a possible explanation of a rather odd phenomenon.

We can speculate a little further. Three seals with the name of Henry Beck of Lusby in Lincolnshire all have the same design, a cross with the ends splayed and curled round; the documents they attest are dated 1227, 1231 or are undated.[57] Subsequently the arms of the Beck family (among them Anthony, bishop of Durham 1283–1311) were this same symbol, a cross moline. But need it follow that we can carry this coat of arms back to the early thirteenth century? The personal mark of one generation might, given an appropriate turn in family fortunes, be the coat of arms of the next. Many coats of arms of the later middle ages may have had a rather humbler origin than as a mark of recognition borne by a knight in armour. Social aspiration, good fortune or simply the spread of heraldry will have moved them up in the world. Certainly, however, it was not social pretensions that account for the wide ownership of seals in thirteenth-century England; it was the demand for written charters of confirmation by those to whom land was given or sold.

[57] P.R.O., DL25/2929, 2930, 2931 (this last seal occurs also on 3213 and 3214).

Chapter 9

Robert Mannyng's History of Arthurian Literature

Lesley Johnson

Robert Mannyng of Brunne's *Chronicle of England*, completed according to the *explicit* on Friday 15 May 1338, belongs to the large group of medieval 'genealogical narratives', to use the term coined by Howard Bloch, which are structured around a linear pattern of descent from a founding father.[1] The founding father in this case is Brutus, who is the first to organise a human society on the island of Britain, and who serves as a point of origin for the succession of kings of Britain, and subsequently of England, which Mannyng traces in his narrative. The culmination of this continuous sequence in the *Chronicle* is the reign of Edward I and the narrative ends with an account of Edward's death when Mannyng's written sources finish too:

---

[1] As yet we do not have a modern edition of the *Chronicle*. For Mannyng's account of pre-Saxon history (which will be referred to as Part i of the *Chronicle*) see Frederick Furnivall's edition, *The Story of England by Robert Mannyng of Brunne*, Rolls Series, lxxxvii, 2 vols. (London, 1887) which is based on the text in London Lambeth Palace, MS 131 and which will be cited by line number in my text.

For Mannyng's narrative of post-British history (which will be referred to as Part ii), see T. Hearne's edition, *Peter Langtoft's Chronicle (as Illustrated and Improved by Robert of Brunne)*, 2 vols (Oxford, 1725), which is based on the text in London, Inner Temple, MS Petyt 511 and which will be cited by page number (since Hearne does not supply line numbers). R. Stepsis has edited the post-British section of the *Chronicle* in an unpublished Ph.D dissertation (Harvard, 1967). For a brief account of the three manuscripts of the *Chronicle* (which, in addition to the Petyt and Lambeth Palace MSS noted above, includes the fragment in Oxford, Bodleian Library, MS 13679 [Rawlinson D 913]) see E.D. Kennedy's entry on Mannyng's *Chronicle* in *A Manual of the Writings in Middle English, 1050–1500*, general editor, A. Hartung, vol.8. xii: 'Chronicles and other Historical Writing' (Connecticut, 1989), pp.2,625–28. Kennedy supplies a comprehensive bibliography of secondary material on the *Chronicle* and clears up the confusion over the number and identity of the manuscripts which contain copies of the *Chronicle*. His discussion thus supplements that of Stepsis, 'The Manuscripts of Robert Mannyng of Brunne's *Chronicle of England*', *Manuscripta*, xiii (1969), 131–41. For the closing lines of Mannyng's text see the *Chronicle*, ii, p. 341 and the comments about the scribal errors in the dating of this *explicit* in R. Crosby's study, 'Robert Mannyng of Brunne: A New Biography', *PMLA*, lvii (1942), 15–28, at 15, n. 5. For H. Bloch's discussion of the characteristics and function of genealogical narratives see his *Etymologies and Genealogies: A Literary Anthropology of the French Middle Ages* (Chicago, 1983), especially pp.64–87.

> Now must I nede leue here, of Inglis forto write,
> I had no more matere of kynges lif in scrite.
>
> (ii, p. 341)

In Bloch's view, this kind of historical narrative seeks to 'establish the most ancient ancestry possible and to create the most coherent continuity between [a] mythic beginning and the present'.[2] But if narratives such as Mannyng's, and the sources on which he draws, seek to legitimise national communities by tracing their origins, as Bloch suggests, they also register the difficulty of tracking down a single generative line which may link the line of Brutus, and the political community he represents, with that of Edward I. The sequence of kings which Mannyng traces cannot be accommodated to a single genealogical line of descent. The origin stories included in the *Chronicle* are multiple not single; the identity of those in power and those whom they govern and represent is subject to redefinition and change as is the very name and geo-political dimension of the site of Mannyng's narrative:

> [Brutus] regned ffoure and twenty, ʒer
> In al Bretaigne fer and ner.
> Al was Brutaigne, by elde tales,
> Engelond, Scotlond and Walys,
> Þyse þre were þenne al on,
> Þat erest was cald Albyon;
> Albion highte þyse londes þre,
> ffor þey ar closed al wiþ þe se.
>
> (i, 1937–44)

The boundaries of Albion itself are naturally defined, but they rarely coincide with those of the various communities who inhabit the land and it is the fluctuating identities of these communitites which provide Mannyng with his historical subject matter.

Mannyng's access to the past is of course through the texts of other historical 'fathers'. Before embarking on the 'geste' of the English, which forms the second part of his *Chronicle*, Mannyng follows his authority, Pierre de Langtoft, in calling on Bede to aid him in his historiographical task:[3]

---

[2] *Etymologies and Genealogies*, p. 81.

[3] For an account of the highly complex textual tradition of the *Chronicle* of Pierre de Langtoft and a full description of the twenty-one extant medieval manuscripts see J.C. Thiolier's discussion in his edition of *Pierre de Langtoft: Le Règne d'Édouard Ier* (Créteil, 1989), pp.1–220. The text of Langtoft's *Chronicle* in London, British Library, MS Royal 20 A XI appears to be closest to that reworked by Mannyng and, in Thiolier's classification, it belongs to the third edition of the second redaction of Langtoft's work. For the Latin *incipit* to the post-British section of Langtoft's *Chronicle* which contains the prayer to Bede see Thiolier's edition, pp.37, 42 and T. Wright's edition of *The Chronicle of Pierre de Langtoft*, Rolls Series, xlvii, 2 vols. (London, 1866), p. 278. Wright's edition (which is based on the second redaction of Langtoft's work according to Thiolier) is the only complete edition of the *Chronicle* and will be cited by page numbers in my text.

When Peres [i.e. Pierre de Langtoft] first bygan his werk,
He bisoughte an holy clerk
To gyue hym grace wel to spede, –
Þat holy man highte seint Bede, –
ffor in his bokes mykel he fond;
He made ffyve bokes of Engelond,
And y schal prey hym þat ilke weys,
Als he ys corseint and curteys,
He gyue me grace wel to seye,
And rightly þys in rym to leye,
Þys story þat ys seyd þorow Peres,
Þat alle be payed þat hit heres.

(i, 16,720–30)

The roll call of authorities on insular history in the *Chronicle* also includes Gildas (i, 10,597, 10,602, 14,737 etc.), William of Malmesbury (ii, p. 25), Henry of Huntingdon, who receives special praise as a 'compilour' (ii, pp.6–7), Geoffrey of Monmouth (i, 163–76, 10,595–604), and Wace (i, 57–70, 177–86).[4] But the relationship between these writers and Mannyng's 'genealogical' narrative cannot be represented in terms of a straightforward pattern of textual filiation. The 'story of England' is a composite one, as Mannyng recognises, but it is also a selective one since his textual authorities do not relate the same story even when their subjects coincide. Thus, although a genealogical narrative such as Mannyng provides may indeed reflect a 'deep, though historically determined, mental structure that assumed power to be legitimised through recourse to origins', the interests and processes of legitimisation contained in the narrative may not be such a simple matter as Bloch's comments imply.[5]

I open with these general observations on the function and form of genealogical narratives because I wish to indicate some of the larger issues about national identity and the mediation of a continuous history of British and English political communities which may be at stake in Mannyng's 'story of Inglande'. It seems to me that we have yet to explore the potential of these kinds of narratives as vehicles, not only for promoting the interests of certain communities of interest, but also for registering the discontinuities and cultural diversity amongst present and former possessioners of the realms of the island. My specific concern in this essay, however, will not be with these larger issues, but with just two passages which Mannyng adds to the Arthurian section of his *Chronicle*

---

[4] Some of these citations (notably to Gildas, William of Malmesbury, and Henry of Huntingdon) are prompted by those in Langtoft's *Chronicle*. For a discussion of the relationship between Langtoft's and Mannyng's works, see M. Thümmig, 'Ueber die altenglische übersetzung der reimchronik Peter Langtoft's durch Robert Manning von Brunne', *Anglia* 14 (1892), 1–76.

[5] *Etymologies and Genealogies*, p. 82.

which comment on the developing history of Arthurian narrative in the early fourteenth century, but which also suggest something of the broader interests of Mannyng's *Chronicle* as a whole. In the first passage Mannyng briefly considers Arthur's position as an historical subject; in the second, Mannyng places the record of Arthur's reign within a wider narrative context and suggests some kind of explanation for why so much material about Arthur is contained in the 'grete bokes . . . Writen and spoken of ffraunces vsage' (i, 10,971–72). Before discussing these passages in more detail, however, it is perhaps necessary to elaborate a little further on Mannyng since his work has attracted comparatively little critical attention and his *Chronicle*, at least, is still relatively inaccessible.

It is an axiom of Mannyng's small twentieth-century audience that his work is too little known and studied.[6] Mannyng's assertion in the introduction to his *Chronicle* that he writes 'not for þe lerid bot for þe lewed' (i, 6) perhaps has done little to excite the interest of modern academics, and yet he is a writer who clearly aspires to be recognised and remembered for his literary labours which provide his English audience with a manual for their spiritual welfare (*Handlyng Synne*) and a guide to their history (the *Chronicle*). Most of our biographical information about Mannyng derives from the literary portraits with which he prefaces both works. We learn from the prologue to *Handlyng Synne* that Mannyng came from Bourne in Lincolnshire and lived in the Gilbertine priory of Sempringham for fifteen years (under the priorship of John of Camelton for ten years and then under the priorship of John of Clynton). He began his reworking of the 'frenshe . . . manuel de pecchees' (the thirteenth-century *Manuel des Pechiez*) in 1303 when 'Dane Felyp was mayster' (*Handlyng Synne*, 73).[7] Further biographical information is provided in the introduction to Mannyng's *Chronicle* (completed in 1338):

[6] For the limited bibliography on Mannyng's work see Kennedy's survey (cited above n. 1). In the most recent and most detailed discussion of the *Chronicle*, T. Turville-Petre describes this work as being 'entirely neglected': see 'Politics and Poetry in the Early Fourteenth Century: The Case of Robert Mannyng's *Chronicle*', *Review of English Studies*, xxxix (1988), 2.

[7] Mannyng's *Handlyng Synne* has been edited by I. Sullens (Binghampton, 1983) and all quotations will be taken from her text and cited by line number. Sullens describes the nine extant copies of *Handlyng Synne* on pp.xxiii–xxxiii. For bibliographical information on the *Manuel des Pechiez* see Sullens, n. 1, pp.xxxviii–ix. The identities of the ecclesiastics mentioned by Mannyng are discussed by Sullens in n. 2, p. xxxix and by Crosby in 'Robert Mannyng of Brunne: A New Biography', 20–21, 27–28. The information Mannyng supplies about his time with these priors suggests that the prologue could not have been composed before 1317 and was written sometime after he had begun work on *Handlyng Synne* in 1308. Crosby notes, 16–17, that Mannyng's comments on the royal wards kept at Sempringham and Sixhills (*Chronicle*, ii, p. 243) confirm his connection with these Gilbertine houses.

> Of Brunne I am, if any me blame,
> Robert Mannyng is my name;
> Blissed be he of God of heuene
> Þat me, Robert, with gude wille neuene;
> In the third Edwardes tyme was I
> when I wrote alle þis story,
> In þe hous of Sixille I was a throwe;
> Danz Robert of Malton þat ȝe know,
> did it wryte for felawes sake,
> when þai wild solace make.
>
>   (i, 135–44)

That Mannyng had spent some time in Cambridge earlier in his life is implied by a narratorial aside which asserts that he 'þat wrote and mad þis ryme' witnessed a feast there, given by Robert Bruce, on behalf of his brother Alexander (ii, pp.336–37). These references form the basis for Ruth Crosby's 'new biography' of Robert Mannyng, published in 1942, which corrected some of the mistaken conclusions of Mannyng's early editors and which itself was written 'in the belief that one of Chaucer's most interesting predecessors in the art of storytelling deserves to be better known than he is'.[8] Crosby concludes that Mannyng was born *c.* 1283; perhaps spent some time at Cambridge (*c.* 1298–1302); was a canon at Sempringham from 1302–17, where he produced his version of *Handlyng Synne*; and spent some time at the priory of Sixhills before completing his *Story of England* in 1338. In addition to this autobiographical information, evidence from the will of Avice de Crosseby of Lincoln, who died on 25 August 1327, suggests that Mannyng may have been a chaplain in Lincoln around this time, as Edith Seaton has pointed out.[9]

The presence of these introductory portraits in *Handlyng Synne* and the *Chronicle* suggest that Robert Mannyng was a writer of a certain literary self-consciousness and this impression is confirmed by the narrator's evident concern in the *Chronicle* with the form and function of his historical narrative. Much of the long introduction to the *Chronicle* is taken up with the narrator's defence of his choice of a 'light' English prosodic form which has been chosen to facilitate communication and accessibility in whatever context his work might be received:

> Als þai [i.e. Langtoft and Wace] haf wryten and sayd,
> haf I alle in myn Inglis layd,
> In symple speche as I couthe,
> Þat is lightest in mannes mouthe.
> I mad noght for no disours,
> ne for no seggers, no harpours,

---

[8] 'Robert Mannyng of Brunne: A New Biography', 15.
[9] 'Robert Mannyng of Brunne in Lincoln', *Medium Aevum*, xii (1943), 77.

> Bot for þe luf of symple men
> Þat strange Inglis can not ken;
> ffor many it ere þat strange Inglis
> In ryme wate neuer what it is; . . .
> And my witte was oure thynne
> So strange speche to trauayle in; . . .
> And þerfore for þe comonalte
> Þat blythely wild listen to me,
> On light[e] lange I it began,
> for luf of þe lewed man,
> to telle þam þe chaunces bolde,
> Þat here before was don and tolde.
>
> (i, 71–128)[10]

However, the apparently humble stance of the writer/narrator as he describes his own stylistic skills and, by implication, the tastes and abilities of his non-learned audience is belied, in practice, by the performance which follows. Mannyng's principal authority for his version of British history is the *Roman de Brut* (finished in 1155), but Mannyng proves his 'light' language to be as flexible as that of Wace's narrative ('rymed . . . in Frankis fyne', i, 180) by the way in which he frequently imitates the flamboyant and highly stylised descriptive passages which characterise the work of the earlier French writer.[11] Moreover, when Mannyng moves to follow the narrative of post-British history provided by Langtoft he responds to the different prosodic media of Langtoft's verse which, he notes, is 'rymed' in 'oþer ways' (i, 190). Mannyng not only uses longer six-stress rhyming couplets as the basis

---

[10] For a parallel to Mannyng's use of the term 'lyghte' (i.e. 'simple') to describe his language (in antithesis to 'strange speche', i.e. 'difficult or unusual language') see Richard Rolle's comments in the prologue to his *English Psalter*: 'In þis werk I seke no straunge Inglis, bot the lightest and comunest', *The English Writings of Richard Rolle*, ed. H.E. Allen (Oxford, 1963), p.7. 91–92. See O.E.D. 'strange' and M.E.D. 'English' 2cb: 'strange English'. I can find no support for Thiolier's suggestion that 'strange Inglis' = 'anglo-normand', *Pierre de Langtoft*, p. 20. Mannyng's use of a variety of terms for prosodic forms and stanzaic arrangements elsewhere in this passage deserves further study because its technical precision is itself so unusual (for a text composed in English) and because the precise meaning of some of these terms has yet to be explained (see, for example the M.E.D. entries for 'baston' and 'entrelace'). It is worth noting that Mannyng does not present the tradition of literary composition in English as an homogeneous one: even though he opts for apparently simple language and a simple prosodic form, more sophisticated literary styles are available. This elaborate introduction to the *Chronicle* is extant only in the Petyt MS.

[11] Wace has been characterised with some justice as 'parmi les auteurs de son siècle le meilleur technicien dans l'art de la description', by I. Arnold, the editor of the *Roman de Brut*, 2 vols. (Paris, 1938–40), p. lxxxvii. For examples of Mannyng's reworkings of Wace's virtuoso passages (albeit abbreviated), compare 1803–48 with the *Roman de Brut*, 1,111–69; 11,153–98 with the *Roman de Brut*, 10,327–58; 12,053–96 with the *Roman de Brut*, 11,190–238.

for this part of his narrative (instead of four-stress couplets), but also imitates Langtoft's excursions into 'ryme couwee', to use Mannyng's term (i, 85), which is used for the sections that add a special emotive emphasis to Langtoft's account of Edward I's reign.[12] In fact Mannyng's very attentiveness to the stylistic quality of the French writers whose work he follows, or has read, confirms his own ambitions as a self-conscious stylist who

> . . . fulle fayn wald bringe
> In Inglis tonge þer faire saiynge.
>
> (i, 197–98)

In practice, if not in theory, Mannyng's apparently simple English verse style proves to be compatible with the 'faire saiynge' that he wishes to bring to the 'Inglis tonge' (i, 198).

The ambitious and self-conscious quality of Mannyng's performance as a compiler of the 'story of Inglande' is also suggested by the sheer range of material which the *Chronicle* encompasses. Mannyng's narrative is not a simple translation but is more of an encyclopaedic compilation which draws on a wide range of vernacular and Latin resources. The verse chronicles of Wace and Langtoft provide Mannyng with his basic narrative frame: a version of 'þe Brute' (i, 32) spliced together with the narrative 'þat calle men now þe Inglis gest'(i, 38).[13] Although Langtoft's narrative covers the whole period, Wace's version of events up to the establishment of Saxon hegemony is preferred by Mannyng because it provides a more comprehensive account of British history and follows the Latin source (the book translated from British by 'Geffrey Arthure of Minumue', i, 163) more closely:

---

[12] As Stepsis has pointed out in the introduction to his edition of Part ii of Mannyng's *Chronicle* (cited above n. 1), there is a greater variety of prosodic forms in Part ii. The number of stress patterns in the lines varies on occasions and internal rhyme, assonance, and alliteration are used as additional cohesive devices. The macaronic tail-rhyme sections which Langtoft uses to provide emotive sequences for the account of Edward I's campaigns against Scotland (Thiolier, *Pierre de Langtoft*, pp.21–22) are partly translated, partly imitated, by Mannyng in English. Although it has been suggested that parts of 'original' soldiers' songs are preserved in these sections of Langtoft's poem, it seems more likely that these passages have been composed by Langtoft and reworked by Mannyng, to supply an emotive commentary on events and thus, ultimately, to heighten the king's prestige. This seems to be the tentative conclusion of R.M. Wilson's slightly contradictory discussion in *The Lost Literature of Medieval England*, 2nd edn. (London, 1970), p. 206.

[13] A parallel of sorts to Mannyng's act of compilation may be found in one of the manuscripts (dated 1350–1410) which preserves part of Langtoft's work. London, College of Arms, MS Arundel XIV ('E' in Thiolier's edition, pp.61–9) contains a copy of Wace's *Roman de Brut*; a copy of Gaimar's *Estoire des Engleis*; a version of *Haveloc le Danois*; and Langtoft's account of the reign of Edward I. It also contains a copy of Chrétien de Troyes's *Perceval*.

> One Mayster Wace þe ffrankes telles,
> Þe Brute, all þat þe Latyn spelles, . . .
> And ryght as Mayster Wace says
> I telle myn Inglis þe same ways;
> ffor Mayster Wace þe Latyn alle rymes
> Þat Pers ouerhippis many tymes.
>
> (i, 57–64)[14]

But Mannyng supplements this narrative with material drawn from the Latin sources of Wace and Langtoft (notably from Geoffrey of Monmouth's work), from Bede, and from other bookish sources (in Latin and in the vernacular).[15] However, not all of these sources are cited by name, nor are they cited with the precision which distinguishes one of Mannyng's references to Bede's work:

> Þyse wordes of seint Bede y tok,
> Þe fifte chapitre of þe secounde bok.
> (i, 14,961–62)

The impression that the *Chronicle* is not only produced from, but is also placed within, a broad range of bookish works is enhanced by the narrator's comments on points at which the subjects of his work intersect with those developed further in other texts. This is a trait which Mannyng has taken over from the post-British sections of Langtoft's narrative: thus Mannyng, for example, following Langtoft, alerts his audience to a written account of the life of Queen Matilda at Westminster (ii, pp.105–6); to the book which recounts the life of Thomas Becket (ii, pp.131–32); and to the 'romaunce' which relates the events of the crusading campaigns of Richard I (ii, p.

---

[14] The scribe of the copy of Langtoft's *Chronicle* in London, British Library, MS Royal 20 A XI (which is similar to the version used by Mannyng – see n. 3 above) shares Mannyng's views on the superiority of Wace's version of events. See Wright's edition, i, p. 264 and Thiolier, *Pierre de Langtoft*, p. 12 for this passage. Mannyng, however, is attentive to Langtoft's version of British history and even though he follows Wace's fuller narrative, he sometimes changes or supplements Wace's account with information from Langtoft's version (as, for example, in Mannyng's account of Arthur's final, fatal encounter with Mordred, i, 14,271–6).

[15] Mannyng, for example, draws on the *Historia Regum Britannie* for some of the details of his description of the pagan temples (i, 5,755–64); he draws on Bede's *Historia ecclesiastica* for his account of Pope Gregory and the English 'angels' (i, 14, 868–946). In his unpublished dissertation Stepsis has suggested that Mannyng has used material from the Anglo-Norman life of St. Edward, from Nicholas Trevet's *Chronique*, from William of Malmesbury's *Historia regum Anglorum*, and from a 'romaunce' version of a narrative about Richard I to supplement his narrative in the post-British section of his work. For a discussion of the sources used by Mannyng to amplify the Arthurian section of his narrative see E.B. Atwood, 'Robert Mannyng's Version of the Troy Story', *Texas Studies in English*, xviii (1938), 5–13. R.M. Wilson discusses Mannyng's addition of the history of 'Engle' and his references to works about the eponymous hero of England in 'More Lost Literature in Old and Middle English', *Leeds Studies in English*, v (1936), 19–21.

205).[16] But Mannyng also adds further textual details (to the histories of Havelok and Engle, for example) and extends this cross-referencing technique to earlier sections of his narrative so that the events of pre-Saxon history are placed within a broader textual matrix.[17] He draws the attention of his audience to Dares's more detailed Latin account of the Trojan war (i, 145–62); to the books of Merlin's masters 'Blase . . . Tolomer and sire Amytayn' which contain the prophecies of Merlin which Mannyng (following Wace) pointedly excludes from his *Chronicle* (i, 821–28); and to the French books which recount the marvels of Arthur's life (i, 10,961–78 – a passage which I shall discuss in more detail).[18] So although Mannyng's opening stance may be formulated in self-deprecatory terms, his literary practice is ambitious. If his work opens with a modesty topos which relates to his abilities, his medium and, by implication his audience, nevertheless his compilation of the 'story of Inglande' both extends the range of authoritative material available in English and validates that linguistic medium at the same time. Indeed the *Chronicle* may be considered as an exercise in creating an image of its audience as a specifically English community, in which the 'lerid' and 'lewede' divisions invoked at the beginning of the narrative are transcended.

[16] See Wright's edition of Langtoft's *Chronicle*, vol.i, p. 462; vol.ii, pp.9, 1 123 for the corresponding passages.

[17] For Mannyng's references to the story of Engle see n. 15 above. In the Petyt MS of the *Chronicle* the narrator remarks that he has heard more about Havelok, but cannot find any written sources on the subject (ii, pp.25–26). In the Lambeth Palace MS, however, this narrative gap has been filled by an abbreviated account of Havelok's history (of 82 lines). For further information about the Havelok interpolation see G.V. Smithers' edition of *Havelok* (Oxford, 1987), pp.xxii–xxiv and E.K. Putnam, 'The Lambeth Version of *Havelok*', *PMLA*, xv (1900), 1–16.

[18] Atwood acknowledges Mannyng's citation of Dares, but questions his use of *De excidio Troiae historia* in 'Robert Mannyng's Version of the Troy Story'. Mannyng's reference to the books of Merlin's masters suggests that he knew the non-Galfredian version of the *Prophécies de Merlin*: this is a French prose narrative, composed *c*. 1276, which contains a large number of Merlin's prophecies as delivered to 'Maistre Antoine' and 'Maistre Tholomer' (amongst others), interspersed with accounts of Arthurian adventures (drawn from earlier prose cycles). The content of these prophecies is wide-ranging, but they are rather different from those related in Geoffrey of Monmouth's *Historia regum Britannie* and in his *Vita Merlini*: they have a distinctive interest in the politics of the church of Rome. The textual tradition behind these *Prophécies* is complex, as L. Paton has made clear in her edition, 2 vols. (New York, London, 1926). In two fourteenth-century MSS, described by Paton in i, pp.24–28, versions of these non-Galfredian *Prophécies* are interpolated into a much longer account of Merlin's life from the prose cycle tradition which refers to Blaise at some length as Merlin's mentor and scribe. It is possible that Mannyng knew some such narrative compilation which would therefore contain material preserved by 'Blase . . . Tolomer and sire Amytayn' (I, 8,215–7). Very little secondary material is available on these *Prophecies*, but see P. Zumthor's general remarks in *Merlin le prophète* (Lausanne, 1943), pp.101–7 and C. Pickford's resumé in 'Miscellaneous French Prose Romances', *Arthurian Literature in the Middle Ages*, ed. R.S. Loomis (Oxford, 1959), pp.352–54.

The self-conscious historiographical interest of Mannyng's *Chronicle* may be illustrated by the two passages of narratorial commentary which Mannyng adds to his account of Arthur's reign: the first of these occurs in relation to Arthur's twelve-year period of peaceful rule in Britain; the second is added to the account of Arthur's nine-year rule in France. These passages reveal Mannyng's concern for the history of his historical material and offer further insights into the wider context in which he is operating as a compiler of the 'story of Inglande' in English. For these reasons alone, such comments deserve more attention from modern readers of medieval historical narrative than they have received. Both passages draw attention to various ellipses and gaps in the textual record of Arthur's reign and bring certain paradoxes of Arthur's textual ubiquity and invisibility to the fore.

Arthur's twelve-year period of peaceful rule in Britain, which followed his victory over the Saxons and his successful campaigns in Ireland and the Northern Isles, is summed up in a sentence in Geoffrey of Monmouth's *Historia Regum Britannie*: 'Emensa deinde hyeme reuersus est in Britanniam statumque regni sui in firmam pacem renouans moram xii annis ibidem fecit'.[19] In the *Roman de Brut*, however, which is Mannyng's principal source for his account of Arthurian history, Wace adds a section which partly explains how Arthur maintained peace within his court during this period, but which also draws attention to the narrator's inability to document the events of this time in any detail (*Roman de Brut*, 9,747–99). The mechanics of this peaceful period are explained in the *Roman de Brut*, then, by Arthur's invention of a round table for his court which quite literally circumvented any expression of rivalry over status between members of his international entourage (9,747–60). This round table plays a relatively insignificant role in the *Roman de Brut*, but it has earned Wace a place in modern histories of Arthurian literature because he seems to be the earliest writer to attribute such a table to the court of King Arthur.[20] Having indicated one of the ways in which Arthur keeps peace during this time, Wace goes on to alert his audience to the existence of fabulous stories and tales which take the events of this period for their subject but are beyond the bounds of his historical narrative:

[19] See N. Wright's edition of the *Historia regum Britannie, 1, Bern MS* (Cambridge, 1984), 153. All further quotations from this work will be taken from this edition and cited by chapter number. There is no significant discrepancy between the Bern text (which represents the so-called Vulgate recension of the *Historia Regum Britannie*) and that of the Variant recension at this point.

[20] For an overview of critical material on the history of the Round Table and Wace's 'invention' of this device see Beate Schmolke-Hasselmann, 'The Round Table: Ideal, Fiction, Reality' in *Arthurian Literature*, ii (1982), 41–75.

> Que pur amur de sa largesce,
> Que pur poür de sa prüesce,
> En cele grant pais ke jo di,
> Ne sai si vus l'avez oï,
> Furent les merveilles pruvees
> E les adventures truvees
> Ki d'Artur sunt tant recuntees
> Ke a fable sunt aturnees:
> Ne tut mençunge, ne tut veir,
> Tut folie ne tut saveir.
> Tant unt li cunteür cunté
> E li fableür tant flablé
> Pur les cuntes enbeleter,
> Que tut unt fait fable sembler.
>   (9,785–99)[21]

These lines, no less than the preceding account of the round table, have generated a good deal of discussion amongst modern critics over what they reveal about the wider context of Arthurian narrative in the early to mid twelfth century.[22] If little sense of a consensus about their referential value has emerged from the debate, this passage does at least have a clear validating function within the *Roman de Brut* as a whole. It is through narratorial asides such as this that Wace establishes his role as a historiographer and asserts the authority of his version of events.

Unlike Pierre de Langtoft and Mannyng, Wace's technique of authenticating his historical narrative is not to buttress his text with named authorities. Rather Wace validates his narrative by developing the image of his narrating persona as a discriminating clerkly figure who alerts the attention of his audience to material beyond his knowledge, and

---

[21] This passage poses certain problems of translation because Wace plays off the language of events and happenings with those of their literary report: thus 'truvees' (9,790), for example, may mean either 'happened' or 'composed'. In my translation I have indicated such ambiguities because they underline Wace's overall point about his inability to separate what happened in this time from what is said to have happened. 'Both out of respect for [Arthur's] generous behaviour and out of awe for his military prowess, the wondrous happenings were demonstrated/established as true and the *adventures* happened/were composed in the great period of peace of which I am speaking (I do not know whether you have heard of it), which have been so often told about Arthur that they have been turned into/interpreted as fiction: neither wholly lies, nor wholly truth; neither all nonsense, nor all wisdom. So much have the storytellers storytold and so much have the fable-writers spun fabulous tales, in order to elaborate their stories, that they have made everything seem fiction'.

[22] M. Delbouille provides a helpful, sceptical overview of the critical debate generated by this passage in 'Le Témoignage de Wace sur la légende arthurienne', *Romania*, lxxiv (1953), 172–99. See also J.S.P. Tatlock, *The Legendary History of Britain* (Berkeley and Los Angeles, 1950), p. 474.

outside his text (often prefaced by a formulaic profession of ignorance) in order to enhance the value of what he does narrate.[23] In this passage of narratorial commentary about Arthurian fictions, Wace both draws attention to a narrative 'gap' in his material, and takes the opportunity to place his narrative within a wider narrative spectrum which affirms its historiographical quality: his text is not narrated in a way which compromises its integrity. The *Roman de Brut*, according to the narrator's own remarks here, clearly does not belong to the category of literary fiction.

This opportunity for self-reflective commentary is developed in a rather different way in Mannyng's version. He follows Wace's account of the invention of the round table and then goes on to provide a general description of the quantity and quality of the material in circulation 'in ryme' about the adventures which occured in this twelve-year period (i, 10,579–590). But, unlike Wace, Mannyng does not seem to be interested in pursuing the mechanics of embellishing which transform 'truth' into fable. Nor does he dismiss the value of the 'mixed' texts about Arthur. Such works may still be of some use and interest:

> Þer nys no þyng of hym [i.e. Arthur] seyd
> Þat hit ne may be to godnesse leyd.

> (i, 10,589–90)

The gaps and discrepancies which Mannyng focuses on are those which emerge from the records of Arthurian history in authoritative Latin historiography and, in addition, those which emerge from the difference between French and English literary traditions on the subject of Arthur:

> Geffrey Arthur of Monemu,
> He wrot his dedes þat were of pru,
> And blamed boþe Gyldas and Bede,
> Why þey wolde nought of hym rede,
> Syn he bar þe pris of alle cristen kynges,
> And write so litel of his preysynges,
> And more worschip of hym spoke þer was
> Þat of any of þo þat spekes Gildas,
> Or of any þat Bede wrot,
> Saue holy men þat we wot.
> In alle landes wrot men of Arthur,

---

[23] For a more detailed discussion of the development of the role of the clerkly-narrator in the *Roman de Brut* see Chapter II of my doctoral thesis, 'Commemorating the Past' (London, 1990), pp.175–92; Karl Uitti, 'Vernacularization and Old French Mythopoesis with Emphasis on Chrétien's *Erec et Enide*', in *The Sower and his Seed: Essays on Chrétien de Troyes*, ed. R. Pickens (Lexington, 1983), pp.81–115, esp. at 82–3; N.V. Durling, 'Translation and Innovation in the *Roman de Brut*', in *Medieval Translators and their Craft*, ed. J. Beer (Kalamazoo, Michigan, 1989), pp.9–39.

Hys noble dedes of honur:
In ffraunce men wrot and ʒit men wryte,
But herd haue we of hym but lyte.
(i, 10,595–608)

Mannyng thus transforms Wace's narratorial aside into an occasion for reflection upon a broader range of textual issues relating to Arthurian historiography.

Neither Wace nor Langtoft attribute their account of British history to any other authoritative textual source.[24] Mannyng, in contrast, both situates his text of British history within a matrix of named sources and, here as elsewhere (i, 163–76), specifically recognises Geoffrey of Monmouth as one of his authorities, albeit one whose version of history does not wholly coincide with that of Gildas or Bede. Of course Mannyng is not the first to draw attention to this discrepancy between the major sources of insular historiography on the subject of Arthur, but he does appear to be one of the earliest writers to do so in English and his mode of registering the discrepancy by attributing the comments to Geoffrey of Monmouth himself is distinctive.[25]

It is difficult to identify a source for Mannyng's 'quotation' from Geoffrey of Monmouth in the *Historia regum Britannie*. Although Geoffrey of Monmouth opens his narrative with some remarks about the gaps in the Latin tradition of insular historiography which his work will fill, he does not castigate either Gildas or Bede for wilfully ignoring Arthur as a historical subject within their narratives. Indeed, the implication of Geoffrey's opening claims is that previous historiographers working in Latin simply have not had access to the sources of British history, specifically to the 'ancient British book' which he is now translating

---

[24] Wace makes some general references to the source of his narrative (*Roman de Brut*, 9,946, 1,621, 2,310, 10,360), but never attributes the material to a named source. Langtoft, although keen to shore up his narrative of *English* history with named sources, simply refers to the mediation of his narrative of *British* history through a 'latymer' (*Chronicle*, I, p. 64).

[25] For an earlier, and much more vitriolic, assessment of the relative accuracy of the versions of early British history by Geoffrey of Monmouth and Bede, see William of Newburgh's remarks in the preface to his *Historia rerum Anglicarum*, composed at the end of the twelfth century. For further examples of how writers on insular history negotiated these discrepancies in practice (if not, explicitly, in theory), see R. W. Leckie Jr. *The Passage of Dominion: Geoffrey of Monmouth and the Periodization of Insular History in the Twelfth Century* (Toronto, 1981); L. Keeler, *Geoffrey of Monmouth and the Late Latin Chroniclers, 1300–1500* (Berkeley and Los Angeles, 1946). Explicit remarks by vernacular writers on the problems of reconciling the authorities on the subject of British history are not common. But for an elaborate assessment of the grounds for this discrepancy and the possible prejudices of Bede, see Thomas Gray's comments in his *Scalachronica* (composed later than Mannyng's *Chronicle*, c. 1355–63) in M.L. Meneghetti's collection, *I Fatti de Bretagna* (Padova, 1979), pp.69–71.

(*Historia regum Britannie*, 2). Whether or not Mannyng's quotation of Geoffrey's observations is itself a fabrication, this citation in the *Chronicle* allows Mannyng to register the discrepancy over Arthur's historical subjectivity without thereby undermining Geoffrey of Monmouth's authoritative status and, therefore, the version of British and Arthurian history which he supplies. The impression which emerges from this passage is that the historiographical limitation is to be located in the work of the earlier insular historians, not in the *Historia regum Britannie*.

In his elaboration of the wider context of Arthurian narrative Mannyng is not merely concerned with the gaps in the Latin tradition of insular historiography, but he is also attentive to the differences between the material currently available in England and France. This is a topic which Mannyng develops in the second passage of narrative commentary in the Arthurian section of the *Chronicle*, which also seems to be prompted by, and draws attention to, ellipses in the textual record of Arthurian history. The subject on this later occasion is Arthur's nine-year stay in Gaul. The events of this period, which followed Arthur's defeat of the Roman tribune Frollo, are related very briefly in the *Historia regum Britannie* (155). In the *Roman de Brut* Wace adds only a very general description of the marvels of this time:

> Es neuf anz que il France tint,
> Mainte merveille li avint,
> Maint orguillus home danta
> E meint felun amesura.
>   (10,143–46)[26]

The impression that this is a period of manifold adventures, battles and dangers, is enhanced, retrospectively, in Wace's elaboration of the scenes which follow when the British side return from France and are reunited with their families: those who return recount stories about the marvellous events and real battles which have taken place during this time (10,193–96). Wace does not offer any further details of these events, nor any kind of narratorial commentary at this point in his text. Mannyng, in contrast, does draw his audience's attention to other 'grete bokes' which elaborate on the events of Arthurian history, and adds some interesting comments on the relationship, in his own time, between the literary traditions of France and England and their distinguishing features:

> Manye wondres by times sers
> Bytydde Arthur þo nyn[e] ʒeres;
> Many a proud man lowe he brought,

---

[26] 'In the nine years he [Arthur] had possession of France many marvellous events happened to him: he humbled many a proud man, many a law-breaker he brought to justice.'

> Til many felon, wo he wrought;
> Enuyous men he hated alle,
> Þe mysproude ful lowe dide falle.
> Þer haue men bokes of al his lyf,
> Þer are his merueilles red ful ryf;
> Þat we of hym here alle rede,
> Þere were þey writen ilka dede.
> Þyse grete bokes so faire langage,
> Writen and spoken of ffraunces vsage,
> Þat neuere was writen þorow Englischemen,
> Swilk stile to speke, kynde ne can,
> But ffrensche men wryten hit in prose,
> Right as he dide, hym for to alose;
> In prose al of hym ys writen,
> Þe betere til vnderstande and wyten.
>
> (i, 10,961–78)[27]

The historical and textual space which Mannyng identifies here is one occupied by a corpus of French prose narratives which supply a fuller account of Arthur's reign. Evidently Arthurian history continued to be made after the appearance of the *Roman de Brut* in 1155. From the later twelfth century onwards, many more vernacular writers took up the opportunity to explore a historicised ideal of chivalry in Arthur's reign in verse and in prose.[28] Mannyng's remarks in this passage register the scale

---

[27] The last two lines of this passage are not found in the Petyt MS of the *Chronicle*.

[28] For a recent survey of the development of cycles of French prose narratives in the thirteenth century which elaborated on the marvels, adventures and quests of the Arthurian period see the section on 'Le Roman en Prose en France au XIIIe siècle' in the *Grundriss der romanischen Literaturen des Mittelalters*, ed. J. Frappier *et al.*, iv, Le Roman jusqu'à la fin du XIIIe siècle, ed. Jean Frappier and Reinhold Grimm (Heidelberg, 1978), pp.502–622. As yet little work has been done on the circulation of Arthurian material in French prose in early fourteenth-century England, but contemporary sources of information on this topic are difficult to find. The wills, for example, which provide M. Deansley with information about vernacular books in England are of a much later date than Mannyng's *Chronicle*. The list of books which Guy de Beauchamp, count of Warwick, donated to Bordesley Abbey in the early fourteenth century includes some which form part of the cycle sequences ('Un volum en lequel est le premer livere de Launcelot', 'Un volum de la Mort ly Roy Arthur, e de Mordret' etc.): see M. Blaess, 'L'Abbaye de Bordesley et les livres de Guy de Beauchamp', *Romania*, lxxviii (1957), 511–18. The survey by Blaess of 'Les manuscrits français dans les monastères Anglais au moyen âge' *Romania*, xciii (1973), 321–58, also indicates a few French Arthurian holdings. E. Salter briefly discusses the circulation of vernacular texts in her chapter, 'Conditions and Status', in *Fourteenth-Century English Poetry: Contexts and Readings*, ed. D. Pearsall and N. Zeeman (Oxford, 1983), pp.34–42, though again most of her evidence is drawn from the later, rather than earlier fourteenth century. As I remarked earlier (n. 17 above) Mannyng was certainly acquainted with the French prose version of the *Prophécies de Merlin*, and possibly a version of the *Estoire de Merlin*.

of the French prose narratives which had accreted around the history of Arthur's court and its personnel by the early fourteenth century.

This is not the only occasion in Mannyng's 'story of Inglande' where he draws attention to points at which the subject of his narrative intersects with more detailed material provided in other books: this is a trait which can be exemplified throughout his narrative. Here, unfortunately, we are not given enough information to identify which versions of the French prose cycles were known to Mannyng, but the citation is still of considerable interest. By drawing attention to these books of Arthurian narratives at this point in his text, Mannyng may be attempting to rationalise the relationship between their place of production (France) and their subject (Arthurian history): Arthur's nine-year stay in France appears to have stimulated his literary history there and resulted in the 'grete bokes' which can supply the missing history of this nine-year gap in Arthur's textual record and more besides (þer haue men bokes of al his lyf', 10,967). This material, however, is beyond the scope of Mannyng's linguistic and stylistic medium: writers in English, it appears, cannot match the 'faire langage' of these prose narratives composed in French in France.[29] Yet these 'grete bokes' were still accessible and apparently in circulation in England. Whereas earlier Mannyng had remarked that more about Arthur may be found in 'farre bokes . . . þan we haue in þys lond' (10,610–11), here he draws attention to books about Arthur's life in French prose 'þat *we* of hym *here* alle rede' (my italics, 10,969). English readers, it seems, might still read and appreciate these texts even if writers of Arthurian narrative in English did not have the option of imitating their literary form.

Mannyng's remarks in these Arthurian asides, and his literary practice in reproducing Arthurian material from Wace and Langtoft, provide an interesting insight into how narrative traditions about Arthurian history could be mapped out from the viewpoint of an early fourteenth-century English writer. The picture of cultural relations which emerges is a complicated one which subverts some of the well-established divisions (between French and English, literary and historical traditions) which structure modern attempts to reconstruct the history of Arthurian narrative in England. Mannyng's comments, and his literary practice, suggest a relationship both of continuity and difference between narrative

---

[29] See M.E.D. entry 'Prose' 1a for other examples of the (infrequent) use of the term in Middle English. Prose, of course, was used by writers in Middle English both in and before Mannyng's time though not, as yet, for secular narrative subjects such as Arthurian romance. For the use of prose in Middle English see N. Davis, 'Styles in English Prose of the Late Middle and Early Modern Period' in *Langue et Littérature: Actes du VIII Congrès de la Fédération Internationale des Langues et Littératures Modernes, Bibliothèque de la Faculte de Philosophie et Lettres de l'Université de Liège*, clxi (1961), pp.165–84.

traditions in English and French, in different prosodic media, produced in France and England. Whereas the narratives of Wace and Langtoft proved to be assimilable to the medium of verse in England (despite Mannyng's initial reservations), the fair prose of the French narratives which supplied the material for the 'gaps' in Mannyng's account of Arthurian history distinguished them as literary productions of France. Yet if the producers of these 'grete bokes' are to be distinguished from writers working in England, their respective audiences cannot be separated in the same way: the history of the production of Arthurian narratives in England is not necessarily coterminous with the history of the reception of Arthurian narratives, in English and French, in England. Mannyng's comments invoke the presence of an audience in England who have access to these French texts, which we 'here alle rede' (10,969). Mannyng's reference to the intersection between these French prose narratives and his own work also suggests that their contents cannot be separated from the tradition in which he was working. These 'grete bokes' (albeit in French prose) still contribute to the history of Arthurian narrative in England.

The interest in the relationship between the *locus* of events, the language of their report, and the place of their reception which can be seen in Mannyng's remarks on the 'grete bokes' of French prose obviously may be linked to that of his wider project: to compile a 'story of Inglande' in English. Mannyng's introductory comments on his choice of literary language have earned him a mention in English literary histories as an example of the shifting pattern of vernacular usage in the literature of medieval England.[30] More recently, Thorlac Turville-Petre has argued for a more radical interpretation of Mannyng's narrative project, suggesting that both in its contents and form the *Chronicle* represents a militant assertion of English autonomy against a political (and linguistic) Norman Yoke.[31] I have reservations about such a reading of this 'story of Inglande' and find it difficult to trace any kind of consistent opposition between English and Anglo-Norman interests in the narrative, or evidence for the consistent characterisation of the audience of the *Chronicle* which Turville-Petre's interpretation

---

[30] See, for example, R. Berndt's citation of Mannyng's comments on his use of English in 'The Period of the Final Decline in French in Medieval England (Fourteenth and Early Fifteenth Centuries)', *Zeitschrift für Anglistik und Amerikanistick*, xx (1972), 341–69, at 349.

[31] 'Politics and Poetry in the Early Fourteenth Century' (see n. 1 above).

requires.[32] Nevertheless, Turville-Petre is right to suggest that this *Chronicle*, and comparable works, have an important place in any attempt to reconstruct the complex cultural context of fourteenth-century England. Charting the identity of an English community of interest is one of the most important issues at stake in Mannyng's work; but if his genealogical narrative provides a way of affirming the historical identity of the English realm, it also offers an arena for confronting the discrepancies, inconsistencies, contradictions, and complications in that identity. Mannyng's choice of literary language may indeed represent an attempt to enhance the symbolic identification of a language (English) with its historical subject (England), for a locatable community of interest (the English). Yet the mixed linguistic, cultural and historical heritage of England's past and present which the *Chronicle* reveals also indicates that this relationship was not necessarily a contiguous one and nor was Mannyng's mother-tongue as yet the only, or necessary, medium for such a genealogical narrative, the 'story of Inglande'.

I remarked earlier that Mannyng's *Chronicle* is still relatively inaccessible: this is not only because we do not yet have access to a modern edition of the whole text, based on a single manuscript version, but also because this 'story of Inglande' belongs to an 'uncertain and unfamiliar literary category', that of the vernacular verse chronicle.[33] Such texts

[32] Turville-Petre argues that in late medieval England 'a large section of the population regarded the post-Conquest nobility as foreigners holding the English nation in subjection', 'Politics and Poetry in the Early Fourteenth Century', p. 17, and suggests that these English, anti-Anglo-Norman, sentiments are voiced in Mannyng's *Chronicle*. However, the evidence for this polemical anti-Anglo-Norman slant (cited on pp.14–15) is insufficient to substantiate this interpretation of Mannyng's narrative as a whole. Moreover, as Turville-Petre later recognises, it would not be at all easy to separate the 'Norman' from 'English' nobility by the beginning of the fourteenth century (p. 24). The audience invoked by the narrator of the *Chronicle* is more heterogeneous than the opening address to the 'lewed' English suggests. The community of interest which the narrator addresses is defined, at various points in the narrative, in opposition to those who inhabit Wales, Scotland and France. But this English community of interest which is defined by the narrator's use of the pronouns 'we' and 'us' transcends the learned/unlearned categories of Mannyng's opening address. His audience is apparently one which includes those who know Robert Malton, prior of Sixhills ('þat ye know', 142) and has access to narratives in French ('þat we . . . rede', i, 10, 969) and Latin ('as seint Bede doþ vs to wyten', i, 14,781). There is little evidence outside of the *Chronicle* itself which would help us recreate some sense of its contemporary audience with more precision, but there are signs that it was read and reused for more than a century after its composition. The three extant manuscripts date from the later fourteenth and fifteenth century and material from the *Chronicle* was used in the composition of the alliterative *Morte Arthure* (dated *c.* 1400). A paraphrase of Mannyng's version of the 'geste' of the English has been identified in the compilations of historical narratives attributed to Richard Fox of St. Albans (*c.* 1448). For Fox's compilation see L. Matheson, 'Historical Prose', in *Middle English Prose*, ed. A.S.G. Edwards (New Jersey, 1984), pp.218–19.

[33] M. Swanton, *English Literature before Chaucer* (London, 1987), p. 175.

tend to fall between the departmental organisation of medieval studies being, it seems, too literary for the attention of modern readers of medieval historiography and too historical for modern readers of medieval literature (and possibly too derivative for both audiences). Yet these kinds of narratives highlight the arbitrary nature of such disciplinary divisions which the work of John Taylor has done much to overcome. Although my discussion has concentrated on the way in which Mannyng elaborates on the synchronic and diachronic contexts of Arthurian historical narrative in just two narratorial asides, the interest in charting a complex cultural heritage which is evident in these passages is a feature of Mannyng's *Chronicle* as a whole.

Chapter 10

'Welcome, My Brother': Edward II, John of Powderham and the Chronicles, 1318

W.R. Childs

In July 1318, at the height of delicate negotiations which led to the reconciliation of the king with Thomas, earl of Lancaster, at the treaty of Leake, Edward II was confronted by the further problem of a rival claimant to his throne. The episode is interesting in itself, and allows a glimpse of the complex interwoven assumptions and attitudes in the political world of the early fourteenth century. For details about it we are almost entirely dependent on the chronicles.

The only clear information in the records is a writ of July 20, ordering William Montague, the king's steward, John de Botetourt, and Henry Beaufiz to take from the gaol at Northampton a man named as John of Exeter, who was in prison for saying he was the king's brother and claiming that the realm was his. Apart from this writ, there is an entry in the roll of the Marshalsea Court held by William Montague, as steward, at Oxford on 26 July, recording that the sheriff and the mayor of Oxford were both amerced for not appearing before him in response to an order from the king.[1] It is possible that this relates to the same case. John first made his claim at Oxford and the sheriff and mayor of the city may well have been obvious witnesses to summon to his trial in Northampton. Beyond these two entries the records are silent. Fortunately the case is reported in a wide range of chronicles, from the west country, London, and the north, including several of the most trustworthy and well informed. The most immediate version is in the *Annales Paulini*, in the section probably originally compiled by 1320; one of the most sober versions is in the reliable *Vita Edwardi secundi*, written within eight years of the event. Some of the reports written in the next fifteen to twenty years

---

[1] *Calendar of Patent Rolls, 1317–21*, p.273; P.R.O., E 37/4 m. 3. Other published records (notably *Calendars of Close Rolls, Chancery Warrants*, and *Miscellaneous Inquisitions, Abbreviatio placitorum, Foedera*) offer no help. The Wardrobe Book for the year does not survive. The King's Bench roll for the period (P.R.O., KB 27/233) reveals nothing, as the case was heard summarily. There are no other references to the episode in the Marshalsea Rolls at the time (P.R.O., E 37/3 and 4).

are more elaborate, but not necessarily less reliable. The chronicles of Bridlington and Lanercost are generally trustworthy; the longer versions of the short continuation of the French prose Brut preserve plausible detail not found elsewhere; the Dominican, Robert Holcot, who used the event as an *exemplum* in his commentary on the Book of Wisdom, knew Northampton where the claimant was executed; and the Osney Chronicle, although not written until about 1347, nonetheless came from Oxford and might have used eye witness accounts.[2] Although versions vary there is a common core of information, and enough uncontradictory circumstantial detail to reconstruct a reasonable narrative.

In June, about the feast of the Nativity of St. John the Baptist (24 June) according to the usually reliable chronicle of Lanercost, but at Pentecost (11 June) according to the Osney and Meaux Chronicles, a man variously described as *literatus* or *scriptor*, came to Oxford. Three

---

[2] The episode is found in the following chronicles of the early to mid fourteenth century for which approximate dates of composition are provided. *Annales Paulini*, in *Chronicles of the Reigns of Edward I and Edward II*, ed. W. Stubbs, Rolls Series, lxxvi, 2 vols. (1882–83), i, pp.282–83 (this section *c.* 1320); *Nicolai Triveti annalium continuatio*, ed. Antony Hall (Oxford, 1722), pp.26–27 (possibly *c.* 1322); *Vita Edwardi secundi*, ed. N. Denholm-Young (1957), pp.86–87 (1326); *Chroniques de Sempringham*, in *Le livere de reis de Brittanie e le livere de reis de Engleterre*, ed. J. Glover, Rolls Series, xlii, (1865), p.335 *c.* 1326); *Polychronicon Ranulphi Higden*, ed. J.R. Lumby, Rolls Series, xli, 9 vols. (1865–86), viii, p.308 (1320s–1350s); the short continuation of the French prose Brut as in the Anonimalle Chronicle (Brotherton Library, University of Leeds, MS 29), fos. 251v–252 (*c.* 1333); the section of the Anonimalle Chronicle for 1307–34 is shortly to be published, edited by John Taylor and Wendy Childs, Yorkshire Archaeological Society Records Series, cxlvii (1991); *The Brut*, ed. F.W.D. Brie, Early English Text Society, cxxxi (1906), pp.208–9 (*c.* 1333); Robert Holcot, *Super librum Sapientiae*, cited in B. Smalley, *English Friars and Antiquity in the Early Fourteenth Century* (Oxford, 1960), p.325 (*c.* 1334–36?); *Gesta Edwardi de Carnarvan auctore canonico Bridlingtoniensi*, in *Chronicles of the Reigns of Edward I and Edward II*, ii, p.55 (*c.* 1339 and 1370); *Chronicon de Lanercost*, ed. J. Stevenson, Maitland Club (Edinburgh, 1839), as translated in *English Historical Documents*, iii, ed. H. Rothwell (London, 1975), pp.270–71 (*c.* 1346); *Annales Monasterii de Oseneia*, in *Annales monastici*, iv, ed. H.R. Luard, Rolls Series, xxxvi (1869), pp.344–45 (*c.* 1347?); *Scalacronica: The Reigns of Edward I, Edward II and Edward III, as recorded by Sir Thomas Gray*, trans. Sir Herbert Maxwell (Glasgow, 1907), p.65 (1355–57). The imposture was also recorded in late fourteenth- and fifteenth-century compilations: *Chronica monasterii de Melsa*, ed. E.A. Bond, Rolls Series, xliii, 3 vols. (1866–68), ii, pp.335–36; *Thomae Walsingham, quondam monachi S. Albani, Historia Anglicana*, ed. H.T. Riley, Rolls Series, xxviii, 2 vols. (1863–64), i, p.158; *A Chronicle of London from 1089–1483*, ed. Sir Nicholas Harris Nicolas and E. Tyrrell (1827), pp.44–45. The last (B.L., MS Harley 565) drew heavily on the Brut and *Melsa* but wrongly ascribed the incident to 1314–15. The episode was *not* recorded in the following early chronicles: *Flores historiarum*, ed. H.R. Luard, Rolls Series, lxxxxv (1890); *Johannis de Trokelowe et Henrici de Blaneforde, chronica et annales*, ed. H.T. Riley, Rolls Series, xxviii (1866); *Adae Murimuth continuatio chronicarum*, ed. E. Maunde Thompson, Rolls Series, lxxxxiii (1889); *Croniques de London*, ed. G.J. Aungier, Camden Soc. original series, xxviii, (1844); *Chronicon Galfridi le Baker de Swynbroke*, ed. E. Maunde Thompson (Oxford, 1889).

chronicles name him: the short continuation of the French prose Brut calls him John Poydras, son of an Exeter tanner; the long continuation in its English translation calls him John Tanner; and the Lanercost Chronicle calls him John of Powderham, which fits an Exeter origin. Several chronicles relate that he went to the King's Hall in Oxford, where the Carmelite friars were beginning to build a church. This hall, which lay immediately outside the city wall at the north gate, had recently been granted to them by Edward II in fulfilment of a vow made after the battle of Bannockburn.[3] Here John, claiming to be the true heir of Edward I, and therefore king of England, ordered the Carmelites to leave his house. The continuator of Nicholas Trivet's chronicle claimed that John sent specifically for the mayor and people of Oxford to make his announcement, and the *Annales Paulini* record that the mayor and people of Oxford had him seized and sent to the Bocardo prison, the Oxford city gaol which probably received its name from smelling as noisome as a privy or 'boggard'.[4] The explicit involvement of the mayor suggests that the entry in the Marshalsea plea rolls mentioned above may refer to this case.

The arguments offered by Powderham are not well reported, but the author of the *Vita*, one of the earliest writers, already noted that he claimed to be Edward I's son taken from the cradle. The canon of Bridlington also reported that he was changed in the cradle by the midwife for an unknown reason. Two chronicles offer more. The annals of Osney, probably drawing on local Oxford memories, say that the royal nurses through negligence allowed the boy to fall from his cradle into the fire so that he was burned, and, not daring to tell the king, they substituted the son of one of the queen's grooms or drivers (*auriga*), a child of the same age as the prince. Much later the abbot of Meaux recorded the story that the prince had been injured in his cradle by a sow and again the terrified nurse had substituted the son of an *auriga*. Whether the story of the sow was rumour or the abbot's misreading of a text is unclear. Stories of children savaged by pigs were not unknown. In 1268 a request was made for letters patent to certify that a man had lost his ears not in the pillory but when savaged by a pig in his cradle, and in London in 1322 the one-month-old daughter

[3] The grant of the king's manor was made on 1 February 1318, confirmed by the pope in May, and in parliament in October; *Calendar of Patent Rolls, 1317–21*, pp.75, 103–4, 168–9, 237; *Calendar of Papal Letters*, ii, p.175. The version of the short continuation of the French prose Brut in the Anonimalle Chronicle (Brotherton Library, MS 29) wrongly calls the friars *cordeilles* (Franciscan); other versions correctly have *carmes*.

[4] R.B. Pugh, *Imprisonment in Medieval England* (Cambridge, 1968), pp.360–61.

of a shop keeper was killed when a sow bit her head as she lay in her cradle,[5] but this sort of thing seems unlikely to have happened in a royal nursery. Moreover, Edward's nurses seem to have been respectable and to have remained in royal favour. True, Mary Maunsel, his first nurse, may have left within a few months of his birth in 1284, but this was probably because of illness, and she was still in possession of a generous grant in 1317. His second nurse, Alice de Leygrave, and her family were given a series of grants throughout the reign, and she received confirmation of a wardship she held in 1318 itself.[6] The story of the substitution is associated with Edward's known enjoyment of undignified hobbies. The Lanercost chronicler says that many believed the claims at Oxford because Edward II was so manifestly different from Edward I, and the abbot of Meaux repeated the pretender's claim that his case was proved because Edward naturally enjoyed the work of countrymen which reflected the activities of his true father.

The pretender persisted in his claims and so was sent the forty odd miles from Oxford to Northampton where the king and his court had been from 30 June, trying to hammer out an agreement with Lancaster.[7] Even face to face with the king, he continued to press his story. The short continuation of the French prose Brut uniquely records that the king was not greatly impressed. He wished to treat the man as a fool, and to give him a jester's club or 'bauble'. The king's attitude is also reflected in the Lanercost chronicler's description of his address to John – 'Welcome, my brother' – as derisive. However, the author of the *Vita* tells us that the queen was unspeakably annoyed, and most chronicles note that the magnates, when consulted, were condemnatory. An offence so clearly against the king and in his presence was dealt with summarily at court. The Lanercost chronicle has the fullest account of the trial. It reports that time was taken to hold a council meeting and to assemble a large number of people (although, since negotiations with Lancaster were proceeding, most great political figures must already have been on hand), and that the trial was held before the steward of the household, William Montague. Montague's involvement is confirmed by the instruction to him to take Powderham from Northampton gaol. The short continuation of the French prose Brut also indicates a careful trial. It uniquely reports that the man's parents were brought from Exeter, some 180 miles away,

---

[5] *Calendar of Patent Rolls, 1266–72*, p.193; *Calendar of Coroners' Rolls of the City of London, A.D. 1300–1378*, ed. R.R. Sharpe (London, 1913), p.56, no.29.

[6] H. Johnstone, *Edward of Carnarvon* (Manchester, 1946), p.9; *Calendar of Patent Rolls, 1317–21*, p.251.

[7] *The Itinerary of Edward II*, ed. E. Hallam, List and Index Society, 211 (1984), pp.168–71.

which would have taken some days. They were sworn in before the king's council and dared not say otherwise than that he was their son. The Lanercost chronicler reports the alleged words of the steward's judgment, which showed that the court was not certain whether the man had been put up to his claim or had dreamt it up himself; but this did not matter. The judgement was death. The execution took place towards the end of July. The annals of St. Paul's and the canon of Bridlington prefer the feast of St. Margaret the Virgin (20 July), which is the date of the order to deliver Powderham from Northampton gaol; the short continuation of the French prose Brut records the eve of St. James (24 July); and the Sempringham chronicler 'about the feast of St. James', perhaps indicating that the gaol delivery was for the beginning of the trial. By this time Edward himself had moved for a few days to Woodstock, but his presence would not be necessary for the execution. Powderham was drawn through the streets and hanged. Robert Holcot, who knew Northampton well and may have had local informants, refers to his being left to hang for a long time – 'while bones still clung to bones'. The execution is emphasised as a just sentence for a traitor, and the author of the *Vita* combined the words of Exodus 21:17 and 22:28 'He who curses the ruler shall surely die' – to justify it.

Almost all chronicles mention an association between Powderham and the devil, and this possibly influenced two reports of the execution. The Lanercost Chronicle records that he was to be burnt after hanging, and the west country continuator of Trivet records that his heart was burnt; both possibly reflect an awareness of the church's increasing association of witchcraft with heresy. Of those mentioning witchcraft, some chronicles simply imply association with the devil by relating that John came to Oxford accompanied by a cat, or a cat and a dog. Others are more explicit. The annals of Osney explicitly say that the cat was a familiar. The short continuation of the French prose *Brut* mentions that the devil drove him to come with a cat and a little cart.[8] The Lanercost chronicler has the devil tell him to take a tom cat, a dog, and a cock with him to Oxford. The *Scalacronica* records that he was told to make his claim by the devil in the shape of a cat. In several chronicles the pretender confessed to association with the devil once sentence had been passed. The *Annales Paulini* reports his claim that the devil drove him, and that he had believed in magic for seven years. The published Brut has him confess to serving the devil for three years. Robert Holcot related that the devil promised that John would ride through England at the head of an army greater than any of Edward I. The Lanercost chronicler contains the longest

---

[8] 'Charrette'. This may be a misreading of a source or an oblique allusion to the substitution of the son of a carter.

description. Here John confessed that the devil first appeared to him in dreams, and promised him carnal pleasures, which he subsequently enjoyed. Then the devil appeared in daytime, in a field, in the guise of a man and asked John if he had ever found him untruthful. Powderham agreed he had never found the devil false. The devil then promised him riches and the throne of England if he would do homage in return, and also promised to help him fight for it. No doubt this is why the same chronicle mentions John's offer to prove his claim by combat.

The episode's association with dreams and the devil struck similar chords in the minds of the two mendicant writers. The Dominican, Holcot, saw this story as a useful *exemplum* for *lectio* cxc on attitudes to magic in his commentary on the Book of Wisdom, and the digression on the vanity of dreams made at this point in the Lanercost chronicle was probably inserted by the original Franciscan author. He too referred to the Book of Wisdom, and to Jeremiah, and quoted the text: 'Dreams excite the unwary, and as one who catcheth at a shadow and pursueth the wind, so is he who taketh heed to the deceptive visions of a dream' (Ecclesiasticus 34:1–2). This text and Jeremiah 23, on the dreams of true and false prophets, are both texts (of course among many others) also used by Holcot in several lectures on the interpretations of dreams, in which he notes the devil's use of dreams to delude men.[9] Whether Holcot's work was already known to the Lanercost author, or whether they were drawing on a common intellectual stock is not clear, but for both the incident had become closely associated with thoughts on magic and dreams in the context of kingship. Beryl Smalley has pointed to the increasing popularity of commentaries on the Book of Wisdom by the early fourteenth century, partly because it was written as advice to rulers, and thus provided a religious view of political theory on kingship to complement the secular writings *De Regimine Principum*.[10] Certainly the events of Edward II's reign, no less than those of Edward I's after 1297, offered plenty of encouragement and material to those who wished to debate the qualities of just and good kingship.

The witchcraft aspect of the case is interesting, but Powderham's alleged pact with the devil was not an isolated incident. Europe in the early fourteenth century experienced a small flurry of accusations

---

[9] Smalley, *Friars*, p.325; see B. Smalley, 'Robert Holcot O.P.', *Archivum Fratrum Praedicatorum*, xxvi (1956), 13. For the numbering of the lectures I have used the edition of 1506, *Ropertus Holkot super librum Sapientie*, where the *lectio* containing the *exemplum* is numbered clxxxix, and the *lectiones* on dreams are clxxxxi and cci.

[10] Smalley, 'Robert Holcot', 10–11.

of witchcraft.[11] The accusations of the period divided broadly into two kinds: accusations of simple magic or sorcery, including images and charms; and accusations of association with the devil. Many churchmen, like Holcot and the Lanercost compiler, still saw pacts with the devil as delusions, but increasingly in the fourteenth century learned opinion came to see the devil as a real force. Accusations of pacts with the devil also came in two kinds, those close to sorcery of conjuring up demons to serve man, and more serious ones of full diabolism including homage to and worship of the devil. The second sort were less often made at this time, but surface in accusations against the Templars, and against Alice Kyteler in Ireland. One particular characteristic of cases at this period was their involvement of important political figures, especially in France and the papal court, but also in England.

The nine incidents known in England and Ireland between 1300 and 1330 range from simple accusations of sorcery to alleged pacts with the devil. Four had political overtones.[12] The case against Powderham comes in the middle of the period. He is clearly accused of having gone beyond the first stage of conjuring demons to serve him, to that of himself serving the devil. Perhaps it was no coincidence that he came from Exeter, since in 1302 municipal archives there refer to two cases of popular witchcraft. Then, in London in 1311, the bishop was instructed to investigate reports of growing witchcraft in his diocese. In 1314 Juliana of Lambeth, daughter of a converted Jew, was convicted of sorcery.[13] More distantly, Alice Kyteler, faced detailed charges in Ireland in 1324, when her stepchildren accused her of murdering her former husbands. Like Powderham, she had a familiar; hers appeared as a cat, a black hairy dog, or an 'Ethiopian'.[14]

The four political cases start in 1301, when among a wide range of accusations against Walter Langton, bishop of Coventry and Lichfield, had been one of paying homage to the devil. They are rounded off by the allegations in 1330 that the earl of Kent, Edward II's half-brother,

[11] For a recent analysis of both popular and learned accusations, see R. Kieckhefer, *European Witch Trials: Their Foundations in Popular and Learned Culture, 1300–1500* (London, 1976). J.B. Russell, *Witchcraft in the Middle Ages* (Cornell, 1972), pp.167–86 also examines the links of witchcraft with the political trials of this period and the contemporary debates of its links with heresy. Useful details are still to be found in G.L. Kittredge, *Witchcraft in Old and New England* (New York, 1956).

[12] Kieckhefer, *Witch Trials*, pp.108–9, provides a calendar of trials. The trial of Juliana should be added, and the date for the impostor's trial corrected. It was taken from Kittredge, *Witchcraft*, p.242, who drew it from *A Chronicle of London*, ed. Nicolas and Tyrrell (see above note 2).

[13] *Annales Londonienses*, in *Chronicles of the Reigns of Edward I and Edward II*, ed. Stubbs, ii, p.236; *Annales Paulini, ibid.*, p.275–76.

[14] *The Proceedings against Dame Alice Kyteler, Prosecuted for Sorcery in 1324*, ed. T. Wright, Camden Society (1843), pp.1–3.

accused of plotting to release him from prison, had received information that Edward was still alive from a devil conjured up by a friar. The other two cases involve lesser defendants. First there is Powderham, who came from an urban craft background, then there is a group of twenty-seven men from a similar urban background in Coventry who were charged with intending to murder the king, the Despensers and the prior of Coventry through sorcery in 1323.[15]

Clearly accusations of witchcraft, although not as frequent as abroad, were not unusual in England in the first thirty years of the fourteenth century; nor were they unknown in political cases. Here French influence may have shaped attitudes, since court connections were close, and the case against the Templars was rehearsed in England as elsewhere. But English political cases were many fewer. Political stability, for all Edward's faults, was not as shaky as in France, where the deaths of four kings in twelve years gave rise to wild accusations. Accusations of magic and pacts with the devil could make offences seem more horrible and help condemn a man, since witchcraft was popularly feared, yet there was no witch hysteria in England at this time. Powderham was clearly condemned as a liar and a traitor not as a witch; and juries in common law and municipal courts were quite likely to acquit the accused, as they did with the leader of the Coventry group. Moreover, not all chroniclers were impressed with the tales of the devil's participation in Powderham's claim. Several mentioned it without emphasis; the canon of Bridlington was sceptical, and willing to see the man as simply weak in the head; and the level-headed author of the *Vita Edwardi secundi* did not even think the witchcraft aspect worth mentioning.

Despite its interesting overtones of witchcraft, the main importance of this episode for the historian lies in its political significance. Whether the man was unhinged and acting alone, or whether he was manipulated by others, his advent certainly came at a delicate and potentially embarrassing time for the king. The political events of 1317 and 1318 have been carefully worked out.[16] England was hovering on the edge of civil war. The main problem was in Edward's relations with Lancaster, who had withdrawn from his position as leader of the Council in April 1316. Attempts had been made in April, July, and August 1317 to get Lancaster and the king together but in vain. By the autumn of 1317 civil war seemed particularly near. Lancaster blocked the bridges at Pontefract to supplies sent to the king at York, and the king, passing Pontefract Castle on his return in October, was persuaded only with

---

[15] *Select Cases in the Court of King's Bench under Edward II*, iv, ed. G.O. Sayles, Selden Society, lxxiv, (1955), pp.154–57.

[16] J.R. Maddicott, *Thomas of Lancaster, 1307–1322* (Oxford, 1970), pp.208–29; J.R.S. Phillips, *Aymer de Valence, Earl of Pembroke 1307–1324* (Oxford, 1972), pp.125–77.

difficulty not to attack Lancaster. The king hated his cousin for his part in the death of Gaveston, and resented his harping on the Ordinances, which Edward saw as humiliating. Lancaster feared not only the king, but the king's favourites and close advisers; he had heard rumours that the king would kill or imprison him if he came to the meeting in August 1317, and in July 1318 he stated that he had heard that Damory and Montague were conspiring to kill him. The court group's interests were best served by Lancaster's absence, and no doubt they did their best to hinder a reconciliation. Wiser advisers too, both magnates and bishops, had run out of patience with Lancaster's postures, but the growing lawlessness convinced them that the king and Lancaster must be brought together. Negotiations proved extremely difficult, especially over royal grants made against the terms of the Ordinances, over certain of the king's advisers, and over a pardon to Lancaster for his offences. However, the hand of magnates and prelates meeting Lancaster in April 1318 at Leicester was strengthened by the need to face the Scots, who regained Berwick in April and then swept in raids as far south as Yorkshire in May. Accordingly June and July 1318 were devoted to meetings to prepare the full reconciliation of Edward and Lancaster. On 2 June a meeting at Westminster, highly critical of Lancaster's shortcomings, nonetheless produced draft conditions for a reconciliation. The king's side showed its willingness to compromise, with an announcement on 8 June that the king would accept the advice of his earls and barons, with an order on 9 June to resume all grants made since the Ordinances, and with the agreement on 11 June of the elder Despenser, Damory, the younger Audley, Montague, and Charlton not to threaten Lancaster when he came to the king. The bishops of Ely and Norwich and the archbishop of Dublin then went to Tutbury to hammer out the details; in expectation of success a safe-conduct was issued for Lancaster to come to the king on 29 June. By 23 June the talks had failed. It was exactly at this time, between 11 and 24 June, that the impostor was reported in Oxford. There is nothing to show that his appearance affected the talks. There were quite enough problems over resumption and the king's advisers to explain the failure, but any suspicion of manipulation of a pretender might have raised tempers at a crucial moment.

On 4 July another embassy went to meet Lancaster. On 11 and again on 18 July the archbishop of Canterbury expected success, but again talks failed. The unknown writer of a letter of about 21 July ascribed failure to a deliberate reversal of policy by some of the envoys, but Dr. Phillips has argued that it was more likely due to a last stand by the king's favourites, trying to avert a total resumption of grants and a standing council. A further embassy was sent to Lancaster between 20 and 29 July, and at last agreement was reached. A pardon was issued on 31 July to Lancaster for all offences before 25 July, and a further embassy, sent to him on 1 August, resulted at last in his meeting the king to exchange the kiss of peace on 7 August. On 9 August the treaty of Leake recorded their agreement. The impostor's transfer to Northampton, trial and execution all took place during these tense days in July. Again there is nothing to show that the episode affected talks, yet the attention of some magnates and prelates may have been diverted from Lancaster to what was happening at the court in Northampton.

Was the impostor simply acting alone, being weak in the head as the canon of Bridlington suggested? Or was he manipulated by others, a question raised by Montague when he gave judgement, according to the Lanercost chronicler? A foolish half-educated man, using his book-learning to dabble in magic, already convinced that the devil came to him in dreams, might easily be led. Although four chronicles record that he came to Oxford to make his claim, eight others simply record it as being made at Oxford; perhaps he had already moved from Exeter to make his living as a scribe on the fringes of Oxford's university community. Perhaps such a move was influenced by the establishment of a new college at Oxford by Walter Stapledon, bishop of Exeter, at this time. The first buildings were acquired in 1314, and the statutes, drawn up in 1316, declared all the scholars should be from the Exeter diocese. There is nothing to suggest Powderham had any formal link with the college but knowledge of the new establishment might have encouraged him to try his fortune in Oxford.[17] Here, in the Midlands, he and his dreams might come more easily to the notice of active political figures. A carefully arranged 'chance' meeting in a field and some carefully chosen words might be sufficient. The Lanercost chronicler certainly draws a clear distinction between the early dreams and the one appearance in broad daylight of the devil in the guise of a man.

If he were manipulated, who might expect to benefit during the negotiations? The king's favourites clearly wanted to hinder a peace settlement, but it is not easy to see how an attack on the king's position would help them, unless they hoped to attribute the attack to Lancaster and his supporters, and so undermine the earl's position. It is conceivable that Lancaster or some of his supporters might have encouraged an attack on the king's position if they thought it would weaken him, make him more eager for reconciliation, and therefore more willing to meet some of Lancaster's conditions. Certainly Lancaster was difficult to the last, and squeezed more from the king than had first been offered. However, there is no suggestion in the long accusations against him at his trial in 1322 that he was in any way associated with this particular act of treason.

[17] M. Buck, *Politics, Finance and the Church in the Reign of Edward II* (Cambridge, 1983), pp.102–3, 110. I am indebted to Dr. Phillips for reminding me of this coincidence.

Even if it did seem attractive to some of the king's opponents to support a claimant to embarrass the king, it is unlikely that any saw the deposition of Edward as a practical possibility at this time. True, the separation of the person of king and the office of crown, which was aired in the declaration of 1308 against Gaveston, made the deposition of a king theoretically possible, and threats of deposition had been made in 1310 in order to force through the appointment of the Ordainers, and would be again in 1321 by the group pressing the exile of the Despensers,[18] but these were threats to force a particular political outcome, and there is no indication that the king's opponents had given thought to how it might be done, nor to whom they would have instead. In 1310 the king had no children. In 1318 that situation had improved but the future Edward III was only five and a half years old, and John of Eltham was not yet two. The prospect was of a long regency unless a suitable alternative candidate could be found. There was no other branch to turn to as in the fifteenth century. Edward I had clearly been the rightful king, his son was his legitimate heir, and Edward II was accepted as that heir. However, just for a moment, a question was raised about his paternity, and in such a way that no scandal touched Eleanor and Edward I. The story of a changeling offered the possibility of an alternative.

Inspiration for this claim to the throne may have come to the literate Powderham and his manipulators, if such there were, from current stories about fostered royal children. The story of Havelock the Dane provides the nearest parallel. Recorded from the twelfth century, it was given its fullest treatment about now, possibly in the first decade of the fourteenth century.[19] The dispossessed heir to the Danish throne, through circumstances of war and piracy, came to England, was brought up in a fisherman's household at Grimsby, and later became the scullion of a nobleman. This nobleman then usurped the throne from his niece, whom he disparaged by marrying her to his scullion, Havelock. After several adventures Havelock regained his throne and that of his wife. *Havelock*'s most recent editor, while accepting that the poem is essentially an entertainment, also emphasises that its whole theme is that of righting wrong, of kingship, dispossession and rightful heirs.[20] Further inspiration could have been drawn from the story of King Arthur's fostering, although there the fostering household was still aristocratic. The changeling motif is not apparent in these tales, but may have been popularly current. It later surfaced in the Second Shepherds' Play of the Wakefield Pageants, but there the agency for proposed substitution is unnatural, whereas

---

[18] *Vita*, pp.10, 109.
[19] G.V. Smithers, ed., *Havelock* (Oxford, 1987), pp.xvi–xxv, lxiv–xxii.
[20] *Ibid.*, pp.lvii–ix.

the changeling story in the chronicles is explained entirely in human terms.[21]

The reports of Powderham's claim show some conflict over his supposed royal relationship. The order for the Northampton gaol delivery notes he claimed to be Edward's brother, presumably an elder brother if he claimed the throne, and the Lanercost chronicler mentions Edward's jibe of 'Welcome, my brother', but the author of the *Vita* already recorded his claim to be Edward himself and most later chronicles assume the same. Proof of this for some of his readers lay in Edward II's hobbies.

Despite some social mobility in the middle ages, the belief was strong that a man was born to a particular station and that 'blood will out', high or low. The gentle blood of Havelock and Arthur was apparent from an early age, despite their current settings, and Holcot related the tale of a lion who recognised the royal blood of the French prince exposed by his father who doubted his legitimacy.[22] More often references were made to men rising above their station. Romances might show that the upstart commoner could never acquire the bravery and loyalty of the true born knight. The canon of Bridlington criticised the unsuitable greed and pride of Harclay, of respectable family, but, in being made earl of Carlisle in 1322, rising too far.[23] It is not surprising therefore that Edward II's unsuitable hobbies provided fuel to rumours that he was not of royal blood. The earliest contemporary reference to Edward's rustic activities comes in record rather than chronicle source, in a law suit of 1315/16. Robert le Messager, a king's messenger, was accused of saying in July 1314 that it was no wonder that Edward lost the battle of Bannockburn because he did not go to Mass. When asked what Edward did instead, he replied that the king was 'idling, and applying himself to making ditches and digging and other improper occupations'.[24] These criticisms appear in the chronicles too. The author of the *Vita Edwardi secundi*, writing before the end of Edward's reign, lamented his pleasure in rustic pursuits rather than devotion to arms.[25] Higden's description is probably the best known, referring to Edward's liking for 'jesters, singers, actors, carters, ditchers, rowers, seamen and other workers in the mechanical arts'. The canon of Bridlington echoed his words.[26] The Lanercost chronicler explicitly remarked that the impostor was given

[21] A.C. Cawley, ed., *The Wakefield Pageants in the Towneley Cycle* (Manchester, 1958), p.59, line 616.

[22] Smalley, *English Friars*, p.162.

[23] *Bridlington*, p.83.

[24] H. Johnstone, 'The Eccentricities of Edward II', *English Historical Review*, xlviii (1933), 264–67.

[25] *Vita*, p.40.

[26] *Polychronicon*, viii, p.298; *Bridlington*, p.91.

credence by certain foolish people because of Edward's liking from his youth for 'the arts of rowing and driving chariots, digging pits and roofing houses; also that he wrought as a craftsman with his boon companions by night, and at other mechanical arts, besides other vanities and frivolities wherein it doth not become a king's son to busy himself'.[27] It is not surprising that a groom or carter appears as the suggested father of the substituted child. The published *Brut* on the other hand emphasised Edward's aquatic pastimes, reporting that the Scots derided the English defeat at Bannockburn with a song which included chants of 'heavalow' and 'rumbalow', suggesting that a king who preferred rowing to fighting could never hope to win a war.[28] Thomas Gray, who used the *Brut* as a source for his *Scalacronica*, also emphasised that the king amused himself with ships, and among mariners.[29] Yet, even if Edward enjoyed unkingly pursuits, the chroniclers agreed that he looked a king, and it is highly doubtful whether any aristocratic manipulator seriously thought that a man whose background was an upbringing in an Exeter craft family, followed by enough academic training to provide him with a livelihood as a scribe, and who believed he was in contact with the devil, would be considered more suitable. Edward's initial reaction of seeing him as a court jester might well have been the right one in normal times.

But these were not normal times. Edward's relations with Lancaster were near breaking point, and the king and his government seemed unable to keep order internally or protect the north. Perhaps some men's thoughts were turning to the possibility of removing an unsuitable king. Edward himself might well have laughed, but the court rightly saw the claim as treason and they were alarmed enough to execute Powderham to discourage disloyalty in others – 'ad terrorem aliorum' as the continuator of Trivet wrote, a view to be echoed later by Walsingham. Indeed Edward himself on reflection may have been less amused. The weakness of his position was clear to him and, as Dr. Phillips has recently shown, he seems to have wanted to strengthen it by reviving the legend of the Holy Oil of St. Thomas, and trying to arrange a re-anointing with this in 1318. His actions, begun in 1317, were not directly in response to Powderham's claim, but they illustrate the propaganda war being waged at the time. The one extreme of denying Edward's kingship might be balanced at the other extreme by emphasis on Edward as

[27] *Lanercost*, trans. *English Historical Documents*, iii, p.270.
[28] *Brut*, i, p.208; see M. Prestwich, *The Three Edwards* (London, 1980), p.81.
[29] *Scalacronica*, trans. Maxwell, p.65.

anointed king. The strange prophetic writings, which are also examined by Dr. Phillips, further underline the variety and complexity of ideas and the search for meaning in the uncertainty of the times.[30] The challenge reverberated round England. The *Vita* records that rumour of it spread through the whole country, and the short continuation of the French prose Brut noted that there was much gossip after the execution. That chronicles as far apart as the west country, London, Carlisle, and Bridlington recorded the event confirms this. Even in the fifteenth century popular English chronicles continued to include it, and Walter Bower thought it still had meaning enough in fifteenth-century Scotland to use Holcot's *exemplum* in his *Scotichronicon*.[31] In 1318 it looked dangerous. Possibly it raised again in the minds of the magnates the fears expressed in the preamble to the Ordinances, that the people were oppressed and likely to rebel. Possibly the magnates saw a man like Powderham as someone who might find a popular following, since, as the Lanercost chronicler wrote, people were disposed to believe him, given Edward's known hobbies. Possibly they suspected Powderham was being manipulated and wanted no such complications that July. Possibly they were outraged at an offence which might reflect on the queen and on the crown which they were sworn to uphold, even if the treason was directed against Edward personally. Possibly they feared that to leave such an offence unpunished would encourage worse to follow.

The whole episode is important as an indicator of the level to which Edward's reputation had sunk. Who would have dared believe such a claim against Edward I or, later, Edward III? New poems such as *Havelock*, current prophecies, the increasingly popular religious commentaries on the Book of Wisdom, all concerned themselves with themes of good and rightful kingship. The country faced famine, lawlessness, Scottish raids and bitter divisions among the ruling groups. It needed a king who would *be* king, yet the public perception of Edward, a perception actively encouraged by his own servants such as Robert le Messager, was increasingly of a king enjoying uncouth rustic pursuits while his realm disintegrated round him. It is not surprising if criticism of Edward led some to deny he could be the rightful heir. The story also illustrates the continued importance of chronicles to the political historian. Government records provide a single clear reference to the event

---

[30] J.R.S. Phillips, 'Edward II and the Prophets', in W.M. Ormrod, ed., *England in the Fourteenth Century* (Woodbridge, 1986), pp.196–201.

[31] Walter Bower, *Scotichronicon*, viii, ed. D.E.R. Watt (Aberdeen, 1987), p.331. I am indebted for this reference to Dr. Phillips.

but only the chronicles provide guidance to the details of a case which is not only interesting in its overtones of witchcraft and changeling children, but which may, more importantly, have been of considerable, if temporary, political significance in the summer of 1318.[32]

[32] I would like to thank all those who have kindly helped me in discussion or by letter while I have been considering this episode, and especially Dr. Helen Jewell of Liverpool, Dr. Lesley Johnson of Leeds, and Dr. J.R.S. Phillips of Dublin. They are not of course responsible for the views expressed here, or any faults which may remain.

Chapter 11

Richard II and the Crisis of July 1397

Roger Mott

In 1971 an article was published on Richard II's views on kingship in which John Taylor provided some valuable insights into the fragmentary nature of the evidence available, and concluded that his personality and policies only had a decisive effect at the end of his reign when, after the events of July to September 1397, he was able to rule in his own right.[1] These events thus become a major turning point in the reign and merit detailed examination.

An important task and possibly one of the most difficult, is to assess Richard's motives for arresting the duke of Gloucester and the earls of Arundel and Warwick in July 1397, since this marked the beginning of the change. Chronicle and record sources for 1397 are revealing, but we also need to consider the impact of his actions and experiences up to that date. Monarchs like Richard II, who came to the throne and were treated as kings from a early age, had little opportunity for personal development and suffered an unnatural upbringing, which they seem to have found it difficult to overcome. Richard was also handicapped by having a father famous for his military successes in France and Spain, even if the Black Prince proved much less skilful in his administration and government of the principality of Aquitaine. In addition his attitudes must have been influenced by his experiences during the Peasants Revolt, where his positive approach, when those around him were failing to respond, meant that it was he who took the centre stage and who saved the day.

The politics of the 1380s were dominated by three particular issues, which had a central importance in influencing Richard's attitudes. To begin with Richard could reasonably have expected to have ruled in his own name long before 1389, and the fact that the minority was of such an unusual length must have caused him resentment. He began to lay increasing emphasis on his rights as a king, as shown in an appendage to a grant of patronage to Robert de Vere: 'the curse of God and St. Edward and the King on any who do or attempt aught

---

[1] A.J. Taylor, 'Richard II's Views on Kingship', *Leeds Philosophical and Literary Society*, xiv (1971), 189–205.

against this grant'.[2] Secondly, Richard had to deal with royal uncles and other magnates who were older than him and who seemed determined to maintain their power. The main cause of the growing tension was the increasingly hostile reactions of his uncle, Gloucester, and magnates such as the earl of Arundel. As early as 1386 Gloucester was reminding the king that subjects had the right to seek his deposition. Thirdly Richard looked increasingly to his contemporaries and to the younger magnates for companionship and support. His view of their role is expressed in the document creating Michael de la Pole earl of Suffolk which states that 'we believe that the more our royal crown is strengthened by men of quality and energy, especially excellent advisers chosen to direct the public good, the more it gleams and sparkles with gems and precious stones'.[3] In this respect he came to rely particularly on Robert de Vere, whom Froissart describes as 'chief in the king's favour' and by whom 'everything was done and without him nothing'.[4]

These three issues had come to head by 1386–8 in a crisis which saw Richard's favourite, De Vere, defeated at Radcot Bridge and forced to flee to France; Queen Anne pleading in vain on her knees before Gloucester for the life of Simon Burley, the king's under-chamberlain; the use of the Merciless Parliament to condemn Richard's followers and the rule of the Appellants; and Richard being held for three days on the point of being declared deposed. His position had changed by 3 May 1389, when he was able to declare himself of age and to end the rule of the Appellants, but Richard was not the kind of man to forget these experiences: they must have played a part in determining his attitudes in 1397.

The years from 1389 have been seen as the most harmonious period of the reign, in which he had the support or at least the acquiescence of the magnates who counted. But it is also necessary to stress the complexities of the situation. The 1390s gradually saw a build-up of forces similar to that of the 1380s. Richard continued to be something of a 'loner' who clung to his regality and his notions of kingship, which were more highly developed than most monarchs of his day. This meant that although he had to consult with his council and his magnates, he was also concerned, as in the 1380s, with building up his power and support. He seems to have been prepared to seek a working relationship with his opponents but, as time went by, that relationship had to be increasingly on his own terms.

---

    [2] *C[alendar] of P[atent] R[olls], 1381–5*, p.542
    [3] *Reports from the Lords Committees Touching the Dignity of a Peer of the Realm*, [*Rep. Dig. Peer*], v, 69.
    [4] G.B. Stow, 'Richard II in Jean Froissart's *Chroniques*', *Journal of Medieval History*, ii (1985), 334.

Richard relations with the former Appellants deteriorated after 1394, due mainly to the stresses and strains of a situation where there was no great measure of agreement. This breakdown was due especially to the twenty-eight year truce with France and Richard's remarriage, which, together with negotiations over the surrender of Brest and Cherbourg, are reported to have provoked a strong reaction from Gloucester and Arundel. In the early peace negotiations between 1391 and 1393 Gloucester had played a prominent role and had received ample rewards, but after the Cheshire revolt his support for peace wavered, although he did not yet move into outright opposition.[5] His former ally, Arundel, seems to have been hostile to negotiations throughout the 1390s and he may even have had a hand in encouraging the Cheshire rebellion – for by remaining in his castle at Holt he showed that he had, at the least, a policy of interested neutrality.[6] By 1396 Gloucester and Arundel had joined forces again and the truce with France confirmed this. Froissart states that Gloucester criticised Richard's pursuance of peace with France and he is said to have withdrawn to Pleshey castle after an argument with the king over the restoration of Brest to the duke of Brittany.[7] Richard's desire for peace and his admiration for the French court and its artistic achievements contrasted with the attitude of the older nobility, for whom the wars against France and the border activity against Scotland had, over the previous decades, become virtually a way of life. They had gained considerable profits from earlier encounters and however genuine the peace negotiations may have been at the outset, they increasingly became clouded with mutual suspicion and mistrust and in the end it proved impossible to achieve a settlement without recriminations and indeed outright opposition.

Richard's failure to come to terms with the hard core of the Appellants became more serious as the balance of magnate forces once more shifted perceptibly in his favour. He had already developed the powers of

---

[5] *Foedera*, ed. T. Rymer (London 1704–34), vii, 813–22. The Cheshire Revolt of 1393 was directed against Gaunt and Gloucester as leaders in trying to secure a truce: *Annales Ricardi secundi*, Johannis de Trokelowe, ed. H.T. Riley, Rolls Series, xxviii, iii (1866), p.159. The Monk of Westminster says that 'the duke of Gloucester from now on lost popular support'; *The Westminster Chronicle*, ed. L.C. Hector and B.F. Harvey (Oxford, 1982), p.519.

[6] *Historia Anglicana*, T. Walsingham, ii, ed. H.T. Riley, Rolls Series, xxviii, i (1864), p.214; J.G. Bellamy, 'The Northern Rebellions in the Later Years of Richard II', B[ulletin] [of] J[ohn] R[ylands] L[ibrary], xlvii (1965), 265–6.

[7] Stow, 'Richard II', 336. A messenger was sent to Pleshey Castle to obtain replies from the duke to certain proceedings; BL, MS Cotton, Cleopatra FIII f. 8b – printed in *Proceedings and Ordinances of the Privy Council of England*, ed. N.H. Nicholas, i, pp.93–94.

William le Scrope, his chamberlain,[8] and Thomas Percy, his steward, and had paid more attention to magnates such as the earl of Rutland and John and Thomas Holand, but this process now became more marked as Richard relied increasingly, as in the 1380s, on those around him. This can be seen in the diversion of patronage to younger magnates. Rutland became constable of Dover and warden of the Cinque Ports in September 1396; was appointed justice of the New Forest and constable of the Tower of London in April 1397; and was given the Isle of Wight and Carisbrook Castle in June.[9] John Holand, earl of Huntingdon, was appointed as keeper of the West March of Scotland in February 1397 and in March he was given the title of Gonfalonier of the church by the pope.[10] Thomas Mowbray, earl of Nottingham, who was also high in the king's favour, had his position as Earl Marshal considerably strengthened in February and gained the lordship of Gower from the earl of Warwick in June.[11] Another reason for the strengthening of the king's position was the emergence of new magnates, as a result of the creation of John Beaufort as earl of Somerset in February 1397, of the succession of Thomas Holand as earl of Kent in May and of John Montague as earl of Salisbury in June. These three elevations must have put pressure on the older magnates. For example it was stated that John Beaufort should have the seat in parliament between Mowbray and Warwick.[12] All six of these magnates who had improved their position were to act as appellants in the trials of Gloucester, Arundel and Warwick in the parliament of September 1397 along with William le Scrope and Thomas Despenser, who were also strong supporters of Richard's cause.

There was thus a shift in the balance of magnate forces early in 1397, with the emergence of a younger nobility on whom the

[8] In 1396 Le Scrope became keeper of Queenborough, Beaumaris (and Anglesey), Caernarvon and Pembroke Castles, *C.P.R., 1391–6*, p.715; *C.P.R., 1396–9*, pp.10, 16, 36, 82, 153. He was also at this time constable of Dublin Castle and justiciar in Leinster, Munster and Louth, *Rotulorum Patentium et Clausorum Cancellarie Hiberniae Calendarium*, ed. E. Tresham (1828) I, i, 152; *C.P.R., 1391–6*, pp.575, 632, 642, 662, 710, 715; *C.P.R., 1396–9*, p.500.

[9] *C.P.R. 1396–9*, pp.24, 118, 150, 250. He had previously been granted the reservations of the offices of justice of the New Forest and constable of the Tower of London in 1392 (*C.P.R., 1391–6*, pp.12, 16). He had apparently held the office of constable from April 1397, when the earl of Kent died, until September when Ralph, earl of Westmorland, was appointed during pleasure'. Rutland was then reappointed in October 'for life'.

[10] *C.P.R., 1396–9*, p.86; *Calendar of Papal Registers*, iv, pp.294, 300. He was appointed keeper of the castle and town of Carlisle in September 1396 (P.R.O. C 71/74, m.3, 2).

[11] He was granted the reversion of the offices of Marshal of the King's Bench, of the Exchequer and of the King's Household, he was also allowed to bear a gold staff as a sign of office, with special ornamentation (*Rep. Dig. Peer, v*, 112–13). For the judgement over Gower, see 20 Richard II, P.R.O, KB 27/542, rot. 64; SC, 6/1123/5, m.6.

[12] *Rep. Dig. Peer, v*, 116, 122; *C.P.R., 1396–9*, pp.113, 140.

king increasingly relied; this narrowed the basis of his support and accentuated the tension already caused by the truce with France. Gloucester, Arundel and Warwick were now further removed from the process of decision-making and must have felt that their position was increasingly insecure. Both sides by their unyielding attitude made some sort of new crisis inevitable. This occurred in July 1397 when, in the most important turning-point of his reign, Richard II arrested Gloucester, Arundel and Warwick. This was so significant because the subsequent deaths of Gloucester and Arundel and the exile of Warwick enabled Richard to rule effectively in his own name for the first time in his reign and set in train the course of events that was to lead eventually to his deposition.

Historians have concentrated on two differing chronicle interpretations of this crisis. The chronicles of Walsingham claim that the arrests were a carefully meditated plan of Richard's in which he acted suddenly and without provocation, and they provide the main evidence for the idea that he was pursuing a long-term policy of revenge.[13] According to their account Richard invited Gloucester, Arundel and Warwick to a feast so that he could arrest them. Warwick however was the only one to fall into the trap. Richard had to take forces to Pleshey Castle to arrest Gloucester, who was conducted to Calais under the custody of the Earl Marshal. Arundel was persuaded to give himself up to the crown, having been warned of the consequences of refusing to do so. The chronicles describe the public mourning at their capture, and state that Richard's claims that they were arrested for new offences and not for previous misdeeds were meant to counter this. The chronicles also claim that the country was being destroyed by the French, and that Gloucester had stood as an insurance for internal security and a sign of freedom from foreign enemies.

The other interpretation is that of the French chronicles – the *Traison et Mort* and the chronicles of St. Denis and of Jean le Beau – which claim that the arrests of Gloucester, Arundel and Warwick were due to evidence of a new plot against Richard in 1397. The background to this is provided by the Monk of Saint-Denis who says that the restoration of Brest and Cherbourg caused a great deal of annoyance to Gloucester, Arundel and other lords because they had not been consulted, and by Jean le Beau who says that the war-loving nobles had conspired against Richard on several occasions while he was seeking peace with France, because they had found the war a source of considerable profit.[14] In the *Traison et*

---

[13] *Annales Ricardi secundi*, pp.201–7; *Historia Anglicana*, p.223.

[14] *Chronique du religieux de St-Denis, 1380–1422*, ed. L. Bellaguet (Paris, 1839–52), ii, p.476; Jean le Beau, *Chronique de Richard II, 1377–1399*, ed. J.A.C. Buchon, Collection des Chroniques Nationales Francaises, xxv, supplement ii, (Paris, 1828), pp.2–3.

Mort and – especially fully – in Jean le Beau, there is a description of
a great feast at Westminster attended by the soldiers who had guarded
Brest. After dinner Gloucester said to Richard, 'Sire, haven't you seen
the companions who were your soldiers at Brest, who have loyally served
you and who have been badly paid?' Richard replied, 'On my faith uncle
they have been well-paid'. He then assigned them twenty villages around
London where they would live at his expense until they were satisfied.
Gloucester continued 'Sire . . . you ought to conquer your enemies by
feats of arms, as your predecessors did, instead of selling or giving away
that which they have conquered', to which Richard retorted, 'What? –
do you think that I . . . would sell my land for gold? No, but our cousin
of Bretagne has loyally given the sum . . . which our predecessor set for
the town of Brest and since he has truly paid it is right that he should
have it'. In this manner, according to the chronicles, began the quarrel
between Richard and Gloucester which, although temporarily patched
up, left both sides deeply suspicious of each other.[15]

The French chronicles then move on to describe a new plot, mentioning
first a meeting of Gloucester, his godfather, John Moot, abbot of
St. Albans, and the prior of Westminster, John Wratting. In this the
prior told of a vision that he had had of the kingdom being lost by
Richard. Both the abbot and Gloucester agreed with this possibility,
and as a result they agreed to meet again at Arundel in two weeks
time. Meanwhile Gloucester sent letters to Arundel, Warwick, Derby,
Mowbray, Thomas Arundel the archbishop of Canterbury, the abbot of
St. Albans and the prior of Westminster to attend at Arundel Castle.[16]
At this meeting Gloucester discussed his projects and asked for their
reactions. He compared the present with the past and, reflecting that
many kings had lost their crowns by having worked against the public
interest, declared that Richard merited deposition.[17] In the morning those
assembled heard mass celebrated by the archbishop of Canterbury and
recited the sacrament as a bond of attachment. In this they agreed to seize
Richard, Lancaster and York and to imprison them all.[18] The chronicles
now move on to the disclosure of the plot by Mowbray, who broke his
oath and told Richard, submitting himself to his mercy. Jean le Beau
says that Richard assembled a 'parliament of seigneurs' and revealed to
them what had happened, as a result of which they adjudged Arundel to
deserve death. Richard went to Huntingdon's house and from there they
rode to Pleshey to arrest Gloucester and sent Rutland and Kent to arrest

[15] *Chronique de la traison et mort de Richard II*, ed. B. Williams, English Historical Society
(London, 1846), p.2; *Jean le Beau*, pp.4–5.
[16] *Ibid*, pp.5–6; *Traison*, pp.3–5.
[17] *St-Denis*, p.478 contains the greatest detail on this incident.
[18] *Jean le Beau*, p.7; *Traison*, p.6; *St-Denis*, p.478.

Arundel and Warwick.[19] *The Traison et Mort* has a variation on this, saying that Richard dined with Huntingdon and then let the plot be known to the council.[20] None of them mentions an invitation to a feast, which is the pretext for arrests in the other accounts. They do, however, all agree that Gloucester was sent to Calais where he was disposed of.[21]

This is a particularly difficult episode to interpret as strong doubts have been cast on these chronicle accounts. Walsingham's chronicles, which portray the events of 1397 as the culmination of a long-term process of revenge for 1386–88, have been criticised for presenting Lancastrian propaganda intent on blackening Richard's character. At the same time the detailed account of a new conspiracy provided by the French chronicles has been given credence by some historians, and appears to be backed up by Warwick's confession in the parliament of September 1397, in which he claimed to have acted through the duke of Gloucester, the prior of Westminster and the abbot of St. Albans and which was sufficient to secure him a sentence of life imprisonment rather than execution.[22] But more recently John Palmer has cast strong doubts on the authenticity of this story and considers that Warwick's confession refers to his part in the political crises of 1386–88. He also argues that the godfather of the duke of Gloucester, referred to in the French chronicles, was Thomas de la Mare, the previous abbot of St. Albans who died in 1396, and not John Moot, the current abbot. He therefore concludes that the whole story as presented by the *Traison et Mort* is 'sheer fantasy' and that it refers to the events of 1386–8 rather than 1397.[23]

Given that the chronicle accounts are considered so unreliable on this crucial episode, we clearly need to examine Richard's actions in July and August 1397 from record sources. These depict Richard as acting hastily to secure his position. The distribution of patronage shows that Gloucester was given livery of all the lands in Ireland belonging to Thomas, earl of Stafford on 29 June 1397, only two weeks before his arrest.[24] There were also some important grants made to the dukes

[19] *Jean le Beau*, pp.8–10.

[20] *Traison*, p.7.

[21] *Traison*, p.9; *Jean le Beau*, p.10; *St-Denis*, p.552.

[22] Those historians who accept the French chronicles include A. Steel, *Richard II* (Cambridge, 1941), pp.230–32, and R.H. Jones, *The Royal Policy of Richard II* (Oxford, 1968), p.76. For Warwick's confession, see *Historia vitae et regni Ricardi secundi (Vita Ricardi)* ed. G.B. Stow (Philadephia, 1977), p.6; *Adam of Usk, Chronicon*, ed. E. Maunde Thompson (London, 1904) pp.16–17; and *Eulogium historiarum*, ii, ed. F.S. Haydon, Rolls Series, ix (1863), p.375.

[23] J.J.N. Palmer, 'The Authorship, Date and Historical Value of the French Chronicles on the Lancastrian Revolution' *B.J.R.L.*, lxi, (1979), 400–5. Others who reject the story include A. Tuck, *Richard II and the English Nobility* (London, 1973), pp.184–85; A. Goodman, *The Loyal Conspiracy* (London, 1971), pp.65–66.

[24] *C[alendar] [of] C[lose] R[olls], 1396–9*, p.138.

of Lancaster and York early in July which seem designed to secure their loyalty. It was vital to gain the acquiescence of Gaunt, given his overwhelming power, and on 6 July he was confirmed in his position as duke of Aquitaine, just four days before Gloucester's arrest. It would seem unlikely that Richard felt able to act without their foreknowledge, and he followed this on 14 July by pardoning Gaunt the sum of £1,800 and allowing him to unload 46 tuns of Gascon wine. The Duke of York obtained a grant of lands without conditions on 17 July, undoubtedly for a similar purpose.[25]

On 13 July orders were sent to Robert of Legh to raise the Cheshire archers, and these were couched in terms of great urgency. He was told to leave everything else that he was engaged upon and to raise 'a tout le haste que vous purrez pur aucune voie de monde' 2,000 archers. He was also told that he would be well-rewarded for his diligence and was exhorted on no account to drop the matter.[26] On 15 July an order was sent out to all sheriffs saying that Gloucester, Arundel and Warwick had not been arrested for previous offences but for new crimes, evidence of which would be brought forward in the next parliament.[27]

Meanwhile the king's military preparations continued. Further efforts were made to raise forces in Cheshire, orders being sent out to ensure the enlistment of all knights and esquires. Defensive measures were taken in that area, such as those at Flint Castle and the holding of Arundel's former castles of Chirk, Holt, Oswestry and Shrawardyn from August to October with men and munitions.[28] Lancaster, York and Derby brought their retinues at the king's command to a council meeting at Nottingham in August, and they were also ordered to bring their forces to parliament the following month. Orders were sent to all sheriffs in August for all those of the livery of the white hart and others taking the king's fees to be at Kingston upon Thames to ride with the king to Westminster.[29] The king also took financial measures to provide money for this emergency and commissioners were sent out into the counties to raise loans in August and early September.[30] By the time of the assembling of parliament in September 1397 Richard was in a strong position to deal with his opponents.

How then are we to explain Richard actions? We need only to consider

---

[25] P.R.O., C61/105, m. 12; E 159/173, *Brevia directa baronibus*, Trinity m. 6v; *C.P.R. 1396–9*, p.177.

[26] P.R.O., Chester 2/70, m. 7v.

[27] *C.C.R., 1396–9*, p.208.

[28] P.R.O., Chester 2/70, m. 8v, 7v; P.R.O., SC6/1234/7.

[29] *C.P.R., 1396/9*, pp.190, 192; *C.C.R. 1396–9*, p.210, *Rot(uli) Parl(iamentorum)*, iii, 374. Lancaster was to bring 300 men at arms and 600 archers, Bolingbroke 200 men at arms and 400 archers, and York 100 men at arms and 200 archers.

[30] eg. P.R.O., E34/18 marked 15/27 (Essex and Hertfordshire); E101/512/9 (Midlands).

the speculative nature and wide variations of newspaper reporting of the machinations that lie behind present day political events to realise how difficult it is to assess people's motivations, and to separate fact from half-truth or fiction. It is of course much more difficult to decide why medieval monarchs should have acted as they did.

Because historians have concentrated so much on the Lancastrian writers, who were deliberately maligning Richard's character, and on the *Traison* and other related sources, which have been shown to be suspect, there has been a tendency to dismiss all chronicles as unreliable. Yet other sources, such as Froissart, who was 'more critical of Richard and his policies than previously thought', the Evesham Chronicle, and the *Vita Ricardi*, which 'departs from Walsingham and becomes a more important source for Richard's reign' after 1390, should not be so readily discarded.[31] The chronicles do provide insights into the characters and attitudes of key figures such as Richard and Gloucester, and they help to show why there was so much suspicion and mistrust. It is only therefore by attempting to evaluate Richard's actions in the light of both chronicle and record sources that we can hope to arrive at the most likely explanation.

It does seem that by July 1397 Richard was in a position to act. His support was by now strengthened as new younger magnates rose to prominence and as Richard increasingly relied on them for advice. The *Vita Ricardi* says that he followed the advice of the young and unwise and the Kirkstall Chronicle emphasises how, in the final years of the reign, Richard relied too much on the wishes and advice of the young lords. Froissart also stresses their hostility towards Gloucester saying that 'there was not one of the king's servants who did not fear him'.[32] In particular, though, it was the truce with France which reopened old wounds between Richard and Gloucester and Arundel. The *Vita Ricardi* reports that Richard was angry at the failure of Gloucester and Arundel to attend the council meeting in February 1397, while Gloucester, according to Froissart, criticised the peace with France and said that there would soon be serious trouble in the realm. As a result of this Gloucester 'conceived a great hatred' for Richard and could not 'speak well of him', while Richard, on his part, doubted Gloucester more 'than any other of his uncles'.[33] It did not need an elaborate new plot (as in the *Traison*) for Richard to be persuaded to act. All that was necessary

---

[31] Stow, 'Richard II', 333; *Vita Ricardi*, p.6.

[32] *Vita Ricardi*, p.137; *The Kirkstall Abbey Chronicles*, ed. J. Taylor, Thoresby Society, xlii (1952), p.83. *Sir John Froissart's Chronicles*, ed. T. Johnes (London, 1908), xi, pp.349, 359, 360; Stow, 'Richard II', p.336.

[33] *Vita Ricardi*, p.137; *Froissart's Chronicles*, ed. Johnes, xi, pp.342, 339–41; Stow, 'Richard II', p.336.

was for those around Richard to convince him that Gloucester, Arundel and Warwick were presenting a new threat to him.[34] Froissart's version of events is that Richard 'had received positive information that the duke of Gloucester and the earl of Arundel had plotted to seize his person'; that he was 'considerably alarmed' at this; and that he arrested them because he decided 'that it was better to destroy than be destroyed'.[35]

The order to the sheriffs of 15 July makes it clear that they were arrested for new offences 'which shall be declared in the next parliament', and not for their role in 1386–8. This has tended to be dismissed because Walsingham described it as an attempt to prevent disorder and because no new charges were in fact brought forward.[36] But, as the record sources show, events were moving fast in July and August 1397, and Richard was having to react to events. It is therefore not unreasonable to conclude that they were arrested initially because Richard believed that they were threatening his position again.

Nevertheless, within a matter of weeks, it seems to have become clear that new evidence could not be found – Gloucester's later confession only referred to 1386–88 and Warwick's confession in the parliament of September 1397 seems to refer to the same events. This meant that they could not be impeached on new charges: on 28 July an order stated in more general terms that the arrests were for 'a great number of misprisons and oppressions by them committed against the king and people and for other offences against the king and his majesty'.[37] It was probably due to this lack of evidence that the king decided to widen the basis of his accusations and to gain revenge for what he had suffered in 1388.

This shift was not only expedient but also necessary because of Richard's strong desire to fulfil his ideas of kingship, which involved removing all the restrictions that had previously been imposed on him. Having taken the decision to arrest Gloucester, Arundel and Warwick, Richard was determined to be master in his own kingdom. This meant that his opponents had to be appealed of treason in exactly the same way as Richard's followers had been in 1388. The *Vita Ricardi* also stresses that the acts of 1388 had to be annulled because they were against the power of the king and the liberties of the crown.[38] The record of 1386–88 had to be erased if Richard was to exercise untrammeled power.

---

[34] Froissart says that the king's servants advised him that 'there will never be quiet in England' as long as Gloucester lives; *Froissart's Chronicles*, ed. Johnes, xi, p.360.

[35] *Froissart's Chronicles*, ed. Johnes, xi, pp.354, 356, 362; *Froissart Chronicles*, ed. G. Brereton (London, 1968), p.428.

[36] *C.C.R., 1396–9*, p.208; *Annales Ricardi secundi*, pp.206–7; *Historia Anglicana*, p.223.

[37] *C.C.R., 1396–9*, p.147; *Rot. Parl.*, iii. 378; *Vita Ricardi*, p.145.

[38] *Vita Ricardi*, pp.139, 147.

It also gave him the opportunity of throw off the yoke of magnates who had been a thorn in his side for a long time and, having arrested them, he now took the opportunity to destroy them. Richard explained some of his motives in a letter to Albert of Bavaria. Referring to the 1380s he said that 'noblemen . . . have for long and since we were of tender years traitorously conspired to disinherit our crown and usurp our royal power, raising themselves with many abettors of their iniquity to rebel against our royal will, publicly condemning our faithful servants to death and doing whatsoever they pleased at their own will. Thus have they striven damnably to spend their malice even upon our person, having wrongly usurped the royal power by going about among our privy affairs, so that they have left us hardly anything beyond the royal name.' He then went on to explain that in the 1390s although 'our royal clemency, indulged these traitors with time enough to change their hearts and show the fruits of repentence, so deeply-rooted in evil seemed their obstinacy that by the just judgement of God our avenging severity has been meted out to the destruction and ruin of their persons'.[39]

Other sources also stress that Richard was now determined to rule in his own right. The author of the *Vita Ricardi* says that Richard felt that he should rule and govern the kingdom himself, as he was now of full age, wisdom and discretion. He also states that Richard remembered the concessions that he had been compelled to make to the Appellants in 1388 and wished strongly to reverse them. The Kirkstall Chronicler lays emphasis on the long-suffering of the king and says that Richard, newly recalling the injuries that had been inflicted on him in 1388, resolved to avenge them and to bring the kingdom under his control.[40]

Richard showed how much he saw the offences of Gloucester, Arundel and Warwick as an affront to his dignity and his kingship when he stated in his letter that he had not only 'adjudged them to natural or civil death' but also 'since the heinousness of their crimes demanded a heavier penalty . . . we have . . . caused their punishment to be perpetuated upon their heirs . . . (so) that posterity may learn what it is to offend the royal majesty, established at howsoever tender years, for he is a child of death who offends the king'.[41]

Whatever Richard's actual motives were, the results of his actions in July 1397 were to create further suspicion and mistrust. Although his

---

[39] BL, MS Cotton, Galba B 1, 21, printed in J.H. Harvey, 'The Wilton Diptych: A Re-examination' *Archaeologia*, xcviii (1961), 27–28. The dating of this letter is almost certainly 1397 or 1398. A letter from Richard to the Emperor Manuel Paleologus in 1398 provides a similar explanation for his actions; *Official Correspondence of Thomas Bekynton*, ed. G. Williams, Rolls Series, lvi (1872), i, p.285.

[40] *Vita Ricardi*, pp.137–38; *Kirkstall Chronicle*, p.73.

[41] And see '*Vita Ricardi*', p.147.

triumph now seemed complete, and although he was able to rule in his own right for the first time in his reign and to exercise his powers of kingship, this seems to have made Richard more remote so that he became less aware of the true state of affairs in the country. Froissart said that 'in those days there was none so great in England that dare speak against anything that the king did or would do', and in the Articles of Deposition it was stated that people 'when giving their advice according to their discretion were suddenly and sharply rebuked and censured by him so that they did not dare to speak the truth about the state of the king and the kingdom'.[42] This led him unwisely, despite the weakness of his position in England, to plan to go to Ireland in the autumn of 1397, to try to extend his authority both in the Scottish and Welsh Marches and to lead an expedition to Ireland in 1399.

Secondly, Richard may now have been able to rely on his favourites and to institute 'the greatest upheaval in English landed society since the Norman Conquest in 1066',[43] but in practice this shift in powers to his supporters in the localities was deceptive. The control established by the new owners of estates was not very secure, and retainers and officials of the former owners were still much in evidence. This was shown when the former estates of the earl of Warwick were fortified and guarded by his former retainers after Bolingbroke's landing in 1399.[44]

And finally, although Richard was able by the arrests and trials of Gloucester, Arundel and Warwick to remove the influence of magnates who had opposed him, he only succeeded in creating further uncertainty. The earl of March died in July 1398 when he was about to be removed from office and the long drawn-out quarrel between Henry Bolingbroke and Thomas Mowbray must have affected relations between the king and the magnates for much of 1398, and thus have continued and intensified the atmosphere of suspicion that had developed the previous year. Although Richard was able, by the banishments of Bolingbroke and Mowbray, to complete the removal of the lords who had imposed their will on him in 1388, their potential inheritance of estates as a result of the deaths of John of Gaunt in February 1399 and of Margaret, duchess of Norfolk in March created further complications. The duchess's lands were seized, but it was the question of the Lancastrian lands that caused

---

[42] Stow, 'Richard II', p.337; *Rot. Parl.*, iii, 420

[43] T.B. Pugh, *Henry V and the Southampton Plot* (London, 1988), p.2.

[44] On 4 July Warwick Castle was seized and fortified on behalf of the earl, observation points were improved, and moves were made to strengthen the gates of the castle and to repair the earl's stocks of arms and armour (Birmingham Deed no.168234; Warwickshire Record Office, Warwick Castle, MS. 481, m. 3v, 2v). Similar moves were made in the Lancastrian castles of Monmouth, Hay, Kidwelly and Brecon in Wales and Kenilworth in England. See also R.A.K. Mott, 'Richard II's Relations with the Magnates, 1396–9' (unpublished Ph.D. thesis, University of Leeds, 1971), pp.71–73.

the greatest difficulty. In the end Gaunt's lands were taken over, although they were not in fact formally confiscated. It was this that helped to determine Richard's fate: to the leading landowners it was the final blow in the growing insecurity that they felt at the end of the reign. Richard had 'found security for himself' in 1397 'only at the cost of making others feel insecure'.[45] It was the continuation of this process in 1399 that finally cost him his throne.

[45] N. Saul, 'The Despensers and the Downfall of Edward II', *English Historical Review*, xcix (1984), 32.

Chapter 12

Social Outlook and Preaching in a Wycliffite 'Sermones Dominicales' Collection

Simon N. Forde

The success of many religious movements in achieving longstanding popularity has lain in their tapping an emergent sector of society, the members of which have seen a link between the ideals of the movement and their own secular, and often material, aspirations.[1] This seems to have been the case, for instance, with the Puritans in sixteenth- and seventeenth-century England and the Methodists in the following two centuries. With respect to the Puritans, Christopher Hill has described the insecurity of the period thus:

> Big towns were impersonal: a man could starve there unknown to his neighbours. By the seventeenth century many London parish churches could not possibly have held all their parishioners at one time. Ultimately sectarian congregations were to replace the parish as community centre and social security agency in the towns . . . The Tudor poor law, the protestant emphasis on the wickedness of the mass of mankind and the Hobbist war of every man against every man, all seemed to make sense in this society. So too did the Puritan stress on discipline and hard work for the good of the commonwealth.[2]

Likewise, in an article celebrating the 250th anniversary of John Wesley's conversion, a secretary in the Methodist Home Mission commented:

> When the economic base of society was moving from agriculture to industry, and that of politics from a hierarchical system to a more democratic one, the issue could be expressed in religious terms. Joining a Methodist society was one way of expressing allegiance to one side of a social issue. In those conditions, Methodism grew.[3]

But what of earlier religious movements? I wish to examine here the Wycliffite movement that had its origins at Oxford University in the 1370s. It developed in the fifteenth century into a less university-based

---

[1] An earlier version of this essay was delivered at the Sixth Medieval Sermon Studies Symposium held at Dijon on 6–9 July 1988. A report on the conference and a summary of this paper is given in *Medieval Sermon Studies*, Symposium Report, vi (1988), p.4.

[2] C. Hill, *Collected Essays, ii, Religion and Politics in Seventeenth-Century England* (Brighton, 1986), pp.21–22.

[3] *The Independent*, 28 May 1988, p.21.

form, the so-called 'Lollards' who, it has often been argued, constituted a native reform movement that prepared the way for the Protestant Reformation in the sixteenth century.[4] My purpose is to present some of the characteristics of the early Wycliffite thinkers through a *Sermones dominicales* collection that can probably be dated to the decade after Wyclif's withdrawal from Oxford and his death in 1384.[5]

The sermon collection to which I refer is that of Philip Repyngdon, onetime colleague of Wyclif in the Theology Faculty at Oxford but, after having been forced to recant, abbot of St. Mary-des-Prés (Leicester) and bishop of Lincoln, both appointments of national importance. There are three characteristics we shall focus upon here through the medium of Repyngdon's sermons and which will be shown to have been shared by the Wycliffites, even after many of them had recanted. First, they were conservatives; second, they were idealists; and, third, they were stern and industrious. The conservatism is evident in the sermon structure adopted by Repyngdon and in his choice of sources; the idealism is evident in the limited number of clear statements made in the sermons by Repyngdon but which, nonetheless, show that he expected each order of society to fulfil its traditional ideals; and the stern industriousness is evident in the dryness of the sermons, their lack of humour, their length and tone of moral seriousness.

Repyngdon and the Wycliffites were conservatives in the sense that they opposed all things 'new' or 'modern', but also in the sense that

[4] The most recent expression of this interpretation is now the standard study on the Wycliffe movement: A. Hudson, *The Premature Reformation: Wycliffite Texts and Lollard History* (Oxford, 1988). Important earlier studies which develop the links from Wyclif through to the Reformation include the two volumes of collected essays by A. Hudson, *Lollards and their Books* (London, 1985); M. Aston, *Lollards and Reformers: Images and Literacy in Late Medieval Religion* (London, 1984); A.G. Dickens, *Lollards and Protestants in the Diocese of York, 1509–1558* (London, 1959); *idem, The English Reformation* (London, 1964); C. Kightly, 'The Early Lollards: A Survey of Popular Lollard Activity in England, 1382–1428', (unpublished D.Phil. thesis, University of York, 1975); J.A.F. Thomson, *The Later Lollards, 1414–1520* (London, 1965); and H.B. Workman, *John Wyclif: A Study of the English Medieval Church*, 2 vols. (Oxford, 1926).

[5] See S.N. Forde, 'New Sermon Evidence for the Spread of Wycliffism', *De Ore Domini: Preacher and Word in the Middle Ages*, ed. T.L. Amos, E.A. Green and B.M. Kienzle (Kalamazoo, 1989), pp.169–83. The only investigations solely on Repyngdon are the studies by G.G. Perry, 'Cardinal Repyngdon and the Followers of Wycliffe', *Church Quarterly Review*, xix (1884–5), 59–82; M. Archer, 'Philip Repingdon, Bishop of Lincoln, and his Cathedral Chapter', *Birmingham Historical Journal*, iv (1954), 81–97; *idem* (ed.), *The Register of Bishop Philip Repingdon, 1405–1419*, Lincoln Record Society, lvii (1963) and lxxiv (1982); J.R. Archer, 'The Preaching of Philip Repingdon, Bishop of Lincoln (1405–1419): A Descriptive Analysis of his Latin Sermons', (unpublished Ph.D. thesis, Graduate Theological Union, Berkeley, 1984), and S.N. Forde, 'Writings of a Reformer: A Look at Sermon Studies and Bible Studies through Repyngdon's *Sermones super evangelia dominicalia*', 2 vols. (unpublished Ph.D. thesis, University of Birmingham, 1985).

they had a populist tendency, which we know from their constant efforts to disseminate their views widely. The conservative reaction of which Wycliffism is a part goes back, as far as can be identified, to Thomas Bradwardine. Initially, Bradwardine had been sympathetic to the sceptical philosophy of Ockham, but he describes his own conversion in the 1310s and 20s in these terms:

I rarely heard anything of grace said in the lectures of the philosophers . . . but every day I heard them teach that we are masters of our own free acts . . . But afterwards, and before I became a student of theology, the truth before mentioned struck upon me like a beam of grace. It seemed to me as if I beheld in the distance under a transparent image of truth, the grace of God . . . I burn with ardour for God's cause . . . [against] the pestilential Pelagians [whom he more usually calls 'the modern Pelagians'].[6]

The fact that he can use the term *moderni* as a term of abuse against the Ockhamists must itself show that he could draw on a broad sense of dissatisfaction with recent developments.

Throughout the second half of the century there were many people who subscribed to this deep unease with present society and looked backwards to understand the process that had led to it, though the expression of such a sentiment took many forms. For some, perhaps FitzRalph among them, the Mendicant orders represented the factor that was 'new' and the element that had to be removed from the equation. Such anti-mendicancy had a superficial similarity with Wyclif's attitude towards the friars, though his was more complex. Wyclif's later invective seems, in fact, to have been rooted in his support for the Spiritual Franciscan ideal and his consequent disillusion with the Mendicant orders for not living up to these high standards.[7] Some, including Langland, understood this historical process in apocalyptic terms, while others, again such as Wyclif, looked towards a return to fundamentals. While superficially these two approaches might appear distinct, there were major areas of overlap. A recent study of *Piers Plowman* has highlighted the following elements of what is termed Langland's 'reformist apocalypticism': the disendowment of the clergy whereby the clergy would be forced back to its pristine or apostolic state; the concern for false prophets, underlying which was a concern with establishing true leadership in the church; and, thirdly, the anxiety to establish

[6] G.A. Leff, *Bradwardine and the Pelagians: A Study of his 'De causa Dei' and its Opponents* (Cambridge, 1957), p.14. See also H.A. Oberman, *Archbishop Thomas Bradwardine: A Fourteenth Century Augustinian* (Utrecht, 1957), pp.14–16, and J.A. Robson, *Wyclif and the Oxford Schools: The Relation of the 'Summa de Ente' to Scholastic Debates at Oxford in the Later Fourteenth Century* (Cambridge, 1961), pp.24–31, 36–39 and *passim*.

[7] K. Walsh, *A Fourteenth-Century Scholar and Primate: Richard FitzRalph in Oxford, Avignon and Armagh* (Oxford, 1981), pp.349–451, especially pp.377–80, and S.N. Forde, 'Nicholas Hereford's Ascension Day Sermon, 1382', *Mediaeval Studies*, li (1989), 217–18 and 226–29.

the authentic *vita apostolica* in one's own life.[8] Yet a Wycliffite would subscribe to these and many similar points. Albeit in different ways these three elements identify an ideal of the church and society that existed sometime in the past, which they perceived to be absent in the present and which they sought to reestablish in the near future. Closely associated with such an outlook was a lack of faith in present day achievements. Exponents of this outlook tended to place their confidence in acknowledged experts from the past; nor were sermon writers exempt from this.

While we may not be in a position, as we are with the Puritan and Methodist examples, to suggest that their expressions of Christianity had a particular appeal to one emergent and identifiable group within their society, we can say that these characteristics of conservatism, idealism and industriousness were shared by many people, whether or not they were identified as such with the Wycliffites. In that sense they were an expression in ecclesiastical affairs of changes in outlook whose origins cannot solely be found within the dynamics of ecclesiastical bodies.

In terms of preaching, the reaction to 'modern' tendencies took two forms. First, among the Wycliffites and Lollards there appears to have been a complete avoidance of devices such as *exempla* and other *curiosa* which they perceived to detract from the proclamation of God's law.[9] Second, there was the dissatisfaction with the excesses of the modern, university sermon form that relied upon verbally dividing up the brief text that constituted the sermon *thema*. Typical among such views is this comment by Repyngdon:

> Certainly many modern preachers are more concerned with clever divisions than fruitful meanings. Instead they elaborate the divisions so much that they rarely build up love and unity.[10]

It is the effect of obscuring a clear exposition of Scripture to which

---

[8] K. Kerby-Fulton, 'The Voice of Honest Indignation: A Study of Reformist Apocalypticism in Relation to *Piers Plowman*', (Ph.D. thesis, University of York, 1985), published as *Reformist Apocalypticism and 'Piers Plowman'* (Cambridge, 1990).

[9] The most complete study of sermon form in this period and the various reactions to 'modern form' is H.L. Spencer, 'English Vernacular Sunday Preaching in the Late Fourteenth and Fifteenth Century, with Illustrative Texts', 2 vols. (unpublished D.Phil. thesis, University of Oxford, 1982), summarised in part in A. Hudson and H.L. Spencer, 'Old Author, New Word: The Sermons of MS. Longleat 4', *Medium Aevum*, liii (1984), 220–38. See also Forde, 'Writings of a Reformer', ii, pp.193–279.

[10] Oxford, Corpus Christi College, MS 54 (hereafter *Co*), fo.80r: 'Set certe multi moderni predicatorum plus ad curiosas diuisiones quam ad sentencias fructuosas attendunt. Immo tantum circa diuisiones elaborant quod caritatem et vnitatem raro edificant'. All translations from this codex are mine. All transcriptions remain unnormalised, except in the cases of 'i' and 'j' which the scribe does not appear to distinguish for orthographic reasons.

Repyngdon was objecting here. For many like-minded preachers the solution lay in adopting the 'ancient' form of preaching, that of postillation, expounding the entire pericope clause by clause. This was the sermon form adopted by Repyngdon.

We may now turn directly to Repyngdon's sermon collection and describe the form that the above mentioned outlooks took. First, it is necessary to examine the framework in which he used sources in his *Sermones dominicales*. In the prologue to this sermon collection Repyngdon explains his approach:

> Lest the ingulfing darkness of ignorance overtake me, I have cut down on deviations from the catholic understanding of Scripture by collecting the statements of other holy doctors and faithful postillators rather than immodestly offering my own.[11]

In this short extract alone we notice the lack of confidence in his own abilities and those of his contemporaries; we see his concern for maintaining orthodox understandings that were formulated in the past and we see too his use of the term 'faithful' which was the description preferred by members of the Lollard movement to their derogatory nickname.[12] Unfortunately, Repyngdon says no more in the prologue about this process of 'collecting statements of holy doctors and faithful postillators'. However, a number of similar fourteenth-century *Sermones dominicales* collections are quite explicit about the procedure. An unidentified Parisian Dominican, for instance, introduced his sermons on the gospels and epistles thus:

> In writing these particular expositions I have not resorted to my own talents which are inadequate but the works of other doctors of the Sacred Page, choosing the best postillas and expositions that they have written, inserting them in turn after each stage of the text and with the prearranged abbreviation before each, and after each Gospel exposition adding some essential notes to the content of the text from the sermons of the renowned doctor, Ugo Vinac [Hugo de Prato Florida].[13]

---

[11] *Ibid.*, fo. 1r: 'Ne ignorancie tenebra inuolutum me contingat, a Scriptura catholica intelligencia exorbitare decreui pocius aliorum sanctorum doctorum et fidelium postillatorum sentencias colligere quam mea ingerere inpudenter, non subtilibus set rudibus mei similibus morem gerens' (the final clause of which is left untranslated).

[12] A. Hudson, 'A Lollard Sect Vocabulary?', in M. Benskin and M.L. Samuels (eds.), *So Meny People Longages and Tonges: Philological Essays in Scots and Mediaeval English Presented to Angus McIntosh* (Edinburgh, 1981), pp.16–17.

[13] Guilelmus Parisiensis (Dominican Professor of Theology), *Postilla super Epistolas et Evangelia de tempore et sanctis et pro defunctis* (Ulm, 1486), fo. Aii: 'Non meum quod exiguum est ingenium consului proprias dictans expositiones, sed aliorum sacre pagine doctorum libris inuitens eas quas melius scripserunt postillas et expositiones perfunctorie exarando post quemlibet passum textus ponens cum premissione tituli vniuscuiusque quod scripsit. Abiiciensque post quamlibet Dominicalis euangelii expositionem necessaria notabilia pro materia textus, ex sermonibus eximii doctoris Hugonis de Prato sumpta'.

This Dominican proceeds to list the half-dozen doctors and the interlinear and ordinary glosses from which his compilation is made, together with the abbreviations used for these authorities in his sermons. An almost identical introduction is found in the Wycliffite *Glossed Gospels*, except here the 'user instructions' are even more explicit, a reflection perhaps of the broader readership envisaged for this particular reference book.[14]

For Repyngdon's part he seems to be able to assume that his readership will be familiar with such compilations and, unfortunately, considers it unnecessary to state the dozen or so works upon which he is basing his sermon collection.[15] Unfortunately, that is, because it would have been a great timesaver for present-day researchers. Nonetheless, all but possibly one postillator have been identified. Many of Repyngdon's sources are named and where there occurs an isolated quotation from a particular source, such as Aquinas or canon law, Repyngdon often provides a full reference for it. But for the central sources we often have to work from abbreviations of authors: *Jan.* for *Ianuensis*, that is Jacopo da Varagine; *Nott.* for William of Nottingham, the fourteenth-century biblical scholar, and not the earlier provincial of the English Franciscans; and *Gor.* for Nicolas de Gorran. Yet several hide under the introductions *quidam postillator ...*, *alius postillator ...* or simply *postillator dicit*. Under this guise lay Guillaume Peyraud, for instance.

Having identified the basic sources from which Repyngdon worked, it is possible to identify three categories of source. The first category consists of sources selected for the literal or historical level of exegesis, the second those for the allegorical levels and the third those used when Repyngdon raised contentious topics. We are now in a position to return to Repyngdon's conservatism through examining each of these categories of sources in turn.

In the first category we can say that for the synoptic gospels Nicolas de Gorran was the most widely-used biblical commentator, supported, especially for readings from Luke, by Bede's homilies on Luke, and for readings from Matthew (and to a lesser extent Luke) by pseudo-Chrysostom's *Opus imperfectum in Matthaeum*. For John's Gospel Gorran was less extensive and thus William of Nottingham was preferred, supported by Augustine's commentary on John. Other works were

---

[14] H. Hargreaves, 'Popularising Biblical Scholarship: The Role of the Wycliffite *Glossed Gospels*', in W. Lourdaux and D. Verhelst (ed.), *The Bible and Medieval Culture*, Mediaevalia Lovaniensia, ser. i, stud. vii (Leuven, 1979), pp.180–81.

[15] The source citations are discussed in greater detail in Forde, 'Writings of a Reformer', i, pp.193–240 and the wider ramifications in *idem*, 'Theological Sources Cited by Two Canons from Repton: Philip Repyngdon and John Eyton', in A. Hudson and M.J. Wilks (ed.), *From Ockham to Wyclif*, Studies in Church History, subsidia, v (Oxford, 1987), pp.419–28. The following paragraphs are drawn from these studies.

cited, such as Nicolas de Lyre and major patristic and early medieval writers such as Isidore, particularly when a textual problem arose, at which point Repyngdon occasionally offers his own reading of the passage. Lyre's commentaries, like Wyclif's own, were too cursory for the detailed and lengthy exposition that Repyngdon envisaged for his collection of Sunday gospel sermons.

In the second category, the sources for the allegorical or spiritual exegesis, fall the *Sermones dominicales* collections, principally those of Jacopo da Varagine and Guillaume Peyraud, though the collection of Jean (Halgrin) d'Abbeville was also used. Jacopo regularly provides three sermons on each gospel pericope, normally on three major clauses in the Gospel, but sometimes all on the same clause, or *thema*. His sermons are exclusively allegorical, as indeed are Peyraud's and the particular sermons selected from d'Abbeville. By contrast, Peyraud provides up to six or seven sermons per pericope, often with specific *ad status* sermons among them. Peyraud's sermons are less symmetrically balanced than Jacopo's, often employing long lists of up to a dozen points, but he avoids the more esoteric analyses, of the properties of plants or animals, say, that characterise Jacopo's sermons. Peyraud appears concerned with ecclesiastical affairs and often criticises contemporary shortcomings. Together these authors provided the allegorical exegesis in Repyngdon's collection. The problem for Repyngdon lay in dividing up these groups of sermons by Jacopo or Peyraud, given that they did not deal equally with every clause of the pericope, and then in redistributing them throughout an entire pericope alongside the literal analysis which was the principal structure of his sermons.

At first sight the favour shown to Jacopo da Varagine may appear quite puzzling, in that one might imagine that his continual imposition of triads, his allegorical, even esoteric, exegesis and his hierarchical view of society would all be quite uncongenial to the likes of Repyngdon. In fact, this problem may arise from our mistaken expectations of what really constitutes Wycliffism and may reinforce the impression that it is far more traditional than radical.

In the third category of sources fall all those that Repyngdon used when discussing contentious topics. Three such topics concerned tithes, almsgiving and whether the merits of ministers affect the efficacy of the sacraments. Perhaps not surprisingly, he cites Aquinas and Duns Scotus as representatives of scholasticism, though they are safe, authoritative representatives nonetheless. Of more significance, perhaps, is the favour he shows in these discussions to earlier works, particularly pseudo-Dionysius, St. Bernard and Robert Grosseteste, and also to canon law. This selection, and the way Repyngdon uses it, indicates that he is striving to understand divine law and to enforce strict morality and that he by no means rejects a hierarchical model of society; he appears to be seeking from the past some objective standard upon which he can rely. The interest in Grosseteste is particularly significant since it seems to have been Wyclif and his colleagues who 'rediscovered' Grosseteste, perhaps detecting in him the vigour and outspokenness which was also their mark.

The point about choosing so many authorities who may have seemed as old-fashioned in that academic context as, say, the Victorians do today, is that it belies the idea that Repyngdon, or the Wycliffites in general, were forward-looking, radical reformers, if by that we mean they wanted an egalitarian or 'democratic' church in the way that we understand these concepts. Rather, they wanted to restore the church from the aberration that they felt was the present and recent past. Indeed they considered themselves to be orthodox and consciously conservative, in a way that many of their contemporaries, including their influential ecclesiastical opponents, were not.

The second characteristic that we are examining, their idealism, was manifested in Repyngdon's sermons through the expectation that each individual should live up to the ideal of his or her station and in opposing behaviour that appeared to blur the distinctions between the orders of society. By opposing such developments they were thrown back on traditional interpretations of the ideal for each social order. This is the case with Wyclif's support for the Spiritual Franciscans, which was mentioned earlier, and his belief that monks should return to the wildernesses; for him this would represent an enforced return to their roots.[16] Repyngdon talked too of the secular realm, stressing the regal responsibilities of the usurper king, Henry IV. The principal responsibility involved enforcing a strong rule of law to rid the injustice and oppression by nobles that was associated with his weak predecessor, Richard II.[17] Nonetheless Repyngdon's idealism can also be seen through his views on the true role of the preacher and we shall examine this outlook now. In order to do so it will again be important to consider not only the content of the sermons but also their format.

Clear, authorial statements in Repyngdon's sermons, by which I mean statements that do not have a source elsewhere, are very limited. There are short sentences that link extracts drawn from his source, but these are rarely controversial. That is why interpreting the choice of sources becomes so important. Nevertheless there are two ways through which Repyngdon does make lengthy and sometimes contentious statements.

---

[16] See for instance, John Wyclif, *Tractatus de simonia*, 7, ed. S. Herzberg-Fränkel and M.H. Dziewicki, Wyclif Society, xvi (London, 1898), pp.97–98.

[17] In G. Williams (ed.), *Official Correspondence of Thomas Bekynton*, 2 vols., Rolls Series, lvi (1872), i, pp.151–54, and E.M. Thompson (ed.), *Chronicon Adae de Usk A.D. 1377–1421* (London, 1904), pp.65–69.

First, he produces his own material on a subject that has developed from his exegesis of the gospel text and, secondly, he both inserts extra sermons into the existing Sunday gospel scheme and academic discussions that include his own conclusions into existing sermons. In the first group come his discussions of twelve requirements of a preacher and of the ten signs, drawn from Bradwardine's *De causa Dei*,[18] from which Repyngdon argues that the apostolic church is the normative model against which the contemporary one should be judged. In the second group come the anomalous sermon for Ascension Thursday and a sermon on a Sunday epistle (not a gospel), which discuss preaching and simony respectively, and the academic discussions in the Fourth-after-Trinity and Trinity Sunday sermons, which debate almsgiving and the question whether the efficacy of sacraments is dependent on the merits of ministers.[19] The way in which Repyngdon constructs these authorial passages can be illustrated by the two passages on preaching drawn one from each group.

The twelve requirements of a preacher are found in the Sexagesima sermon, from Luke 8:4, 'And when a great multitude came together', the introduction to the parable of the sower. The first three requirements reflect on the preacher's self-awareness of his responsibilities. First, he should lead a life that was praiseworthy and therefore involve poverty, and should be well-informed before proceeding to teach others, though, naturally, he should not boast of his holy lifestyle. Likewise he should attribute the authority of the preaching *magisterium* to God and not to himself and, thirdly, he should put prayer before teaching. On other occasions he cited authorities or made asides to the effect that preachers should assiduously study Scripture and that worldly comfort will make preachers soften the harshness of the scriptural message. The demanding responsibilities of a preacher are immediately clear. The fourth to seventh requirements of a preacher concern sermon form and the use of Scripture. They are that the preacher should prefer the meaning of words to the words themselves, seek the authorial intent in the Scriptures, should not seek mysteries everywhere in Scripture and should steer a middle path with regard to divisions within sermons, carefully avoiding excessive division of the material. It has already been mentioned that the adoption of such a sermon form was characteristic of the conservatism associated with the Wycliffites. The remaining requirements of a preacher are less controversial and the characteristic of idealism is difficult to show here, but it can be seen in the Ascension Thursday sermon.

The sermon for the feast of the Ascension is one of three 'anomalous'

---

[18] The latter is discussed at *Co*, fos.134v-36v.

[19] The Ascension Thursday sermon is not extant in *Co*. For the other passages see *Co*, fos.344v-51r, 255r-57v and 211r-20r respectively.

sermons;[20] anomalous, firstly, because it does not fit into the Sunday gospel scheme – Ascension Day being a Thursday – and, second, because there are unique features that suggest that they were composed after the main body of sermons. For instance, while the core fifty-two sermons of this sermon collection are constant to all the complete extant manuscripts, only one or two out of the three anomalous sermons are ever found in any one manuscript. Further, the anomalous sermons are polemical, short and deal with a single verse from the lection. This is the case with the Ascension Thursday treatment of preaching.

On this occasion Repyngdon showed uncharacteristic outspokenness and demonstrated his high expectations of prelates and his perception of their contemporary shortcomings, especially with regard to preaching. A typical example in this sermon occurs when he states three requirements for ecclesiastical promotion, the third of which being 'a knowledge of the Scriptures which is implied by the passage that "a cloud received him"', a clause from the day's lection [Acts 1:9].[21] To expound this clause Repyngdon quotes Grosseteste, who proceeds to justify the equation of clouds with the mysteries of the Scriptures, and pseudo-Chrysostom, who provides the analogy that the rains (from the clouds) are the teachings (from Scripture). Repyngdon chose to continue the analogy:

> But it must be noted that very many are taken up today without the clouds. Others are dense clouds but do not rain, which is a sure sign for an epidemic.[22]

Grosseteste is again cited to reinforce the danger of promoting clerics with inadequate biblical learning:

> Imagine a feeble person who is strictly enjoined to feed lavishly and splendidly a great crowd suffering from hunger, yet he does not possess even one loaf. Imagine further that, despite this injunction, since he has nothing, or perhaps very, very little to give he does not bother even to seek out the crowd. Then imagine that having by chance obtained a little piece of food he stupidly throws it away.[23]

Grosseteste summarises such behaviour as 'arrogant presumption, negligent and a stupid waste'. But the point is forced home:

[20] For the distribution of these 'anomalous' sermons within the various manuscripts see Forde, 'New Sermon Evidence', pp.173–74.

[21] Worcester, Cathedral Library, MS F.121 (hereafter *W*), fo.146r: 'Tercium requisitum in vero assumptum est sciencia Scripturarum que innuitur in hoc quod nubes suscepit eum'. Oxford, Lincoln College, MS lat. 85 (hereafter *Li*) and Bodleian Library, MS Laud misc. 635 (hereafter *B*) both read 'assumpsit' for 'suscepit'.

[22] *W*, fo. 146v: 'Set hic notandum quod nimis multi assumuntur sine nubibus hiis diebus. Alii sunt nubes dense set non pluunt quod est signum epidemie satis manifestum'.

[23] *Ibid.*, fo.146v: 'Pone aliquem tibi in opem qui nec forte vnius panis habet copiam qui se obliget districte ad pascendum copiose et splendide turbam plurimam fame periclitantem et adice quod sic obligatus sit necligens ad querendum cum eciam nil habeat vel paruissimum, et si forte paruum cibi habeat illum stulte abicit'.

Today many pastors are like that. For when they take up a pastoral office they are enjoined to feed the crowd of people subject to them. They are suffering from a hunger of God's word and require the bread of the teaching of true faith and moral precepts. In this lies salvation and without it there is no salvation.[24]

The advice that follows on what should be preached supports the thesis that elementary catechetical instruction constituted the primary tier of preaching content, but that collections of sermons such as Repyngdon's constituted a higher level:

Many [of these pastors] are feeble because they know neither how to expound a single article of faith nor a single precept of the Ten Commandments . . . Moreover, many of them despise the wisdom, knowledge and teaching that they reject.[25]

Grosseteste continued in this vein, but Repyngdon quoted him in his entirety and obviously found such opinions congenial. Repyngdon had expressed in his own words his views on the calibre of contemporary prelates earlier in this same sermon:

Christ ordered his preachers to go into the world, not to sit or stand or lie around. For those who sit, stand or lie in the world are those who seek rest in temporalities. And what, I ask, could be more foolish than seeking rest in something that is continually on the move?[26]

This final phrase suggests an unease with fluidity and a yearning for stability. Surely this is what underpins the desire to reestablish traditional models of behaviour for each group within society at a time when society was indeed in flux? In these standards to be expected of prelates we see a clear example of an idealistic rather than, say, a pragmatic or cynical, approach.

Finally we can say that the sermons reflect the industriousness that was frequently lauded in this period. They are stern and earnest in the

[24] *Ibid.*, fo.146v: 'Tales sunt pastores multi. Cum enim assumunt officium pastorale obligant se ad pascendum turbam populi sibi subiecti fame verbi Dei periclitantis pane doctrine vere fidei et moralium preceptorum in quibus consistit salus et sine quibus salus non est'. The most relevant variant reading from the two other extant MSS. Is the addition of 'hodie' before 'pastores' in *Li* and *B*; my translation follows this variant here.

[25] *W*, fo.146v: 'Multi nec vnicum fidei articulum nec vnicum de preceptis decalogi populo sciunt exponere, et velut tot panum indigentes quot sunt articuli fidei et precepta moralia saluti necessaria que exponere nesciunt. Et cum hos panes non habeant obligati tum ad pastum ex hiis panibus discere ea que nesciunt necligunt. Imo et multi eorum sapienciam atque doctrinam despiciunt scienciam que repellunt'.

[26] *Ibid.*, fo.146r: 'Precipit eciam Christus suis predicatoribus quod eant in mundum non quod sedebant aut stent vel iaceant. [Illi autem in mundo sedent, stant vel iacent] qui in temporalibus requiem querunt. Et quid queso stulcius quam in re tali quietem querere que in continuo motu est'. The parenthetical variant, which my translation follows, is from *Li; B* also has it, though here 'sedent' and 'stant' are inverted. The omission in *W* can be readily explained as a haplographic error.

way that they seem to lack a sense of humour and have a tone of moral seriousness. Above all, Repyngdon's sermons were lengthy, running to about 650,000 words, or over two hours' reading or recital time for every sermon. Since I do not believe that they represent, in any way, *reportationes* of delivered sermons,[27] the literary magnitude of the project becomes more obvious. There are several statements by Repyngdon that exhort the idea of hard work and individual responsibility.[28] It appears therefore that this personal belief had a practical expression in such moral seriousness and in the conservatism and the preaching ideal that I have identified. The entire *Sermones dominicales* project seems to epitomise the industriousness in which Repyngdon believed.

It is not surprising that the paradigm for judging Wycliffism has consistently been that of doctrinal orthodoxy. This, of course, was the definition adopted in 1377 by Pope Gregory IX in reaction to Wyclif's published views on dominion, the eucharist and endowment. Likewise, the list of ten heresies and fourteen errors was the basis for the trials of Repyngdon and Hereford at the Blackfriars Council of 1382.[29] A similar, but extended, form of doctrinal investigation was the method by which inquisitors were to examine the later Lollards. Nonetheless, this paradigm is inadequate. It confuses and ignores the outlooks that the Wycliffites shared with their contemporaries, whether within the university or wider society. At the outset I indicated briefly how FitzRalph and Langland, among others, shared certain of these outlooks with these Wycliffites. Contemporaries often recognised these overlaps, though they and modern historians have habitually resorted to the test of doctrinal orthodoxy to

[27] The case for this assertion is argued at some length in Forde, 'Writings of a Reformer', i, pp.241–79.

[28] Perhaps the most remarkable is a passage attributed to Augustine which, in its context, is primarily attacking voluntary mendicancy, but it is hereby affirming the values mentioned here. The context is the exegesis of Matthew 6:27 ('Behold the fowls of the air: for they sow not, neither do they reap'). The argument, in brief, is that if one has the human resources available to achieve something one should use these, otherwise to rely on God in these circumstances would be putting him to the test. *Co*, fo. 324*r-v: 'Hic insuper dicit Augustinus: "Quidem dixerunt non debere hominem laborare set diuine prouidencie se totaliter committere". Set istum errorem repellit dicens: "Si adest temporis facultas debemus adquirere victum laborando alias si velimus sicut volatilia volare aut natatilia natare hoc esset Deum temptare. Si vero imminet necessitas debemus nos diuine prouidencie committere et tunc ille nos pascet sicut aues". Et ponit exemplum de Paulo et Petro: "Paulus quidem mortem fugit et tamen Christus Petrum a vinculis liberauit. Paulus itaque per auxilium humanum euadere poterat. Ideo si miraculosum operacionem exspectasset Deum indubie temptasset Petrus vero quia humano carebat auxilio, ideo confidenter se auxilio commisit diuino".'

[29] For the documents in question and a contemporary narrative of this perod, see W.W. Shirley (ed.), *Fasciculi zizaniorum magistri Johannis Wyclif cum tritico*, Rolls Series, v (1858), pp.319–25, and for the background to this collection see J. Crompton, '*Fasciculi zizaniorum* I and II', *Journal of Ecclesiastical History*, xii (1961), 35–45 and 155–66.

establish whether such connections are valid. It is one of the contentions of this essay that we shall continue to misread the connections among individuals in this sphere if we fail to recognise the importance of shared social outlooks and only study the sectarian beliefs associated with Wyclif and his earliest colleagues.

Chapter 13

John Gerson and Hierarchy

David Luscombe

Many spokesmen seeking to solve difficulties in the church during the conciliar age found help in the notions of hierarchy advanced in the writings of Denis the Areopagite. But these were invoked and interpreted in varying ways. Commonly Denis was used to support the case for papal monarchy as by Giles of Rome[1] and by François de Meyronnes,[2] and later by the Eugenians, especially Turrecremata.[3] Jean Gerson, while upholding papal monarchy, was one who found in Denis support for a conciliar viewpoint. He used him too to defend the rights of the clergy.

Even after the extensive studies of A. Combes, there is still reason to suggest that Gerson was during his career increasingly liable to have recourse to Denis.[4] Whether in teaching or in preaching in Latin

---

[1] See the masterly study by Y. Congar, 'Aspects ecclésiologiques de la querelle entre mendicants et séculiers dans la second moîtié du XIIIe siècle et le début du XIVe siècle', *Archives d'histoire doctrinale et littéraire du moyen âge*, 36ème année (1961), pp.35–151. Also, my 'The *Lex divinitatis* in the Bull *Unam Sanctam* of Pope Boniface VIII', *Church and Government in the Middle Ages: Essays Presented to C.R Cheney*, ed. C. Brooke *et al.* (Cambridge, 1976), pp.205–21.

[2] See my forthcoming paper on 'François de Meyronnes and Sovereignty', to appear in *The Church and Sovereignty: Essays in honour of Michael Wilks*, ed. D. Wood, Studies in Church History, Subsidia series (Blackwell, Oxford).

[3] See A.J. Black, *Monarchy and Community: Political Ideas in the Later Conciliar Controversy, 1430–1450* (Cambridge, 1970).

[4] Especially see A. Combes, *Jean Gerson, Commentateur dionysien: Les Notulae super quaedam verba Dionysii de Caelesti Hierarchia. Texte inédit.* Études de philosophie médiévale, xxx (Paris, 1940); *Jean de Montreuil et le Chancelier Gerson: Contribution à l'histoire des rapports de l'humanisme et de la théologie en France au début du XVe siècle*, Études de philosophie médiévale, xxxii (Paris, 1942); *Ioannis Carlerii de Gerson de mystica theologia*, ed. A. Combes, Thesaurus Mundi: Bibliotheca Scriptorum Latinorum Mediae et Recentioris Aetatis (Lugano, 1958); A. Combes, *Essai sur la critique de Ruysbroeck par Gerson*, 4 vols. (Paris, 1945, 1948, 1959, 1972). Important though these studies all are, they yield little to our purpose. For an account of *Gerson and the Great Schism* see J.B. Morrell's book under this title (Manchester, 1960). J.B. Schwab, *Johannes Gerson, Professor der Theologie und Kanzler der Universität Paris: Eine Monographie* (Würzburg, 1858) is far from having been superseded. That hierarchy and order are central to Gerson's understanding of the church is explained by L.B.

continued

or in the vernacular, or in participating in the affairs of the great councils, Gerson very extensively wove Denis's themes, both mystical and hierarchical, into his writings. In the Faculty of Theology in Paris he extolled Denis not only as the convert of St. Paul but also as the father of lights who had brought to the people of Gaul the light of faith.[5] He hailed Denis as an example to be followed in the difficult work of uniting the Latin and Greek churches,[6] and he fought the abbey of Saint-Denis in an attempt to persuade the monks to renounce their claim to possess the head of their patron saint.[7] It was entirely natural for him to launch himself upon a verbal flight up to the realms of the Seraphim and Cherubim and of the other angelic orders which set the example to be followed in the church on earth.[8]

For the church militant mirrors and is arranged like the angelic society. *Christianitas* can only be conserved by maintaining the order found in heaven and which is *hierarchia*, engaged in the activities of purifying, illuminating and perfecting. The pope and cardinals imitate the first three orders of angels in hierarchising and in not being hierarchised by others; the patriarchs, archbishops, bishops and priests imitate the middle hierarchy in being hierarchised and in heirarchising their subjects; the laity and religious (*populi et simplices religiosi secundum*

---

continued

Pascoe, *Jean Gerson: Principles of Church Reform*, Studies in Medieval and Reformation Thought, vii (Leiden, 1973). Valuable comments and references are also found in D.C. Brown, *Pastor and Laity in the Theology of Jean Gerson* (Cambridge, 1987).

[5] 'Instrumentalis auctor fuit Dionysius Areopagita, theosophus ionicus, primum philosophus, dehinc conversus a Paulo et factus episcopus Athenarum, post missus a Clemente in Galliam, qui nonagenarius passus est anno ab incarnatione 96, et ita tempore passionis erat 27 annorum aut circiter. Notentur ea quae prologi et legendae dicunt de eo. Hic potest dici a Gallis pater luminum quia lumen fidei eis dedit'. *Notulae super quaedam verba Dionysii de coelesti hierarchia* (1240), ed. P. Glorieux, *Jean Gerson: Oeuvres complètes*, iii, *l'oeuvre magistrale* (Paris, 1962), no.98, here 217–18. The phrase *pater luminum* is adopted from the opening sentence of the *Celestical Hierarchy*. Hereafter the ten volumes of Gerson's *Oeuvres complètes* 'ed. Glorieux'.

[6] 'Nonne sanctus Dionysius Galliae Apostolus natione Graecus fuit per quem suscepimus veram pacem. Fidem Christianam, nec hoc fuit sine magna fortitudine & labore; ideo simili modo laborandum est, quod Graeci ad nos revertantur, praesertim Universitas, de qua fuit Sanctus Dionysius pro tempore quo erat Athenis', *Sermo coram rege pro pace et unitate Grecorum*, ed. E.du Pin, *Iohannis Gersonii opera omnia*, 4 vols. (Antwerp, 1706), tom. ii, col.151C.

[7] Letter from Gerson to the abbot of Saint-Denis, *c.* October 1408, ed. Glorieux, ii, no.27, pp.103–5.

[8] 'Le royaume des cieux se institue en certaines ordres ou ordonnances essentielles et permanentes que nous appellons hierarchies. C'est la determination Saint Denis en son livre que pour ce il appela de hierarchie celeste, par l'instruction Saint Pol', *Quomodo stabit regnum*, ed. Glorieux, vii, 980.

Dionysium) imitate the lowest hierarchy because they are hierarchised but lack the authority to hierarchise others.[9] Hierarchical activity aims to lead all members of the church to union with God: 'ut infima reducantur ad suprema per media'.[10] References by Gerson to the hierarchical activities of purging, illuminating and perfecting and to the hierarchical states which support such activities are numerous. In his *Notulae super quaedam verba Dionysii de coelesti hierarchia* Gerson distinguishes a triple hierarchy: the celestial or angelic order, the ecclesiastical which is the order in the church, and the supercelestial which is the Trinity. Thus the church is constituted as a hierarchy to lead men back to God (*reducere in Deum*). Founders of religious orders and those who bestow honours on churches help to lead men back to God.[11] The three hierarchies resemble each other. Thus the Roman curia should correspond to the first order of the angelic hierarchy and should therefore consist of men suspended in contemplation like the Seraphim, splendid in wisdom like the Cherubim, steadfast in fairness like the Thrones.[12]

'Sed Heu, quid de calamitate praesentium temporum querar misera'. In the church of Gerson's time there was much that resembled hell in which no order is to be found but only horror. Many learned and worthy men are not ordained; many ignorant and unworthy men occupy the highest grades in the church. Many in the hierarchy of the church do

---

[9] *De postestate ecclesiastica* (6 February 1417), ed. Glorieux, vi, no.282, p.227. Later in the same work (p.240), which was presented at the council in Constance, Gerson suggests (*juxta probabilem valde sententiam*) that there are properly only two hierarchical states in the church: the greater prelates (bishops, archbishops and upwards) who succeed the apostles, the lesser prelates (curates) who succeed the seventy-two disciples. These perform the hierarchical actions of purifying through correction, enlightening through teaching and preaching, and perfecting by the ministry of the sacraments. Gerson believes that the church has three *ordines principales (supremus, infimus* and *medius)* but is *principalius* a church of prelates rather than of laity: 'Ecclesia consistit principalius in ordine primo et secundo quam in tertio qui est ordo laicorum, et maxime feminarum, quibus actus hierarchici nullo modo conveniunt nec ordines sacri, nec praedicatio publica vel solemnis, juxta prohibitionem Apostoli', *De orationibus privatis fidelium* (Lyon, 27 February 1429), no.507, ed. Glorieux, x, 135, 4th consideration. Unless the church on earth respects its prelates it cannot properly imitate the celestial hierarchy. c. *Quomodo stabit regnum*, ed. Glorieux, vii, 982. On Gerson's clericalism – the laity formed the *ecclesia audiens* – see the comments of Brown, *Pastor and Laity*, pp.38–40, 44.

[10] *Quomodo stabit regnum*, ed. Glorieux, vii, 981. On this phrase (which is not found in Denis, *De divinis nominibus*, to which Gerson refers), see Luscombe, 'The *Lex divinitatis*'. Also Denis, *Celestial Hierarchy* 4, 3 (J.P. Migne, *Patrologia graeca*, iii, 181A, 210AB); 8, 2 (3, 239 CD); *EH* 1, 2 (3, 373A). Cf. Gerson, *Sermon* (1392), 'Nimis honorati sunt', ed. Glorieux, vii, no.361, 728.

[11] Ed. Glorieux, iii, no.98; here pp.208, 222.

[12] Sermon preached before Pope Benedict XIII at Tarascon, 1 January 1404, ed. Glorieux, v, no.212, p.77.

not perform their hierarchical actions of purifying, enlightening and perfecting.[13] Much of Gerson's recourse to Denis was for the purpose of finding solutions to the problems of the Schism. His use of Denis was not simply oratorical or literary. In his polemical, ecclesiological treatises, in his sermons and statements, Gerson develops hierarchical terminology into a weapon which powerfully and customarily shapes and gives substance to his argument that it is of the essence of the church to be ruled by a monarch but also to be gathered together in councils; the church is in character a congregation or gathering. Throughout the Councils of Pisa and Constance, Gerson spoke repeatedly on the theme that the creator, not man, instituted the whole supernatural hierarchy of the church, from the supreme pontiff right down to the lowest official. This hierarchy is especially able to purify, enlighten and perfect the world when it is brought together in council.[14] The whole network (*junctura*) of grades, dignities and offices exists, and will never be destroyed, because Christ, the spouse of the church, has infused into all its members a living seed which enables the hierarchical order as a whole to conserve and to propagate itself until the end of time. Popes and bishops, being mortal, will come and go but the collective structure of grades, dignities and administrative offices is an essential and permanent part of the church, for they were impregnated into the primitive church by Christ.[15] Schismatical splits in this sub-celestial hierarchy are therefore abhorrent.

Gerson adheres to Denis's neo-platonic scheme: hierarchy functions properly only if the entire hierarchy is maintained; the middle term could not be lost without the whole triplicity becoming meaningless. The church is governed by a monarchy but the papal fullness of power is not exercised over all immediately; ordinary bishops have the right to

---

[13] *Mémoire* in oratorical form, written to justify the summoning of the Council of Pisa, *c.* 19 June 1409, and later submitted to Pope Alexander V, ed. Glorieux, v, no, 221, pp.212–14.

[14] *Propositio facta coram Anglicis* (i.e. to the English party journeying to Pisa), 29 January 1409, ed. Glorieux, vi, no.271, here p.132. (An English translation of this work has been published by G.R. Dunstan, 'Jean Gerson, *Propositio facta coram Anglicis*: A Translation' in *The Church in Pre-Reformation Society: Essays in Honour of F.R.H. Du Boulay*, ed. C.M. Barron and C. Harper-Bill (Woodbridge, 1985), pp.68–81). Sermon, 'Ambulate dum lucem habetis' (Constance, 23 March 1415), ed. Glorieux, v, no.210, p.40. See also Brown, *Pastor and Laity*, p.41.

[15] *Sermo post recessum Joannis XIII* preached at the council of Constance, 23 March 1415, ed. Glorieux, v, no.210, pp.40, 43–4. Cf. *De auferibilitate sponsi ab ecclesia*, first written 1409 but presented at the Council of Constance on 20 April 1415, ed. Glorieux, iii, no.102, pp.296–97. *Propositio facta coram anglicis*, ed. Glorieux, vi, no.271, pp.132–33. Cf. *De postesate ecclesiastica* (6 February 1417), ed. Glorieux, vi, no.282, p.222. The essential parts are: papacy, cardinalate, patriarchate, archiepiscopate, episcopate, sacerdotium.

perform their hierarchical acts to their own flocks.[16]

Gerson's various and varying attempts to define the church, in the *Propositio facta coram Anglicis* and in other later works, all rest, and in very large measure, upon a constant, unvarying insistence that the ecclesiastical hierarchy as a whole is a life-bearing divine institution which finds its unity through being gathered together in entirety. As Denis and others had written, it is of the nature of being to be one.[17] What, then, can and what cannot be lawfully done within the whole hierarchical structure to heal divisions? Clearly, no part of the hierarchy may be mutilated or rearranged. Cardinals, bishops and curates are all successors of the apostles and of the disciples.[18] Papal authority must be included in a general council, even if there is at the time no pope.[19] But changes in appointments procedures may be made and individual office-holders, including popes, may be replaced in their offices.[20] The church as a whole is indissolubly wedded to Christ, its head, but its marriage with its secondary head, the vicar of Christ, is not indissoluble. Moreover, a general council representative of the whole hierarchical state of the church, while it cannot take from the papacy its plenitude of power, may place certain restrictions upon its use and a council may meet frequently.[21] In his *On Investigating Teachings* (1423), Gerson spells out the rights and powers of ecclesiastical authorities; he upholds the powers of councils to declare doctrine which is in accord with Scripture and seems to regard the powers of pope and prelates as primarily juridical. Gerson's church is in this work neither Dionysian nor not Dionysian. Doctrinal competence is placed as much inside as outside the hierarchy.[22] On the other hand, the 'constitution' of the church, unlike that of other societies, cannot be changed. Whereas a civil polity may, for example, cease to be monarchic and become aristocratic, the church cannot cease to be a monarchic polity because it was instituted as such by Christ.[23] Because

[16] *De plenitudine potestatis ecclesiasticae*, ed. Glorieux, vi, no.283, pp.250–51. This short work is a sequel to Gerson's *De potestate ecclesiastica* of 1417.

[17] 'Tradit divinus Dionysius, et post eum Boetius et Augustinus, quibus experientia suffragatur, quod res quaelibet non minus diligit aut appetit congregationem sui ipsius quam propriam entitatem, nimirum quia ens et unum convertuntur', *Propositio facta coram Anglicis*, ed. Glorieux, vi, no.271, p.127. Cf. the *Sermon* preached at Tarascon, 1 Jan. 1404, ed. Glorieux, v, no.212, p.84.

[18] *De consiliis evangelicis*, ed. Glorieux, iii, no.88, p.25 and *Quomodo stabit*, ed. Glorieux, vii, p.984 and *De statu pape*, ed. Glorieux, ix, no.424, pp.28, 31.

[19] *De postestate ecclesiastica* (6 February 1417), ed. Glorieux, vi, no.282, p.222.

[20] Cf. *De auferibilitate sponsi ab ecclesia*, (1409, 1415), ed. Glorieux, iii, no.102, p.297.

[21] *Sermo post recessum Joannis XIII*, preached at the Council of Constance on 23 March 1415, ed. Glorieux, v, no.210, pp.44–45.

[22] Ed. Glorieux, ix, no.456, pp.458–75.

[23] *De auferibilitate sponsi ab ecclesia* (1409, 1415), ed. Glorieux, iii, no.102, pp.298–99 (8th consideration). Here Gerson attacks Marsillius of Padua.

Christ constituted the church as a monarchy on the model of the church triumphant, no one may grant or receive hierarchical rank (the power to purge, illuminate and perfect) without the real or assumed authority of the supreme hierarch.[24] But a pope who is a heretic may be deposed and replaced because such an action in no way destroys the sacramental unity of the church.[25]

According to Denis – as understood by Gerson – the church is a kingdom made in the likeness of the kingdom of heaven. The kingdom of Christianity will endure if it is faithful to the order established as an exemplar in the kingdom above. The kingdom of heaven is arranged into certain essential, permanent orders which we call hierarchies, as Denis demonstrated in his *Celestial Hierarchy*, and those men who are saved will enter one of these nine orders according to their individual merits. There is in the church too an essential hierarchic order, which is both stable and permanent, just as, for example, there is a personal *regimen* in every man, for each of man's members is joined to another in an inalterable way and his body should be subject to his own reason. In the church the prelates and curates have been set over men to hierarchise them or purge, illumine and perfect them. There should be no resistance to these dispositions. Lucifer was punished for wishing to transgress his own order or hierarchy; Adam was expelled from his terrestial paradise for the same reason and Giles of Rome gave this as a reason for the evils which befell the order of the Temple.[26]

God does sometimes change this order. The Annunciation to Mary was entrusted to Gabriel who did not belong to the lowest angelic choir. The pope may perhaps in particular instances also waive the obligation upon people to confess to their own curates. But he cannot wholly and permanently cancel the subordination of all parishioners to their curates, as is achieved by the Bull *Regnans in excelsis* issued by Pope Alexander V in 1409. The sermon Gerson preached in 1409, as well as the protest made by the university of Paris under his chancellorship in 1410, against the Bull *Regnans in excelsis*, are very largely couched in hierarchical terms.[27]

---

24 *De potestate ecclesiastica* (6 February 1417), ed. Glorieux, vi, no.282, pp.227–28.

25 *De auferibilitate sponsi ab Ecclesia* ((1409, 1415), ed. Glorieux, iii, no.102, p.309.

26 However, as Brown points out in *Pastor and Laity* p.45, doctors of theology illuminate the whole church, including the upper ranks of the ecclesiastical hierarchy. To this extent Gerson modifies Denis's scheme. See *Quomodo stabit regnum*, ed. Glorieux, vii, p.980. Also, *Ecce pareo*, ed. Glorieux, ii, p.36. On Giles of Rome and Gerson see R. Scholz, *Die Publizistik zur Zeit Philipps des Schonen und Bonifaz' VIII.* (Stuttgart, 1903), pp.124, 165.

27 *Sermo contra bullam mendicantium*, ed. E. du Pin, *Iohannis Gersonii opera omnia*, ii, pp.431–442; *Contra bullam regnans in excelsis* (5 March 1410), ed. Glorieux, x, no.495, p.30; *Oblata reformatoribus in Constancia per nuncios universitatis Parisiensis*, ed. H. Finke, *Acta Concilii Constantiensis*, 4 vols. (Münster, 1896–1928), ii, pp.694–98. For the circumstances see Finke, here, pp.570–73. Cf. also Gerson, *De postestate ecclesiastica*, ed. Glorieux, vi, no.282, p.215 (on penitentiars and *privilegiati*).

The Bull shakes the hierarchic order of prelates; the pope (*qui magnus est theologus*) must have made a mistake, for curates, who are lesser or minor prelates, are more perfect than simple religious (that is, members of religious orders other than priors, abbots and provosts who are like curates). Denis – according to Gerson – shows this in his *Ecclesiastical Hierarchy*. It is curates who have the responsibility of preaching to parishioners and of hearing confessions. The Mendicants have no right to do these things or to solemnise marriages or to administer the sacraments, except where curates consent. Members of religious orders along with the laity are the lowest hierarchy in the church. The Bull must therefore be quashed.

Gerson was also concerned with secular monarchy. In a sermon on the feast of St. Louis (25 August, ?1391) he developed the theme that glory belongs to kings on earth only by way of imitation and participation in the divine example. Gerson invoked as an analogy scholastic discussions concerning the goodness that attaches to ordinary external human acts. Such goodness as exists in these derives wholly from the intrinsic goodness of internal acts. An external act may possess goodness but only through its participation in and its resemblance to the goodness in the interior act. So too in a kingdom of men, glory arises from its imitation of good (Ecclesiasticus 23:3: 'gloria magna est sequi Dominum'). Kingdoms are found in three types. The natural kingdom is an intrinsic, monastic state among men subject to right reason and justice. The civil kingdom is the political type regulated by civil and positive laws. The divine kingdom is the evangelical society responding to the precept of charity. Glory and peace can be produced in each of these by the inculcation of virtues according to the teachings of Plotinus, Macrobius and Denis. The four cardinal virtues (prudence, temperance, fortitude and justice) are relevant to men, whatever their kingdom. In the monastic kingdom, their function is purificatory; in civil society, it is political or enlightening; and in the divine Kingdom it is perfective among minds who are both purged and enlightened. These functions correspond to the three hierarchical states or activities of which Denis wrote: those of purifying, illuminating and perfecting.[28]

Gerson expressed views on other subjects along similar, customary lines derived from the thinking of Denis. Jurists say that episcopacy is an order distinct from that of the priesthood but theologians describe it not as a new order but as a hierarchical power above the priesthood.[29]

---

[28] Ed. Glorieux, v, no.219, pp.179–190.
[29] *De potestate ecclesiastica*, ed. Glorieux, vi, no.282, p.215 *in fine*.

The reason why women cannot be either bishops or priests is that theirs is the subject sex and therefore incapable of exercising hierarchical domination.[30] The subjection of all lay believers to the sacerdotal and episcopal order is spelt out: priests and bishops must rule the faithful by the three hierarchical activities, purging them by baptism and sacramental absolution (or in the case of rebels by the penalties of excommunication or interdict); illuminating them through preaching and teaching; perfecting them by administering the other sacraments.[31] Unlike Wyclif, Gerson did not deny hierarchical authority to those in a state of sin.[32] If episcopal status were to be put in jeopardy on account of sin, the hierarchy of the church would itself be put into doubt.[33]

[30] *Ibid.*, ed. Glorieux, vi, no.282, p.215; *De orationibus privatis fidelium*, ed. Glorieux, x, no.507, pp.135–36, 4th, 6th and 8th considerations.

[31] *De potestate ecclesiastica*, ed. Glorieux, vi, no.282, p.219, cf. *Sermo de officio pastoris* (29 April 1408, at Reims) on the wrongness of indifferently granting the authority to preach, for this would confuse the ecclesiastical hierarchy; ed. Glorieux, v, no.215, p.129. As Combes commented: 'Pour un esprit de cette famille, la conception d'une origine démocratique du pouvoir spirituel est littéralement impensable. Hiérarchiquement parlant, il reçoit tout, il ne donne rien', *Jean de Montreuil et le chancelier Gerson: Contribution à l'histoire des rapports de l'humanisme et de la théologie en France au début du XVe siècle*, Études de philosophie médiévale, xxxii (Paris, 1942), p.477.

[32] '. . . hic enim fuit error vetus Waldensium et pauperum de Lugduno, qui per Wicleff et sequaces suos renovari quaesitus est, sed juste damnatus. Cur ita? Ne hierarchicus ordo potestatis ecclesiasticae maneat instabilis, vagus et incertus cum nemo sciat an amore vel odio dignus sit . . .', *De potestate ecclesiastica*, ed. Glorieux, vi, no.282, p.212. Cf. *De orationibus privatis fidelium*, (Lyon, 27 February 1429) ed. Glorieux, x, no.507, pp.136–37, 7th and 10th considerations. See Brown, *Pastor and Laity*, pp.41–42. Also, D. Luscombe, 'Wyclif and Hierarchy', *From Ockham to Wyclif*, ed. A. Hudson and M. Wilks, Studies in Church History, Subsidia 5 (Oxford, 1987), pp.233–44.

[33] 'Status episcopalis, sicut non acqiritur in aliquo per solum titulum fidei vel caritatis, ita non deperditur per solam haeresim vel peccatum mortale, non interveniente humana destitutione vel divina revelatione; alioquin status Ecclesiae hierarchicus prorsus esset incertus cum suo usu vel exercitio, quod non est conveniens dicere de politia a supremo legislatore constituta', *De statu papae et minorum praelatorum* (before June 1409), ed. Glorieux, ix, no.424, p.30.

Chapter 14

Contrasting Chronicles: Historical Writing at York and Durham at the Close of the Middle Ages

Barrie Dobson

'The form which historical writing took in the Middle Ages is an index of the intellectual standards of monasticism.'[1] By that severe if not altogether unpersuasive criterion, it might well be supposed that the intellectual life conducted by the major monastic, cathedral and mendicant communities of fifteenth-century England must have lacked both the excitement and the intellectual curiosity enjoyed by their predecessors. Not for nothing perhaps has John Taylor's own indefatigable interest in the medieval English monastic chronicle tended to slacken after the *annus mirabilis* of 1399; and even Dr. Antonia Gransden has recently concluded her detailed survey of the last stages of the monastic tradition of English medieval historiography with the melancholy reflection that this tradition 'was all but dead well before the end of the fifteenth century'.[2] Although the gradual disintegration and final collapse of the most impressive genre of historical writing ever produced in medieval England is impossible to deny, that decline has perhaps never been altogether satisfactorily explained. No longer does it seem plausible to account for the demise of the monastic chronicle so many decades before the demise of the monasteries themselves in such general and over-simple terms as the supposed moral decline or 'spiritual rusticity' of the fifteenth-century English religious.[3] Perhaps, as John Taylor himself has done much to document, the emergence during the previous century of increasingly large numbers of secular clerks and laymen who practised the art of historical writing outside the precinct

---

[1] J. Taylor, *Medieval Historical Writing in Yorkshire*, St. Anthony's Hall Publications, 19 (1961), p.25.

[2] J. Taylor, *English Historical Literature in the Fourteenth Century* (Oxford, 1987), pp.174–94; A. Gransden, *Historical Writing in England*, ii, *c. 1307 to the Early Sixteenth Century* (London, 1982), pp.342–424.

[3] D. Knowles, *The Religious Orders in England*, iii (Cambridge, 1959), pp.456–68; H.O. Evenett, 'The Last Stages of Medieval Monasticism in England', *Studia Monastica*, ii (1960), 387–419; and cf. C. Harper-Bill, *The Pre-Reformation Church in England, 1400–1530* (London, 1989), pp.36–43.

walls of England's religious houses was crucial in bringing an end to the ascendancy of the latter in this field?[4] Even so, it remains not a little surprising that so few members of what were still in the 1530s the most closed and self-regarding religious communities in the country should have responded to this new challenge by demonstrating a detectable interest in perpetuating the memory of either their past or their present. To take the example of the English Benedictine monk most central to John Taylor's own interests, why did Ranulf Higden of St. Werburgh's Abbey, Chester, have no real successors after his death in 1363–64?[5]

It need hardly be said that so large a problem is easy to pose but impossible to answer in this short essay. Indeed a full explanation of the collapse of the tradition of historical writing in late medieval English religious houses would almost certainly necessitate a full-scale analysis not only of the well-known internal contradictions and uncertainties of purpose within that tradition, but also of the new patterns of sensibility which transformed the corporate attitudes of monasteries and cathedrals alike during the decades before and after 1400. Such at least are the conclusions which seem to emerge from the following very cursory review of what apparently happened to the practice of writing historical work within the two most important religious communities of northern England in the fifteenth century, the Benedictine community of St. Cuthbert at Durham and the metropolitan cathedral church of St. Peter at York. Here, if anywhere in the late medieval northern province, one would self-evidently have expected a continuing obsession with the spiritual glories of the past and the not inconsiderable material successes of the present; but at both these major *ecclesiae matrices* of the north it is hardly an exaggeration to state that by the second half of the fifteenth century the tradition of writing the history of the past, or indeed the present, had reached almost if not quite vanishing-point. Despite the extraordinary differences between the constitutional structures, the religious observances and the composition of the clergy serving these two cathedrals, they were eventually alike in failing to sustain a creative interest in the history which gave them their sense of self-identity and their international fame.[6] More ironically still, the fragments of historical

---

[4] J. Taylor, 'Letters and Letter Collections in England, 1300–1420', *Nottingham Medieval Studies*, xxiv (1980), 65–70; *idem, Historical Literature*, pp.14–16, 24–36.

[5] J. Taylor, *The Universal Chronicle of Ranulf Higden* (Oxford, 1966), pp.110–51. Dr. Gransden makes the important point that neither Higden's many continuators nor those other 'massive histories' of the period, the *Brut* and John of Tynemouth's *Historia aurea*, tried to reproduce his own encyclopaedic and universal approach: *Historical Writing*, ii, pp.56–57.

[6] See the surveys of the two cathedrals in G.E. Aylmer and R. Cant, eds., *A History of York Minster* (Oxford, 1977), pp.44–108, and R.B. Dobson, *Durham Priory, 1400–1450* (Cambridge, 1973).

composition occasionally being produced in both cathedrals at the very end of the middle ages are surprisingly similar in suggesting a final involuntary return of the full-blown flower of the English monastic chronicle to its origins, a reversion to 'annals' at times even less sophisticated than those once produced by the major Anglo-Saxon churches of the pre-Conquest church.

Nowhere in the fifteenth-century north, perhaps nowhere in England, is this contraction of historical horizons more poignant than within St. Cuthbert's great religious community at Durham. For within twenty or so years of the original transformation of Durham cathedral into a Benedictine cathedral priory at the hands of Bishop William of St. Calais in 1083, the monk Symeon and his contemporaries had already validated their spiritual ascendancy in the north by what amounted to the creation of a sustained historical vision of the whole of northern British history since the age of Bede.[7] This vision was of course expressed in its most lengthy and influential form within the *Libellus de exordio atque procursu istius, hoc est Dunelmensis Ecclesiae*, almost certainly composed by the monk Symeon who actually witnessed the translation of St. Cuthbert's remains to their new shrine behind the cathedral's new high altar in 1104. According to the *Libellus*, the fundamental key to the history of the see of St. Cuthbert from its foundation at Lindisfarne by St. Aidan in 635 until the death of Bishop William of St. Calais in 1096, was a remarkable and at times astonishing spiritual continuity throughout the violent political vicissitudes of more than four hundred years. It followed, to cite a celebrated phrase from the *Libellus* itself, that in 1083 Bishop St. Calais 'was not instituting a new monastic order but restoring an old one'.[8]

Symeon provided the model which nearly all his successors at Durham were to emulate. At the centre of all the many diverse and often confusing works of history produced within or near the cathedral during the next three centuries lay the monks' continued determination to demonstrate that St. Cuthbert remained the tutelary and ever-watchful protector of their community. It was no doubt for this reason above

[7] T. Arnold (ed), *Historia ecclesiae Dunhelmensis* in *Symeonis monachi opera omnia*, Rolls Series, lxxv (1882), i, pp.1–135; according to this providential interpretation of northern history, the reintroduction of the Benedictine life into St. Cuthbert's own *patria* during the 1070s and 1080s was itself the direct result of the reading of *historia Anglorum* by West Country monks (*ibid.*, p.108).

[8] *Ibid.*, p.11. To that extent, and somewhat unusually, the monks of Durham exploited Anglo-Saxon history to validate a post-Conquest initiative. Cf. R.W. Southern, 'Aspects of the European Tradition of Historical Writing, 4: The Sense of the Past', *Transactions of the Royal Historical Society*, 5th ser., xxiii (1973), 243–63; J. Campbell, 'Some Twelfth-Century Views of the Anglo-Saxon Past', *Peritia*, iii (1984), 131–50.

all that already by 1200 'History writing at Durham . . . tended to parochialism'. However such historical parochialism achieved some not inconsiderable successes on the banks of the Wear: few saints of twelfth-century England, for example, were as fortunate as the comparatively obscure Godric of Finchale in attracting three *vitae* at such rapid speed.[9] More obviously still, the succession of Durham monks and others who added continuations to the *Libellus de exordio* from the mid twelfth to the mid fourteenth centuries were by no means naive in their concepts of how arguments and *exempla* from the historic past could enhance the morale and welfare of their present community. The 'domestic' histories produced at Durham by the anonymous twelfth-century continuators of the *Libellus*, then by Geoffrey of Goldingham in *c.* 1215, and, above all, by the perspicacious Robert de Graystanes (who completed his section of the history of Durham in 1336) now all urgently deserve editions less antique than those of Henry Wharton and James Raine the elder.[10] When such editions finally emerge, it may well appear that no monastic cathedral in medieval England displayed a more sustained expertise in writing genuinely local history, and in squaring some difficult circles, than did these Durham chroniclers. At one level, Graystanes and his colleagues consistently used historical evidence, and the historic past itself, against the unwelcome intrusions of bishops like Antony Bek and Lewis de Beaumont; at another, they were increasingly at pains to produce highly flattering images of those bishops in order to make the latter seem not entirely unworthy successors of St. Cuthbert himself.[11]

As will be seen, this progressive tendency to write the history of the contemporary church of Durham in terms of its *Gesta episcoporum* (the title, significantly enough, by which the *Libellus de exordio* was soon to be best known) became thoroughly entrenched in the mid fourteenth century, exactly when the accounts of those episcopal *gesta* start to show obviously signs of perfunctory, excessively episodic and even banal compilation, 'an

[9] H.S. Offler, *Medieval Historians of Durham* (University of Durham, 1958), p.13, a lecture to which this essay is much indebted. Cf. J. Stevenson, ed., *Libellus de Vita et Miraculis S. Godrici*, Surtees Society, xx (1847); A. Gransden, *Historical Writing in England, c. 550 – c. 1307* (London, 1974), pp.270, 308–9.

[10] For Raine's (excessively severe in the light of his own editorial lapses) animadversions on the 'utter worthlessness' of Wharton's 1691 edition of Coldingham, Graystanes and 'Chambre' in *Anglia Sacra*, see *Historiae Dunelmensis Scriptores Tres*, Surtees Society, ix (1839), pp.vii-xv, 3–123.

[11] After his death in 1311, even Bishop Bek, the source of so many of the convent's tribulations, received from Graystanes the posthumous tribute that by his benefactions 'he honoured the church of Durham more than any of his predecessors' (*Scriptores Tres*, p.91).

historical tradition in full dissolution'.[12] All the more remarkable was the
apparently single-handed attempt by one of St. Cuthbert's monks, John
Wessington, to revivify the proud tradition of historical writing on the
Durham peninsula. John Wessington, professed as a Durham monk in
1390 and then a student at Durham College, Oxford, before becoming
sacrist and chancellor of his convent in the years preceding his election
as prior in November 1416, now holds a respected place among the ranks
of the most learned Benedictines of fifteenth-century England.[13] Within
a historical context, he fills a more exemplary role as the most dedicated
northern English scholar to write at length about the past between 1400
and 1540. If therefore seems all the more ungenerous to suggest that
on close acquaintance John Wessington may prove to be an example
of that not uncommon late medieval literary figure, the historian who
promises more than he performs. To some extent such is admittedly
a provisional judgement, above all because Wessington was a prolific
author in a variety of different genres. Few of his treatises and *libelli* have
been analysed in detail, all the more serious a deficiency in the case of a
writer who was so systematically derivative from earlier chronicles and
records. Indeed his careful assembling of historical evidence for use in
preparing legal or other briefs on his community's or his bishop's behalf
is unfailingly impressive, even if he may sometimes cast his net too widely
and irrelevantly.[14] What Wessington's large and diverse output proves
beyond question is that he, and no doubt many of his fellow monks, were
still thoroughly imbued with – and sustained by – the Durham historical
tradition as the latter emanated from Bede. However, what it equally
proves is that Wessington was largely uninterested in, or incapable of,
adding substantively to that tradition.

Such a conclusion seems to emerge most clearly from Prior Wessington's most considerable literary achievement and the one most germane
to the subject of this essay – his large-scale survey of the history of
the see of St. Cuthbert. Wessington's revised and reorganised history

[12] See Oxford, Bodleian Library, MS Fairfax 6, fos. vi *verso*, 213; MS Laud Misc. 700, fo.
14v; Offler, *Medieval Historians*, pp.14 and n. 31, 16. The first detailed demonstration that
from the pontificate of Bishop Richard de Bury onwards the Durham *Gesta Episcoporum*
ceases to be a coherent chronicle written by one historian was provided by N. Denholm-
Young's 'The Birth of a Chronicle', *Bodleian Quarterly Record*, vii (1932–4), 325–28.

[13] Knowles, *Religious Orders*, ii (1955), 190–93; Dobson, *Durham Priory*, pp.81–113,
378–86.

[14] Contemporary lists of Wessington's written works survive as Dean and Chapter of
Durham Muniments [hereafter cited as DCD], Misc. Charters, 5727 (a) and (c); Reg.
II, fos. ix *verso-x verso*. Cf. *Scriptores Tres*, pp.cclxviii–xxi; and for an attempt to identify
all surviving tracts associated with the prior see R.B. Dobson, 'The Priory of Durham
in the Time of John Wessington, Prior 1416–1446' (unpublished D. Phil. thesis, Oxford,
1962), pp.580–86.

of the origins and development of the church of Durham (*De exordio et status ecclesie cathedralis quondam Lindisfarnensis, post Conchestrensis, demum Dunelmensis, ac de gestis pontificum eiusdem*) was first identified by Sir Edmund Craster in his remarkable paper on the 'Red Book' of Durham; but the work has received, rightly or wrongly, virtually no scholarly attention since Craster's discoveries of over sixty years ago.[15] Of the three manuscripts of the history still known to survive, all written in the first half of the fifteenth century, the first and draft version (Bodleian Library, MS Laud Misc. 748, fos. 6–67), fills almost sixty leaves of closely-written and often interlined text, so comprising a work incomparably larger than any other associated with the prior. According to Craster's persuasive analysis, this Laud manuscript not only forms the earliest version of Wessington's 'new' history but is also itself divided into two parts, of which fos. 6–47 provide a revised draft of the history of the see from its origins to the pontificate of Hugh du Puiset (1153–95), while fos. 50–67 take the story of the bishopric of Durham from 1174 to 1356 and seem to be an original draft.[16] There is little doubt that the revised draft of MS Laud Misc. 748 was the original source of the two other extant texts of Wessington's new history, namely those to be found within Lincoln's Inn Library, MS Hales 114 (the '*Liber Ruber*' itself) and British Library, MS Cotton, Claudius D. VI. As the latter is the most handsomely executed copy of the three, decorated on its first page with the armorial shields of the see and priory of Durham as well as that of the Wessington family itself, Craster was inclined to believe that this was the final prestige edition of the history, presumably destined for the common monastic library at Durham.[17] It might be equally possible to conjecture that after Prior Wessington had instructed a scribe to complete MS Claudius D.IV for the convent's library from the first part of his original draft, he decided to have a third, rather less accomplished, copy (MS Hales 114) made for use in the monastic chancery, where it was certainly preserved in the early sixteenth century.[18] Nor does there seem any firm reason to suppose with Sir Edmund Craster that there must at some time have existed yet a fourth copy of Wessington's history, now lost but once consulted and summarised by John Leland.[19]

[15] H.H.E. Craster, 'The Red Book of Durham', *English Historical Review*, xl (1925), 504–19.

[16] *Ibid*, 508–11; MS Laud Misc. 748, fos. 6–67.

[17] Craster, 'Red Book', pp.513–14.

[18] Lincoln's Inn, MS Hales 114, fo. 1 (where Thomas Swalwell, monastic chancellor at the beginning of the sixteenth century, has written his signature); cf. *Scriptores Tres*, p.ccccxxii.

[19] Craster, 'Red Book', 514; and for Leland's consultation of other manuscripts at Durham see his *Itinerary*, ed. L. Toulmin Smith (London, 1907–10), v, pp.129–31.

On all the evidence available, for the rest of the middle ages Prior Wessington's revisionist history of the see of St. Cuthbert circulated not at all outside the Durham cloister and perhaps not very widely within it.

Nevertheless, and despite its inadequacies, Wessington's *Libellum de exordio et statu ecclesie cathedralis quondam Lindisfarnensis* provides a unique opportunity to explore the historical mentality of an intelligent and devout Durham monk at the beginning of the fifteenth century. The first draft of the history (MS Laud Misc. 748) is of particular interest in this connection, as it seems to have been written and partly dictated by Wessington himself during his years as monastic chancellor shortly before 1416.[20] What is immediately clear is that Wessington had no intention of abandoning the traditional canon of historical work at Durham as it was represented in his community's library. Thus for the whole of the pre-Conquest history of the church of Lindisfarne, Chester-le-Street and Durham, the 'new' history relied predominantly on Symeon's so-called *Historia Dunelmensis ecclesiae*. However Wessington was at pains, for it seems to have been his major intention, to elucidate and expand from other sources Symeon's narrative whenever the latter seemed to be in danger of becoming too bare and unadorned. Thus the third book of Bede's *Ecclesiastical History* (known as *De gestis Anglorum* at Durham) and the third book of Henry of Huntingdon were cited on the very first page of Wessington's history.[21] Although Wessington's frequent insertions can sometimes spoil the simplicity of Symeon's account of the early days of the Durham church, his new arrangement of familiar historical material usually reveals a comparatively skilful practitioner of 'scissors and paste', at least for the period before the pontificate of Hugh du Puiset.

From the late twelfth century onwards, however, Prior Wessington's new history of Durham (as represented in the unrevised draft of MS Laud Misc. 748, fos. 50–67) is a good deal less satisfactory. The prior's decision not to revise this section of the Laud Misc. manuscript nor to use it as the basis for a lengthier edition of a Durham history may be the result of lack of leisure after his election to the priorate of 1416; but it is quite possible that he himself realised its inadequacy. This inadequacy is all the more disappointing in that the modern historian would prefer to read Wessington's comments on this later rather than pre-Conquest period, particularly if he had taken his narrative down to his own lifetime. The prior however presumably never had any intention of continuing

---

[20] The early folios of MS Laud. Misc. 748 contain instructions to the copyist (e.g. 'Nota hic processum in parvo libro ad talem signum' at fo. 52) which are probably in Wessington's own hand.

[21] MS Laud Misc. 748, fo. 6.

his composite chronicle into the fifteenth century; and to criticise him
on those grounds would be to misrepresent his aims and position as
a historian. There was a more prosaic reason why Wessington did so
little justice to the period in Durham's history from 1174 to 1356: he left
himself too little space. Within only eighteen folios (50–67) of the Laud
Misc. manuscript, the prior made what must now seem a foredoomed
attempt to combine the domestic account of events at Durham provided
by Geoffrey de Coldingham and Robert de Graystanes with enlarged
references to events of national or European importance. The only
purpose these references now serve is to suggest what historical episodes
of the preceding two hundred years seemed most significant to a Durham
monk writing in the early fifteenth century. It is not surprising that an
English Benedictine should end his chronicle with brief accounts of the
three most famous military victories of the fourteenth century (Crecy,
Neville's Cross and Poitiers) as well as of the *mortalitas* of the first
onslaught of the Black Death, misdated by a not untypical slip of the
pen to 1368.[22] More revealing are Prior Wessington's reserved comments
on the great monastic reforming legislation of the 1330s promulgated by
Benedict XII, 'qui, anno pontificatus sui tercio, pro statu monachorum
constituciones edidit gravissimos ... quas penas papa Clemens VI
misericorditer commutavit'.[23] However, much the greater part of the
section of Wessington's history from the 1170s to the 1350s is devoted to
the internal history of his convent and especially to its notorious disputes
with various bishops of Durham and archbishops of York, apparently still
the main focus of local historical interest in his cloister well over a century
later.[24]

As Sir Edmund Craster pointed out, perhaps the greatest fascination of
John Wessington's revised *Libellus de statu Lindisfarnensis, id est Dunelmensis
ecclesiae* is the unrivalled light it throws on what historical texts were

[22] *Ibid.*, fos. 66–67; and for Wessington's understandable interest in English humiliations at the hands of the Scots after Bannockburn see fos. 61–62. For a recent important
discovery of one of Wessington's sources for Border affairs during the reign of Edward
III, see H.S. Offler, 'A Note on the Northern Franciscan Chronicle', *Nottingham Medieval
Studies*, xxviii (1984), 45–59.

[23] *Ibid.*, fo. 64v.

[24] For his accounts of these most searing episodes in the recent ecclesiastical history of
the north, Wessington depended primarily on Robert de Graystanes's chronicle but
seems to have occasionally used, less astutely than Graystanes himself, one of the latter's
own most important sources, the so-called *Annales Dunelmenses*: cf. MS Laud Misc. 748,
fo. 57v, and F. Barlow (ed.), *Durham Annals and Documents of the Thirteenth Century*, Surtees
Society, clv (1945), p.64.

actually available to a serious student of the past in close proximity to what was probably the most substantial single collection of historical texts in the late medieval north.[25] To an exceptional extent not only can the sources Wessington consulted and copied be identified but so too can the very manuscripts in which he encountered them. Thus the texts which make up at least three-quarters of Wessington's history seem to derive from two books only: the *Gesta episcoporum* (Symeon and his continuators), especially in the copy now preserved as Bodleian Library, MS Fairfax 6, and the fine three-volumed edition of the *Historia Aurea* still extant as Lambeth Palace, MSS 10–12.[26] Besides these two central authorities, Wessington naturally drew especially heavily on a variety of less substantial Durham historical works and saints' lives, far too numerous to list here. Most interesting of all Wessington's sources to the modern historian, although there is no clear evidence that he appreciated its significance himself, was the *Libri summi altaris ecclesie Dunelmensis*, skilfully reconstituted and then printed by Sir Edmund Craster.[27] Except for copious citation, as in nearly all his work, from the notorious Durham 'foundation' charters of the twelfth century, Wessington's history made much less use of the convent's muniments than might have been supposed; but for information on more general history he was eager to exploit the respectable if not particularly voluminous collection of *Libri historiarum* preserved within the monastic cloister at Durham in the early fifteenth century.[28] Several of these volumes are now less than easy to trace; but at least it is tempting to suppose that the copy of Ranulph Higden's *Polychronicon* used extensively by Wessington may have been the one owned and eventually bequeathed to the community of St. Cuthbert by Bishop Thomas Langley of Durham.[29]

[25] For a longer (but not at all comprehensive) account of historical works available in the early fifteenth-century Durham libraries than is possible here see Dobson, 'Priory of Durham', pp.491–501; cf. Craster, 'Red Book', 516–19.

[26] At least part of MS. Fairfax 6 was written by 'Petrus plenus amoris' (fos. vi *verso*, 1), conceivably the monk Peter of Durham who was monastic librarian in 1366 (DCD, Misc. Charters, 4297). Lambeth Palace MS 12, fo. 254, has an entry inserted by John Fishburn, Prior Wessington's chancellor: for this work see V.H. Galbraith, 'The *Historia Aurea* and Sources of the St. Albans Chronicles, 1327–77', *Essays in History Presented to R.L. Poole*, ed. H.W.C. Davis (Oxford, 1927), pp.379–98.

[27] Craster, 'Red Book', 523–29.

[28] B. Botfield, ed., *Catalogi veteres librorum ecclesiae cathedralis Dunelm*, Surtees Society, vii (1838), where most of the 'history books' and 'chronicles' inventorised at pp.30, 56–57, 107 still survive and can be identified. Cf. A.J. Piper, 'The Libraries of the Monks of Durham', in *Medieval Scribes, Manuscripts and Libraries: Essays presented to N.R. Ker*, ed. M.B. Parkes and A.G. Watson (London, 1978), pp.213–49.

[29] *Catalogi veteres*, p.120; but (surprisingly perhaps) no copy of the *Polychronicon* now seems to survive at Durham; Taylor, *Universal Chronicle*, pp.152–59.

Such were some of the standard sources, by no means an exhaustive list, available to the historical enquirer within the early fifteenth-century Durham cloister. They were to be pressed into service by Wessington again and again throughout his lifetime, not only to illuminate his full-scale history of St. Cuthbert's see but also to document his many other tracts and treatises. Many of the latter indeed prove a good deal more lucid and coherent than the former, and in particular it might well be argued that Wessington proved more successful as a pioneering prosopographer than as a traditional monastic historian. Perhaps the most instructive of several possible examples is provided by his longest and most ambitious work on Benedictine history and theory, a treatise beginning with the words 'Quia de ortu sacrosanctae religionis monachorum plerisque vertitur in dubium' which occupies the first twenty-five folios of Durham, MS B. III. 30. In this case Wessington's purpose was to provide a commentary upon a series of images or pictures of celebrated Benedictine monks, apparently painted on wood, already in place at the altar of Sts. Benedict and Jerome within the cathedral church.[30] After detailed research, the biographies of no less than 148 different individuals (not all of them Black Monks) were written on parchment and attached to two or more wooden boards or *tabulae* placed in the vicinity of the altar for consultation by monks or visitors to the cathedral.[31] In this case Wessington also produced a separate list of the twenty-five authorities he had consulted in order to provide the biographical information he was purveying in this popular and condensed form.[32] Although this work (like several of his treatises) had the incidental polemical purpose of disputing the claims of Canons Regular to greater antiquity than the Benedictines, it is of even more importance in revealing how extensively, as will be seen later, the late medieval cathedral community might rely upon written *tabulae* for communicating historical knowledge. *Quia de ortu* also confirms that the painstaking compilation of biographical data constituted what was in many ways Wessington's own most successful form of historical writing.

If so, the strengths and limitations of John Wessington's work as a historian, however exceptional it seems at first sight, nevertheless still exemplify the general transformation from narrative discourse to

---

[30] DCD, MS B. III. 30, fos. 1–25, briefly described in W.A. Pantin, ed., *Documents Illustrating the Activities of the General and Provincial Chapters of the English Black Monks, 1215–1540*, ii, Camden 3rd. ser., xlvii (1933), p.xiv. For the position of the altar in question see J.T. Fowler (ed.), *The Rites of Durham*, Surtees Society, cvii (1903), p.112.

[31] As Wessingham refers to *in supremo gradu superioris tabule* (DCD, MS B. III. 30, fo. 6) there seems no doubt that there was more than one of these tables or boards at the altar; for the popularity of *tabulae*, see below, note 59, and G.H. Gerould, '*Tables* in Mediaeval Churches', *Speculum*, i (1926), 439–40.

[32] DCD, MS B. III. 30, fo. 5; cf. Dobson, *Durham Priory*, p.382.

episodic biography which forms the central characteristic of historical writing at late medieval Durham and, as will be seen, at York. It is therefore perhaps all the more unfortunate that the prior's most ambitious work should have failed to exploit the art of biography more directly. Wessington did indeed close his history of St. Cuthbert's see with versions of those brief biographies of Bishops Richard de Bury and Thomas Hatfield, as well as of Prior John Fossor, which James Raine misleadingly printed as the early chapters of the misnamed Durham chronicle of William de Chambre.[33] However, in his arrangement of these biographical passages, the prior also helps to confirm the now established view that the latter were written piecemeal in the late fourteenth century and mark the more or less complete disintegration of the medieval Durham tradition of creative historical interpretation.[34] It was a disintegration which Prior Wessington, despite his creditable intentions, had been unable to arrest; but it was a disintegration too which managed to avoid becoming completely and positively terminal. For at intermittent and confusing intervals throughout the long period from the late fourteenth century until the death of Bishop Cuthbert Tunstall in 1559, new biographies of the last medieval bishops and priors of Durham were grafted on to at least a few of the copies of the convent's standard history as originated by Symeon, the *Gesta episcoporum Dunelmensium*.

Admittedly the correct interpretation of the slightly random scraps of biographical information which bring the medieval Durham chronicle tradition to its close in the early sixteenth century is no easy matter. Several of the manuscripts of the *Gesta*, like that in the library of York Minster which Raine selected as his primary copy text, actually end with the death of Bishop Richard de Bury in 1345;[35] but in other manuscripts the gradual process of subsequent accretion can certainly be observed, if through a glass somewhat darkly. Most instructive of all in this regard are the later folios of Bodleian Library, MS Fairfax 6, from which were subsequently copied the identical Durham biographies in Bodleian, MS Laud Misc. 700. The late fourteenth-century compiler of MS Fairfax 6 adopted the standard Durham practice of dividing his composite account of the *Gesta episcoporum* up to the pontificate of Bishop Bury into 184 separate chapters; but by the middle of the sixteenth century

---

[33] MS Laud Misc. 748, fos. 63–66; *Scriptores tres*, pp.127–42.

[34] Denholm-Young, 'Birth of a Chronicle', 326–28; Offler, *Medieval Historians*, pp.16–17. The collapse of sustained continuity in historical writing at Durham during these years is particularly well reflected in the different hands at work within the relevant sections of Bodleian Library, MS Fairfax 6 (fos. 281–84).

[35] York Minster, MS XVI 1. 12, fos. 225v–27. As Professor Offler has shown (*Medieval Historians*, p.24, n. 40), the late fourteenth-century continuations to the *Gesta Episcoporum* are too confusingly diverse to be easily summarised – or explained.

his successors had succeeded in adding a further twenty-seven chapters to make a grand total of 211.[36] Although none of these chapters is of substantial length, at the very least they reveal some slight attempt to maintain a record of who the late medieval bishops of Durham and their priors actually were. In fact these 'chapters' of biographical notes are of highly uneven quality, at their most specific in the cases of Bishops Bury, Thomas Hatfield, John de Fordham and Walter Skirlaw before a more or less complete attenuation of information follows for most of the fifteenth century. Thus the one-sentence entry on Prior John Wessington himself records merely the dates of his election, his priorate and his burial, the last erroneously.[37] Only with Bishop Thomas Ruthall (1509–23) and Prior Thomas Castell (1494–1515) does there emerge a partial and final revival of what is nevertheless by now an acutely emaciated chronicle tradition.[38] As Prior Castell and his industrious monastic chancellor, Thomas Swalwell, exemplify to perfection, the last generations of Durham monks continued to be absorbed in the glories of their community's past; but that absorption no longer took the form of rewriting that past but rather of copying and recopying, with however pious an intent, historical material already in the convent's library.[39]

By one of the more curious but perhaps inevitable ironies of historical writing in the late medieval north, a not dissimilar fate befell the church of York at approximately the same period. Admittedly the metropolitan cathedral of York had never developed a sustained tradition of historical enquiry to rival that of Durham. Although the miscellaneous chronicles and associated works produced at York from the twelfth century onwards are not of course without their considerable interest, especially where the controversial issue of Canterbury's primacy over York was at stake, they failed to promote either authors of the calibre of those often encountered at

[36] MS Fairfax 6, fos. 290–96; MS Laud Misc. 700, fos. 146–55v. Cf. F. Madan, H.H.E. Craster and N. Denholm-Young, ed., *Summary Catalogue of Western Manuscripts in the Bodleian Library at Oxford*, ii (2) (Oxford, 1937), pp.773–75.

[37] MS Fairfax 6, fo. 292v; Laud Misc. 700, fo. 149v; *Scriptores Tres*, p.147. In this entry the prior is named as 'Washington', yet another indication that these mid fifteenth-century Durham biographies must often have been written decades after the death of the bishop or prior in question.

[38] MS Fairfax 6, fos. 293v–94; *Scriptores Tres*, pp.151–54. Appropriately enough, much the most valuable entry in the closing chapters of the Durham *Gesta* is the account of St. Cuthbert's last celebrated medieval miracle, the healing at his shrine in 1503 of Richard Poell, one of Henry VII's servants.

[39] Perhaps the most revealing example is the collection of Cuthbertine and other historical tracts (British Library, MS Horley 4843) transcribed in 1528 by William Tod, one of the last monks and first canons of the cathedral: A.B. Emden, *A Biographical Register of the University of Oxford, A.D. 1501–1540* (Oxford, 1974), p.570; B. Colgrave, ed., *Two Lives of Saint Cuthbert* (Cambridge, 1940), pp.28–29.

Durham or an analogous sense of spiritual and constitutional development over the centuries.[40] Of the two most plausible explanations for the comparatively undistinguished late medieval historiographical tradition at York Minister – that so indisputably venerable a metropolitan 'temple' needed no historical validation for its authority over its province; and that only a small minority of the senior cathedral clergy committed their loyalties to the Minster by residing there – neither seem completely adequate. Moreover, the scarcity of interesting historical writing at the Minster seems all the more surprising when contrasted with the diverse and impressive work produced elsewhere in late medieval Yorkshire: as John Taylor has shown, the celebrated fourteenth-century monastic chronicles produced at Bridlington, Guisborough, Jervaulx, Kirkstall, Meaux, Ripon, Tynemouth and St. Mary's York itself cumulatively far outweigh such historical work then being written south of the Trent.[41] Nor is it too hard to discover interesting examples (admittedly much more sporadic) of historical enquiry in fifteenth-century Yorkshire, for instance by Thomas Pickering, abbot of Whitby from 1462 to 1475, who was capable of investigating the genealogies of several armigerous families in a way not easy to parallel among the Benedictine monks of southern England.[42] Much more obviously, by the fifteenth century there was a large readership for historical work among both the senior clergy resident in the city of York and also those lay and clerical members of Yorkshire society who bought their books there. Whether or not (as seems likely) the city's craft of *escriveners de tixt* themselves copied works of history for some of their customers, record has now been found of no less than thirty-five to forty bequests of chronicles or histories in the late medieval probate registers of the diocese of York.[43] The majority of these bequests are sadly unspecific; but in the case of Sir John Morton's legacy of a copy of Higden's voluminous *Polychronicon* to

[40] See Taylor, *Historical Literature*, pp.25–26. With the major exception of Hugh the Chanter's so-called *History of the Church of York from 1066 to 1127*, ed. C. Johnson (London, 1961) revised, M. Brett, C.N.L. Brooke and M. Winterbottom (Oxford, 1990), nearly all the highly diverse later medieval historical literature associated with York Minster is to be found printed in J. Raine, ed., *Historians of the Church of York* [hereafter cited as *HCY*], Rolls Series, lxxi (1879–94), ii.

[41] Taylor, *Historical Writing in Yorkshire*, pp.16–32. Thanks to the same author's own recent analysis of the highly complex composition of the *Anonimalle Chronicle*, the Benedictine monks of St. Mary's, York, can also now be seen as the creators of northern England's most ambitious, if derivative, fourteenth-century national political chronicle (*Historical Literature*, pp.133–45).

[42] B.L. MS Harley 3648, fo. 5; D.N.B., Pickering; C.L. Kingsford, *English Historical Literature in the Fifteenth Century* (London, 1913), pp.279–91.

[43] J.A.H. Moran, *The Growth of English Schooling, 1340–1548: Learning, Literacy and Laicization in Pre-Reformation York Diocese* (Princeton, 1985), pp.12, 15–16, 202–3; cf. M. Sellers, ed., *York Memorandum Book*, Surtees Society, cxx, cxxv (1912, 1915), i, pp.56–57.

Robert Semer, rector of St. Michael's, York, in 1431, the same volume passed from Semer to Whitby Abbey twelve years later in 1443. There can be no better illustration of an increasing appetite for similar types of historical writing among late medieval Yorkshire knights, secular clergy and religious alike, of an 'affection' for traditional history which was to survive even the Reformation.[44]

Within such a county context, the failure of the city of York itself, despite its inhabitants' proud awareness that they lived in *une citee de graunde reputacion et tutdys nomee le secounde Citee du Roialme*, to develop a genre of urban history even remotely comparable with that of the London city chronicles of the later middle ages might be thought at least slightly surprising.[45] Faced with precisely this deficiency, in 1430 Roger de Burton, the most enterprising of York's late medieval common clerks, took the highly unusual step of copying into twenty-seven folios of the city's official 'memorandum book' a copy of a *Cronica de successionibus et gestis notabilibus archiepiscoporum Eboracensium* from St. Paulinus to the death of Archbishop John Thoresby in 1373. Not only does Burton's unexpected initiative prove that the history of a cathedral and its pastors could intrigue and interest a fifteenth-century city council: the *Cronica* he copied is in fact nothing more nor less than the standard history of the church of York for all late medieval readers wanting information on the topic.[46] The composite York *Cronica archiepiscoporum*, which might be interpreted as a much less substantial counterpart of the Durham *Gesta episcoporum*, is also in urgent need of more critical attention than it received at the hands of its last editor, in this case James Raine the younger. However, the latter was almost certainly correct to suggest that in its fullest, early sixteenth-century version the *Cronica archiepiscoporum* falls into three sections: the first of these was compiled in the early twelfth century; the second was written (almost certainly not, as Twysden and Raine supposed, by a Dominican friar called Thomas Stubbs) soon after the death of Archbishop Thoresby in 1373; while the third and final

    [44] York, Borthwick Institute of Historical Research, Probate Register 2, fo. 653v; J. Raine, ed., *Testamenta Eboracensia*, ii, Surtees Society, xxx (1855), p.14; D. Hay, *Annalists and Historians* (London, 1977), pp.118–19.

    [45] York City Archives [hereafter cited as YCA], York Freeman's Register (D. 1), fo. 348. The only major library catalogue to survive from late medieval York reflects no particular interest in the history of the church or city there: see M.R. James, 'The Catalogue of the Library of the Augustinian Friars at York', *Fasciculus Joanni Willis Clark dicatus* (London, 1909), p.77.

    [46] The clear if not elegant hand is probably Burton's own: YCA, A/Y, fos. 219v–46v; *York Memorandum Book*, ii, p.101.

section was completed at some time in the archiepiscopate of Thomas Wolsey (1514–30).[47] Of these three parts of the York *Cronica*, the first two are much the most sophisticated; and they alone, placed together in eighty-eight consecutive chapters, form the contents of most surviving manuscripts of what became a not unpopular work. Extant texts of this late fourteenth-century version of the *Cronica* suggest that it circulated quite widely outside York Minster in attractively written quarto editions, like the present Bodleian Library, MS Barlow 27, itself perhaps similar to the manuscript used as his copy text by Roger de Burton within the York city council chamber in 1430.[48]

However it is the much less popular third section of the *Cronica archiepiscoporum* which is of interest here in revealing that from the late fourteenth century onwards (and at York just as much as at Durham) there occurred a dramatic disintegration of the previous conventions of historical writing. In some ways this disintegration is even easier to observe at York Minster than at Durham Cathedral Priory because at the former no one of Prior Wessington's interests and stature as a historian ever emerged. As in the similar case of the analogous biographical notices of the prelates of Durham, those at York were composed at erratic and now unascertainable intervals in the period between the late fourteenth and early sixteenth century. Accordingly the *Cronica*'s brief descriptions of the deeds of the last thirteen medieval archbishops of York (from Alexander Neville in 1374 to Thomas Wolsey in 1514) vary considerably in interest and information. Like the Durham *Gesta episcoporum*, the biographies of these York archbishops are usually at pains to record, not always accurately, the precise dates of the pontificates in question. However, it is noticeable that at Durham it was the date of consecration but at York the date of enthronement in the cathedral which was thought most worthy of attention.[49] Thus in 1477 and 1481 Archbishops Lawrence Booth and Thomas Rotherham were commended for enthronement ceremonies in the Minster accompanied by *magna convivio in palatio suo* and *magno honore* respectively; by contrast, Archbishop Thomas Savage (1501–7) was implicitly rebuked for 'being the first of his line who omitted the feasts and solemnities customary on the installation of archbishops of York'.[50] A more important difference between these Durham and York biographies is that the former often include quite

---

[47] *HCY*, ii, pp.xx–xxvii, 312–445. Internal evidence strongly suggests that the first and second parts of the chronicle were written by, or at the instructions of, members of the senior cathedral clergy at York.

[48] Bodleian Library, Oxford, MS Barlow 27, fos. 1–62, of which *HCY*, ii, pp.422–45, provides a full and quite accurate transcription.

[49] *Scriptores Tres*, pp.144–51; MS Barlow 27, fos. 47v–58v.

[50] *Ibid.*, fos. 56v, 57v, 59v; *HCY*, ii, pp.438–39, 442.

detailed and invariably highly laudatory accounts (especially in the case of Thomas Castell) of the cathedral priors, while at York the deans and other dignitaries of the Minster tend to be mentioned only when they were in bitter dispute with their archbishop.[51] However, both at Durham and at York, the late medieval prelate of the see (very rarely present within his cathedral community of course) was praised above all for his building enterprises. Here again there are significant differences of emphasis between the two dioceses. Whereas a bishop of Durham was most likely to be eulogised for his contribution to building works within his cathedral precinct, a fifteenth-century archbishop of York normally attracted more attention for his lavish extensions to his favourite palaces at Bishopthorpe, Southwell, Scrooby and (above all) Cawood.[52] As the late medieval prelates of the north might well have wished, it was indeed as great builders that they were most vividly remembered by the last if limited historians of their sees.

On closer examination there remains another and more revealing difference between the *Gesta episcoporum* of Durham and the *Cronica archiepiscoporum* of York. Whereas the former is invariably complimentary about the achievements of the bishops of St. Cuthbert's see, the biographies of the last thirteen medieval archbishops of York are much more likely to oscillate between adulation and hostility. Not surprisingly, the extreme examples of these two very different attitudes were those provoked by the tempestuous regimes of Archbishop Alexander Neville (1374–88) on the one side and of Archbishop Richard Scrope (1398–1405) on the other. For the careers of both these politically embattled metropolitans, the biographical notices within the York *Cronica* are an important, sometimes original and often neglected source. It is naturally no surprise to learn from the latter that Neville, 'unmindful of the oath he swore to God and St. Peter on the day of his enthronement', made a deliberate onslaught on the liberties and praiseworthy customs of the church of York; and in view of the cult of the martyred Scrope at York Minster itself it is even less surprising that his death was portrayed as a sacrilegious crime against an 'athlete of Christ'.[53] Much less to be expected are two other and more specific revelations: that one of Alexander Neville's greatest offences was to despatch six of York cathedral's vicars choral to Beverley Minster for over two years in the 1380s, and that it was also four vicars choral who carried, *non absque timore*

[51] *Scriptores Tres*, pp.152–54; MS Barlow 27, fos. 48, 59v.

[52] *Scriptores Tres*, pp.145, 146, 155–56; MS Barlow 27, fos. 47v, 54, 55v, 58v.

[53] MS Barlow 27, fos. 47v–49; *HCY*, ii, pp.422–25; cf. R.B. Dobson, 'Beverley in Conflict: Archbishop Alexander Neville and the Minster Clergy, 1381–8', in C. Wilson, ed., *Medieval Art and Architecture in the East Riding of Yorkshire* (British Archaeological Association, 1989), pp.152–54.

et tremore, Scrope's decapitated corpse into the east end of the cathedral choir on the day after his execution.[54] In a quite different and happier context, neither Archbishop Thomas Arundel's consecration of a stone altar in the vicars' chapel within their Bedern nor Archbishop William Booth's appropriation of the church of Nether Wallop to their college was allowed to be forgotten.[55] But then the more closely one examines these miniature biographies of the late medieval archbishops of York, the more clear it becomes that it was the latter's benevolence towards the Minster's college of vicars choral which tends to be warmly appreciated and carefully recorded. If so, what are the possible implications for the vexed issues of the composition and authorship of the last section of the *Cronica archiepiscoporum*?

More than a century ago James Raine the younger hazarded the 'conjecture' that the author of this third and final section of the chronicle of the archbishops of York might have been William Melton, chancellor of the Minster from 1498 to 1528. It now needs no urging at all that there could be few more implausible candidates for such a role than this sophisticated Cambridge-educated disciple of Erasmus, tutor of John Fisher and reader of Thomas More's *Utopia*.[56] In the writing of brief conventional lives of English prelates, William Melton – like Erasmus and More – can have had little interest at all. Indeed it now seems necessary to direct attention towards an altogether different element within the cathedral clergy. Is it not most likely that by the early sixteenth century the duty of sustaining the decaying tradition of medieval historical writing in the mother church of the northern province had passed to the Minster's vicars choral – among the most obscure rather than the most distinguished servants of St. Peter at York? Perhaps not altogether coincidentally, a highly similar development seems to have occurred at another of the church of York's minsters, Ripon, where one of two surviving metrical chronicles of the see was begun by a vicar and chantry priest of the 1370s, John de Alhalowgate, and completed by a *simplex presbyter* of Ripon in the next century.[57] In all these cases, as at Durham, the compilers of the biographical sketches also often reveal their local origins by displaying a knowledge of the epitaphs then to be

---

[54] MS Barlow 27, fo. 53; *HCY*, ii, pp.428–33. Not surprisingly, the circumstances of Richard Scrope's execution made him the only fifteenth-century archbishop of York to stimulate a minor outburst of hagiographical and biographical literature: see *HCY*, ii, pp.xix-xx, 292–311; J.W. McKenna, 'Popular Canonization as Political Propaganda: the Cult of Archbishop Scrope', *Speculum*, xlv (1970), 608–23.

[55] MS Barlow 27, fos. 49v, 55v; *HCY*, ii, pp.425, 436.

[56] *HCY*, ii, p.xxv; *Testamenta Eboracensia*, v, Surtees Society, lxxix (1884), pp.258–59; Aylmer and Cant, *York Minster*, p.73; B. Bradshaw and E. Duffy, eds., *Humanism, Reform and the Reformation: The Career of Bishop John Fisher* (Cambridge, 1989), pp.25–26.

[57] *HCY*, ii, pp.xxviii–xxx, 464; Taylor, *Historical Writing in Yorkshire*, pp.23, 32.

read on the tombs and effigies of recently deceased pontiffs within their cathedral churches.[58] More significantly still, and in Yorkshire as well as at Durham, these miniature biographies of prelates seem not infrequently to be related to – and perhaps derive from – what a late medieval visitor to a major church would have been able to read for himself on boards or *tabulae* as he wandered through the nave, transepts and aisles.[59] Here too the writing of history at England's two great northern cathedrals seems to have come full circle. As the most distinguished and scholarly monks of Durham and canons of York in the late middle ages lost interest in producing historical work themselves, so what historical writing there was perhaps came to be increasingly addressed by the lesser cathedral clergy to the pilgrim and the tourist. If so, this melancholy story of medieval northern historcial writing in decline may not, after all, be without a cautionary moral to impart for the future of the English historical profession in the 1990s.

[58] E.g., MS Barlow 27, fos. 50–51, 56v; *HCY*, ii, pp.427–28, 437–38; *Scriptores Tres*, pp.133–34, 145, 148, 149–50, 154.

[59] For the view that the historical narratives fastened to the two surviving late medieval *tabulae* at York Minster were designed to instruct and edify pilgrims and visitors to the cathedral, see Aylmer and Cant, *York Minster*, p.108, n. 227; cf. a paraphrase of these narratives in J.S. Purvis, 'The Tables of the York Vicars Choral', *Yorkshire Archaeological Journal*, xli (1967), 741–48; and for their use by the cosmographer, John Foxton, at the close of the fourteenth century, see J.B. Friedman, 'John Sifferwas and the Mythological Illustrations in the *Liber cosmographiae* of John de Foxton', *Speculum*, lviii (1983), 391–418. The use of such 'tables' to provide historical information is very evident at Ripon (*HCY*, ii, pp.xxviii, 446) and Durham (see above note 31 and, for a life of Bishop Bury on a *tabula pensilis*, Denholm-Young, 'Birth of a Chronicle', 326). As the examples recently collected in Gransden, *Historical Writing*, ii, p.495, suggest, the role of *tabulae* as an important agency for the transmission of historical knowledge in the later middle ages deserves much more attention than it has ever received. I am grateful to both Dr. Gransden and to Dr. David Smith for their generous assistance during the writing of this chapter.

Chapter 15

Women in the Plumpton Correspondence: Fiction and Reality

Joan W. Kirby

When Simone de Beauvoir observed some years ago, in *Le deuxième sexe* (1949), that with the exception of Sappho, Christine de Pisan, Mary Wollstonecraft and Olympe de Gouges, the history of women had been written entirely by men,[1] she was apparently unaware of the work of Eileen Power, whose pioneering essay on the 'Position of Women', based principally on de Pisan, the Ménagier de Paris and the fifteenth-century letter collections, had been published in 1926.[2] Since then historians of both sexes have turned their attention to aspects of marriage, the family, the legal status of women and evidence as to the extent of their awareness of, and submission to the dominant sexual ideology that restrained them.[3]

In spite of its contradictions, medieval theory about women, as created by the church and the aristocracy, was overwhelmingly derogatory. To churchmen woman was the detestable 'daughter and heiress of Eve, burdened with the yoke of Original Sin, and . . . the gateway to Satan'.[4] To the fifteenth-century aristocracy living in a world of 'decaying feudalism' and 'dying knighthood', for whom war, if no longer seen as the sole justification for their existence, remained the most laudable occupation for those of noble blood, belief in woman's inborn inferiority was reinforced by her irrelevance, save for her role

---

[1] S. de Beauvoir, *Le Deuxième Sexe*, 2 vols. (Paris, 1949), i, p.170.

[2] E.E. Power, 'The Position of Women', in *The Legacy of the Middle Ages*, ed. G.C. Crump and E.F. Jacob (Oxford, 1926), pp.401–33.

[3] E.g., R.H. Helmholz, *Marriage Litigation in Medieval England* (Cambridge, 1972); C. Richmond, 'The Pastons Revisited: Marriage and the Family in Fifteenth-Century England', *Bulletin of the Institute of Historical Research*, lviii (1985), 25–36; S. Shahar, *The Fourth Estate: A History of Women in the Middle Ages* (London, 1983); E.E. Power, *Medieval Women* (Cambridge, 1975); *The Role of Women in the Middle Ages*, ed. R.T. Morewedge (New York, 1975); *Women in the Medieval World: Essays in Honor of John H. Mundy*, ed. J. Kirshner and S.F. Wemple (London, 1985); A.M. Lucas, *Women in the Middle Ages: Religion, Marriage and Letters* (London, 1982).

[4] Shahar, *op. cit.*, pp.23–24; I. Origo, *The World of San Bernadino* (London, 1963), p.53; E.E. Power, *The Legacy of the Middle Ages* (Oxford, 1926), p.401; *idem, Medieval Women* (Cambridge, 1975), p.9.

in the procreation of children.[5] It was also fostered by the immense popularity of Jean de Meun's *Romaunt de la Rose* and the *Lamentations* of Matheolus – misogynistic works whose authors were denigrators of women.[6]

Belief in the total inferiority of a woman's mind and judgement to those of her husband was held to justify wifely obedience and submission. Yet while convinced of the propriety of his wife's fictional role, what the fifteenth-century landowner really needed was not patient Grizelda, but rather a vigorous, loyal helpmate to defend the home, run the household and estates, and keep him supplied with money during his prolonged absences; one, furthermore, whose counsel was undimmed by lack of knowledge.

The reality of women's role in contemporary society is vividly demonstrated in the Paston Letters, where Margaret Paston, for example, emerges as loving wife, hard-headed manager, harsh parent and stout-hearted defender of the family's 'livelode'. The Plumpton Letters, though less numerous, vibrant or politically informative, are, on this subject at least, almost equally revealing. They compromise some 260 letters from over a hundred correspondents, including kings, peers, courtiers, gentry, lawyers, estate officials, ecclesiastics and kinsmen, written between 1416 and 1552. The originals, now lost, were transcribed in the early seventeenth century into a small folio paper volume for the use of Sir Edward Plumpton (1581–1654), for whom also, a coucher book was compiled containing transcripts of over a thousand items of family evidence commencing in the twelfth century. The two manuscripts provide an unique source for the history of this northern knightly family.[7]

First mentioned in 1166 as holders of a knight's fee of the Percy barony of Spofforth, the Plumpton estates lay solely in Yorkshire until, in 1393, Sir William Plumpton secured the wardship and marriage of a midlands heiress as bride for his son Robert (d. 1421). Alice Foljambe brought her husband lands in Nottinghamshire, Derbyshire and Staffordshire that raised the family temporarily to equality with the comparatively small

---

[5] D.M. Stenton, *The English Woman in History* (London, 1957), p.29; C. Allmand, *The Hundred Years War* (Cambridge, 1988), p.43.

[6] B. Gottlieb, 'The Problem of Feminism in the Fifteenth Century', in *Women in the Medieval World*, ed. Kirshner and Wemple (London 1985), p.342.

[7] The L[etter] B[ook] and C[oucher] B[ook] are in the L[eeds] C[ity] A[rchives] (Accession 1731). The author, who is working on a new edition of the Plumpton Correspondence, wishes to thank Mr. W.J. Connor and Mr. Brett Harrison for their help. References to the letters unless otherwise stated are to *[The] P[lumpton] C[orrespondence]*, ed. T. Stapleton, Camden Society, o.s., iv (1839). See also J. Taylor, 'The Plumpton Letters, 1416–1552', *Northern History*, x (1975), 72–87; K.R. Dockray, 'The Troubles of the Yorkshire Plumptons in the Wars of the Roses', *History Today*, xxvii (1977), 459–66.

number of knightly families with important interests in more than one county.[8]

Apart from the single letter addressed to Sir Robert by the citizens of York on the 24 May 1416, the Plumpton Letters were written mainly to Sir Robert's son Sir William (1404–80), and to the latter's son another Sir Robert (1453–1523), whose tenure as head of the family saw its fortunes reduced to ashes. Among the most vivid letters in the Plumpton collection are those written to Sir Robert Plumpton by his two wives, Agnes and Isabel, at a time when the family's fortunes were at their nadir. The verdicts in a prolonged dispute over the Plumpton inheritance having gone against him, Sir Robert's estates, including Plumpton itself, had been awarded to his adversaries, led by the notorious lawyer-administrator, Richard Empson, whose success in diverting the rents and dues of his tenants eventually reduced Sir Robert to financial straits that became ever more desperate as his determined efforts to have the verdicts reversed involved him in high legal costs.[9] Whilst her husband was in London wrestling with lawyers and labouring influential officials, Agnes remained in command at Plumpton, charged by Sir Robert to see above all else that 'the manor and the place of Plumpton be surely and stedfastly kept'.[10] Meanwhile, as he feasted with friends who had supported him at the trial, Sir Robert at first felt sanguine about the possibility of restoring his position. Five months later, however, so great was his need of funds that he reproached his wife for failing to send the money she had promised:

> Best beloved . . . Soe it is I mervaile greatly, that yee send mee not the money that yee promised mee to send with John Waukar within 8 days after you and I departed, for I am put to a great lacke for it . . . for my cost is very sore and chargeable at this tyme . . . Therefore, deare hart, I pray you to remember mee . . .[11]

Dame Agnes exerted herself loyally. Through her eight surviving letters, written between November 1502 and April 1504 (the year of her death), we see the family at bay, grappling with recalcitrant tenants and facing prosecution by the archbishop of York for distraint upon their cattle; powerless to prevent the felling and sale of timber, and stung by the disgrace of having one of their servants arrested. Worst of all was the diminishing supply of cash as one by one the sources dried up, and Dame Agnes was driven to declare that she knew not where to turn to raise one penny more.[12] Only once, in her anguish, does she admonish

---

[8] CB, 294, 313.
[9] J.W. Kirby, 'A Fifteenth-Century Gentry Family: The Plumptons of Plumpton and their Lawyers, 1461–1515', *Northern History*, xxv (1989), 106–19.
[10] *PC*, p.cx. Transcription in LCA, Acc. 1731, 9.
[11] *Ibid.*, p.cxiii.
[12] *Ibid.*, pp.167–74, 184–88.

her husband:

> Sir, I marvell greatly that ye let the matter rest so long, and labors no better for your
> selfe, and ye wold labor it deligently . . . Sir, I beseech you to remember your great
> cost and charges, and myne, and labor the matter that it myght have on end. . . .[13]

Soon after Agnes's death in 1504 Sir Robert married Isabel, daughter of
Ralph, Lord Neville, and the unfortunate girl was immediately thrust
into her predecessor's uncomfortable shoes. Dame Isabel's sole surviving
letter could hardly have been more discouraging. After reporting her
inability to raise money from the sale of timber, except, as she had
foretold, at a give-away price forced upon them by common knowledge
of their predicament, she begs him 'For God's sake take an end, for we
are brought to beggerstaffe, for ye have not to defend them withall'.[14]
  Clearly the wives of the military aristocracy required a far wider range
of accomplishments than those advocated in the courtesy books, for
example, as traditionally suited to noble girls. Since most daughters left
home at an early age, by whom can they have been taught these skills if
not by the châtelaines of the great households to which they were sent for
training and service? Christine de Pisan's vignette of the lady in charge
of a country estate – rising early and watching from her window to make
sure her labourers set off betimes for the fields, tramping the balks and
coppices to oversee their work, supervising the harvest, and alive to all
the tricks by which her servants and suppliers might seek to defraud her[15]
– was probably true to the experience of most gentry women, who if they
were required to defend their homes could, like Margaret Paston, Alice
Knyvett, and Joan Pelham, equal their husbands in courage, defiance
and resource.[16] Such heroism is usually construed in traditionally male
terms; but what of the recurring 'precarious adventure' of childbirth,
upon which Agnes Plumpton embarked at least thirteen times?[17] This too
called for heroism that gave the lie to the buzzing trumpet of opprobrium
that blared from pen and pulpit.
  Behind the heroics and the masculine tasks she might need to perform
was the 'uneventful, jog-trot of domesticity', in which domain the mistress

---

[13] *Ibid.*, p.186.
[14] *Ibid.*, pp.198–99.
[15] Christine de Pisan, *The Treasure of the City of Ladies*, transl. S. Lawson (London, 1985),
pp.130–33.
[16] *The Paston Letters*, ed. J. Gairdner, 6 vols. (London, 1904), i, p.82; C[alendar of] P[atent]
R[olls], 1461–67, p.67; J. Taylor *English Historical Literature in the Fifteenth Century* (Oxford,
1987), pp.232–33.
[17] M.B. Rose, 'Making Gender the Question', *Journal of British Studies*, xxv (1986), 338.

of a large household was assisted by a sizeable male bureaucracy.[18] Unfortunately the Plumpton Letters contain few references to household purchases. There are requests for material for clothing and an order for barrels of salt salmon to be sent from London, doubtless to be added to the stock of preserved fish maintained by most families, chiefly for use on days of abstinence and in Lent. Dame Isabel Plumpton was understandably dismayed that shortage of money made it impossible for her to lay in her Lenten stores in time to take advantage of lower prices, but despite their straitened circumstances she did not forget to remind her husband of her stepchildren's need of books.[19]

In spite of their loyal and energetic support, Agnes and Isabel Plumpton became impatient with what they regarded as Sir Robert's unrealistic and wasteful excursions into litigation. Clearly their relationship with him was one neither of inferiority nor superiority, but of the kind of rough-and-ready partnership which characterised the Pastons and, on contemporary testamentary evidence, many other husbands and wives.

In view of the importance of a successful marriage partnership it is surprising that consideration of the personal character of the proposed partners played so little part in matchmaking. Edward Plumpton, it is true, told his cousin and patron Sir Robert Plumpton that the widow he was courting was 'amyable and good', and Germain Pole, writing to promote a love match between his sister-in-law, Eleanor Plumpton, and his kinsman, Randal Mainwaring, assured Sir Robert that the latter was 'as godly and as wyse a gentleman, as any is within a m. myle, of his hed'. Nevertheless, both correspondents gave far more weight to the financial than to the personal advantages of the unions they proposed.[20] Edward Plumpton's lady had

> xx marc of good land . . . and a ryall manor buylded therupon to give or sell at her
> pleasure. She hath in coyne in old nobles, C – in ryalls, C – in debts, XL – in plate,
> CX, with other goods of great valour . . .[21]

Having no land himself the marriage would, he claimed, enable him to be more serviceable to his patron. The bait offered by Germain Pole, that Eleanor's suitor 'wilbe contented to take lesse with hir than any

---

[18] S.H. Mendelson, 'Stuart Women's Diaries and Occasional Memoires', in *Women in English Society, 1500–1800*, ed. M. Prior (London, 1985), pp.188, 190; Shahar, *op. cit.*, pp.151, 160; I. Pinchbeck and M. Hewitt, *Children in English Society*, i, *from Tudor Times to the Eighteenth Century* (London, 1969), pp.29, 31.

[19] *PC*, pp.10, 13, 31, 37, 198–99; H.S. Bennett, *The Pastons and Their England*, 2nd edn. (London, 1968), p.56.

[20] *PC*, pp.126, 192.

[21] *Ibid.*, p.123.

man in Ingland wold doe, being of his avyowre, because of the great love and favour that is betwyxt them', would, he knew, be a powerful inducement.

Through the marriages of his sons and six of his seven daughters, Sir Robert's father, Sir William Plumpton (1404–80), forged links with a small group of neighbouring families: Clifford, Middleton, Aldburgh, Hammerton, Darrel, Beckwith, Goldsburgh and Gascoigne, most of whom were drawn into the fateful settlements of 1464 on the marriages of his two young granddaughters.[22] Like Sir Thomas Brews, who wrote to Sir John Paston that he was loth to give one daughter a disproportionately large dowry at the expense of her sisters, Sir William provided his daughters with roughly similar portions, which, although paid by instalments, must have been a considerable drain on his resources, but family pride demanded that disparagement in marriage be avoided at all costs.[23]

Suitable marriages were usually formed through the willingness and ability of relations, particularly the head of the lineage, friends and employers, to act as intermediaries and provide finance and credit.[24] Sir Robert Plumpton having provided Edward Plumpton's deceased first wife with a rent out of Studley Roger for her jointure, it was essential that his approval be sought in the hope that he would do as much for her successor. Godfrey Green, Sir William's attorney and distant relation, wrote to his patron in some anxiety. A young tradesman who wished to marry his sister, Isabel, having found favour with the girl's employer, the latter and some of her friends were willing to advance money to enable him to go into business on his own account. 'Lyvelode he has none', wrote her brother, 'a Norfolk man and of birth no gent, as I can understand; what he is worth in goods I cannot wytt. Mercers deals nott all together with ther owne proper goods'. What with the fear on the one hand of incurring a great lady's displeasure and on the other of alienating the head of the family by acquiescing in a dishonourable match, brother and sister were at a loss. Sir William was urged to make his views known without delay. The girl's feelings towards her suitor were obviously

[22] CB, nos.374, 541, 570, 555, 579, 534, 535, 604. See also M.J. Bennett, 'A County Community: Social Cohesion Amongst the Cheshire Gentry, 1400–1425', *Northern History*, viii (1973), 30; A.J. Pollard, 'The Richmondshire Community of Gentry during the Wars of the Roses', in *Patronage, Pedigree and Power in Later Medieval England*, ed. C.D. Ross (London, 1979), pp.47–48, 51.

[23] *Paston Letters*, v, p.272; R.H. Houlbrooke, *The English Family, 1450–1700* (London, 1984), p.237; E.E. Power, *Medieval Women*, p.41; Stenton, *op. cit.*, p.95; Richmond, 'The Pastons Revisited', 29.

[24] M. Slater, 'The Weightiest Business: Marriage in an Upper Gentry Family in Seventeenth-Century England', *Past and Present*, (1976), 28–29; Houlbrooke, *op. cit.*, p.47; F.R.H. Du Boulay, *An Age of Ambition* (London, 1970), p.89.

considered irrelevent.[25] Sir Robert himself wrote to a Nottinghamshire squire suggesting that a gentlewoman of his acquaintance would make a suitable wife for his eldest son. The gentleman was delighted. This was the more so since Sir Robert had provided him with a second string to his bow, and he made no bones about his intention to accept the highest bid.[26] In the face of such opportunism it is well to remember that the jointure settled on the young couple by the bridegroom's family bore some relation to the size of the dowry. Furthermore, it was the mutual consent of the parties that constituted the marriage bond, though in practice, especially among the nobility and gentry, this was not always forthcoming.

Several generations of Plumpton heirs were the victims of infant marriages, which, although in general comparatively rare, were a means whereby a father might avoid the dangers of wardship: sale of the marriage and, possibly, a match inimical to the interests of the family.[27] It was not the desire to avoid feudal incidents, however, that prompted Sir William Plumpton to sell the marriages of his two granddaughters, Margaret, aged four, and her younger sister Elizabeth, the daughters of his deceased son William, but the desire thereby to acquire the substantial premiums they commanded as heirs at law of the Plumpton estates. (We have a glimpse of Margaret in her future father-in-law's household, speaking pretty French and learning her psalter.)[28] But Sir William was playing a dangerous and cruel game of deception with the lives of three women. By concealing his own marriage to his second wife, Joan Wintringham, which according to later evidence, had taken place at least ten years before 1463 (when the first of these two marriage contracts was signed), he condemned her to years of dishonour, and his two granddaughters to eventual disherison in favour of a son, the future Sir Robert, who may have been illegitimate.[29]

Meanwhile, the devious knight was trifling with the affections of a certain Mistress F.S. to the extent of raising her hopes of marriage. 'I conceive that there is displesure hanging', wrote Hugh Pakenham, '. . . that ye comfort not my said Mistress S. ne none of her frends in the matter ye know of, for the which I have bene often called upon sith Paske'. There is a hint that Sir William was not unaccustomed to extricating himself from similar entanglements, for the writer advises him

---

25 *PC*, p.11.

26 *Ibid.*, p.137.

27 M. Ingram, 'Spousals Litigation in the English Ecclesiastical Courts c. 1350 – c. 1640', in *Marriage and Society: Studies in the Social History of Marriage*, ed. R.B. Outhwaite (London, 1981), pp.38–39. CB, nos.294, 313.

28 *PC*, p.8.

29 CB, nos. 581–83.

to write to the lady 'excuseing the non accomplishment of her desire in such wis as yee can well enough, and soe put her out of despaire'.[30] The seductive power of money could also bring the disillusionment of a broken promise. For example, the 'young, little, well-favoured and witty' woman with an income of £40 a year whom Richard Cely first saw in Northleach church, and with whom he exchanged wine and a roast hen, and enjoyed 'ryught gode comynecacyon', was let down when, nine days after leaving Northleach, Richard was persuaded to espouse the daughter of a wealthy mercer who offered a dowry of 500 marks. His brother, George, broke off his matrimonial negotiation on hearing of the appearance on the marriage market of a young widow whose deceased husband, a rich stapler, had made her the sole heir to his estate.[31]

The corollary of the essentially practical and unromantic view of marriage was a fairly tolerant attitude towards illegitimacy – an attitude fostered by the church, whose violent opposition to abortion and infanticide overrode its view of the heinousness of the sins of the flesh.[32] It is not unlikely therefore that Sir William's two bastard sons, William and Robert (significantly, they were given the favoured family Christian names), were brought up within the family. He provided for them by granting to each a life estate in land, and Sir Robert continued to support them. Bastardy was much more of a problem where the mother was unmarried – servants living away from home were especially vulnerable. Canon law might insist on the duty of a father to provide for his offspring, and permit an unmarried mother to sue for support in the ecclesiastical courts, but to what extent the courts were able to enforce their judgements in these cases we do not know. Neither do we know what befell when a father did not acknowledge paternity.[33] One such poor girl was sent by her master to Sir Robert with a letter explaining that one of the Plumpton servants had fathered her child. In her desperation she would have run away, but that her master took pity on her and had since maintained the child at his own expense. He now appealed to Sir Robert to hear the girl's story and deal justly with her. A similar offence was treated by Margaret Paston with characteristic severity. Hearing the report of two ploughmen that they had seen one of her son Edmund's servants making love to a woman in the 'Kinyneclosse', she demanded his instant dismissal. Edmund, who valued the man's services and thought there was no great wrong

---

[30] *PC*, p.15.
[31] *The Cely Letters 1472–1485*, ed. A. Hanham, Early English Text Society (1975), nos. 165, 215.
[32] Pinchbeck and Hewitt, *op. cit.*, pp.201–02; Shahar, *op. cit.*, p.113.
[33] Shahar, *op. cit.*, pp.113–17.

in 'swhyne[ing] a quene', begged his brother, John, to give the man employment.[34]

Where there was discord in marriage the legal disabilities of the wife could indeed make her life a 'little hell'. One of Sir William's sisters, Dame Isabel Thorpe, was wretchedly lonely, having 'neither woman nor maide with her, but herselfe alone', and a husband who was always in trouble. Christine de Pisan's advice to such women was in all circumstances to do their wifely duty with gentleness, tact and good humour. After all, even a bad husband might so provide for his wife as to enable her to enjoy a comfortable widowhood.[35]

It is well to remember that the hen-pecked husband is an ancient figure of fun, and the scold a well-documented nuisance. As Eileen Power observed, a man might dream of patient Grizelda but find himself married to the Wife of Bath. Richard Ampleforth's foolish wife caused a serious rift between her husband and Thomas Saxton, one of the earl of Northumberland's men. The earl, tiring of their clamour, passed the matter to Sir Robert Plumpton, desiring him 'to exammen it, and therupon to shew your lovying diligence . . . to sett the sayd parties at agreement'. The woman finally admitted her responsibility and, through an intermediary, assured Sir Robert of her repentence.[36]

The relationship between husband and wife being all-important in the medieval aristocratic family, the mother's role was probably often that of a mediator between the children and their father. As Margaret Paston could sometimes be cajoled into secretly helping her sons, so it was to his mother that Sir Robert Plumpton's grandson and namesake wrote from the Inner Temple appealing for funds to keep him solvent until Easter. Mother and son appear to have been close, for in another letter he wrote to her as one 'which hath shewed to me so much kindeness, besides all motherly kindeness', urging her to study the gospels in the light of the new doctrine on the authority of Scripture, in which he deemed it his bounden duty to instruct her.[37] Robert may have been the first of the Plumpton heirs to study at an Inn of Court, but times were changing, and for those with landed interests to protect, some knowledge of the increasingly complex law of property was essential. Nevertheless, service in a great house was still regarded as the principal road to social advancement as well for noble girls as for boys; but because the best situations for the former

---

[34] *PC*, p.109; *Paston Letters*, iv, 231–32. On the legal disabilities of women, see F. Pollock and F.W. Maitland, *The History of English Law*, 2 vols., 2nd edn., (London, 1968), ii.
[35] *PC*, pp.xxxix–xl; LB, pp.178–79.
[36] *PC*, p.77.
[37] *Ibid.*, pp.231–34; D. Herlihy, *Medieval Households* (London, 1985), pp.120–21.

were comparatively few, there was fierce competition to place daughters in the coveted position of lady-in-waiting to a noble mistress. Indeed, the fortitude and resourcefulness of so many gentry women must have been learnt in the great households where they were brought up, which because of the preponderance of men in all departments, were almost always actively hostile to their presence.[38] Sir William Plumpton sought Brian Rocliffe's help in obtaining a place for his niece, Isabel Marley, in the household of Joan, Lady Ingoldesthorpe, where she was later reported to be 'right wele and greatly . . . bounden to my Lady'.[39] By contrast, Jane Stonor was unhappy in the post obtained for her by the queen (Elizabeth Wydeville), but was told she must subordinate her wishes to the interests of her family, who dared not risk giving offence by removing her without the queen's express approval.[40] Another daughter who pined for home, Dorothy Plumpton, wrote to Sir Robert from Templehurst where she was in service with her step-grandmother, Lady Darcy. Her discontent apparently arose from finding herself in a position she considered demeaning. On discovering the reason for the girl's dissatisfaction, however, her mistress proved sympathetic, and promised to find a situation more suited to her rank, either within her own household or elsewhere. Dorothy therefore besought her father to make his wishes known, and

> to send a servant of yours to my lady and to me, and shew now by your fatherly kyndnesse that I am your child; for I have sent you dyverse messuages and wryttings, and I never ansere againe. Wherfore, Yt is thought in this parties, by those persons that list better to say ill than good, that he have litle favor unto me; the which error ye may now quench, yf yt will like you to be so good and kynd father unto me.[41]

Neither Sir Robert nor his father baulked the duty of providing dowries for their many daughters. But what was the fate of gentlewomen who could not be married, whether for lack of dowries or because of some physical or mental handicap? Such women were at a disadvantage compared with the daughters of tradesmen or peasants, who could be usefully employed in the shop, at the spinning-wheel or in the fields. Katherine Chadderton's request to her brother, George Plumpton, to obtain for her 'any goodly young woman, that is a good woman of

[38] K. Mertes, *The English Noble Household* (London, 1985), pp.57–59; M. Girouard, *Life in an English Country House* (London, 1978), p.27. C.D. Ross, 'The Household Accounts of Elizabeth Berkeley, Countess of Warwick, 1420–21', *Transactions of the Bristol and Gloucester Archaeological Society*, lxx (1951), 80–105.

[39] *PC*, pp.10, 15.

[40] *The Stonor Letters and Papers*, 1290–1485, ed. C.L. Kingsford, 2 vols., Camden Society, 3rd ser., xxix-xxx (1919) i, 122–23.

[41] *PC*, pp.202–03.

her body and pay, iiij and xx or more (and I would have one of my owne ken an theare were any)' suggests one possibility. Thus Thomas Roos of Ingmanthorpe left ten marks to his niece, Janet Gower, 'for her good, kind and favourable service'.[42] For the medieval noblewoman the natural and obvious alternative to marriage was the veil. 'Religious houses paralleled aristocratic households in their communal life, their hospitality and their employment of servants . . . What more natural than that they should provide education for aristocratic children and a safe harbour for their unmarried daughters?'. For an outlay of £10 7s.10½d. that included her dowry (£3), the cost of her habit and bed (£3. 13s. 6½d.), expenditure on entertainment after the ceremony (£3 11s. 4d.), and the preacher's gratuity (2s.), young Elizabeth Sewardby could be settled for life as a nun;[43] whereas it cost Sir William Plumpton £123 6s. 8d. to marry his daughter Elizabeth to Thomas Beckwith, Esq., of Clint, and Sir William Gascoigne 1,000 marks to obtain the hand of Robert Constable for his daughter Dorothy.[44]

Amongst the matters discussed by Hugh Pakenham in his letter to Sir William Plumpton was the news that his daughter, Agnes, had been clothed in the habit of the order of St. Dominic at Dartford Abbey, one of the largest, richest, and most observant nunneries in the country. She must have been at least sixteen at the time of her profession, and may have been sent there as a young child to be educated. We know nothing of her subsequent history: had she a vocation for the quiet, disciplined, observant life, or did the years drift by in an endless procession of fretful, discouraged days?[45]

Convents were also convenient retirement homes for widows who felt the need to attend more closely to the welfare of their souls, once their sons had come of age and they had fulfilled their secular responsibilities. Thus Elizabeth Pole, having administered the estate of her grandson during his minority, and been much troubled over the affairs of her younger son, Thomas, confided to Sir Robert that she was weary of 'grett tuggs

---

[42] *Ibid.*, p.xxxix; LB, pp.175–79; *Test[amenta] Ebor[acensia]*, iv, Surtees Society, liii (1869), pp.223–26.

[43] E.E. Power, *Medieval English Nunneries* (Cambridge, 1922), pp.4, 6, 19–20, 25, 29, 99; N. Orme, *From Childhood to Chivalry: the Education of the English Kings and Aristocracy, 1066–1530* (London, 1984), pp.60, 65; Stenton, *op. cit.*, p.43; Shahar, *op. cit.*, pp.8, 39–41, 140; M.W. Labarge, *Women in Medieval Life* (London, 1986), p.74.

[44] CB, no.541; *The Parliamentary Representation of the County of York 1258–1832*, ed. A. Gooder, 2 vols., Yorkshire Archaeological Society Record Series (1935, 1938), i, pp.218–19.

[45] PC, p.15; Power, *Medieval English Nunneries*, pp.1, 2, 573; *Victoria History of the County of Kent*, ed. W. Page, ii (1926), pp.181, 187.

of husbandry' and proposed to retire to a dwelling within the precincts of the friary at Derby, where she would 'keep a narrow house' with but a few servants, and so end her days.[46] The arrangements made with her eldest son by Dame Alice Plumpton, widow of another Sir William who was executed for his part in the rising of 1405, were not unusual in the circumstances. Robert was to provide his mother, her three younger children and their nurse with a suitable 'table' free of charge for one year, together with a chamber, possibly in the manor house at Kinalton, and sufficient light and fuel. Should she wish to remain under his roof for a longer period she was to be provided with her 'table' at a charge of 12d. for herself, 8d. each for her elder daughter and one gentlewoman, and 6d. each for the two younger children and a chamberer.[47] Dame Alice's future plans were obviously uncertain, but Joan Wintringham, having no dependent offspring, published her intention never to remarry by receiving the veil as an avowess. On succeeding his father, Sir Robert showed his affection for his mother by immediately increasing her life estate, and she apparently continued to live at Plumpton Hall.[48]

Those well provided for in widowhood, like Joan, Lady Ingoldesthorpe, whose path crossed that of Sir William more than once, enjoyed greater freedom in law than any other type of woman in medieval society. Sister of John Tiptoft, the humanist earl of Worcester, and widow of Sir Edmund Ingoldesthorpe, a prominent Cambridgeshire knight with extensive lands in Norfolk and seven other counties, including Yorkshire, she co-founded a chantry and lending library in the church at Pott Shrigley, where she was portrayed in the east window. Among her feoffees were John Morton, archbishop of Canterbury, John Alcock, bishop of Ely, Sir Reginald Bray and John Vavasour, a justice of the court of Common Pleas. Her ultimate heir was her great-grandson, John Stonor.[49]

For those less fortunate, widowhood could be perilous. Whether rich or poor there were those, often members of the family, who sought to relieve

---

[46] *PC*, pp.162–63, 190, 101; Power, *Medieval English Nunneries*, p.39; Shahar, *op. cit.*, pp.44–45; Stenton, *op. cit.*, pp.40–41.

[47] CB, no.325.

[48] *Test. Ebor.*, iii, Surtees Society, xlv (1865), p.344. CB, nos. 701–03.

[49] J. Wedgwood and A. Holt, *History of Parliament: Biographies of Members of the House of Commons, 1453–1509* (London, 1936), p.493; *Calendar of Fine Rolls, 1452–61*, p.167; M.J. Bennett, 'Sources and Problems in the Study of Social Mobility: Cheshire in the Later Middle Ages', *Transactions of the Historic Society of Lancashire and Cheshire*, cxxvii (1978), 63; J.P. Earwaker, *East Cheshire Past and Present*, 2 vols. (1880), ii, pp.325–27; P.W. Fleming, 'Household Servants of the Yorkist and Early Tudor Gentry', in *Early Tudor England*, ed. D. Williams (Bury St. Edmunds, 1989), p.35 n.; *Inquisitions post mortem, Hen. VII*, i. 436, 1085–88.

a widow of her property; but whereas the wealthy could afford the best legal advice, those of more modest means could not, and were advised by Christine de Pisan, herself widowed whilst still a young woman, to settle their cases out of court and so avoid putting themselves at the mercy of others.[50] Hence Dame Joyce Percy, lady-in-waiting to the countess of Shrewsbury and widow of Sir Robert Percy of Scotton, importuned the earl of Shrewsbury for the recovery of her right to land in Arkendale which she alleged Sir Robert Plumpton had denied her. The earl having complained to the abbot of Lilleshall, as tenant-in-chief, the latter threatened to dismiss Sir Robert from the stewardship of the abbey's Yorkshire lands if he refused to comply. As the widow of one of the earl of Northumberland's retainers, Dame Isabel Ilderton was able to enlist that nobleman's influence. In a letter to Sir William Plumpton, Earl Henry directed him to order the return of Dame Isabel's expropriated cattle, 'for she hath no other mean to help herself with, unto that a determination be had betwixt Thomas Ilderton and her, of the livelyhed that standeth in travers betwixt them'. Another 'poore widdow . . . grieveously vexed in her sons' was Ellen Helme of Flasby, whose landlord intervened to enlist Sir William's good offices as arbitrator.[51]

Finally, in times of civil unrest and conflict the cost of loyalty could be high, for women as well as for men. Whilst many of the gentry were experienced trimmers, the fortunes of others, including the Plumptons, were decided by their unswerving loyalty to their lords and patrons, and so to the wider cause of Lancaster or York.[52] As the combatants rode towards Towton, or Barnet, or Tewkesbury, for example, did their women-folk glimpse the abyss into which their lives might suddenly collapse? Between 1350 and 1500, 20 per cent of English secular peers died violent deaths, and 25 per cent of them never reached their fortieth year.[53] One woman who 'tasted the bitter dregs of defeat' after the death of her husband on the field of Tewkesbury and the summary execution of her son immediately after the battle, was Lady Delves, whose agreement to certain land transfers was sought by Sir Robert Plumpton. Left to survive in a dangerous and unfriendly world, it is small wonder that Edward Plumpton was unable to persuade her

---

[50] Labarge, *Women in Medieval Life*, p.28; C.C. Willard, 'A Fifteenth-Century View of Women's Role in Medieval Society: Christine de Pizan's *Livre des Trois Vertus*', in *The Role of Women in the Middle Ages*, ed Morewedge, pp.103–4; Bennett, *Women in the Medieval English Countryside* (London, 1987), pp.30, 151, 155, 158, 160; Shahar, *op. cit.*, pp.12, 98.

[51] PC, pp.26, 27, 29, 65–66.

[52] J.T. Rosenthal, 'Other Victims: Peeresses as War Widows, 1450–1500', *History*, lxxii (1987), 213–30.

[53] J.T. Rosenthal 'Medieval Longevity: The Secular Peerage, 1350–1500', *Population Studies*, xxvii (1973), 287–93.

to make up her mind, and reported that she was 'variable in hyr promys'.[54]

Like the Pastons, the women we meet in the Plumpton Correspondence were as sensitive to the honour of the family as the men, and could defend it fiercely. As wives and mothers they were vitally important and were appreciated and trusted accordingly; girls received the best available training, were provided with substantial dowries and married in accordance with family policy; widows and others in need of assistance could invoke the power of good lordship either directly or through intermediaries. While it is no more possible to generalise about women in late medieval society than in any other period, it may be said that then – as before and afterwards – men wrote about precepts more often than they lived by them.[55]

---

[54] Wedgwood and Holt, *History of Parliament: 1453–1509*, pp.267–68; 'A Chronicle of Tewkesbury Abbey', ed. C.L. Kingsford, in *idem, English Historical Literature in the Fifteenth Century* (Oxford, 1913), p.377; *PC*, pp.90, 100, 102.
[55] J. Leyerle, 'Marriage in the Middle Ages', *Viator*, iv (1973), 415.

Chapter 16

'Medievalism' in Counter-Reformation Sicily

A.D. Wright

The *Monarchia Sicula* was the claim of the kings of Sicily to control of the island church. In essence this involved the crown's assertion of legatine authority over the church as a result of an original papal delegation. In practice such control was extended by other, additional means, claiming distinct origins, such as nomination to bishoprics and review of papal missives. The asserted rights of the *Monarchia* allowed the crown and its ministers to defend all other such mechanisms of control, on the grounds that the inherent legatine jurisdiction was sufficient to determine all contested questions involving the church in the island.

It was only in the eighteenth-century pontificate of Benedict XIII that the papacy finally and reluctantly accepted defeat in its resistance to the claims of the *Monarchia Sicula*.[1] These claims to a legatine authority over the Sicilian church asserted by royal government in the island were thus to survive, by an irony, to the age of Garibaldi. In the seventeenth century however the papacy still contested the claims of the Spanish monarchs, predecessors of the Piedmontese and Bourbon rulers of the island. The assertion that a bull of 1098 established the grant by Urban II to Count Roger I of legatine rights, unaffected by a subsequent concordat of 1192, was the basis of Habsburg claims to be heirs of the Norman and Hohenstaufen rulers of Sicily.[2] But these Habsburg claims involved a degree of antiquarianism, a conscious search indeed for archival proof of what the crown's servants privately admitted was an uncertain and obscure case.[3] The revival and extension of such claims were intended to counter the advance of papal jurisdictional assertion, in the gradually

---

[1] L. von Pastor, *The History of the Popes from the Close of the Middle Ages*, 40 vols. (London, 1891–1953), xxx (1940), p.13; cf. L. Fiorani, *Il Concilio Romano del 1725* (Rome, 1978).

[2] Pastor, *History*, xxix (1938), pp.186–87; xxxiv (1941), pp.135–46; G. Catalano, 'Le Ultime Vicende della legazia apostolica di Sicilia (1711–1871)', in *Studi sulla legazia apostolica di Sicilia* (Reggio Calabria, 1973), pp.[43] ff.; F. Scaduto, *Stato e Chiesa nelle due Sicilie*, 2 vols. (Palermo, 1969), i, p.147.

[3] Archivo General de Simancas, Spain [A.G.S.], Estado, Negociación de Roma, Legajo 1000, fo.28: 20 Mar. 1614; Sicilia, Leg.1147, fo.190: 22 Nov. 1577: similar uncertainty about the precise basis of Sicilian royal patronage rights too.

recovered confidence expressed at Rome during and after the Council of Trent. The timing of this renewed conflict was not coincidental.[4] Nor did the papacy of the Counter-Reformation regard the obstacle to ecclesiastical supervision presented by the claims of the *Monarchia Sicula* as an isolated and purely insular difficulty. Quite apart from the implications of the *Monarchia* for the other island of Malta, which in ecclesiastical terms was a part of the Sicilian world at this date, there was the danger involving the kingdom of Naples, with its long-running history of resistance to papal jurisdictional assertion.[5] The papacy, as in 1639 for example, feared the use of the Sicilian rights claimed under the *Monarchia* to support and extend the Habsburgs' existing regalism in the Neapolitan kingdom.[6] The Habsburgs had equally shown a determination to maintain substantial control over the church in Sardinia, based on other claims and arguments, from the time of the Council of Trent onward.[7] It was not surprising then that the literary battle over the *Monarchia*, culminating in the famous attack on its historicity by Baronius in his *Annales*, met a Spanish response which was in no way confined to Sicily itself.[8] The belated Spanish reaction involved the prohibition of the offending work not only in that island but in due course throughout the Iberian and Mediterranean kingdoms of the Habsburgs. The irony that the prohibition in Sicily should be published during the interim vice-regal government of an ecclesiastical president of the kingdom, Archbishop Doria of Palermo, confirmed the Roman view that the *Monarchia* represented an oppressive and unacceptable interference in the life of the Catholic church there.[9]

The post-Tridentine royal creation of a permanent judicial tribunal, that

[4] E. Cochrane, *Italy, 1530–1630* (London, 1988), p.45.

[5] Pastor, *History*, xxix, pp.187–88; cf. Cochrane, *Italy*, pp.43, 200; Fiorani, *Concilio Romano*.

[6] Pastor, *History*, xxix, p.195; cf.xxxii (1940), pp.422–23, 598; xxxiii (1941), p.98.

[7] Sardinia remained under the Council of Aragon when the other Italian possessions of Spain passed to the jurisdiction of the royal Council of Italy: H.G.Koenigsberger, *The Government of Sicily under Philip II of Spain* (London, 1951), p.25; G. Catalano, 'Controversie giurisdizionali tra Chiesa e Stato nell' età di Gregorio XIII e Filippo II', *Atti dell' Accademia di Scienze, Lettere e Arti di Palermo*, ser.iv, xv, 2 (1955), pp.5 ff.: at 34, 154, n.62.

[8] A.D. Wright, 'Federico Borromeo and Baronius', in *Baronio Storico e la Controriforma*, ed. R. De Maio *et al.* (Sora, 1982), pp.169–82; *idem*, 'The Venetian View of Church and State: Catholic Erastianism?', *Studi Secenteschi*, xix (1978), 101; *idem*, 'Relations between Church and State: Catholic Developments in Spanish-Ruled Italy of the Counter-Reformation', *History of European Ideas* ix, 4 (1988), 386, 389, 391–2; Catalano, *Studi sulla legazia*, p.55; J. Pérez Villanueva, 'Baronio y la Inquisición Española', in *Baronio Storico*, p.48, n.126.

[9] A.G.S., Estado, Sicilia, Legs.1163, fo.203; 1164, fos.22 f., 43, 47, 72, 125; 1165, fos.2, 31; 1166, fo.27; 1167, fo.57; 1170, fo.76; 1891, fos.26, 226; 1892, fo.13; cf. fo.298; cf. Leg.1887, fo.91: 1609–20; Consejo de Italia, Secretaría Provincial, Sicilia: Varios: Legs.1380; 1510: 1617–33; A. Borromeo, 'Il Cardinale Cesare Baronio e la Corona Spagnola', in *Baronio Storico*, p.160; Scaduto, *Stato e Chiesa*, i, 318, 335; cf.339; Catalano, *Studi sulla legazia*, p.65; Wright, 'Venetian View', 85; cf. Pastor, *History*, xxix, pp.186–7.

of the judge of the *Monarchia*, was indeed attacked, on occasion at least, by the Sicilian hierarchy itself. Bishops in the island were not necessarily Italian but might be Spaniards, as were the Inquisitors in the island, and despite their nomination by the crown, they sometimes objected to the obstruction of their own authority by this royal tribunal.[10] Yet, as Cardinal Doria and others pointed out, this court was not the only obstacle to the implementation of Tridentine reform which the conciliar decrees had made precisely the responsibility of diocesan bishops. The operation of the court certainly prevented appeals to Rome or the reception in the island of a papal nuncio.[11] The tribunal's proclaimed supremacy in all things spiritual and temporal in the island undoubtedly inhibited the authority of the metropolitan archbishops of Sicily, by entertaining appeals not only from their own provincial courts but also directly from inferior, diocesan courts.[12] The choice of a lowly cleric, or even a lay jurist, as judge of the *Monarchia*, to review the decisions or reverse the orders of archbishops and bishops, certainly undermined the Tridentine, reasserted concept of clerical dignity.[13] The operation of the *Monarchia* prevented the papacy sending Apostolic Visitors to inspect Sicilian dioceses or providing Apostolic Vicars for sees which were left

[10] Despite the supposed rights of Sicilians at each alternate vacancy in any one see. A.G.S., Estado, Negoc. de Roma, Leg.968; Sicilia, Leg.1161, fo.67: [1596]–1604; Secr. Prov., Sicilia: Varios: Leg.1319: 1604–6; Archivio Segreto Vaticano: Segreteria di Stato: Spagna [A.S.V. Spagna]: vol.xxx, fo.410 r, 15 May 1584; Pastor, *History*, xxix, pp. 186–87; Scaduto, *Stato e Chiesa*, i, pp.172–73, 221; ii, pp.41, 52; Catalano, 'Controversie', 101, 204–5, 207–8, 268–69; id., *Studi sulla legazia*, p.49 and n.1, p.52; cf. A.C. Jemolo, *Stato e Chiesa negli scrittori politici italiani del seicento e del settecento*, 2nd edn., ed. F.M. Broglio, (Naples, 1972), p.173, n.114; A. Borromeo, 'Contributo allo studio dell' inquisizione e dei suoi rapporti con il potere episcopale nell' Italia spagnola del cinquecento', estratto dall' *Annuario dell'Istituto Storico Italiano per l'età moderna e contemporanea* (Rome, 1979); P.B. Gams, *Series episcoporum* (Ratisbon, 1873), pp.943 ff.; T. Davies, *Famiglie feudali siciliane. Patrimoni redditi investimenti tra '500 e '600* (Caltanissetta-Rome, 1985), p.22; cf. R. Quazza, *Preponderanza spagnuola 1559–1700*, 2nd edn. (Milan, 1950), p.264; cf. F. Nicolini, *Scritti di archivistica e di ricerca storica* (Rome, 1971), p.261.

[11] A.G.S., Estado, Negoc. de Roma, Leg.939, fo.47; Sicilia: Legs.1155, fo.50; 1161, fo.271; 1162, fo.145; 1163, fo.52; cf. Legs.1890, fo.262; 1892, fos.13 f.: 1605, 1607, 1619; Secr. Prov., Sicilia: Varios: Legs.1466, 1510: 1581–1685; Scaduto, *Stato e Chiesa*, i, p.261; ii, pp.41–42, 98; Catalano, *Studi sulla legazia*, p.52; *idem.*, 'Controversie', pp.50 ff.; A.D. Wright, 'Catholic History, North and South', *Northern History*, xiv (1978), 142–44.

[12] A.G.S., Estado, Negoc. de Roma, Leg.968: [1596]; Sicilia, Leg.1892, fo.13: 3 Apr. 1619; Secr. Prov., Sicilia: Varios: Legs.1450, 1473: 1613–28.

[13] A.G.S., Estado, Negoc. de Roma, Leg.968: [1596]; Secr. Prov., Sicilia: Varios: Leg.1380: 28 Oct. 1617; Scaduto, *Stato e Chiesa*, i, pp.172–73; cf. Catalano, *Studi sulla legazia*, p.52.

vacant or ungoverned for abnormally extended periods.[14]

The authority of the crown over the Sicilian church was maintained in other, complementary ways too. The bishops nominated by the king could not, in practice, be forced to present themselves in Rome for examination as to their suitability according to Tridentine standards. Nor could they be forced to present themselves in person at Rome for the periodic reports on their dioceses which the post-Tridentine papacy tried to demand of European and even overseas bishops. The crown opposed such examination or the exaction of personal *ad limina* visits on the grounds that Sicilian sees were transmarine, and so not comparable to continental dioceses.[15] Urban VIII was aware that individuals could easily escape the control of episcopal authority in Sicily by securing letters of protection from the judge of the *Monarchia*. He and his predecessors were also well aware that many other individuals in the island equally escaped episcopal jurisdiction by virtue of being familiars of the Inquisition. For the Inquisition in the island was powerful, a part of the distinct Spanish Inquisition, not of the Roman Holy Office.[16] It was similarly the independent Index of Spain, not the Roman Index of prohibited literature, which had force in Sicily.[17] Moreover the post-Tridentine papacy was hampered in its negotiations with the crown over the condition of the church in Sicily by the constant Roman need for Sicilian grain, especially in years of particular shortage in the papal states or in Jubilee years.[18]

While such considerations affected papal representations over ecclesiastical rights and their obstruction throughout the possessions of Spain, the reliance on Sicilian grain, preferably supplied free or at least untaxed, obviously tempered papal interventions in the case of Sicily itself. This was not only true in years when extra numbers of pilgrims flocked to Rome, to marvel at the outward display of spiritual and temporal

[14] A.G.S., Estado, Negoc. de Roma, Legs.929, fos.16, 111 f.; 930; 939, fos.47, 49; 946; 972; 990; Sicilia, Legs.1147, fo.190; 1148, fos.13 f., 65; 1161, fos.105, 271: 1577, 1581, 1605; Secr. Prov., Sicilia: Varios: Leg.1510: 1577–1633, especially for 1585–7 and 1602–4; cf. Catalano, 'Controversie', 50 ff., 191 f. and n.16.

[15] A.G.S., Estado, Negoc. de Roma, Legs.929, fos.111 ff.; 930; 972: 1577, 1600; Secr. Prov., Sicilia: Varios: Leg.1510: [1633]; A.S.V. Spagna, xxx, 480 r ff., 512 r–v; xxxi, 220 r ff.; xxxii, 108 r–v: 5 Nov. 1584–13 Apr. 1586; Scaduto, *Stato e Chiesa*, i, p.241.

[16] A.G.S., Estado, Sicilia, Leg.1147, fo.184: 1577; Pastor, *History*, xxix, pp.186–87.

[17] A.G.S., Estado, Negoc. de Roma, Legs.947, 981: 1586, 1605; Sicilia, Leg.1164, fo.125: 1 Apr. 1611; Scaduto, *Stato e Chiesa*, i, p.335; cf.339.

[18] A.G.S., Estado, Negoc. de Roma, Legs.947; 968; 981; 1855; Sicilia, Legs.1149, fo.34; 1161, fos.273, 285; 1162, fo.128; 1885, fos. 12, 69, 186, 321; 1887, fo.251; Secr. Prov., Sicilia: Varios: Legs.1453, 1454; Napoles: Visitas y Diversos, Libro 96 passim: 1580–1631; A.S.V. Spagna, vols.xxx ff.: e.g. xxx, 446r ff., 484r ff.: 13 Aug., 26 Nov. 1584; J. Delumeau, *Vie économique et sociale de Rome dans la seconde moitié du XVIe siècle*, 2 vols. (Paris, 1957–9), ii, 634 ff.: cf. *Nunziature di Napoli*, ed. P. Villani et al., vols.1–3, (Rome, 1962, 1969, 1970), ii, nos. 458 ff.: 1587.

authority increasingly displayed by the Counter-Reformation papacy.[19] Roman resistance to exceptionally unsuitable nominations for Sicilian bishoprics nevertheless proved counter-productive for another reason. Royal refusal to make alternative nominations left sees vacant, and the resulting lack of pastoral oversight was an even worse result.[20] The crown in any case put forward its own claims to competence in visitation not only of Sicilian abbeys (many of which were indeed held *in commendam* by absentees – cardinals and curialists among them); but also of dioceses in the island.[21] Furthermore, all papal documents sent to the island were subject to the vice-regal *executoria*, and without this review and approval they were without force.[22] The royal chaplain at Palermo admittedly exercised a less ambitious jurisdiction than that of his equivalent at Naples. Even so this did not preclude ceremonial and jurisdictional rivalries, involving the chaplain, the archbishop of Palermo and the viceroy.[23]

The viceroys of Sicily relied on the clerical first estate in the island's parliament for leadership in the granting of supply to the crown.[24] The clergy never paid their grant until papal permission had been obtained. This indeed was one of Rome's very few means of breaching the otherwise almost absolute control of the Sicilian church by the crown,[25] and one of the papacy's few means of balancing Roman dependence on

---

[19] The Spanish Inquisition in Sicily was involved in the control of grain supplies too: A.W. Lovett, *Philip II and Mateo Vázquez de Leca: The Government of Spain (1572–1592)* (Geneva, 1977), p.23.

[20] A.G.S., Estado, Negoc. de Roma, Leg.929, fo.16; A.S.V. Spagna, xxxi, 112 r ff., 121 r–v, 134 r–v, 158 r–v, 183 r ff., 192 r ff., 220 r ff.; xxxii, 92 r–v, 94 r, 108 r–v, 178 r ff.; xxxiii, 8 1r ff.; xxxiv, 59 r ff.; 94 r ff.; xxxv, 362 r–v; 26 June 1584–3 Mar. 1590; cf. Scaduto, *Stato e Chiesa*, ii, 24 f.

[21] A.G.S., Estado, Sicilia, Legs.1148, fo.65; 1154, fos.112 ff.; 1162, fos.78 f.; 1164, fos.1–2; 1886, fo.215: 1578, 1584, 1609; Secr. Prov., Sicilia: Varios: Legs.1319, 1403: 1583; A.S.V. Spagna, xxxv, 93 r ff.: 1 Apr. 1589–2 Jan. 1610; cf. J. Lynch, *Spain under the Habsburgs*, 2 vols. (Oxford, 1965, 1969), i, 246; cf. G. Benzoni, *Venezia nell'età della controriforma* (Milan, 1973), p.67.

[22] This included the controversy over the revised post-Tridentine issue of the bull *In Coena Domini*, against infraction of ecclesiastical jurisdiction. A.G.S., Estado, Sicilia, Legs.1147, fos. 184, 190; 1148, fos.8, 13, 14, 57; 1170, fo.75: 1577–18; Secr. Prov., Sicilia: Varios: Legs.1380; 1450; 1510: 1573–1633 (and indeed 1679–82); Scaduto, *Stato e Chiesa*, i, pp.52, 273; cf. Catalano, 'Controversie', 34, 154 n.62, 216 ff., 226 ff.; Borromeo, 'Contributo', pp.249–58.

[23] A.G.S., Estado, Sicilia, Legs.1136, fos.286 f.; 1159, fo.46; 1166, fo.72; 1895, fo.106: 1571, 1600, 1613, 1623; Secr. Prov., Sicilia: Varios: Legs.1319; 1510: 6 Aug. 1633; Catalano, *Studi sulla legazia*, p.65.

[24] A.G.S., Estado, Sicilia, Legs.1148, fo.65; 1161, fo.42; 1164, fos.22 f.; 1165, fo.80; 1892, fo.13: 1578–1619; Catalano, *Studi sulla legazia*, p.52.

[25] A.G.S., Estado, Sicilia, Legs.1147, fos.103, 170; 1148, fo.65; 1160, fos.152, 218; 1161, fo.42: 1577–1604; cf. Scaduto, *Stato e Chiesa*, i, 285; cf. Sardinia too: Catalano, 'Controversie', 9 n.9.

Sicilian grain supplies.[26] Papal concern at the pastoral neglect evident in post-Tridentine Sicily was clear, while so much energy was spent in jurisdictional rivalries between competing manifestations of royal and allegedly legatine authority: not just as between bishops and the judge of the *Monarchia*, but also involving viceroys, inquisitors, commissioners of the *cruzada*, the occasional crown visitor, the *Gran Corte*, the military orders, the royal chaplain general.[27] Yet Roman solicitude extended even to the preservation of the distinctive Greek rite of the island's Basilian monasteries. Against proposals from Philip II that these houses should be reduced to Latin uniformity, a Roman commission of cardinals argued that the Basilian communities were an important sign of the true catholicity of the church, even if there had been no Greek-speaking laity remaining in Sicily; and indeed there were Greek-rite Albanians in the area of Palermo.[28] The spiritual impoverishment, by post-Tridentine standards, of much of the native population of Sicily however remained, whatever Rome's concerns. The defence of royal patronage rights and claims to legatine authority effectively excluded much of the new post-conciliar initiatives: the educational work of the Jesuits at Messina remained an exception, far from typical of Sicilian religious life under Spanish rule.

The parliament of Sicily, in its periodic debates on fiscal supply to the crown, dealt with appeals for financial relief from religious and charitable institutions.[29] Such requests were forwarded to the royal court for ultimate decision. The relatively early development of Jesuit education in Sicily, precisely at Messina, has perhaps obscured the more general participation of some new orders of the Counter-Reformation in Sicilian religious life after the Council of Trent.[30] But even such contributions to pastoral and charitable endeavour were effectively confined to Messina and to Palermo (together with adjacent Monreale). The state of religious instruction and lay practice in the greater part of the island remained evidently poor,

[26] A.G.S., Estado, Sicilia, Legs.1162, fo.145; 1885, fos.12, 69, 186, 321; 1887, fo.251: 1592–1627; Secr. Prov., Sicilia: Varios: Leg.1454; Scaduto, *Stato e Chiesa*, i, 261; ii, 42; cf. J.F. Guilmartin, *Gunpowder and Galleys* (London, 1974), pp.30f.

[27] A.G.S., Estado, Sicilia, Leg.1892, fo.13: 3 Apr. 1619; Secr. Prov., Sicilia: Varios: Leg.1450: 1628; cf. Scaduto, *Stato e Chiesa*, i, 316.

[28] A.G.S., Secr. Prov., Sicilia: Varios: Libros 776, fos.1 ff.; 779, fos.26v f.: 1627; A.S.V. Spagna, xxxiii, 85r ff., 103r ff.; xxxv, 362r-v: 17 Oct. 1586–15 Mar. 1598; cf. Scaduto, *Stato e Chiesa*, i, pp.400 f.; cf. Bessarion's fifteenth-century attempt to reorder the Basilian houses of Sicily and Southern Italy: D. Hay, *The Church in Italy in the Fifteenth Century* (Cambridge, 1977), p.59.

[29] A.G.S., Estado, Sicilia, Leg.1161, fos.42, 65, 67 f.; Koenigsberger, *The Government of Sicily*, pp.149 ff.; cf. *idem*, 'The Italian Parliaments from their Origins to the End of the 18th Century', *Journal of Italian History*, i, 1 (1978), 18–49.

[30] G.P. Brizzi, *La formazione della classe dirigente nel Sei-Settecento* (Bologna, 1976), pp.20 ff.; cf. M. Ruiz Jurado, *Origenes del noviciado en la compañía de Jesús* (Rome, 1980).

if the evidence from the Inquisition in Sicily is taken into account. It was not essentially for overt heresy, nor even for alleged Judaising[31] or enforced conversion to Islam among captured islanders,[32] that so many young and apparently able-bodied men were condemned at *autos* to the galleys. The blasphemy for which such lengthy sentences were passed was clearly part of the common language of port and countryside, little affected by any systematic catechism or by any confraternities for the suppression of blasphemy, such as were found elsewhere in post-Tridentine Italy.[33]

Thus parliamentary requests for the traditional crown grants to Sicilian religious establishments, made from the fruits of vacant sees, included in 1604 the Jesuits of Messina, but also the Carmelites, the Minims and the Ministers of the Sick there; as well as the *convertite* or house of reformed prostitutes. The Theatines of Palermo were also mentioned; and it was suggested that the canons of Messina cathedral deserved a large sum, in the light of a claim that the impoverished cathedral needed aid to make it more worthy of its archiepiscopal status.[34] The viceroy provided an assessment of these suggestions. The Jesuits were indeed deserving, as they were involved in educational provision. The Ministers of the Sick had an excellent reputation for charity, but seemed to be misapplying themselves to the erection of large churches: (similar misplaced pastoral ambitions were evident at Milan in fact). The Carmelites and the Theatines of Palermo deserved well, and the latter had already received help from the viceroy. The house of the *convertite* was a most worthy cause and in great need. The claim of the Messina canons however was sheer importunity.[35] Such judgements reflected of course the perpetual rivalry between Palermo and Messina,[36] as well as viceregal concern about the ever greater economic and financial distress of the island.[37]

In the interior of the island the real state of religious practice and

---

[31] A.G.S., Estado, Sicilia, Leg.1171, fos.130 f.; cf. fo.144: 30 Apr., 29 May 1609.

[32] *Ibid.*, Legs.1161, fos.169f.; 1162, fos.101 f.; 1163, fos. 172 f.: 13 Mar. 1605 – 3 Apr. 1609.

[33] *Ibid.*, Legs.1161, fos.169 f.; 1162, fos.101 f.: 1605–6.

[34] *Ibid.*, Leg.1161, fo.67. The Theatines were also involved in education and the award of degrees at Messina: ed. M. Campanelli, *I Teatini. L'inchiesta di Innocenzo X sui regolari in Italia*, ed. G. Galasso, i (Rome, 1987), pp.65 f. and n.320; Scaduto, *Stato e Chiesa*, ii, pp.7 ff., 12 ff., 14 ff., 18, 97, 150, 158.

[35] A.G.S., Estado, Sicilia, Legs.1161, fos.65, 68, 75; 1892, fo.185: 1604, 1620; cf. Leg.1158, fo.3: *convertite* of Palermo.

[36] *Ibid.*, Sicilia, Legs.1144, fos.155, 158, 173 ff., 192; 1171, fo.144: 1575, 1609; cf. Napoles, Leg.1881, fo.192; Secr. Prov., Sicilia; Varios: Legs.1403; 1473; 1510: 1604, 1608, 1632. Koenigsberger, *The Government of Sicily*, p.154.

[37] A.G.S., Estado, Sicilia, Legs. 1147, fos.103, 170; 1148, fo.65; 1160, fos.152, 218; 1161, fo.42; 1162, fo.145; 1165, fo.32; 1166, fos.3 f.; 1167, fo.40; 1887, fo.193; 1889, fos.153, 175; 1890, fos.269, 272; 1891, fos.26, 226 f.; 1892, fos.16, 82, 89 f., 165: 1577–1604, 1607, 1611–20; Scaduto, *Stato e Chiesa*, i, p.261; ii, p.42.

lay instruction had to depend on other forces. Some examples can
be found of post-Tridentine episcopal activity in such matters as
diocesan synods, foundation of seminaries, or attempted reform at
female convents.[38] Arguably in the hinterland the decrepit Benedictine
and Basilian houses, with their absentee abbots, commendators resident
in Spain or Rome, their loss of alienated revenues and their poor
discharge of such pastoral duties to the laity as they owed, were more
characteristic.[39] One absentee cardinal, reflecting on the conditions at
his commendatory abbey, suggested the replacement of the monastic
community by a secular priest, to act as the abbot's curate and administer
the sacraments, and even the community itself agreed that this would
be better.[40] The state of temporal administration could be just as bad,
despite the commendator's natural desire to maximise his income. At one
monastery so many prosecutions would have been necessary to recover
the abbey's debts that the legal costs would have been greater than the
returns; and crown consent for a token settlement with the debtors could
not be refused.[41]

The Spanish inquisitors in the island gave attention also to the
behaviour of foreign ships' crews, even after the Anglo-Spanish peace
of the early seventeenth century.[42] The plan of an English exile and
adventurer to revive the failing Sicilian economy by the readmission
of a Jewish mercantile community was resisted, to preserve the racial
and supposed religious purity of the island.[43] More generally however
the Spanish Inquisition, with its large number of armed familiars,

---

[38] A.G.S., Patronato Real, Leg.22, [22–32]; Estado, Negoc. de Roma, Legs.981; 991:
1605–31; Sicilia, Legs. 1150, fo.114; 1160, fo.93; 1164, fos.42 f.; 1886, fos.213 f., 271;
1887, fos.68, 75; 3478, fos.66, 68f., 71; Secr. Prov., Sicilia: Varios: Legs.1319; 1403; 1510:
1581–1620; A.S.V. Spagna, xxx, 410r, 446 r ff., 484r ff.; xxxi, 112r ff., 134r-v, 158r-v, 183r
ff., 192r ff.; xxxii, 178r ff.; xxxxiii, 81r ff.: 15 May 1584–11 Nov. 1586; Scaduto, *Stato e Chiesa*,
i, pp.211 ff., 366 f.; ii, pp.96, 98, 112 f., 125, 128 ff., 136 f.; Catalano, 'Controversie', 79;
ed. M. Campanelli, *I Teatini*, pp.66: seminary at Messina; D. Balboni, 'Il Baronio e la
riforma liturgica post-tridentina', in *A Cesare Baronio, Scritti Vari*, ed. F. Caraffa (Sora,
1963), pp.315–22: p.319; P. de Ribadeneyra, S.J., *Vida de los Padres Ignacio de Loyola, Diego
Laínez* [etc.], [*Historias de la Contrarreforma*, ed. E. Rey] (Madrid, 1945), pp.liii, 441 f., 471.
[39] A.G.S., Secr. Prov., Sicilia: Varios: Libro 776, fos.1 ff.; A.S.V. Spagna, xxxi, 19 r ff.;
xxxiii, 85r ff., 103r ff.; xxxv, 362r-v: 29 Jan. 1584 – 15 Mar. 1598.
[40] A.G.S., Secr. Prov., Sicilia: Varios: Leg.1403: 25 Nov., 16 Dec. 1583.
[41] A.G.S., Secr. Prov., Sicilia: Varios: Leg.1403: 30 Jan. 1581; cf. Scaduto, *Stato e Chiesa*,
ii, pp.34 f., 40 f., 55.
[42] A.G.S., Estado, Sicilia, Legs.1155, fo.105; 1161, fos.170, 142, 216; 1885, fos.268, 273:
4 Dec. 1586 – 18 June 1605.
[43] *Ibid.*, Leg.1171, fos.130 f., 144: 30 Apr., 29 May 1609. For Shirley (or Sherley), Sir
Anthony: *Dictionary of National Biography*, 63 vols. (London, 1885–1900), vol.lii, ed. S. Lee
(1897), pp.121–24; cf. C. Roth, *The Jews of Malta* (London, 1931), pp.187, 207.

contributed to violence and disorder within the island, involving in the process lengthy and dramatic confrontations with competing represent-ations of royal authority, specifically the viceroys and the judicial *Gran Corte*.[44] The commissioners of the *cruzada*, the indulgence still issued effectively for cash payment after the Council of Trent in Spain itself and increasingly in Spain's other dominions, also deployed armed familiars; indeed the personnel of the commissioners and the Inquisition in Sicily sometimes overlapped.[45] The royal chaplain general might use the prelatical status associated with the office as a basis for grandiose schemes to establish a quasi-episcopal jurisdiction, centred on one of the island's abbeys.[46] But at the cathedral of Monreale, with its two chapters, monastic and secular, the archbishops who held the richly endowed see had few pastoral duties. With the occasional exception, such prelates were frequently absentees, the beneficiaries of Spanish patronage extended to curialists or clerical members of princely families for essentially political reasons.[47]

These inhibitions on the Sicilian episcopate in any pursuit of the reform of clergy, regulars and lay religious practice, which the Tridentine decrees had made specifically the responsibility of diocesan bishops, were paralleled in a minor degree in Malta too. The agreement, in the post-conciliar decades, that the Spanish crown should choose a bishop for that island from a short-list prepared by the Grand Master of the Knights did not necessarily produce a nomination acceptable to the papacy.[48] The unfortunate prelate, in any case, might easily find himself

[44] A.G.S., Estado, Sicilia, Legs.1147, fos.81, 109, 170, 184; 1148, fos.7, 55, 58; 1149, fo.1; 1154, fos.112 f.; 1155, fo.105; 1160, fos.96, 230; 1161, fos.67, 80, 216; 1162, fo.128; 1885, fo.200; 1891, fo.35; Secr. Prov., Sicilia: Varios: Leg.1380: 1577–1618; Koenigsberger, *The Government of Sicily*, pp.85 f., 161 ff., 166 ff., 169 f.; Scaduto, *Stato e Chiesa*, i, pp.264 ff., 312, 314 ff., 317–18, 320; Borromeo, 'Contributo', 256–57; cf. C.F. Black, *Italian Confraternities in the Sixteenth Century* (Cambridge, 1989), p.76. The state of law and order in Sicily was perhaps never very healthy.

[45] A.G.S., Estado, Sicilia, Legs.1165, fo.32; 1166, fos.3 f.; 1167, fo.40; 1885, fo.25; 1887, fo.193; 1889, fos.153, 175; 1890, fos. 269, 272; 1891, fos.26, 226 f.; 1892, fos.16, 82, 89 f., 165: 1611–20; Secr. Prov., Sicilia: Varios: Legs. 1380; 1450: 1593–1680.

[46] A.G.S., Secr. Prov., Sicilia: Varios: Legs. 1319; 1510: 6 Aug. 1633; cf. Catalano, *Studi sulla legazia*, p.52.

[47] A.G.S., Estado, Negociación de Roma, Legs.981; 991; 995: 1605–31; Sicilia, Legs. 1161, fo.104; 1164, fos.1, 42 f.; 1886, fos.213 ff., 217, 271; 1887, fos.68, 75; 1891, fo.1; 3478, fos.66, 68 f., 71: 1604–11, 1618; Secr. Prov., Sicilia: Varios: Leg.1403: 15 Feb. 1611–16 Oct. 1631; A.S.V. Spagna, xxx, 410 r, 446 r ff., 484 r ff.; xxxi, 112r ff., 134r-v, 158r-v, 183r ff., 192r ff.; xxxii, 178r ff.; xxxiii, 81r ff.: 15 May 1584– 11 Nov. 1586; Scaduto, *Stato e Chiesa*, ii, pp.34 f., 97; Gams, *Series*, p.951; Balboni, 'Il Baronio', p.319; Ribadeneyra, *Vida*, pp.liii, 441 f., 471: Cardinal Farnese had employed Jesuits at Monreale even before the reforming activity of Cardinal de Torres.

[48] A.G.S., Estado, Sicilia, Leg.1148, fo.65: 21 May 1578; A.S.V. Spagna, xxxii, 154 r-v: 31 May 1586; Catalano, 'Controversie', 58 ff.

subsequently reprimanded at Rome, for practical submission to the Sicilian *Monarchia*.[49] The inclusion of Malta in a Sicilian archiepiscopal province meant that the viceroy in Sicily was insistent on the jurisdiction of the *Monarchia* over the church in Malta, just as in other off-shore islands, such as the bishopric of Lipari.[50] At this date the possibilities for Roman intervention in Maltese affairs were clearer in relation to the Knights of Malta, not least when these were in dispute with a Grand Master.[51] A papal envoy, such as Gaspare Visconti, subsequently successor to Charles Borromeo at Milan, might assert Roman authority, despite the need to assure the viceroy in Sicily of goodwill towards the interests of the Spanish crown in the religious affairs of Malta.[52] The *Monarchia Sicula* within the Italian possessions of Spain came closest to the conditions created by the royal *patronato* in the Spanish overseas empire.[53]

The Spanish Inquisition was also operative in Sardinia, even though in that island the Inquisitors also had their disputes with the viceroys. Nevertheless the crown via the latter effectively controlled the bishops, and so the life of the church.[54] The poverty of insular sees presented the bishops with great difficulties in any attempts to improve religious practice, for example by the erection of seminaries.[55] Non-residence, even after the Council of Trent, was thus a feature not unknown among Sardinian

---

[49] A.G.S., Estado, Negoc. de Roma, Leg.981: Feb., Apr. 1605.

[50] *Ibid.*, Negoc. de Roma, Leg.981; Sicilia, Leg.1895, fo.87; Secr. Prov., Sicilia: Varios: Legs.1473; 1510: 1605–32; cf. Catalano, 'Le Ultime Vicende', pp.[43] ff.

[51] A.G.S., Estado, Sicilia, Leg.1151, fo.28.

[52] *Ibid.*, Legs.1150, fo.142; 1151, fos.28, 222: 1581; Pastor, *History*, xix (1930), p.116; cf. *Nunziature di Napoli*, ii, no.198: 18 July 1581; F. Ughelli, *Italia Sacra*, 10 vols. in 7 (Venice, 1717–22), iv, col. 276 D; P.P. Bosca, *Decadis Quartae Historiarum Mediol. Sive de Pontificatu Gasparis Vicecomitis Libri Duo* (Milan, 1682), pp.13–23; cf. p.49. Malta originally lacked a permanent papal representative: P. Brezzi, *La diplomazia pontificia* (Milan 1942), p.15 n.6. But by 1645 the (Italian) Inquisitor in Malta was acting as nuncio there: Pastor, *History*, xxx (1940), p.355; and already in 1635 Urban VIII appointed Chigi (bishop of Nardò and future Pope Alexander VII) Inquisitor and Apostolic Visitor in Malta, where he settled a disputed election of the Grand Master: Pastor, *History*, xxxi (1940), pp.14–15; cf. also xxxii, p.572; cf. A.P. Vella, *An Elizabethan-Ottoman Conspiracy* (Valetta, 1972), pp.29–31, 71, 143, 159.

[53] A.D. Wright, 'The Institutional Relations of Church and State in the Overseas Iberian Territories', *Hispania Sacra*, xl (1988) [1989], 693–99; cf. A. Garrido Aranda, *Organización de la Iglesia en el Reino de Granada y su proyección en Indias. Siglo XVI* (Seville, 1979); C. Hermann, *L'Eglise d'Espagne sous le patronage royal (1476–1834)* (Madrid, 1988).

[54] D. Scano, *Codice diplomatico delle relazioni fra la S. Sede e la Sardegna*, ii, *Da Gregorio XII a Clemente XIII* (Cagliari, 1941), pp.xi f.; Borromeo, 'Contributo', pp.258–74; cf. A.G.S., Estado, Negoc. de Roma, Legs.947; 981: 1586, 1605.

[55] Scano, *Codice*, p.425. But for what could be achieved: R. Turtas, *La Casa dell'Università: La politica edilizia della Compagnia di Gesù nei decenni di formazione dell'Ateneo sassarese (1562–1632)* (Sassari, 1986); idem, *La nascita dell'università in Sardegna: La politica culturale dei sovrani spagnoli nella formazione degli Atenei di Sassari e di Cagliari (1543–1632)* (Sassari, 1988).

bishops, just as with the bishops of impoverished sees in the Kingdom of Naples.[56] Papal authority over the Sardinian church was limited in practice by the vice-regal operation of the *exequatur*, designed to allow review of all Roman documents reaching the island, not just benefice provisions as in the case of the Milanese *placet*.[57] The papacy persisted, into the seventeenth century, to argue against the automatic assumption of rights of presentation to Sardinian sees by the successors of Charles V to the Spanish crown.[58] But this had little practical result in affecting the choice of suitable bishops, any more than did objection to the *spogli* of deceased bishops being contested and confiscated, as in Spain itself.[59] Bishops in Sardinia thus naturally looked to the Spanish crown for such protection of their activities as they could hope for.[60] A bishop who was thought to be courting Roman favour by emulation of Charles Borromeo was explicitly noted as attempting at the Spanish court the unacceptable.[61]

The Neapolitan kingdom by contrast, for all the traditional legal assertions of local independence in this papal fief, potentially allowed more freedom to bishops intent on implementing Tridentine reforms.[62] A nuncio resided at the vice-regal court to reinforce the efforts of the nuncio in Spain in support of the Neapolitan episcopate, even though the exercise of his faculties in the kingdom was long contested, and he might have his own disputes with the papal collector.[63] Financial disputes, over the *spogli*

---

[56] Scano, *Codice*, pp.lxxiv f.; A.G.S., Estado, Negoc. de Roma, Leg.986; Sicilia, Leg.1893, fo.159: 1607,1621; Gams, *Series*, pp.839–40; cf. Borromeo, 'Contributo', p.267; *Nunziature di Napoli*, i, nos.160, 162, 164 f., 168, 172, 364, 367, 372; ii, nos.329 ff.: 1573–85.

[57] Catalano, 'Controversie', 34, 154, n.62.

[58] A.G.S., Estado, Negoc. de Roma, Legs.929, fos.111 ff.; 930; 990; 1000, fo.8: 1577, 1609, 1614; cf. Sicilia, Leg.1147, fo.190: 1577; Catalano, 'Controversie', 101, 204 f., 207 f., 268 f.: Sicily too.

[59] Catalano, 'Controversie', p.57; cf. p.193, n.19.

[60] A.G.S., Estado, Negoc. de Roma, Leg.1000, fos.10, 49: 28 Jan., 20 May 1614.

[61] *Ibid.*, Leg.937, fos.24 f.: 14 Nov. 1580; cf. Borromeo, 'Contributo', pp.262, 275–6; cf. R. Turtas, 'Pastorale vescovile e suo strumento linguistico: i vescovi sardi e la parlata locale durante le dominazioni spagnola e sabauda', *Rivista di storia della Chiesa in Italia*, xlii, 1 (1988), 1–23.

[62] A.G.S., Estado, Negoc. de Roma, Legs.968, 971; Napoles, Legs.1092, fos.87, 101, 122; 1096, fo.91: 1590–99; *Nunziature di Napoli*, i, nos.210, 212, 213, 249, 312, 406; ii, nos.58, 94, 95, 97, 102, 107, 112–14, 133; iii, nos.205, 208 ff.: 1573–90; V.I. Comparato, *Uffici e Società a Napoli (1600–1647). Aspetti dell' magistrato nell' età moderna* (Florence, 1974); P. Caiazza, 'Nunziatura di Napoli e problemi religiosi nel Viceregno post-tridentino', *Rivista di storia della Chiesa in Italia*, xlii, 1 (1988), 24–69.

[63] A.G.S., Estado, Negoc. de Roma, Legs.929, fo.15; 930; 968; Napoles, Leg.1097, fo.34; Secr. Prov., Napoles, Visitas y Diversos, Libro 95; A.S.V. Spagna, xxxiii, 7r ff., 35r ff., 81 r ff., 85r ff.; cf.xxxiv, 352r ff.: 7 Oct. 1586 – 15 Oct. 1596; *Nunziature di Napoli*, i, nos.2, 45, 82, 142 f., 150, 152, 205, 207; ii, p.xv f., nos.3 ff., 13, 14, 18, 21, 24 f., 34 and *passim*; iii, pp.[ix] ff.: 1570–7; Comparato, *Uffici*, pp.44 ff.; Scaduto, *Stato e Chiesa*, i, pp.269, 341 f.

of both deceased bishops and clerics, over the *fabbrica di S. Pietro*, or over *decime* specially ordered by the papacy to be collected from the clergy of the kingdom, were not lacking.[64] Private admissions, in royal circles, that local royal officials on occasion oppressed bishops or failed to protect them, did not prevent unwavering insistence, even when cardinals acted at times as viceroy, on royal control of all relations between the Neapolitan church and Rome.[65] The issue of the *exequatur* for all Roman documents addressed to the kingdom was one of the greatest questions in the repeated attempts to secure a comprehensive jurisdictional agreement for the whole of the Spanish possessions.[66] The royal chaplain general at Naples, naturally a subject of the crown, advised the vice-regal authorities on the issue of each *exequatur*, despite Roman attempts to resist the chaplain's pretensions.[67]

The chaplain general moreover extended his claims of jurisdiction, via other royal chaplains, beyond the city of Naples or the royal galley fleet, to the other dioceses of the kingdom.[68] Papal support, with the help of the nuncio, for diocesan bishops nevertheless secured some relative success in establishing episcopal control over allegedly exempt institutions, such as the church of Altamura or the basilica of

[64] A.G.S., Estado, Negoc. de Roma, Legs.922, fos.19, 20, 25, 28; 930; 946: 1572–85; Napoles, Leg.1098, fo.25; Secr. Prov., Napoles, Visitas y Diversos, Libro 108, fos.244v ff.; cf. Sicilia: Varios: Leg.1381: 1602; A.S.V. Spagna, xxxii, 270r ff., 297r ff.; xliii, 378r ff., 397r-v: 1586–94; *Nunziature di Napoli, passim*, esp.i, nos.3, 5, 9, 18, 19, 21 ff., 134 f.; ii, nos.3, 4, 7, 8, 11, 13, 14, 18, 21, 24 f.; iii, p.x, nos.44–6, 49, 120, 248: 1570–91; Scaduto, *Stato e Chiesa*, ii, pp.19, 21, 29 ff., 64, 71; Catalano, 'Controversie', 55 f., 58 ff.

[65] A.G.S., Estado, Negoc. de Roma, Legs.922, fos.19–20; 968: 1596–1604; Napoles, Legs.1063, fo.133; 1093, fo.102; 1884, fos.69, 85, 123, 294; Secr. Prov., Napoles, Visitas y Diversos, Libros 98, 107; cf. Estado, Sicilia, Legs.1161, fo.67; 1164, fos.72, 125; Secr. Prov., Sicilia: Varios: Leg.1473: 1592–1604; A.S.V. Spagna, xxxii, 297 r ff.: 22 Aug. 1586; *Nunziature di Napoli*, i, nos.11 f., 86, 142–4, 150, 152, 175, 178, 181, 184 ff., 203, 360, App.I–II; ii, no.1: 1570–77; C. Russo, *I monasteri femminili di clausura a Napoli nel secolo XVII* (Naples, 1970), p.86; cf. G. Cozzi, *Il Doge Nicolò Contarini. Ricerche sul patriziato veneziano agli inizi del seicento* (Venice-Rome, 1958), p.294.

[66] A.G.S., Estado, Negoc. de Roma, Legs.929, fo.16; 937, fos.26 f.; 968; 978, fo.83; Napoles, Legs.1094, fos.262 f.; 1095, fos.144 f.; 1097, fos.24, 33 f.; 1098, fo.25: 1564–1622; cf. Milan, Leg.1301, fos.466r ff.: 1611; Secr. Prov., Napoles, Visitas y Diversos, Libros 94, 96: 1602; cf. Sicilia: Varios: Leg.1381: 1620–61; A.S.V. Spagna, xxxiii, 424r ff.; xxxiv, 32r-v, 210r ff.; xliii, 378r ff., 397r-v: 1587–94; *Nunziature di Napoli*, ii, nos.7 ff., 14–8, 21, 23–5, 33–4 and *passim*; iii, nos.40, 123: 1577–89; Russo, *I monasteri*, pp.15, 41, 85 f.; Comparato, *Uffici*, pp.190 f. and n.77; cf. Scaduto, *Stato e Chiesa*, i, p.341 f.

[67] A.G.S., Estado, Negoc. de Roma, Leg.937, fos.26 f.; Napoles, Leg.1097, fo.35; Secr. Prov., Napoles, Visitas y Diversos, Libros 94, 98, 100, 104, 105: pre-1565 to 1625; *Nunziature di Napoli*, ii, nos.361, 368, 371, 429 ff.; Russo, *I monasteri*, pp.13, 81 ff., 143 ff.: 1585–1673; Scaduto, *Stato e Chiesa*, i, pp.185 f., 201, 340, 347 ff.

[68] A.G.S., Estado, Napoles, Leg.1097, fo.35; Secr. Prov., Napoles, Visitas y Diversos, Libros 93, 98, 104: pre-1565 to 1625.

St. Nicholas at Bari.[69] In such disputes the presence of Greek-rite priests in parts of the kingdom could be a further complication.[70] But only some of the bishops in the kingdom, in any case, were presented by the Spanish crown. Other diocesans, as at Naples itself, were papal appointments, despite continued disputes with Spain over this.[71] The papacy might thus on occasion succeed in appointing to a Neapolitan see as vigorous a disciple of Charles Borromeo as his Welsh former vicar general, Lewis Owen, despite Spanish reluctance.[72] Even where royal patronage was involved, and non-Italian appointments, as at Brindisi and Oria, held by Cardinal Granvelle, papal support for pastoral reorganisation, as in the separation of these two sees, could triumph over Spanish objections.[73] Some Spaniards and some Italians among the episcopate however were anxious to complete their life of often secular service to the crown by securing translation to Spain itself.[74] Pensions imposed on Neapolitan sees, as on Sicilian sees, could also be burdensome, quite apart from the essential poverty of many of the smaller dioceses.[75]

In Naples itself however the archbishops pursued, in the face of Spanish resistance, Tridentine reform of clergy and regulars. Discipline of delinquent clerics could be problematic, despite the supposed agreement over procedure with the secular courts.[76] As with breach of sanctuary by secular officials, such difficulties often necessitated recourse to Rome and the intervention of the nuncio.[77]

[69] A.G.S., Estado, Negoc. de Roma, Legs.929, fos.111 ff.; 930; 968; 981; 990; 1000, fo.8: 1577–1625; Napoles, Legs.1094, fos.262 f.; 1097, fo.35; 1880, fo.180; Secr. Prov., Napoles, Visitas y Diversos, Libros 54, fos.176r ff.; 94; 104; 105: 1564–1622; cf. Sicilia: Varios: Leg.1319; Libro 776, fos.3v ff.; A.S.V. Spagna, xxxiii, 89r-v: 17 Nov. 1586; *Nunziature di Napoli*, ii, nos.141, 152 f., 168, 302, 304 ff., 338, 355, 357, 359 ff., 364 ff., 372 ff.: 1579 to post-1585; Comparato, *Uffici*, p.79 n.128: 1562; Scaduto, *Stato e Chiesa*, i, pp.186, 201.

[70] A.G.S., Secr. Prov., Napoles, Visitas y Diversos, Libros 94, 95, 104, 105; Scaduto, *loc. cit.*

[71] A.G.S., Estado, Negoc. de Roma, Leg.990; Napoles, Leg.1884, fo.107: 1594–1622; Secr. Prov., Napoles, Visitas y Diversos, Libros 39, fos. 21r ff.; 44; 110: 1574–1621; A.S.V. Spagna, xxx, 483r-v; xxxi, 233r ff.; xxxiii, 35r ff.; xxxiv, 504r ff.: 1584–8.

[72] A.G.S., Secr. Prov., Napoles, Visitas y Diversos, Libro 44; A.S.V. Spagna, xxxiv, 59r ff., 196r ff.: 1587–94.

[73] A.G.S., Estado, Negoc. de Roma, Leg.995; Napoles, Legs.1093, fo.48; 1106, fo.96: 1592–1610; Secr. Prov., Napoles, Visitas y Diversos, Libros 44, 93, 110: 1587–1621; A.S.V. Spagna, xxxii, 138r ff.: 12 May 1586.

[74] A.G.S., Estado, Negoc. de Roma, Leg.990: 12 Mar. 1609.

[75] *Ibid.*, Legs.978, fo.83; 981; Secr. Prov., Napoles, Consultas, Leg.10: 1603–5.

[76] A.G.S., Estado, Napoles, Legs.1095, fo.285; 1097, fo.34; 1103, fo.184; 1104, fo.45; 1599–1607; Secr. Prov., Napoles, Visitas y Diversos, Libro 95; *Nunziature di Napoli*, i, nos.2, 9: 1570; Comparato, *Uffici*, pp.44 ff.; Scaduto, *Stato e Chiesa*, i, pp.269, 341 f.

[77] A.G.S., Estado, Napoles, Legs.1095, fo.285; 1096, fo.180; 1097, fo.20: 1599; Secr. Prov., Napoles, Visitas y Diversos, Libro 102; Comparato, *Uffici*, p.189 and n.73; p.248 and nn.12, 13; p.261 n.41; Scaduto, *Stato e Chiesa*, i, 276; Borromeo, 'Contributo', p.229.

This was so particularly at moments of great tension, as with the involvement of Campanella and other ecclesiastics in the Calabrian rebellion,[78] or the anti-tax riot in the time of Archbishop Acquaviva.[79] The distinct *chierici selvaggi* of Calabria also posed a more permanent problem.[80] Reform of female convents in the city of Naples was most strongly contested, however, when Cardinal Gesualdo began the implementation of Tridentine improvements at the convent of S. Chiara, which claimed royal protection.[81] The aim of extending reform to other female convents was countered by vice-regal plans to declare these also to be under royal patronage and mount armed guards.[82] Vice-regal opposition to episcopal in place of regular control was clear, not only in support of local objection on grounds common in Counter-Reformation society.[83] Also explicit was the objection to any reduction of female convents to places for those with a proven vocation alone: the economic ruin of the nobility could be the only result of a ban on depositing undowered daughters in convents, or the imposition of deterringly strict enclosure.[84]

The vice-regal government was less clearly supportive of resistance by confraternities and *luoghi pii* to archiepiscopal control, asserted on the basis of the Tridentine decrees.[85] After long disputes, the Spanish crown was advised to accept episcopal control in the spiritual, as

---

[78] A.G.S., Estado, Napoles, Legs.1095, fo.285; 1096, fos.105 f., 111, 119, 123, 178, 180; 1097, fos.2, 24, 33 f.: 1599–1600; Scaduto, *Stato e Chiesa*, i, p.271; T. Campanella, *Supplizio*, ed. L. Firpo (Rome, 1985).

[79] A.G.S., Estado, Napoles, Legs.1103, fos.162, 170, 184; 1104, fo.45: 1606–7.

[80] A.G.S., Secr. Prov., Napoles, Visitas y Diversos, Libros 54; 95; *Nunziature di Napoli*, iiii, no.264: 15 June 1591; cf. A. Musi, 'Fisco, religione e Stato nel Mezzogiorno d'Italia (secoli XVI–XVII)', in *Fisco religione Stato nell' età confessionale*, ed. H. Kellenbenz and P. Prodi (Bologna, 1989), pp.427–57, at 449–50 and nn.; cf. G. Griffiths, *Representative Government in Western Europe in the Sixteenth Century* (Oxford, 1968), pp.81 ff., 112: Sicily also (1552–72). The married *chierici selvaggi*, unlike lay sacristans and parish clerks elsewhere in Italy, asserted an absolute claim to the immunities of clerical status.

[81] A.G.S., Estado, Negoc. de Roma, Leg.968; Napoles, Leg.1097, fos.34 f.: 1596–1600; Russo, *I monasteri*, pp.11 ff., 38 ff.

[82] A.G.S., Estado, Negoc. de Roma, Leg.968; Napoles, Leg.1095, fo.109: 1596–97; Russo, *I monasteri*, pp.14, 16, 52, 54 ff., 82, 121.

[83] A.G.S., Estado, Negoc. de Roma, Leg.968; Napoles, Legs.1094, fos.262 f.; 1096, fo.109; 1097, fo.35: 1596–1600; *Nunziature di Napoli*, i, nos.146, 179: 1573; Russo, *I monasteri*, pp.15, 41 ff., 55, 57 f., 69 ff., 75 ff., 82 ff., 85 f., 99, 107; Scaduto, *Stato e Chiesa*, i, pp.200 f.; cf. J.P. Sommerville, 'The Royal Supremacy and Episcopacy "Jure Divino", 1603–1640', *Journal of Ecclesiastical History*, xxxiv, 4 (1983), 555 and n.39.

[84] A.G.S., Estado, Negoc. de Roma, Leg.968; Napoles, Legs.1095, fo.109; 1097, fo.34: 1596–7; Russo, *I monasteri*, pp.7 ff., 14, 41 ff., 52, 57 f., 83 f., 103 f., 121; cf. A. d'Addario, *Aspetti della Controriforma a Firenze* (Rome, 1972), pp.279–97.

[85] A.S.V. Spagna, xxxiii, 300r ff.: 10 July 1587.

opposed to temporal, affairs of such charitable foundations.[86] A similar compromise, limiting the range of enforceable penalties at episcopal disposal, was often the result in contests over 'mixed cases'. Such cases, most commonly involving moral offences, brought laity before the ecclesiastical courts.[87] Where bigamy[88] or witchcraft[89] were concerned, however, as opposed to concubinage,[90] blasphemy or usury for example,[91] the ad hoc inquisitorial authority delegated by Rome to a local bishop or to the nuncio, sitting with or without such a bishop, might be involved.[92] The absence of a permanent tribunal of the Roman Holy Office in the kingdom was the paradoxical result of popular reaction to any rumour of royal plans to introduce the distinct Spanish Inquisition. The results of such local sensitivity, as during the troubles of Osuna's vice-regal government, which involved the noble and popular *seggi* of Naples, the

[86] A.G.S., Estado, Napoles, Leg.1097, fo.35; Secr. Prov., Napoles, Visitas y Diversos, Libros 39; 54; 100: 1570–1621; A.S.V. Spagna, xxxiv, 43r ff., 283r ff.: 1587–8; *Nunziature di Napoli*, i, nos.146, 179; ii, nos.361, 368, 371, 429 ff.: 1573 to post-1586; Russo, *I monasteri*, pp.81 ff.; Comparato, *Uffici*, p.248, p.261 n.41; Scaduto, *Stato e Chiesa*, i, p.201; cf. E. Novi Chavarria, 'L'attività missionaria dei Gesuiti nel Mezzogiorno d'Italia tra XVI e XVIII secolo', in *Per la storia sociale e religiosa del Mezzogiorno d'Italia*, ii, ed. G. Galasso and C. Russo (Naples, 1982), pp.159–85, for the context of the work of the New Orders of the Counter-Reformation in the Mezzogiorno.

[87] A.G.S., Estado, Negoc. de Roma, Leg.922, fo.54; Napoles, Leg. 1063, fo.133; Secr. Prov., Napoles, Visitas y Diversos, Libros 54, fos.51r ff., 107: 1573; A.S.V Spagna, xxxiii, 424r ff.: 1587; *Nunziature di Napoli*, i, nos.11 f., 175, 178, 181, 184 ff.: 1570–3; Comparato, *Uffici*, p.189, p.261 n.41; Scaduto, *Stato e Chiesa*, i, pp.248 ff.

[88] A.G.S., Estado, Negoc. de Roma, Legs.978, fos.246, 259 f.; 980; 981; 1858; Napoles, Legs.1100, fos.141 ff., 202; 1102, fo.254: 1605; Secr. Prov., Napoles, Visitas y Diversos, Libro 107; *Nunziature di Napoli*, ii, nos.289, 291, 293 ff.: 1584 onwards; Comparato, *Uffici*, p.191 n.78; cf. Spanish Inquisition and bigamy cases in Sicily: A.G.S., Estado, Sicilia, Legs.1161, fo.170; 1162, fo.102; 1163, fo.173: 1605–9; cf. Borromeo, 'Contributo', pp.251–4; cf. H. Kamen, *The Spanish Inquisition* (London, 1965), pp.197 ff.; *idem., Inquisition and Society in Spain in the Sixteenth and Seventeenth Centuries* (London, 1985), pp.183, 185, 206.

[89] A.G.S., Estado, Negoc. de Roma, Leg.981: 1591–1605; Secr. Prov., Napoles, Visitas y Diversos, Libros 54, fos.51r ff.; 106, 107: 1591.

[90] A.G.S., Secr. Prov., Napoles, Visitas y Diversos, Libro 107; A.S.V. Spagna, xxxv, 53r-v: 1589; *Nunziature di Napoli*, ii, nos.289, 291, 293 ff.: 1584.

[91] A.G.S., Secr. Prov., Napoles, Visitas y Diversos, Libros 54, fos.51r ff.; 107; Scaduto, *Stato e Chiesa*, i, p.394; ii, pp.29 f., 64; cf. P. Sarpi, *Discorso dell' Origine, forma, leggi, ed uso dell' Ufficio dell'Inquisitione* [Geneva] (1639), pp.10 f., 132 ff., 138f.

[92] A.G.S., Estado, Negoc. de Roma, Legs.947; 978, fos.246, 259 f.; 980; 981; 1858: 1569–1605; Napoles, Legs.1096, fos.125, 178, 180; 1097, fos.2, 20; 1100, fos.141 ff., 202; 1102, fo.254; 1104, fo.115; 1105, fo.92: 1599–1608; Secr. Prov., Napoles, Visitas y Diversos, Libros 48; 60; 106; 107: 1565; *Nunziature di Napoli*, I, nos.331 ff.: 1568–1605; Comparato, *Uffici*, p.191 n.78; Borromeo, 'Contributo', pp.220–21, 228–33; Quazza, *Preponderanza*, p.264; cf. R. Villari, *La rivolta antispagnola a Napoli: Le origini 1585–1647* (Bari, 1967), p.77, n.123.

reform of the Neapolitan Dominicans, and diplomatic tensions with Venice, could produce major conflict between royal authority and that of the Roman Holy Office, supported by the papacy.[93] In general however this occasional representation of the Holy Office by bishops or nuncios led to vice-regal co-operation, for example in the matter of handing over wanted persons to Rome.[94] In other affairs the laity were defended by the secular courts against any energetic exercise of episcopal authority according to Tridentine priorities, such as attempted recovery from lay persons of unfulfilled pious bequests or alienated church properties and revenues.[95]

The concern of the Counter-Reformation papacy to resist the claims of the *Monarchia Sicula* thus derived from both specific and more general conditions. On the one hand the unsatisfactory state of religious practice in Sicily itself was evident, and the immediate aim was therefore to counter wherever possible the damaging isolation of the church in that island, exemplified by the revived exercise of supposedly legatine rights by the crown. But the papacy did not view the dispute over the *Monarchia* in isolation, any more than did the lawyers who advised the Spanish monarchs on the jurisdictional disputes with the reinvigorated post-Tridentine church in Spain itself, Portugal under Spanish rule, Sardinia, Lombardy, Naples or Sicily.[96] The specific caution at Rome over the potential use which might be made of the *Monarchia* claims to fortify existing regalism in the kingdom of Naples was not unjustified. For precisely after the Council of Trent, from the last decades of the

---

[93] A.G.S., Estado, Negoc. de Roma, Leg.978, fo.246; Napoles, Legs. 1095, fo.285; 1096, fos.123, 178, 180; 1097, fos.2, 20, 24, 33 f.; 1102, fo.254; 1104, fo.115; 1881, fo.192: 1599–1618; Secr. Prov., Napoles, Visitas y Diversos, Libro 107; *Nunziature di Napoli*, i, nos.331 ff.; ii, nos.264, 266: 1575–83; Comparato, *Uffici*, pp.289 ff., 297 f. and n.19; Scaduto, *Stato e Chiesa*, i, pp.303 ff., 348; Villari, *Rivolta*, pp.73–79; Nicolini, *Scritti di archivistica*, p.261; F. Yates, *Giordano Bruno and the Hermetic Tradition* (London, 1964), pp.363–65; A. Zambler, 'Contributo alla Storia della Congiura Spagnuola contro Venezia', *Nuovo Archivio Veneto*, xi (1896), 15 ff.: p.19 n.1.

[94] A.G.S., Estado, Negoc. de Roma, Leg.978, fo.246; Napoles, Legs. 1102, fo.254; 1880, fo.180: 1617; Secr. Prov., Napoles, Visitas y Diversos, Libros 94; 104, 105; 107; Scaduto, *Stato e Chiesa*, i, pp.303 ff., 348.

[95] A.G.S., Estado, Negoc. de Roma, Legs.992, fo.19; 929, fo.15; 991; Napoles, Leg.1063, fo.133; Secr. Prov., Napoles, Visitas y Diversos, Libros 54, fos.51r ff.; 107; 108, fos.244v, ff.; A.S.V. Spagna, xxxiv, 109r ff., 342r ff.: 1588; *Nunziature di Napoli*, i, nos.3, 5, 9, 11 f., 18 f., 21 ff., 134 f., 175, 178, 181, 184 ff., 248 ff.; ii, nos.3 f., 7 f., 11, 289, 291, 293 ff.: 1570–84 and onwards; Comparato, *Uffici*, p.189, p.261 n.41; Scaduto, *Stato e Chiesa*, i, pp.186, 200, 248 ff., 348; ii, pp.19, 21.

[96] A.G.S., Estado, Napoles, Legs.1095, fos.145, 147; 1097, fo.34: 1597–1600; cf. Milan: Leg.1301, fos.466r ff.: 1611; Secr. Prov., Napoles, Visitas y Diversos, Libro 99; A.S.V. Spagna, xxxi, 183r ff.; xxxiv, 210r ff.: 1584–8; cf. W.J. Bouwsma, *Venice and the Defense of Republican Liberty* (Berkeley, 1968), p.491.

sixteenth century onwards, the royal lawyers in the kingdom began a new stage in the elaboration of extensive theories about the subordination of ecclesiastical to secular jurisdiction there.[97] In extended compilations of supposed precedents and alleged parallels from other states, the *Monarchia* and its operation in Sicily were cited, alongside references to other parts of Italy and other kingdoms of Europe.[98] Such legal treatises were of course a reaction to the Tridentine and post-conciliar reassertions of papal and episcopal authority, and such Counter-Reformation reassertions produced a more acute reaction at Naples because of the vexed political relationship between the papacy and the kingdom.[99] These legal opinions however were only in one sense the precocious foundations for the more sweeping arguments of a later age, the era of Vico and Giannone.[100] In their own epoch they rather represented a conscious antiquarianism, opposed to the demands of Trent,[101] as much as did the 'medievalism' by which the Habsburg rulers of Sicily revived and defended their claims to an innate legatine power in the island.

[97] A.G.S., Secr. Prov., Napoles, Visitas y Diversos, Libros 39; 44; 47; 48; 54; 60; 93; 94; 95; 96–99; 100, 102; 104; 105–8; 110; Comparato, *Uffici*, pp.189 f.; Scaduto, *Stato e Chiesa*, i, p.53.

[98] A.G.S., Secr. Prov., Napoles, Visitas y Diversos, Libro 54, fos.95r ff., 126r ff.

[99] A.G.S., Estado, Napoles, Legs.1084, fo.70; 1092, fo.102; *Nunziature di Napoli*, i, nos.385–86; ii, nos.81, 84, 89, 90, 96–97, 143, 173, 261, 263–4, 266: 1580–91; cf. C. Russo, *Chiesa e comunità nella diocesi di Napoli tra cinque e settecento* (Naples, 1984).

[100] A. Lauro, *Il Giurisdizionalismo pregiannoniano nel Regno di Napoli: Problemi e bibliografia* (Rome, 1974); cf. V.I. Comparato, *Giuseppe Valletta: Un intellettuale napoletano della fine del seicento* (Naples, 1970).

[101] A.G.S., Estado, Napoles, Leg.1097, fo.35; *Nunziature di Napoli*, i, nos.146, 179: 1573; cf. Russo, *I monasteri*, pp.42 f., 55, 57 f., 69 ff., 82 ff., 107; Scaduto, *Stato e Chiesa*, i, pp.200 f.

Chapter 17

The First Medievalist in Leeds:
Ralph Thoresby, F.R.S., 1658–1725

G.C.F. Forster

Writing in 1939, David C. Douglas (who was shortly to become professor of medieval history at Leeds) asserted that, 'between 1660 and 1730 a long succession of highly distinguished Englishmen brought to its proper culmination the best sustained and the most prolific movement of historical scholarship which this country has ever seen'.[1] The developments in historical studies to which Douglas alluded had been powerfully stimulated since the later fifteenth century by a variety of influences: the accession of a new royal dynasty; the growth of printing and bookselling; the spread (however selectively and haltingly) of education and literate habits; the great cultural watershed of the Reformation; the search for 'primitive' elements in Christianity, associated with Protestant teachings, and in human society at large, prompted by geographical discoveries which also boosted archaeological studies. If these cultural and intellectual influences drove men towards the study of the more remote past, they also pointed to the investigation of the middle ages, of which there was already greater knowledge, as well as more records and an abundance of physical remains, religious and secular.[2] Medieval studies under Elizabeth I and the early Stuarts had a strong utilitarian purpose too: it seemed possible that an understanding of medieval records could elucidate the origins of contemporary political problems and suggest solutions to them by establishing the precedents.[3]

These close links between historical research and contemporary religious and political arguments continued after the Restoration, when 'strong tides of sectarian zeal, of pristine patriotism, and of political conviction' inspired 'an immense energy' in medieval scholars.[4] Their

[1] D.C. Douglas, *English Scholars*, 1660–1730, 2nd edn. (London, 1951), p.13.
[2] F.S. Fussner, *The Historical Revolution* (London, 1962), *passim*; T.D. Kendrick, *British Antiquity* (London & New York, 1970), pp.114–15.
[3] P. Styles, 'Politics and Historical Research in the Early Seventeenth Century', in L. Fox (ed.), *English Historical Scholarship in the Sixteenth and Seventeenth Centuries* (London, 1956), pp.49–72; S. Piggott, *Ruins in a Landscape* (Edinburgh, 1976), pp.1–24.
[4] Douglas, *Scholars*, pp.19–22.

'special type of erudite curiosity' and the 'riot of learning' in which it was displayed, was more firmly engaged than ever before with the close examination of original sources and the careful consideration of the evidence which they presented. The work of these scholars resulted in great advances in medieval scholarship; their achievements were warmly welcomed by educated people and enabled them to claim for history an independent position as a branch of learning.[5]

Another aspect of the growing zest for antiquity since the later fifteenth century was the study of English topography and local history. A consequence of the enhanced pride and influence of landed families, and of their concern with status, genealogy, heraldry and titles to property, this development also served utilitarian purposes: in a period of sharp social rivalries, an active land market, and keen litigation about landownership, it was clearly sensible to have a sound record of ancestry and possessions. The careful, detailed examination of the records and antiquities of the countryside by county gentry, clergy and lawyers resulted in the publication of major topographical works on many English counties, and during the period 1660–1730 notable advances in local history were made, particularly because the leading medievalists of the day frequently strengthened their work by local enquiries. In an atmosphere favourable for historical research the common interests and intellectual industry of many scholars countrywide came to fruition in 1695 in a new, collaborative edition of William Camden's *Britannia* (first published in 1586).[6] An important contributor to that volume was Ralph Thoresby of Leeds.

An outline of Ralph Thoresby's life is readily constructed from the autobiographical details which were recorded in some of his writings, notably in the diary which he began, at his father's behest, in his nineteenth year.[7] Ralph Thoresby was born at a house in Kirkgate, Leeds on 16 August 1658. His family were well-to-do cloth merchants; his grandfather had been an alderman of Leeds; his father, John Thoresby, was a Puritan of strict religious principles who had served in Lord Fairfax's parliamentarian army and remained a moderate Nonconformist after the Restoration, in danger of persecution for his beliefs. Young Ralph therefore grew up in an atmosphere of political

---

[5] *Ibid.*, pp.19–22, 25, 26, 28, 29.

[6] *Ibid.*, pp.256–58; Fussner, *Revolution*, p.34 and chap.8, *passim*; W.G. Hoskins, *Provincial England* (London, 1963), pp.208–12; *idem, Local History in England* (3rd edn., 1984), pp.18–23.

[7] J. Hunter (ed.), *The Diary of Ralph Thoresby, F.R.S.*, 2 vols. (London, 1830); *Biographia Britannica*, 7 vols. (London, 1747–66), vi, pt. 1, pp.3931–43; see also D.H. Atkinson, *Ralph Thoresby, the Topographer; His Town and Times*, 2 vols. (Leeds, 1885, 1887), a rambling compilation which nevertheless provides a useful guide to the contents of the diary.

upheaval and religious tension with repercussions on his own family which made the issues – Protestantism, Dissent, Popery – of immediate and lifelong interest to him. His father's religious persuasions and scholarly interests, especially in history and antiquities, had a deep influence upon him, especially after the death of his mother in 1669. After his formal education at a private grammar school in Leeds, Ralph did not enter a university but joined his father's cloth merchanting business. He was partly trained by a kinsman and merchant in London where, apart from attending sermons and sightseeing, he spent his spare time in examining church monuments. In 1678 his father sent him to Holland, a country with which the West Riding cloth industry had close trading links, so that he could study the language and learn more about the business, but after falling ill he had to return home prematurely. Once recovered he resumed a pleasant enough life, working with his father, accompanying him on business journeys, hearing sermons, reading systematically and making notes on the lives and writings of great churchmen of the past, but his contentment was shattered by the sudden death of John Thoresby in October 1679. In his twenty-second year, therefore, Ralph Thoresby, now bereft of his father's wise guidance, was faced as the eldest surviving son with a host of family and business responsibilities.

Despite his father's careful training Ralph Thoresby did not take kindly to merchanting, for which he had little aptitude, and it was in any case a difficult period for the cloth trade. The business did not prosper, while Thoresby's marriage in 1685 to the daughter of another Leeds merchant brought further family duties and financial burdens. Thoresby could not afford to give up business and even sought to improve his fortunes by joining in a partnership to run a rape-seed mill, a project which was ultimately unsuccessful. He did not evade public duties, however, and at various times was involved in charitable administration as well as in manorial business and the affairs of the Dissenting chapel of which he was a member; following his eventual decision to became a communicant of the Church of England he was appointed to membership of Leeds Corporation, serving (albeit reluctantly) on the town's governing body from 1697 until 1713.

Yet, as Thoresby himself admitted, his real interests lay elsewhere: in the study of books, especially about religion and the church, and in history and antiquities, to which he devoted a large part of his time. His growing collection of 'coins and curiosities' and his work on manuscripts, monuments and pedigrees, brought him into regular contact with like-minded antiquaries in Yorkshire and beyond. He mostly delighted in showing his collections to visitors, and he freely shared his knowledge and his material with others. His growing reputation, especially as a numismatist, brought him the invitation to contribute to the *Britannia*.

His exacting scholarly work for that undertaking enhanced his standing in the world of learning and provided an introduction to an ever-widening circle of scholars.[8] It also concentrated Thoresby's interests in local history, especially that of earlier times, and he seems to have become increasingly concerned with local antiquities and archaeological remains, particularly those of Roman Britain. His observations in this field led to the bestowal of another honour on Ralph Thoresby: in 1697, following the publication of some of his Romano-British investigations in the *Philosophical Transactions*, he was elected a Fellow of the Royal Society.[9]

Thoresby was now confirmed in his historical studies and, after a serious illness during his fortieth year and a crisis in his religious beliefs which led to his joining the Established Church, he gradually withdrew from business life. Despite some financial embarrassments and straitened circumstances he committed himself fully to his real interests: the collection and study of evidence for the past. By the early 1690s he had decided to work systematically on a topography and history of Leeds and its neighbourhood, but amidst Thoresby's manifold scholarly interests this work did not proceed rapidly, and the plan proved too ambitious for completion. In the event two separate works were published: the *Ducatus Leodiensis* (1715), a topographical survey; and the *Vicaria Leodiensis* (1724), part only of the projected history.[10] With advancing years Thoresby's progress had been hampered by ill-health, although his diary shows that he continued his studies until he was overtaken by serious illness in 1724. He died on 17 October 1725 and was buried without epitaph or memorial in Leeds Parish Church, the fabric and monuments of which he had faithfully recorded and published.

To some extent Thoresby's diary charts the development of his historical interests and enquiries, and something of his approach and mental outlook can be discerned in the nature of his work, the materials he gathered, his reading, his collections and, ultimately, his writings. Thoresby himself claimed that he had 'A Natural Propension to the Study of Antiquities' and that his inclinations were excited when, as a schoolboy, he heard the vicar of Leeds declare that Leeds was a place of great antiquity mentioned by Bede; he professed an 'innate affection' for his birthplace and came to realise that he lived in an area which merited description because of the richness of its buildings and landscapes.[11] His more general antiquarian interests were indulged in the visits he made to London and Holland during his apprenticeship to merchanting, and

---

[8] Below, pp.259 ff.
[9] Below, p.263.
[10] Below, pp.265–67.
[11] Ralph Thoresby, *Ducatus Leodiensis* (London, 1725), pp.v–vi.

from his early twenties he developed his lifelong practice of recording inscriptions, transcribing documents, taking notes from books, collecting, compiling lists, pedigrees and catalogues.[12] Thoresby's journeys on business or family affairs to York, London and Northumberland, and later to Oxford, Cambridge, East Anglia, Lancashire, Cheshire, the Borders and Edinburgh, widened his outlook and his knowledge of antiquities.[13] He prepared for his travels carefully, by reading the works of Camden, Speed and Fuller on the places to be visited. He became increasingly observant of the details of buildings and monuments but was usually content with a limited antiquarian approach. The comments he noted in his diary retain some value for topographers, but unlike Celia Fiennes and other travellers he rarely noted any observations about social life, though in 1702 he made remarks on the festivities at Preston Guild,[14] and he frequently included descriptions of scenery, or of the gardens, statuary and vistas at country houses.[15]

Thoresby's journeys enabled him to visit fellow antiquaries, examine their collections and work in libraries and museums. As early as 1680, for example, he was to be found at Stittenham (Yorks. N.R.) studying manuscripts in Sir Thomas Gower's possession.[16] The good offices of Humfrey Wanley gave him access to the Cottonian Library; he was permitted to transcribe manuscripts in the Harleian Library, where he refused to break off for refreshment; he visited the public records housed in the Tower of London and professed himself 'mightily pleased' with their arrangement.[17] Two other collections afforded him particular pleasure. First, with his skill and unquenchable interests in heraldry and genealogy he greatly valued the opportunity afforded to him by Peter Le Neve, the Herald, to work on the manuscript pedigrees at the College of Arms, where he was still making transcripts at the age of sixty-five.[18] Secondly, in the latter part of his life he repeatedly enjoyed the generous and considerate hospitality of the philanthropist Lady Elizabeth Hastings at Ledston Hall (Yorks. W.R.), where they spent many hours looking at books, discussing religious questions and elucidating manorial rolls; he was transcribing benefice documents there

---

[12] *Diary*, i, pp.2, 3, 4, 6, 8, 9, 14, 18, 19.

[13] *Ibid.*, pp.64–69, 98–108, 118–24, 136–51, 173–74, 234–35, 261–82, 293, 302, 303, 380 ff., 422–33.

[14] *Ibid.*, pp.389ff.

[15] E.g., *ibid.*, pp.234–35; *Diary*, ii, pp.133–34.

[16] Diary, i, pp.50–51.

[17] *Ibid.*, pp.334, 342; *Diary*, ii, pp.26, 31, 40–41; C. Jones & G. Holmes, eds., *The London Diaries of William Nicolson, Bishop of Carlisle, 1702–1718* (Oxford, 1985), p.477. Humfrey Wanley (1672–1726), librarian and cataloguer.

[18] *Diary*, i, p.343; ii, pp.373, 375. Peter Le Neve (1661–1729), Herald, Norroy King-at-Arms and antiquary.

for the parishes of Harewood and Ledsham as late as 1724.[19]

Thoresby's practice of studying and copying a very wide range of manuscript sources reflected one of the more recent characteristics of historical research. Another, also noticeable in his approach, was that historical enquiries were increasingly pursued for their own sake: Thoresby was not a controversialist and moreover was initially unselective in gathering evidence from manuscripts.[20] His apparently haphazard approach to sources perhaps owes something to the influences exercised upon him by the work of three notable Yorkshire antiquaries: Dr Nathaniel Johnston, John Brearcliffe and John Hopkinson. Between 1679 and 1681 Thoresby saw Hopkinson's large assemblage of pedigrees, as well as the miscellaneous collections of transcripts and manuscripts concerning Yorkshire compiled by these men, and this material was made available to him; it set him on his life's work.[21]

Thoresby was never discouraged by the hard labour involved in transcription, and he undertook all of it himself, for unlike some of his contemporaries he could not afford an amanuensis. Moreover, he tried to improve his Latin and used various works to gain some knowledge of Anglo-Saxon. Although his earlier studies were partly devoted to ecclesiastical records – those of Fountains Abbey, for example – there was no unifying purpose behind them: he was a collector and copyist of historical sources, rather than an editor or writer.[22] It was only when he decided to prepare a history of Leeds that his researches in original sources took on a clearer, more systematic direction.[23]

Two other aspects of Thoresby's work claim attention. One is the variety of general reading that he undertook. Prompted by his interest in antecedents of the religious issues of his time he read published sermons, controversial works, and classics of church history, amongst them Foxe's *Book of Martyrs*, Fuller's *Church History*, Strype's *Annals of the Reformation* and his lives of Archbishops Parker and Grindal. The range of his historical interests caused him to read Sir John Spelman's book on King Alfred and Elizabeth Elstob's *English-Saxon Homily*, as well as Clarendon's *History of the Rebellion*, the manuscript of Oliver Heywood's diary, and the writings of Bishops Burnet and Stillingfleet. He

---

19 *Diary*, ii, pp.172, 302, 409–10. Lady Elizabeth Hastings (1682–1739).
20 Fussner, *Revolution*, pp.34, 98.
21 *Diary*, i, pp.29–30, 39, 110–11; below, p.258.
22 *Diary*, i, pp.225, 258, 259, 260, 290, 307, 308, 408.
23 Below, p.263.

maintained his habit of serious reading and note-taking, and expressed chagrin when illness began to keep him from his books.[24]

Finally, Thoresby's knowledge of Latin and Anglo-Saxon caused him to investigate local place-names and prompted him to become a keen field archaeologist, visiting places with Roman or Scandinavian names in search of remains, inspecting ancient sites, tracing possible fortifications and Roman roads in the neighbourhood of Leeds. He recorded archaeological finds and reported several of them to the Royal Society, to the advantage of his own scholarly reputation.[25]

The *Musaeum Thoresbyanum*, which Thoresby founded, had its origins in John Thoresby's own coin cabinet, together with the collection of coins purchased by him from the 3rd Lord Fairfax's executors in 1671 and subsequently augmented. The English tradition of collecting had developed since the sixteenth century, beginning with manuscripts and coins, then books, and examples of material culture. During the later seventeenth century the number of 'cabinets of curiosities' increased and comprised antiquities of all kinds and dates, contemporary artefacts, and specimens of the natural world (including oddities). This concern with physical remains was essentially a Royal Society approach; collections of the kind described (sometimes called 'virtuosi cabinets') were favoured by the Royal Society and frequently owned by its Fellows, who through their contacts among the Fellowship were able to disseminate information and observations throughout the country.[26]

Building on his father's collection, therefore, and fired by his own enthusiasm, Ralph Thoresby developed the collecting habit early in life. With his bookish and antiquarian turn of mind he lost no opportunity to visit London booksellers, attend book auctions (including the first one ever held in Leeds in 1692) and call at shops selling antiquities. He purchased or begged coins, medals and curiosities of all kinds. He sought archaeological finds. He was fired with a particular enthusiasm for collecting autographs of famous people, dead or alive. 'Nothing can come amiss . . .', he wrote to Thomas Hearne, and although he was referring to autographs the phrase supplies unwittingly the clue to his

---

[24] *Diary*, i, pp.30–31, 83, 449–51, 453, 454, 457, 467, 468; ii, pp.51, 58, 65, 91, 174 ff.

[25] *Ibid.*, i, pp.90, 107, 123, 139, 309, 311–12, 354, 358, 363–64, 367, 376, 399, 403; *Ducatus*, p.ix; Piggott, *Ruins*, p.18; below, p.263.

[26] Kendrick, *Antiquity*, p.166; Piggott, *Ruins*, pp.107, 110; E. Gibson, ed., *Camden's Britannia* (London, 1695, repr. Newton Abbot, 1971), p.731; C.E. Doble, D.W. Rannie, H.E. Salter, eds., *Remarks and Collections of Thomas Hearne*, i–v, ix, Oxford Historical Society, ii, vii, xiii, xxxiv, xlii, lxv (Oxford, 1884–1914), ix, p.56; R.W. Unwin, 'Cabinets of Curiosities', *The Historian*, xix (1988), 13; P.C.D. Brears, 'Ralph Thoresby: A Museum Visitor in Stuart England', *Journal of the History of Collections*, i (1989), *passim*.

determined but unselective approach to collecting, for there is little
to suggest that Thoresby always subjected the objects he obtained to
critical examination. Nevertheless he took the advice of other collectors
and obtained catalogues of collections existing elsewhere. Moreover, his
own collections were furthered by his knowledge of the other 'cabinets'
which he visited on his travels.[27]

With his unremitting urge to collect Thoresby eventually built up
not simply a 'virtuoso cabinet' but a large and varied museum. It
was well housed with his library in an extension to the family
house in Kirkgate, Leeds, carefully arranged, well looked after, and
properly listed, frequently with notes of provenance or of the means
of acquisition. The catalogue of Thoresby's museum published (at
the request of various scholars) with the *Ducatus Leodiensis* shows
that it comprised an astonishing quantity and variety of objects:
books, manuscripts, coins, antiquities, natural and artificial rarities.
The main items included: some 2,400 coins, half of them Roman but
with an important collection from Anglo-Saxon, Viking and medieval
times; Bibles and commentaries including Caxton and Aldine editions; a
multitude of manuscripts, many of them original, some copies, including
charters, monastic deeds and other texts, ecclesiastical records, the *Scala
Mundi* (a collection of extracts from chronicles of which Thoresby was
especially proud), and a copy or abstract of part of the *Polychronicon*, once
the property of Dean Laurence Nowell; numerous autographs; copies
of portraits; scientific, archaeological and religious objects, including
architectural fragments from York Minster; and a mass of curiosities,
many of them clearly spurious.[28]

Coins and medals were Thoresby's primary interest. He built up one
of the finest collections – one correspondent, Sir Andrew Fountaine,
called it 'the completest nest' – in the country.[29] Thoresby, who
clearly understood the value of numismatic evidence, especially for
the historical periods for which written sources were limited, acquired
a formidable knowledge of coins. As early as 1683 he had lent coins
and information for a new edition of Spelman's *Life of Alfred*, the work
of Dr. Obadiah Walker, and he was soon in correspondence with other
numismatist-antiquarians, including Archdeacon William Nicolson and
Dr. John Sharp, archbishop of York. In consequence he agreed in 1693

[27] *Diary*, i, pp.156, 159, 161, 230; *Hearne's Collections*, i, 208–9; Unwin, 'Cabinets', 16–17;
Brears, 'Museum Visitor', *passim*

[28] *Ducatus*, pp.269–568; *Diary*, i, p.230; Piggott, *Ruins*, pp.106–7; R. Flower, 'Laurence
Nowell and the Discovery of England in Tudor Times', *Proceedings of the British Academy*,
xxi (1935), 50, 53, 55, 69. For a list of the manuscripts of the Polychronicon, see J. Taylor,
The Universal Chronicle of Ranulf Higden (Oxford, 1966), pp.152–58.

[29] *Diary*, ii, pp.28–29. Sir Andrew Fountaine (1676–1753), virtuoso and Warden of the
Mint.

to supply coins and material for the new edition of the *Britannia*.[30] By then he was recognised as one of the foremost numismatic experts of his time, and it was this reputation which, more than anything else, induced the publishers and the editor, Edmund Gibson, to press him to help with other revisions of the *Britannia*. The note about his coins, which he entered in his additions to the West Riding sections of the new edition, helped to attract to the museum both enquirers and visitors from all parts of the country.[31] The visitors included nobility and gentry, travelling merchants, lawyers, judges on circuit, clergy, scholars and 'virtuosi'. The most welcome were obviously those who actually understood the significance of the collections as well as those who augmented them by their gifts. The fame of 'the ingenious Mr. Thoresby's museum' was enhanced by the publication of the catalogue in 1715, but well before that date Thoresby occasionally admitted to finding the visitors a tiresome distraction: 'Thus am I exposed, like a common innkeeper, to guests of all complexions'.[32]

The widespread interest aroused by the museum, and the recognition by reputable scholars of its value, especially as a repository of pre- and post-Conquest coins, of books and manuscripts, accounts for the concern about its fate expressed by many when they heard of Thoresby's death.[33] Their anxiety was not misplaced. The family proved not to be interested in the collections, which were dispersed: the more valuable contents were auctioned and the remainder discarded.[34] This was a major loss to collecting in general, as well as to Leeds, because Thoresby's museum was important for its manuscripts and books, natural historical and ethnographical collections, varied antiquities, as well as for its most impressive coin cabinet, and it was unquestionably one of the most interesting of the first generation of English museums.[35]

The fame of Thoresby's museum, his manifold antiquarian interests, and his industry and seriousness brought him into contact with a wide circle of scholars (many of them early Fellows of the Royal Society), who were keen to draw on his knowledge and collections or to exchange information

[30] *Ibid.*, i, pp.152, 165, 235, 258; below, p.262. Obadiah Walker (1616–99), Oxford Romanist and ejected Master of University College; William Nicolson (1655–1727), Oxford scholar, Archdeacon and later Bishop of Carlisle, subsequently Bishop of Derry; John Sharp (1645–1714).

[31] J.J. Saunders, 'Ralph Thoresby and his Circle' (unpub. M.A. thesis, London Univ., 1936), pp.63–64. Edmund Gibson (1669–1748), Oxford scholar, Bishop of Lincoln and of London.

[32] *Diary*, i, pp.87, 131, 132, 133; ii, p.65.

[33] *Hearne's Collections*, ix, pp.56, 104–5.

[34] Atkinson, *Thoresby*, ii, pp.425–43 gives an account of the dispersal of the museum.

[35] Piggott, *Ruins*, pp.106–7; Brears, 'Museum Visitor', *passim*.

with him.[36] During his lifetime the Church of England was the major repository and patron of English learning, and Thoresby's decision to join the Established Church may have strengthened his contacts with the many clergymen-scholars who, despite strong attachments to different traditions of churchmanship, shared a common enthusiasm for medieval antiquities. Historians of the church, therefore, were numbered amongst Thoresby's circle, along with Anglo-Saxon scholars, collectors and editors, genealogists and local historians.[37]

In Yorkshire Ralph Thoresby had a group of friends with strong antiquarian interests: he discussed historical matters with two Leeds men, William Milner, an alderman, and Richard Thornton, the recorder, and Thomas Kirke of Cookridge (Yorks. W.R.);[38] he conducted a lively correspondence with the humorous rector of Barwick-in-Elmet, George Plaxton;[39] he conferred with Archbishop Sharp about coins; and he had serious, learned conversations with the much-admired Lady Elizabeth Hastings. He was acquainted with several artists, including some of the artistic coterie of York, among them Henry Gyles, the glass painter, William Etty the younger, and Francis Place.[40] Some of Thoresby's most fruitful local connections, however, were with the Yorkshire antiquaries who carried on Roger Dodsworth's great work of collecting and copying manuscripts. The transcripts possessed by Dr. Nathaniel Johnston of Pontefract, the voluminous material about the Halifax area accumulated by John Brearcliffe, an apothecary, and, above all, the pedigrees collected by John Hopkinson of Lofthouse (a lawyer and herald's deputy who had assisted Sir William Dugdale) were sources of assistance and instruction to Thoresby in his younger days.[41] He was also able to draw upon the important collections of material about the history of the diocese of York built up by his friend, James Torre.[42] Later Thoresby was in touch with the Rev. Abraham de la Pryme, F.R.S., the historian of Hull, to whom he lent transcripts. He was able to profit from de la Pryme's researches, corresponding with him about the descent of local families and about the newly-discovered text of the Henrician visitation commissioners' report

[36] Much of the biographical data in this section is drawn from Saunders, thesis, esp. chap.4 and from Douglas, *Scholars, passim*.

[37] J. Hunter (ed.), *Letters of Eminent Men Addressed to Ralph Thoresby*, F.R.S., 2 vols. (London, 1832), *passim*; Douglas, *Scholars*, pp.246, 254; Fussner, *Revolution*, pp.110–11.

[38] Thomas Kirke (1650–1706), virtuoso and distant relative of Thoresby.

[39] E.M. Walker (ed.), 'Letters of the Rev. George Plaxton, M.A., Rector of Barwick in Elmet', in *Miscellanea*, xi, Publications of the Thoresby Society, xxxvii (1945), *passim*.

[40] *Diary*, ii, pp.70, 113, 170–71, 364–65, 366. James Parmentier made a portrait of Thoresby in 1703 and George Vertue engraved his likeness in 1712 (Atkinson, *Thoresby*, ii, pp.193–94). See DNB.

[41] *Diary*, i, pp.29–30, 39, 110, 151, 314; *Letters*, i, pp.65–67, 135. See DNB.

[42] *Diary*, i, pp.225–27, 330, 452–53. James Torre (1649–99), antiquary and genealogist.

on the northern monasteries; he also discussed with him his own opinions about the possible sites near Leeds of the decisive battle of Winwaed in 655 A.D.[43]

With his interest in the Anglo-Saxon period stimulated by his coins, as well as by Bede's references to the Leeds area, Thoresby developed a working knowledge of Anglo-Saxon, and although he could hardly be considered a 'Saxonist' it was only to be expected that, given the flourishing contemporary state of Anglo-Saxon studies, he would be in contact with many of the leading 'Saxonists' of his day. He was able to provide them with evidence drawn from his numismatic collection, and he drew on their learning. Although he does not seem to have met Edward Thwaites, the Oxford scholar, he knew the Rev. Dr. John Smith, a critical editor of Bede's *Ecclesiastical History*, who consulted him about the provenance and authenticity of a Bede manuscript.[44] Thoresby benefited from an introduction to Humfrey Wanley who afforded access to the Harleian collection.[45] He came to be on friendly terms with the Rev. William Elstob and his sister, Elizabeth; they discussed problems of editing and translation with him, and he secured from his friends a number of subscriptions to one of the Elstobs' publications.[46]

Thoresby was on terms of close friendship with three distinguished Anglo-Saxon scholars: Archdeacon William Nicolson, Dr. Edmund Gibson and Dr. George Hickes.[47] Nicolson was associated with most of the learned men of his day, and he was first in touch with Ralph Thoresby no later than 1690. They had common interests in coins and topography as well as in manuscript sources, for Nicolson wished to establish the history of the ancient kingdom of Northumbria. They corresponded about the interpretation of coins, runic inscriptions, the Bewcastle Cross and ancient boundaries. Thoresby lent coins to Nicolson, who gave him suggested readings of obscure passages in manuscripts and explanations of place-names; they visited each other's collections and collaborated over the new *Britannia*; Thoresby supplied references and comments for Nicolson's bibliographical works, and Nicolson gave assistance with the *Ducatus*; their co-

[43] *Ibid.*, i, pp.332, 456; *Letters*, ii, pp.3–5; *Hearne's Collections*, v, p.106; C. Jackson, ed., *The Diary of Abraham de la Pryme, Surtees Society*, liv (1870), pp.188–89, 255–58; W.T. Lancaster (ed.), *Letters Addressed to Ralph Thoresby*, F.R.S, Publications of the Thoresby Society, xxi (1912), p.134; Atkinson, *Thoresby*, ii, pp.76–78; F.M. Stenton, *Anglo-Saxon England*, 3rd edn. (Oxford, 1971), p.84. See DNB.

[44] *Diary*, ii, p.213; *Letters*, ii, pp.39–40; Douglas, *Scholars*, chap.3.

[45] *Diary*, ii, pp.40, 41.

[46] *Ibid.*, pp.27–28, 131; *Letters*, ii, pp.160–63, 199–200; *Nicolson's Diaries*, p.500. William Elstob (1673–1715) and Elizabeth Elstob (1683–1756), editors and translators.

[47] George Hickes (1642–1715), Nonjuror and deprived dean of Worcester.

operation and learned correspondence were sustained over many years.[48]

Thoresby's standing as a numismatist brought him to the notice of Edmund Gibson, a major 'Saxonist', who valued his work for the *Britannia*. Their common interest in early coins and 'old musty monuments' resulted in a long-standing friendship during which Gibson encouraged his research and writing and – as Bishop of London – extended patronage to Thoresby's two clergyman sons.[49] Thoresby first met the celebrated Dr. Hickes in 1701 to discuss Anglo-Saxon charters and later lent Northumbrian coins and some notes for inclusion in Hickes's vast *Thesaurus*; they corresponded frequently, and Hickes gave Thoresby variant readings of some Anglo-Saxon sources as well as place-name derivatives.[50]

Thoresby's working interests were not confined to the pre-Conquest period, however, and they brought him into contact with several later medievalists, among them the most notable collectors and editors of the day. Thus he had a slight acquaintance with Thomas Madox and with Thomas Rymer, who several times showed him choice items in the public records.[51] He enjoyed a much more fruitful connection with Dr. Thomas Gale, a fellow Yorkshireman, and Thomas Hearne. Gale, widely known for his editions of medieval chronicles, corresponded with Thoresby about a variety of Yorkshire antiquarian topics, gave him useful information and learned advice and proposed him for the Royal Society. He may have used Thoresby's copy of part of the *Polychronicon* for the version which he published, and he certainly borrowed *Scala Mundi* (a chronicle collection) from him.[52] Like many others, Thomas Hearne, controversialist, man of letters and meticulous editor, began corresponding with Thoresby about coins but the range of their correspondence broadened considerably: Roman finds, disputed passages in Asser's *Life of Alfred*, autographs and royal letters, ecclesiastical records in Dodsworth's manuscripts in the Bodleian, detail in medieval chronicles, the new *Britannia*.

[48] *Diary*, i, pp.196, 271–72, 275 ff.; *Letters*, i, pp.116–17, 120–22, 124–27, 257–58, 316, 317; *Nicolson's Diaries*, pp.611, 626, 627, 629 and fn. 90; F.G. James, *North Country Bishop* (New Haven, 1956), pp.11, 74–75, 79, 87.

[49] *Diary*, i, pp.305–6; *Letters*, i, pp.150–51; ii, pp.199–200; N. Sykes, *Edmund Gibson* (1926), pp.9, 13–14, 16–17, 56; Atkinson, *Thoresby*, ii, p.404. Thoresby supplied Gibson with material for the new catalogue of manuscripts in Oxford and in libraries elsewhere. See *Diary*, i, pp.305–6; *Letters*, i, pp.205, 211; R.W. Hunt (ed.), *A Summary Catalogue of Western Manuscripts in the Bodleian Library at Oxford*, i (Oxford, 1953), pp.xxv–xxxv.

[50] *Diary*, i, p.343; ii, pp.20, 29, 32; *Letters*, i & ii, *passim*. The *Thesaurus* is the classic foundation for the study of English diplomatic.

[51] *Diary*, i, pp.296–97, 456; ii, pp.24, 156; *Letters Addressed* (Thoresby Soc. xxi), pp.111, 112. Thomas Madox (1666–1727), legal antiquary, historian of the Exchequer and Historiographer Royal; Thomas Rymer (1641–1713), author and editor of *Foedera*.

[52] *Diary*, i, pp.360–61; *Letters*, i, pp.141, 157, 231–35, 282–83, 298–99, 303–4, 308–9; Douglas, *Scholars*, p.173. Thomas Gale (?1635–1702), Dean of York.

Quarrelsome though Hearne is known to have been, he and Thoresby collaborated smoothly, checking references and transcribing documents for each other.[53]

Thoresby's circle also included some of the best known church historians of the day, notably John Stevens, and the Rev. John Strype. Stevens, a Roman Catholic, translated, abridged and supplemented Dugdale's *Monasticon*, for which Thoresby supplied a number of transcripts including material on orders omitted by Dugdale.[54] He conducted a long correspondence with Strype which first raised the evidence for Cranmer's ownership of Kirkstall Abbey, Leeds. Thereafter Strype presented numerous autographs to Thoresby, and the two men discussed Strype's researches on the Elizabethan archbishops. Thoresby provided him with extracts from the records of the Puritan 'Exercises' held in the West Riding with Grindal's encouragement, as well as notes from manuscripts concerning Archbishops Hutton and Matthew of York.[55]

Thoresby's other antiquarian correspondents included Bishop White Kennett, who shared his interest in local history and antiquities, Edmund Calamy, to whom he gave details of Yorkshire clergy, two Scottish scholars, Sir John Clerk of Penicuik and Sir Robert Sibbald, as well as Arthur Collins, who obtained from him genealogical material for his work on baronets.[56] He was frequently in touch with Heralds, notably Peter Le Neve, about pedigrees; he had a working acquaintance with Edward Llwyd, exchanging coins and information about inscriptions and archaeological finds; and he assisted John Warburton with his mapping of the West Riding, trying unsuccessfully to engage Leeds Corporation's support for the undertaking.[57]

As his diary and accumulated correspondence show, from the 1680s to the 1720s almost every notable scholar – in antiquities, letters, science and the church – was an acquaintance, a correspondent or a friend of Thoresby, who had earned their respect. He clearly enjoyed the company of men with similar interests and sought introductions to them. He maintained regular

[53] *Letters*, ii, pp.48–49, 68–70, 88–90, 107–9, 120–22, 135–39, 369; *Hearne's Collections*, ii, p.140; v, p.151; S. Piggott, *Ancient Britons and the Antiquarian Imagination* (1989), p.97. Thomas Hearne (1678–1735), librarian and Nonjuror.

[54] *Diary*, ii, pp.270, 309; *Letters*, ii, p.376. John Stevens (d. 1726), translator and editor.

[55] *Diary*, ii, pp.38–39; *Letters*, ii, pp.46–47, 51–53, 74–77, 145, 190–92, 234–35, 244–46, 247–49, 255–57, 363–69, 385–86. John Strype (1643–1737), ecclesiastical historian and biographer.

[56] *Diary*, ii, pp.97, 115, 120, 183, 388–89; *Letters*, ii, pp. 242–43, 393–94; Piggott, *Ruins*, pp.137, 140–41. White Kennett (1660–1728), historian, topographer, philologist and Bishop of Peterborough. For Calamy, Clerk, Sibbald and Collins see DNB.

[57] *Diary*, ii, pp.30, 118, 364; *Letters*, i, pp.203–4, 207; ii, pp.189, 261–69; *Hearne's Collections*, i, p.96; Atkinson, *Thoresby*, ii, pp.314–16, 319–21. Edward Llwyd (1660–1709), Celtic scholar, naturalist and archaeologist, keeper of the Ashmolean Museum. John Warburton (1682–1759), Herald, mapmaker and antiquary.

contact with even the most eminent scholars, writing to them in admiring but confident terms, and benefiting from their criticism, collaboration and encouragement in the work he had set himself.

As Thoresby was initially a collector, it was fitting that he first became known to the world at large as a direct consequence of his 'cabinet'. He gave numismatic material and inscriptions to Archdeacon Nicolson for the Northumbrian portion of the new, revised *Britannia*, and he also lent coins and notes to Dr. Obadiah Walker for the numismatic section of that collaborative work, to which some of the most distinguished scholars in the country had been invited to contribute. Thoresby's opportunity came in September 1693 when Dr. Thomas Gale, who had been expected to supply revisions for all three Ridings of Yorkshire, professed himself unable to do more than provide additions for the North Riding; Thoresby was promptly invited to correct and amend the West Riding section. With his local background he was an obvious choice and may well have been recommended to the editor, Dr. Edmund Gibson, and the publishers by Nicolson and Walker. Drawing on his already extensive antiquarian knowledge and stock of notes, he set to work on his annotations within days of receiving an interleaved copy and submitted them by January 1694. Three months later, however, he firmly refused to undertake work on the North Riding when Gale's text failed to materialise. Nevertheless, Thoresby's contribution was substantial, one of the longest in the book; it comprised the correction of errors in the original, together with amendments and additions to repair omissions and bring the main text up to date. It was an exacting task which Thoresby discharged to the satisfaction of the editor and thereby established his scholarly reputation. Accordingly, in 1707, when Gibson contemplated another revision of the *Britannia*, he invited Thoresby to prepare new material on all three Ridings of Yorkshire and, later, to revise all the entries about historic coins, tasks which Thoresby undertook willingly and purposefully. This further edition, however, was not issued until 1722, but the delay in publication gave him the opportunity for a later revision of his contributions, the text of which provided additional proof of his knowledge of Yorkshire's early and later medieval history and antiquities, and the extent of his researches.[58]

Thoresby's active interest in the Romano-British period, pursued through fieldwork and the study of place-names, as well as by collecting,

[58] *Diary*, i, pp.246–47, 248ff; ii, pp.9, 35, 55; *Letters*, i, pp. 137–38, 141, 149–50, 151–52, 156–57; ii, pp.69, 80–81, 84, 97–103, 200–1; *Letters Addressed* (Thoresby Soc., xxi), pp.26–27, 157; James, *Bishop*, pp. 72, 75; Piggott, *Ruins*, pp.46, 48, 110–11, 136–37; *idem, Ancient Britons*, p.134; Atkinson, *Thoresby*, ii, pp.316–17. The second of Gibson's editions did not appear until 1722. (*Camden's Brit.*, 1695, preface).

provided him with material for further publications. He attended a meeting of the Royal Society as guest of Dr. Gale in 1695 and soon afterwards, through the good offices of Dr. Martin Lister, F.R.S., a family friend, he had two communications published in the Society's *Philosophical Transactions*: one mentioned a Roman altar in his possession and then described the possible remains of Roman pottery furnaces which he had recently seen in the neighbourhood of Leeds; the other reported the discovery of Roman altars near Hadrian's Wall. Dr. Gale was subsequently instrumental in securing Thoresby's election to the Royal Society, an honour he greatly valued.[59] When in London he endeavoured to attend the meetings, where he was warmly received, and joined in learned discussions with Fellows of the eminence of Sir Hans Sloane, Sir Christopher Wren, Sir Godfrey Copley, and John Evelyn. In the *Philosophical Transactions* he published some thirty contributions, mainly about various antiquities (including a detailed account in 1702 of a Roman site found at Adel, Yorks. W.R.), but also recording natural observations, unusual occurrences, 'prodigies' and other curiosities.[60]

Before his early publications in the *Britannia* and the *Philosophical Transactions* Thoresby had already embarked on what was to be his main work, the history of Leeds and its neighbourhood. In 1682 he had translated one of the town's earlier Latin charters into English, and from 1691 at the latest he busied himself increasingly with the antiquities of his birthplace. As often as possible he immersed himself in the laborious investigation of a wide range of sources: Domesday Book, monastic charters and deeds, archbishops' registers and other diocesan records, manorial surveys, borough charters and the records of the corporation, J.P.s' court books, heraldic visitations, and the evidences for chantries, charities and recusancy. He worked on the parish registers to establish pedigrees, to compute the growth or decline of the population, and to trace the incidence of epidemics. As well as drawing on the genealogical collections of other Yorkshire antiquaries, he was not afraid to ply the distinguished scholars in his circle with questions or to beg for information:[61] in 1696–97, for example, Drs. Gale and Gibson vainly checked the Kirkstall Chronicle in the Cottonian Library for him, in search of information about the abbey or Leeds itself.[62] By that time Thoresby had probably decided to divide his proposed work into two

[59] *Diary*, i, p.198; *Letters*, i, pp.282–83, 298, 307–8; M. Hunter, *The Royal Society and its Fellows*, 1660–1700 (Chalfont St Giles, 1982), p.45; Atkinson, *Thoresby*, i, pp.392–401.

[60] *Diary*, i, pp.339 ff., 411 ff.; ii, *passim*; Unwin, 'Cabinets', 17; Atkinson, *Thoresby*, i, pp.401–43; *Biog. Brit.*, vi, pt. 1, p.3934.

[61] *Diary*, i, pp.132, 200 ff., 215, 217, 219–20, 225, 229, 260, 290, 297, 307–8, 311, 314, 347, 350, 361, 366, 369; ii, pp.4, 30–32, 49, 55, 62, 87, 408, 459.

[62] *Letters*, i, pp.235, 241, 282, 283–84. For the documents see J. Taylor (ed.), *The Kirkstall Abbey Chronicles*, Publications of the Thoresby Society, xlii (1952).

parts, a topographical survey and a history, and in 1695 he obtained
Gibson's approval for this design, which may have been influenced by
William Somner's fine topographical work, *The Antiquities of Canterbury*,
which Thoresby had read during the previous year.[63]

Despite Thoresby's industry progress was slow. In May 1699 Gibson
urged him to organise his material, prepare it for the press, and 'remember
the general fate of collectors, whose misfortune it has been, never to consider
either the uncertainty of human life, or the uselessness of their own materials
unless put together by the same hands that gathered them'.[64] Thoresby, a
natural collector, was not yet ready and continued with his researches and
other studies, confessing in 1707, 'I find the Topography and Hist. of this
Parish (in the method I propose) more tedious than I expected'.[65] His
friends continued to give encouragement and advice. Thomas Hearne,
for example, expressed general approval of the plan for the Topography
but counselled him to keep it as short as possible by reducing detail,
printing evidence (as Dugdale did) in marginal or footnote references,
confining notes on monuments to those of the 'really eminent' and
excluding material on antiquities if already published. Mr. Plaxton's
advice was equally sound: write a short book, avoid flowery epithets,
draw conclusions in plain words, and 'force not your style beyond that
of an historian'.[66]

Thoresby was still not ready to publish his Topography but by 1709
he had prepared a specimen draft which he submitted for criticism to
three of his most valued and learned friends, Drs. Hickes, Gibson and
Nicolson. They unanimously advised speedy publication, Gibson adding
a firm warning against 'that endless itch of collecting more'. When, more
than a year later, Thoresby's work had still not gone to press, his friends
vehemently repeated their exhortations, and at last, in 1712, Thoresby
travelled to London to submit his manuscript to the printer.[67] He had
received good advice about the arrangements for printing and publishing
from Gibson and from Dr. Gale's son, but progress was delayed by
difficulties with the printers and the engravers.[68]

Thoresby's *Ducatus Leodiensis* was published at last in 1715. In the
preface the author expressed his long-standing interest in the subject,
explained the nature of the book's contents, defended his approach
(especially to the inclusion of numerous pedigrees) and acknowledged

[63] *Diary*, i, p.260; *Letters*, i, pp.205–6; W. Somner, *The Antiquities of Canterbury* (1640; rev.
edn., 1703, repr. Wakefield, 1977).

[64] *Letters*, i, p.367.

[65] *Hearne's Collections*, ii, p.19.

[66] *Ibid.*, iii, p.235; *Letters*, ii, pp.88, 134–35.

[67] *Diary*, ii, pp.33–34, 35; *Letters*, ii, pp.144, 148–49, 160, 253–54, 282–83, 291–92,
293–95.

[68] *Diary*, ii, *passim*; *Hearne's Collections*, iv, pp.53, 143.

the assistance of his friends and associates, including Hickes, who had contributed a glossary. The *Ducatus* is, as Thoresby had planned, an ample topography of Leeds and its neighbourhood cast in the traditional form of a perambulation, which allowed for historical and genealogical digressions, extensive transcripts, and numerous etymologies (many of them dubious). It presents a detailed description of the town as it was at the end of the seventeenth century, with shorter accounts of the out-townships in the ancient parish and of villages in the immediate vicinity. Leeds had changed considerably since the Elizabethan period, but remains and traditions of medieval buildings (since lost) still survived. Although he did not have a keen visual sense, and it was not his purpose to provide an architectural description, Thoresby gives sufficient incidental detail to afford an impression of the general appearance of the town, and his book includes plates by two of the foremost topographical artists of the day, both friends, William Lodge and Francis Place.[69]

To the topographical account in the *Ducatus* Thoresby attached the extensive catalogue of his museum as well as additional material, and some of the attention paid to his book was perhaps occasioned by interest in his collections; thus a large part of a lengthy review in the *Philosophical Transactions* was devoted to the catalogue. In general the *Ducatus Leodiensis* was well received and was even reviewed in a French periodical, although there are hints of carping criticism.[70] Hearne, for example, wrote of his 'great delight and satisfaction', but wished that the topographical and historical parts of Thoresby's work had been published together and the catalogue separately.[71] John Anstis, Garter King-at-Arms, Bishops Gibson, Nicolson and Kennett all sent warm letters of congratulation, and Strype thanked Thoresby for his 'laborious and exact work'.[72]

Strype's comment was not wide of the mark, for although Thoresby's *Ducatus* is not a chronological or analytical history, it is a work based on the author's original researches, supplemented by material carefully accumulated by fellow antiquaries. Thoresby was not always critical and was disposed to enhance the dignity of his native place, an approach which led him to misapply evidence about Leeds Castle, Kent, to his own town: hence the glaring errors (against which contemporaries had warned him) concerning the location both of a siege by King Stephen and the imprisonment of Richard II. Nevertheless, the *Ducatus Leodiensis* remains in general a trustworthy and competent local topography which

---

69 *Ducatus, passim.*

70 Atkinson, *Thoresby*, ii, p.263 ff.

71 *Letters*, ii, p.303; *Hearne's Collections*, iii, p.235; v, p.88 Hearne noted in his private diary that among many good observations Thoresby had shown insufficient critical judgement towards the more extraordinary and dubious natural and human curiosities.

72 *Letters*, ii, pp.304–6, 323, 347, 393–94.

records evidence not preserved elsewhere, establishes much about the historical antecedents of modern Leeds, and retains its usefulness for later enquirers.

Following the success of his Topography, Thoresby continued his historical work, collecting material for the further revision of the *Britannia*, and for his contributions to the *Philosophical Transactions*, but he was mainly occupied with the historical part of the *Ducatus*. By 1718, prompted by the vicar of Leeds and conscious of advancing years, he had decided to write first the ecclesiastical portion of his proposed History.[73] With his strong personal piety and abiding interest in church history the prompting was perhaps not unwelcome to him. The manuscript went to press in 1723 but progress was again delayed by difficulties with the printer, as well as by Thoresby's uncertain health; the prelims were eventually seen through the press by Bishop Gibson, and the *Vicaria Leodiensis* was published in 1724.[74] A small octavo of 250 pages with some illustrations, the *Vicaria's* main purpose was, 'the Retrieving the Memories of those valuable Persons who have fill'd this Vicarage'.[75] It was based on the numerous ecclesiastical manuscripts consulted during the preceding years, on the main published authorities, and on works of reference duly cited in the footnotes.

The *Vicaria* is at best only a partial history of the church in Leeds, concentrating heavily on incumbents and benefactors. Of the former, the book includes a list with biographical notices which become more detailed during the fifteenth century; the more informative accounts are, inevitably, those of the post-Reformation vicars. In admitting that details of the recent clergy were well known to many, Thoresby showed that he realised the value of recent and contemporary history: 'If no Man write what every Man knows, it must at last happen that none will know what none have ever written'.[76] Recognising that strictly parochial evidences were sometimes scanty, he supplemented his history both with memoirs of certain archbishops directly concerned with church affairs in Leeds, and with accounts of several benefactors to the parish. Archbishop John Thoresby, with whom the author claimed a family connection, is treated at length, and the volume includes a copy of some of his religious writings. The contents of the *Vicaria* extend to Thoresby's own time with an account of the early-eighteenth-century scheme for the 'new church' in Leeds, with which the author was closely involved. He includes transcripts of a number of medieval and sixteenth-century documents concerning the benefice, tithes and advowson, thereby presenting evidence for the ecclesiastical

---

[73] Atkinson, *Thoresby*, ii, pp.315.

[74] *Diary*, ii, *passim*; Atkinson, *Thoresby*, ii, p.404; Ralph Thoresby, *Vicaria Leodiensis* (London, 1724).

[75] *Vicaria*, preface, unpaginated.

[76] *Ibid*.

arrangements of the parish before and during the Reformation.[77] Whatever its value as a quarry, however, the *Vicaria*, with its slender text and restricted theme, lacked the appeal of the *Ducatus* and attracted little more than local interest during Thoresby's lifetime.

At his death Thoresby left behind some unpublished writings, including an incomplete draft of the early political section of his proposed History. This fragment, published posthumously in the *Biographia Britannica*, is a survey of 'these Northern parts' in pre-Conquest times. It is well organised and proceeds almost to the end of the sixth century A.D. drawing on the available sources and using the evidence of the author's own fieldwork and coins. The material is often handled uncritically, but the account affords some insight into the contemporary state of Romano-British studies.[78] The text of Thoresby's diary also survived and it, together with the accumulated correspondence in which Thoresby was for long involved, provides an invaluable source for contemporary historical and antiquarian investigations.

In commending Ralph Thoresby to the readers of the *Britannia*, Gibson said that he was one 'of whose abilities and exactness the large collection of Curiosities he has made himself Master of, is a sufficient argument'.[79] He was already one of the most notable numismatists of his day, and although Richard Gough (writing in 1780) remarked on his 'credulity', he nevertheless placed him second only to John Tradescant as a collector.[80] In his approach to the study of history and antiquities, as well as to the acquisition of objects for his museum, he was in many ways cast in the traditional Tudor mould.[81] He was often neither critical nor selective and was hampered by 'some want of judgement', an intellectual limitation which caused him to concern himself with the unimportant rather than the important, and with 'little niceties' and minutiae.[82] He set out to discover antiquities and record facts and to transcribe documents, but he made little or no attempt to analyse them or explain their significance. He tended to accept his sources at face value and sometimes either strained the evidence which they presented or failed to grasp the full import of his material.

Nevertheless, however restricted in scope and lacking in analysis and interpretation Thoresby's writings may be, they are competent and useful,

---

[77] *Ibid.*, *passim*; G.C.F. Forster, 'Holy Trinity Church in the History of Leeds', in *Miscellanea*, xvi, Publications of the Thoresby Society, liv (1979), pp.281–92.

[78] *Biog. Brit.*, vi, pt 1, pp.3934–43.

[79] *Camden's Brit.*, preface, p.2.

[80] R. Gough, *British Topography* (London, 1780), ii, p.436.

[81] Fussner, *Revolution*, p.98.

[82] *Letters*, ii, p.294; *Hearne's Collections*, iii, p.352; v, p.88; Gough, *Brit. Topog.*; ii, p.436.

for he undoubtedly possessed some merit as an antiquary. Gibson found the *Ducatus Leodiensis* 'more instructive and entertaining' than might have been expected'; Kennett admired 'the immortal service you have done your native town' and praised 'the vast improvement you have made to parochial antiquities'.[83] One could go further. The *Ducatus* was a pioneering work, for Thoresby could not draw upon any earlier writings about the town and district. It also had the quality of comparative novelty because, apart from Somner's *Canterbury*, no other large topographical survey of a provincial town had then been published.

Finally, Thoresby played a valuable and influential role in a web of learned correspondents who preserved and disseminated information about historical sources.[84] His friendship or acquaintance with many of the most formidable scholars of his day linked him closely with the wider world of learning and enhanced his own knowledge. John Anstis once described him as 'a plain, honest, well-meaning, industrious gentleman'.[85] He was all these things and probably rather more, for although he was not as sound or distinguished a medievalist as his learned correspondents, he had nevertheless won both their respect for his knowledge of manuscripts, artefacts and coins, and their gratitude for the generosity with which he shared it. In gaining their esteem, Thoresby brought honour on himself as a figure of more than local standing, secured for Leeds a place on the map of English learning and made his own contribution, modest yet enduring, to the study of the past.

---

83 *Letters*, ii, pp.148, 393–94.
84 Saunders, thesis, esp. chap.4.
85 *Hearne's Collections*, iv, p.372.

List of Subscribers

Miss R.S. Allen
P.J. Armstrong
Robert Black
Robin Blades
Brenda Bolton
Dr. R.H. Britnell
Dr. Richard F.M. Byrn
Dr. Marjorie Chibnall
Dr. Lesley Childs
John Cox
Prof. Barrie Dobson
B.S. Donaghey
Dr. A.I. Doyle
Simon N. Forde
G.C.F. Forster
John Gillingham
Dr. C. Given-Wilson
Dr. Antonia Gransden
R.F.S. Hamer
Miss Barbara F. Harvey
Prof. P.D.A. Harvey
R. Higgins
Dr. J.R.L. Highfield
Andrew James
Dr. H.M. Jewell
Lesley Johnson
Dr. Michael Jones
Dr. P.J. Jones
Michael J. Kennedy
Miss Ann J. Kettle
Dr. J.A. Kiff-Hooper
Joan W. Kirby

Judith Loades
Dr. G.A. Loud
Warwick Lowe
Prof. David Luscombe
Dr. J.P. Martindale
Dr. A.K. McHardy
David John Meeson
Dr. Edward Miller
Roger Mott
Tom Moulton
Dr. J.J.N. Palmer
Dr. G.R. Rastall
Peter Richardson
Dr. H.W. Ridgeway
Prof. J.S. Roskell
Peter Rycraft
Dr. N.E. Saul
Prof. Peter Sawyer
Catherine A. Sheppard
Sir Richard Southern
Prof. George B. Stow
Dr Idelle Sullens
Dr. John Thompson
Dr. J.A.F. Thomson
J.F. Wade
Prof. Ernest Wangermann
Prof. Michael Wilks
Dr. Ian Wood
Elaine M. Wood
A.D. Wright
Claire Wright